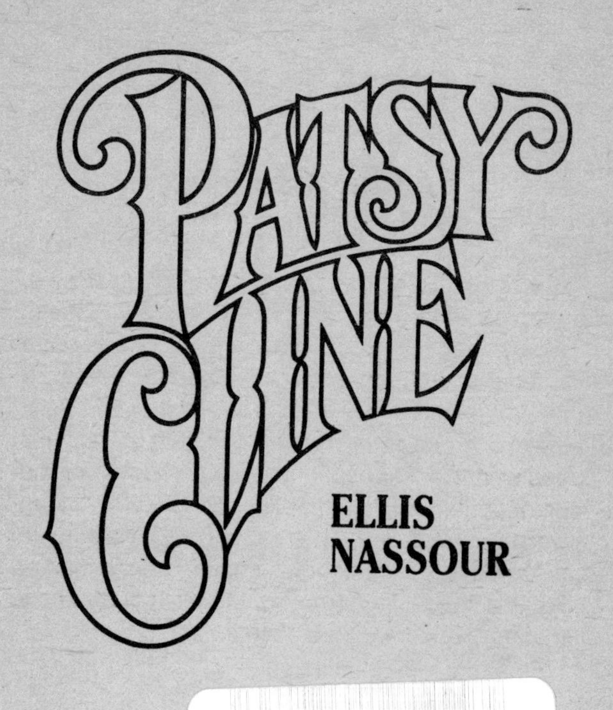

ELLIS NASSOUR

LEISURE BOOKS NEW YORK CITY

For Hilda Hensley and Charlie Dick . . .
thanks for the memories.

Cover photograph by Hal Buksbaum/MCA Records

A LEISURE BOOK

Published by

Dorchester Publishing Co., Inc.
6 East 39th Street
New York, NY 10016

Printed in the United States of America

"A revealing and absorbing book on the late, great Patsy Cline's ride to the top of the charts and into the hearts of millions of fans . . . What a dame! . . . a winner!"

—Liz Smith, *New York Daily News*

Patsy wasn't just good, She was great, sensational! I only wish more of her had rubbed off on me. When she sang a ballad — you know, a real good tearjerker — and you'd see her crying, Patsy wasn't faking. No! She was into her music that much. She was that good.

Her whole life was singing. She was born for show business. When you saw her perform, you knew that, nobody else could come close. I don't think there is anybody even around today who can! she had a charisma that was equal to someone like Elvis or Johnny Cash, two artists she admired very much. There are entertainers who come along that just have that certain something. She was definitely one of them.

—from the Introduction
by Dottie West.

FOR THE FIRST TIME. . .

the true story of the legendary

Patsy Cline

About The Author

ELLIS NASSOUR contributes celebrity profiles to such publications as *The New York Times*, Woman's World, and CountryStyle. He has done extensive entertainment work for the New York *Daily News* and Grit and is the author of "Rock Opera: Creation of Jesus Christ Superstar." He has written and been an assistant director for the prestigous Blackfriars Guild, and is now working with the Veterans Ensemble Company. Nassour is a frequent lecturer on the entertainment media. He is a native of Vicksburg, Mississippi and now makes his home in New York.

Contents

Introduction
by
Dottie West

Patsy Cline could never be summed up in a nutshell. The closest I'd come is to say that she was *real*.

I first met Patsy in Nashville, backstage at the Grand Ole Opry in the years it was held downtown on Saturday nights at the Ryman Auditorium. In 1957, after I had seen Patsy on "Arthur Godfrey's Talent Scouts" and gotten her record of "Walkin' After Midnight," I wrote her a fan letter—the only fan letter I've ever written. And she answered it, saying she hoped we'd get to meet.

We did, when I finished Tennessee Tech and came to town for Starday Records, and when I made a point of "bumping into her."

Before long we were visiting each other as good friends. Patsy would come in off the road, or I would return home, and we'd call each other and get together to talk shop. When I wasn't working, I'd even go out on tour with Patsy, riding in the back seat of her car, and help with her wardrobe. More than anything, I watched her. And I learned from her. It was unbelievable the way I looked up to her.

Until I watched Patsy on stage, I just sang songs. After I learned her secret, I sure tried to approach things differently.

Patsy not only put feeling but also her entire self into her music. I knew I'd never be able to duplicate Patsy Cline, but I became determined that I would set out to try.

The main thing I learned from Patsy was to show emotion—to be unafraid to say the words with the feeling they deserved. Patsy would say, "Find one person to sing to and sing your song just for that one person. Try to cast a spell over the audience and make each of them think he or she is that one person."

That was, perhaps, the best advice anyone has ever given me. I know I might not have found that way of getting across the feeling of a particular song if it hadn't been for Patsy.

Patsy wasn't just good, she was great, sensational! I only wish more of her had rubbed off on me. When she sang a ballad—you know, a real good tearjerker—and you'd see her crying, Patsy wasn't faking. No! She was into her music that much. She was that good.

Her whole life was singing. She was born for show business. When you saw her perform, you knew that. Nobody else could come close. I don't think there is anybody even around today who can! She had a charisma that was equal to someone like Elvis or Johnny Cash, two artists she admired very much. There are entertainers who come along that just have that certain something. She was definitely one.

Patsy enjoyed the recognition she received when it all started to *finally* happen. You didn't want to talk to Patsy about dues paying! She'd say, "Well, damn it, it's about time. I've been paying dues for years!" She got the biggest kick out of signing autographs and posing for pictures with fans. I'll never forget that whenever she'd have a new record out, we'd get the trade magazines and look for her songs and watch them progress each week.

People will say "so and so can really belt out a song." Probably, next to the word "superstar," that is the most overused expression in the entertainment business. But with Patsy, well, she almost didn't have to have a microphone. Her voice was so strong. And she would just cry out her songs.

Patsy had soul—one of the most soulful voices I've ever heard. For a simple human being, she had so much heart and feeling. It was no wonder I looked up to her. And we were about the same age.

Nobody could sing the blues like Patsy. I think, in a lot of ways, her troubles might have added to her greatness as a singer. But then, amazing lady that she was, Patsy could turn around and sing "Bill Bailey" and do it with as much happiness as you could ever hope to give it.

It was no surprise at the end of her sets when she'd have the audience on their feet. She really got them wound up. Whatever I learned about respecting my audiences and fans, I learned from Patsy. She taught me that you depend on the public for your future, that you must be real, and not a phony, with them.

If Patsy had heart on stage, she had a heart of gold off. She was one generous lady, even before she had anything to give. Patsy was always giving her friends things. At one time or another, she must have helped all of us girl singers who were starting out.

I can't begin to tell what she did. Those stories would go on and on. Patsy asked me once what I wore to bed and I told her I didn't have anything special. She gave me this gorgeous, bright, royal-blue bathrobe. It was the prettiest robe I've ever had. And I lost it in the fire when my home burned.

About the only thing I was able to save was the scrapbook of clippings and mementoes Patsy gave me weeks before she was killed. We were at her house crying over all the trying times we were having in the business and about all of Patsy's personal troubles, and she just suddenly gave the book to me.

When I got home I was leafing through it and there was a check for $75 with a note saying, "I know you been having a hard time." It was the money (former husband) Bill and I needed to pay the rent.

Patsy was so kind, giving, full of joy—and she always spoke exactly what she thought. You never had to guess or read between the lines with her. She told it like it was. I loved her all the more for being like that. You always knew where you stood with her. If you were her friend, Patsy didn't know the meaning of "in harm's way." She was the type of person who'd step in front of a locomotive to save you.

In the "era" of country music we came up through, the women did not have the clout they have today. There was Kitty Wells and Jean Shepard—they were big in country—but Patsy crossed over and had massive pop appeal when this was virtually unheard of. She introduced an audience that most likely would have never found time to listen to our music.

More than anyone, Patsy opened the door for us. She made the producers and record labels believe we could sell records and the promoters see that we could draw audiences. Before that, we'd only been used as window dressing.

Patsy Cline was bright and intelligent. No one would think of her as dumb. Oh, no! If they did, they'd sure as hell soon find out! Patsy made the men—singers, promoters, and fans—respect her and the success she achieved. Some of us are feminine and soft, and Patsy had those qualities, but she could also hold her own against any man. When she'd walk on stage, she'd look so beautiful, but if you kicked her, Patsy'd kick you right back.

The saddest thing to me is that Patsy worked so hard for so long and she was only a star—I mean, a really big star—three years. And then she was gone.

I recall that last date—the Kansas City benefit where we shared a dressing room—as if it were yesterday. Patsy went out suffering with a cold and did such a good show she defied anyone to even vaguely remember who'd come on before her. That night, as always, she had everyone on their feet. Patsy was moved and quieted the audience to a roar. "I got here because of you," she exclaimed. "I never could have done it without your support. I love you all!"

The next morning at the hotel Bill and I tried to get Patsy to drive back to Nashville with us since the weather was indefinitely delaying her flight back. She was traveling in a private plane, piloted by her manager Randy Hughes. Hawkshaw Hawkins and Cowboy Copas were with them.

Patsy said yes and then changed her mind, deciding to stay and wait out the weather. Two days later I got the news of the crash on the radio. The more we found out, the more unbearable it became. I was beyond depression. I was numb.

At the prayer service I could hardly stand. I put my hand on the bronze coffin. I wanted to reach out to her. She had been like my own family, my sister. But it was too late. It was a horrible nightmare. It hit hard, losing three prized entertainers. For me, though, it was worse. My Patsy was gone!

I wouldn't take anything in the world for the love and friendship we shared. There'll never be another like Patsy Cline. She was the consummate singer, the consummate human being.

Putting it simply, no matter which way you looked at Patsy, she was dynamic and she was dynamite. She's probably listening to us right now and saying, "Hoss, tell 'em!" If Patsy were here today and writing her autobiography, she'd want to tell it like it was.

What a thought. Oh, if only that could be.

Let me tell you, I miss her.

—Dottie West

Author's Note

Some shocking revelations have come out of my interviews for this biography of Patsy Cline—revelations so shocking, they are a bit frightening when I consider their impact.

When I began writing about Patsy Cline for a magazine series, I never envisioned the end result would be a book. When I began researching into Patsy's life, I only imagined telling a simple story of a girl from the Shenandoah Valley and the Apple Blossom city of Winchester, Virginia, who came up the hard way—determined all the while to become a star.

To that point in time, most of my knowledge of Patsy Cline came from conversations with Loretta Lynn during a period when we worked together and became close. I heard so much about Patsy from Loretta that I collected her records and began listening. Loretta was right, and I discovered quite a remarkable talent.

In Nashville for a Disk Jockey Convention and the Country Music Association Awards in 1970, while visiting one of the hospitality suites, I met Charlie Dick, Patsy's second husband. He was a nice guy.

That was that, until 1977 when I suggested a series on Patsy Cline to commemorate her forty-fifth birthday. Over a three-week period I had several thoroughly enjoyable conversations with Hilda Hensley, Patsy's mother, who is a bright, charming, and quite affable lady. I also contacted Mr. Dick and we spoke about Patsy.

Then came Loretta's *Coal Miner's Daughter* autobiography and the Universal film, and an explosion of interest in Patsy Cline. And now there's a film about Patsy!

I spent the entire summer of 1980 in Nashville, Los Angeles, Dallas, Winchester, in and out of Baltimore, and on the phone, conducting interviews with friends of Patsy's from the early days down through her final years of stardom. Halfway through the summer, as one interview followed another, and as one selfless person after another contacted me offering to share their remembrances of Patsy, a book I never had any inkling of began to take shape. It was too late to stop.

The memories of many of those interviewed were amazing in their total recall—just as some were thoroughly hazy. Often I would hear the same details of a story from three different people, and each time it took place in a different year. The next step—and the most massive of all—was to separate honestly and ethically the truth from fiction.

These interviews gave birth to facets of Patsy Cline that not even some of her very closest associates were familiar with. At the same time, I discovered that many of the artists who knew Patsy well were being overprotective of her memory. Repeatedly I'd hear, "Well, I will tell you this off the record . . . " and "She's not here to defend herself . . . "

Patsy Cline shouldn't have to worry about defending herself against anything. Here was a lady who enjoyed life as it came and with great gusto. She was far from a pin-up girl, but what beauty she may have lacked on the outside she more than made up for by her inner beauty, warmth, and friendship to those in need.

The irony of it all was that while Patsy Cline brought happiness to millions, she never completely found it herself.

Having come to admire Patsy—most of all for the simple reason that Patsy's two children never knew their mother beyond infanthood and have lived with the "legend"—I found myself in a quandary.

Never before in my years of interviewing celebrities had so heavy a burden lay in my decisions. What to reveal and what not to reveal? I have asked myself these questions over and over. Some facts revealed in this biography will surely hurt those who were closest to Patsy, but I decided the truth, rather than the exaggerations that have built up over the years, should be told.

For especially troubling passages I attempted and succeeded in substantiating facts by at least two additional sources. Reconstructing Patsy's life was not an easy task. It was like putting together a giant jigsaw puzzle.

Throughout my interviews it became obvious that many persons responsible for advancing Patsy's career had remained uncredited all these years. It was also my purpose to set the record straight.

So here, in all its vivid detail, is the true, untold story of Patsy Cline. It is a poignant, often humorous, certainly endearing, sometimes painful, and surely controversial story that more than a few have tried to suppress.

Great attention has been paid to recreating the music era Patsy Cline came up in and in recreating scenes from her life. Though it was impossible to present every event in Patsy's life and career, I have attempted to include the important ones. Recording session and record release dates are correct to the best of my knowledge and have been taken from Decca Records archives files.

Much conversation between Patsy and the people she came in contact with is quoted. In some instances, this device is used to flesh out scenes following the context in which the story was told to me. In a majority of instances, relying on those interviewed, this is direct conversation to the best of their memory.

I have tried to build the stories of events in Patsy's life in chronological order, and I apologize for any errors those more learned of Patsy's times may discover. In many cases only approximate dates were known.

For especially devoted Patsy Cline fans who may find the book disillusioning about the star they have loved so many years, I can only ask, "Why should I make apologies?" Patsy surely would not have. I think by learning about the complete woman that was Patsy Cline, not just the recording artist, we come away with the fire and soul that burned within her to make her the star she became.

Two especially good friends of Patsy's—Dottie West and Del Wood—told me that Patsy Cline would want her life told "like it was." This is what I have set out to accomplish.

I pray the story I have unraveled will touch your heart the way it did mine and that, for those who held Patsy dear and for those dear to her, no hurt is kindled.

This was never my intention.

Again and again I have told myself that this is the true story that Patsy Cline, had she lived, would have demanded be told.

—Ellis Nassour
April 1985

Side One

"Love that runs away from me,
Dreams that just won't let me be,
Blues that keep on bothering me,
Chains that just won't set me free..."

—"Just Out of Reach," recorded by Patsy Cline, written by V.P. Stewart. © 1953 by Four-Star Music Co., Inc.

1
"... And Then Goodbye"

Dottie West: **"Patsy, I don't want y'all riding in that small plane. It might crash in this weather...."**

Patsy Cline: **"Hoss, if that little bird goes down, I guess I'll go down with it."**

Monday, December 31, 1962

New Year's Eve is a time of revelry and resolution. Hollywood, New Orleans, New York, everywhere—it's no different an evening: marathon parties, popping corks, clinking glasses, confetti, noisemakers.

Nashville's parties, especially those in the fabled mansions of the country-music artists, need not worry about ranking second place on anyone's charts. Music City, U.S.A., did not get the tag ''Hollywood East'' merely because of its recording technology and roster of stars.

But the eve of a new year, since it marks a beginning as well as an ending, offers—besides the merriment—an occasion to give thanks for what has gone past and for what is to, hopefully, come. And some have more to give thanks for than others.

Such was the case with Mr. and Mrs. Ramsey Hughes and Mr. and Mrs. Charles Dick. And, amid the revelry, they paused to reflect.

Hughes, who preferred to be called Randy rather than by his

given name, was born in 1929 in the small middle-Tennessee town of Murfreesboro and went on to become a Grand Ole Opry sideman on the rhythm guitar. In 1956 he married Kathaloma (Kathy), the fair-haired singing daughter of country veteran Lloyd Copas, better known as Cowboy Copas, "the hillbilly waltz king." Then Hughes decided to branch out. He allowed his musical skills to take a back seat as he took on the stars. Randy became personal manager to such country veterans as Ferlin Husky, Ray Price, Billy Walker, Wilma Lee, and Stoney Cooper, and the Willis Brothers, not to mention Randy's father-in-law.

Friends were not surprised at Hughes' decision. As one put it, "He was a born smoothie, and if you're going to be a manager in this business that's a number one prerequisite."

Hughes got into the business at fifteen as a guitarist, playing with Moon Mullican, Tennessee Ernie Ford, Husky, and George Morgan. In 1949, while living in Florida, he originated the first country variety television shows in Miami.

After logging a million miles on the road as a musician, Randy had found a better way.

Now Randy hooked onto Patsy Cline's rising star. She was the hottest female singer in Country music—with Number One records "I Fall to Pieces," "Crazy," and "She's Got You." But Patsy's impact had gone further. With a voice capable of varied textures and ranges, she was one of the few country entertainers enjoying success in the pop field. Patsy had appeared on network television with Dick Clark on "American Bandstand" and with Tennessee Ernie Ford.

It was television—"Arthur Godfrey and His Talent Scouts" program—that brought Patsy to stardom in January 1957. To date it was the one arena in which she had failed to completely conquer. Randy planned major TV guest spots for Patsy throughout 1963.

Patsy Cline was now the star she had been so determined to become. From the time of her youth in Winchester, Virginia, and throughout the Virginia, West Virginia, and Maryland areas, nothing short of an act of God could have stopped Patsy in her quest to get to the top of the ladder.

After the ovations of the Godfrey show, Patsy came to Nashville to be on the Grand Ole Opry. She told friends she would never forget the reception she received after singing "Walkin' After Midnight." It was, after all, a dream come true.

While still a teenager, Patsy had auditioned for the Opry, but for reasons never explained she was passed over. She returned to Winchester, met Jumbo Rinker and then Bill Peer, and set about paying her dues. Now everybody everywhere knew Patsy Cline.

She had a brand new house, but Patsy was so busy touring she had little time for it, or her precious Julie and new baby boy, Randy. Her husband, Charlie Dick, had now given up his job and, because of Patsy's condition as a result of a near-fatal accident, was frequently accompanying her on the road.

Patsy had three of the top songwriters in country music—Hank Cochran, Harlan Howard, and Willie Nelson—composing material especially for her. Each week saw her big Cadillac being loaded for personal appearances that had her crisscrossing over America's byways from Buffalo to Wichita to Peoria to Ottawa. During the rare times at home, Patsy was selecting furniture for the house, and preparing for the next picture session, the next recording session, the next Opry broadcast. And maybe, as a result of her recent trip with Dottie West to Deland, Florida, another country music movie. Hopefully, it would be a better experience—maybe this time she'd even get paid.

Patsy hated the travel and the *de rigueur* aspects of being a star. She didn't mind the posing for photographs and autographs, but why couldn't she just sing and to hell with everything else? It was, however, all part of the commitment Patsy Cline made. "Country music, they keep saying," Patsy wrote a friend, "is not a business. It's something that's in your blood. Bulldoddy! I am just waiting for the first person to come and tell me that!"

But Patsy was living proof that the saying was correct. Country music—all kinds of music—ran through every vein in her body.

As so often happens, in the process of reaching her goal of stardom, Patsy Cline had become a tormented soul.

She had problems at home, no doubt about that. She was nervous and fidgety as a result of injuries suffered in the accident the year before. Because of female problems, she might never be able to have children again. Charlie, when he was drinking, was abusive, even violent. More than once, Patsy had had him arrested.

Patsy found herself turning more and more to Randy Hughes. Though their brief fling at romance had cooled, they remained the best of friends. With the exception of her mother and Charlie, Randy was closer to Patsy than anyone. He was not only her manager, he was also her confidant. And though Randy had found his niche in the world of show business and business, in general—he was also a stock and insurance broker—there were times, when reflecting on his 18-hour days and the hours spent traveling with his artists, he wondered if he had made the wisest choice. There was just not enough time. He found an answer. Randy decided the one sure way to beat the constant defeat of road fatigue was to take flying lessons. This summer he had gotten his pilot's license and, with all those various commissions rolling in, his very own private plane.

Friday, February 1, 1963

You didn't say "no" to Hap Peebles. It had a way of backfiring. Harry Peebles was the Midwest's largest and best-known promoter and music buyer. He took good care of the acts he booked, was honest and, as a founding member of the Country Music Association, respected.

Since radio airplay helps even good records achieve greater sales, it is natural to find labels, their artists, and promoters courting the favor of disk jockeys.

Since 1956, Jack Wesley Call, under the name Cactus Jack, had been one of Kansas City's most popular record spinners, first on KANS and then KCKN. By January 17, 1963, he was the driving force behind KCMK-FM switching to an all-country format. This, too, was the culmination of every dream he had had.

One week later all his plans were shattered. He lay unconscious and dying at St. Joseph's Hospital. Call's car and a transport truck collided at Sterling Avenue and U.S. 40 in Independence, Missouri. The following day, January 25, country artists and fans lost a friend and big booster of country music when Call lost his tenuous hold on life. He left behind a wife, Anne, and two young sons. And very little money.

Cactus Jack's associate, Guy Smith, went to Peebles and singing star Billy Walker, a good friend of Call's, to ask if a benefit could be arranged to raise funds for the family. Both pledged to do everything they could.

Two years prior, Peebles had been best man at the wedding of country singers Jean Shepard and Hawkshaw [Harold]

Hawkins. The ceremony became a media event. It took place on the stage of the Forum Auditorium in Wichita after an SRO performance also headlining Tex Ritter and the Plainsmen Quartet. Peebles contacted Hawkins, a star of the Grand Ole Opry and a pillar of the Nashville music community.

Walker spoke with his manager Randy Hughes about donating the services of some of his acts. The date was set for Sunday, March 3, at the Kansas City, Kansas, Memorial Building.

Within a few days a line-up of the Who's Who in Country had been promised: Roy Acuff, the King of Country Music and a two-time Republican nominee for governor of Tennessee; Wilma Lee and Stoney Cooper and their Clinch Mountain Clan, popular staples of the Wheeling, West Virginia, Jamboree and now the Grand Ole Opry; Cowboy Copas, not only Hughes' father-in-law but an ever popular entertainer since the fifties who, after a recording decline, was back at the top with the songs "Alabam" and "Signed, Sealed and Delivered"; fast-rising singer Dottie West; Ralph Emery, WSM premier disk jockey and Grand Ole Opry announcer; Hawkins, another popular veteran singer/musician especially known for his theme record "Slowpoke"; and Walker.

Thursday, February 28

George Jones, who was to be appearing in Kansas, was added to the bill, but Walker and Peebles were frantic for another top name. "Since Patsy was such a favorite of Call's, couldn't she make it?"

"I'll talk to Patsy and see," Hughes told Billy, "We got a date in Birmingham Saturday, but if she's willing and we can make it in the plane you can count on us. But, damn, we're gonna be pushing it!"

"If you were coming by car," razzed Billy, "I know you'd make it—the way you drive! Guess you can only get that plane going so fast."

Randy spoke to Patsy and she said, "Hoss, if you can get us there, I'll damn sure do it!"

"Honey, that ole Comanche will get us there with plenty of time to spare."

"Then tell 'em I'm a-coming!"

Saturday, March 2

It was a time when promoters tried to get all they could from an artist. The show producer in Birmingham, Alabama, was no different. The date had been booked when "I Fall to Pieces" was starting to happen for Patsy. She was to do two shows for a total of $400. Then the promoter canceled. He rebooked when Patsy's song was Number 1, telling Randy that all they could pay was $400—take it or leave it. Hughes took it. The date was canceled again. When the promoter called to rebook a third time, Randy asked for $1000 and settled for $800.

Patsy, Randy, and Charlie left New Orleans, where Patsy had done a show early Saturday morning, and flew in Hughes' four-seater plane to Birmingham. The package that night included Tex Ritter, Charlie Rich, Jerry Lee Lewis, and Flatt & Scruggs. The first performance had been sold out for days and now the second show was SRO and still there were 500 fans outside wanting to buy tickets.

The promoter came to Randy and Charlie and asked, "Will Patsy do a third show?" Randy replied, "Not at this price." Patsy overheard and wanted to know what the problem was. "They want us to do another show," Hughes told her. "Well, we'll do it if everyone else does." Because Randy and Charlie liked the promoter they went along with Patsy. They really didn't have much choice. The lady had spoken.

As they were preparing to go to the hotel that night, the promoter came to Randy and Charlie and handed them an envelope. It had a thousand dollars in it. "There," he told them jokingly, "you got what you wanted! And thanks for coming through."

Up in Brunswick, Maryland, a small town some fifteen miles from where Patsy had lived in Frederick with her first husband, Bill Peer and his Melody Boys took an intermission at the Brunswick Moose Club.

Peer and his band had been a Saturday night tradition for fifteen years. He had given Patsy Cline her start in this very same club. Peer stopped to say hello to Fay and Harry Crutchley of Frederick. Fay had been one of Patsy's closest friends before she hit the big time. Peer had been more than that.

"Oh, God, I miss Patsy, don't you?" Fay sighed to Bill.

"Yeah, I sure do," he replied.

"Have you heard anything from her?"

"Are you serious? Not a damn word."

"Hey, Bill, why don't you and the boys do 'Crazy' or 'I Fall to Pieces'? It'll be just like the good ole days."

"You gotta be kidding! You're the one that's crazy. As far as I'm concerned Patsy Cline can just fall to pieces!"

Fay could see that Bill Peer had never really gotten over Patsy.

Sunday, March 3

The lights went on early that morning at 4413 GraMar Lane in the Inglewood section of East Nashville.

Kathy Hughes had received a call from Randy late Saturday to let her know that he, Patsy, and Charlie would arrive around 8 a.m. at Cornelia Field, the private airport in nearby Madison.

"The plan was to let Charlie out to make room for Billy and Dad," recalled Kathy. "Charlie'd also have the weekend receipts and would deposit them. Because of some last-minute complication with the arrangements in Kansas City, Billy needed to get there earlier. He took a commercial flight after the Grand Ole Opry Saturday night. Hawkshaw volunteered to go in Randy's plane in his place.

"Randy was going to refuel and go right on to Kansas, so I knew they wouldn't have time to stop anywhere and have lunch. As it was, they would probably arrive around show time. I was frying a chicken for them to take along. It was going to be a real Southern meal—fried chicken and a loaf of white bread!"

Hawkshaw and Jean lived only a few blocks away, so Hawkins came over that morning to meet Copas.

"While my mother, Lucille, and I prepared the chicken, Hawk and Dad sat in the middle of the kitchen floor playing with our son Larry's gyroscope. It's a sight I will never forget! Two grown men—and Hawkshaw was tall!—sitting on the floor with a child's toy and just having the time of their life."

When she finished the chicken, Kathy, her mother, Larry, and her brother Mike all got ready for church. Then Copas gathered together everyone and Kathy drove to Cornelia Field. It wasn't long before they could spot Randy's plane.

"Everybody got out and Charlie and Patsy told how successful the show had gone in Birmingham. Tex Ritter was also on the bill. I gave Randy the chicken and the loaf of bread. Patsy wanted a piece right away. 'Can't think of the last time I had chicken for breakfast!' she joked.

"We said our goodbyes and kisses were exchanged. Then

they taxied off. Charlie had his car at the airport and he headed home. Their little boy Randy was sick and running a fever. Patsy was worried and Charlie wanted to get back home as soon as possible.

"Mike, Larry, mother, and I got back in the car and went on to services at Grace Baptist Church."

There were to be three shows that afternoon and evening: at 2:00, 5:15, and 8:15. Randy arrived in Kansas City at approximately 12:30. Patsy was especially exhausted, but there was only time enough to check into the new Town House Hotel, change, and get to the auditorium.

Anne Call was backstage to thank each of the artists for their loyalty and donating their services. "You all know how much Jack loved you," she said solemnly.

When Mrs. Call inquired to meet Roy Acuff, a red-faced Peebles explained that he had phoned and canceled at the last minute. Acuff, who had unofficially retired from the Opry after 30 years, agreed to come for the benefit, but on the morning of departure, his wife Mildred "got this funny feeling" about him making the trip. She let him sleep. He missed the plane and could not make other connections. And, Hap pointed out, it was too late to hitch a ride with Randy Hughes as the plane was full.

Peebles started the program with a tribute to Call and the music got underway. As it did a festive atmosphere filled the hall.

It's a day Marie Kerby would never forget: "It was tremendous. We had such an enjoyable time at the show, never once dreaming that it would be the last show for three of our most-loved Opry stars.

"Since fans were not allowed backstage at the shows, we'd sit in our seats until we saw one of the artists, and then we'd run to the hall, which led to the stage entrance, to say hello to them and have pictures taken. As soon as I saw Patsy appear, I rushed to meet her. I found that she was still the same sweet person that I had met a couple of years earlier in spite of all the successes she was having.

"Although she had flown into Kansas City from Nashville, and had been up since early morning, she didn't appear to be tired and was very cooperative when it came to posing for pictures.

"Patsy was very excited about her new album that would

soon be released. She had just been in the studio and felt that this was, perhaps, the best recording session she had ever done. She told us all about her recent engagement in Las Vegas. 'I never worked so hard in my entire life as I did during that five-week period,' she said. 'And I definitely did not like Vegas!'

"She told us she dreaded the thought of going back there, although, as she put it, 'It's one of the necessary evils of being in show business.' "

Of the stars, Copas was the most introverted, but when he and Hawkshaw were not on stage they were in the hallway visiting with fans and watching the other performers.

"During the period he stood on the sideline," Marie recalled, "I believe Hawkshaw was enjoying the show as much as anyone in the audience. You could hear him applaud, cheer, and whistle as each artist completed a number. A few times that day he took his guitar and played for some of the fans who gathered around him.

"Hawk was in a talkative mood and we felt we got to know him as he really was. We talked about fan clubs and about his recent release, 'Lonesome 7-7203,' which he was really happy about. 'You know what King Records went and did?' he laughed. 'They re-released the song on the flip side of another record so more of the radio stations would have a copy of it!'

"There was a funny incident surrounding that song. It was so new that Hawk hadn't had a chance to memorize the words. He didn't sing it on the first show. When he went off stage he discovered he had a copy of the lyrics in his wallet.

"He had so many requests for it that he had George McCormick of the Clinch Mountain Clan stand next to him on the second show and hold the piece of paper while he did the song. Believe me, the audience literally went wild!

"Hawk's main topic of conversation was about his wife Jeanie and their baby Don Robin, who he told us they had named after Don Gibson and Marty Robbins. He talked about his trick horses, and said he'd just built a photo darkroom in the basement of the house so he could develop his own pictures.

"More than anything, though, he talked about the baby that would soon be due. You could tell how he and Jeanie must have been looking forward to that."

Patsy was not feeling well. She had a slight case of the flu and kept razzing Randy that "the way you froze me to death in that plane of yours coming up here has made it worse."

Peebles asked Patsy to try and lie down between shows and she told him and Randy that she would rest. There were so many people wanting autographs, pictures, and to say hello Patsy barely had a chance to sit down.

After the 5:15 show Randy took Patsy back to the Town House, only three blocks away, so she could eat something and take a nap.

She was in good spirits at the 8:15 performance. Patsy sang "She's Got You," "Heartaches," "Am I a Fool," two songs from her February sessions—"Sweet Dreams" and "Faded Love"—and, of course, "Crazy" and "I Fall to Pieces." She had to do the last two; they were her "Over the Rainbow."

At one point Patsy apologized to the audience. "I've got the flu! I think I caught it in New Orleans Friday night. It ain't getting better. So don't be disappointed if my singing's not up to par."

She held her right ear with her finger when she was reaching for the high notes.

Randy planned to leave following the late show with Patsy, Copas, and Billy Walker, but since a press party had been scheduled it was decided to depart early the next morning.

Hawkshaw, who hated small planes, was returning via commercial flight. Walker had bought him an open-end ticket.

Monday, March 4

It was a bitter cold morning. Patsy's flu was no better. She had coughed most of the night. There had been intermittent rainstorms throughout the previous evening and now, in addition to pouring rain, it had become dark and cloudy.

The show didn't end until almost midnight and the press party did not begin breaking up until after one. But Randy was up early to get the bad news: Fairfax Municipal Airport was fogged in. Unless the weather cleared, their morning flight would have to be scratched.

Bad news was the omen of the day.

Billy Walker's phone rang. His dad had had a heart attack. He phoned Hawkshaw, his longtime friend, to tell him, "I just got the call. They don't expect Dad to live. Randy doesn't know what time we'll be able to leave, and I've got to get back to Nashville as soon as possible. I know you didn't want to come up in that small plane, but can I talk you into going back with Randy and letting me have your airline ticket?"

The phone rang in Patsy's room. She desperately wanted a cigarette but she knew it would only make her cough worse. Patsy picked up the receiver.

"Yeah?" Patsy always answered the phone that way, but this time she was a bit gruff.

It was Dottie West.

"Well, hello, hoss! Cheer me up. Ain't heard nothing but bad news this morning."

"I got something to get your spirits up. Hap's gonna buy everyone breakfast and tell us about how much money was raised last night for the Calls."

"I couldn't eat a thing!"

"It'll be the best thing for you. Have some hot tea. Come on down."

Patsy went to the coffee shop in the lobby of the Town House. There was Peebles with several of the artists from the night before.

"Hap, now don't expect me to be cheery. I'm sick as a dog! But, well, when I heard you was buying, I just couldn't resist. I got up out of a sick bed!"

Already Patsy had everyone in stitches.

George Jones told her, "Patsy, honey, on a gloomy day like this, you're like a big ray of sunshine!"

They discussed the success of the benefit. Everyone was shocked when Peebles announced only $3,000 had been raised. The tickets were $1.50 for adults and 50¢ for children, and the first and last shows had been sold out.

Peebles said that the receipts would have to be rechecked. When Billy heard the news after the show he exclaimed, "If you ask me, it looks like somebody's had their hand in the till!"

Patsy was on her third cup of coffee as she and Dottie talked. She didn't want any tea and she wasn't that hungry. Dottie could see Patsy's heart was not in the conversation. She seemed nervous and looked out the windows as the rain came down and the sky darkened.

"Hey, honey, what's bothering you?"

"Oh, we can't take off. The damn airport's fogged in!"

"You can't fly in this weather. Look at it."

"I don't know when we'll be able to leave. Goddamn it, this would happen just when I gotta get home in a hurry."

"What's the hurry?"

"I miss my babies!"

"I know what you mean."

"I haven't seen them in several days and when I left, little Randy was feeling sick. He's not any better. I don't like leaving them for long periods."

"Well, my God, if that's what's worrying you, why don't you drive back with Bill and me? We've got room. Even if we didn't, we'd make room for you! Get your things ready. We're gonna be leaving in just a little while."

Patsy's spirits brightened. "All right!" She echoed throughout the restaurant. "I will 'cause I got things to do at home." She got up. "Let me get upstairs and finish packing. I won't be long."

"Wait. I'll go up with you and get my stuff." Dottie yelled to her husband, "Bill, Patsy's gonna go back with us."

"I'll be ready in a few minutes!"

"Take your time," Bill told her. "We won't leave without you."

Bill asked Hawkshaw if he wanted to go back to Nashville by car.

"I do and I don't," replied Hawkshaw. "I hate to see Randy and Cowboy go back alone. It won't be too crowded, will it?"

West assured him he would make room. "You can stretch out in front and the girls can have the back seat to themselves."

"You got a deal!" Hawkshaw went to speak to Randy and get his bags.

"Patsy and me met in the hall by the elevator," Dottie said. "When it came we put all our luggage on and I pushed the lobby button. The doors opened and Patsy leaned over and started to pick up her suitcase.

" 'Naw,' she blurted. 'I'm gonna go back up.' 'What?' I asked her. 'I'm not gonna ride home in the car. I'll wait for Randy. I think I'll get home quicker.'

"About that same time, Hawk came down to the lobby. 'Where're your bags, Hawk?' Bill asked. He told us he'd changed his mind. 'I'm gonna wait it out with Randy and Cowboy.' I'll never forget Hawk putting his arm around me and saying, 'Heck, this stuff is gonna lift and we'll beat y'all home in the plane.' I gave him a big hug."

Dottie remembers Hawkshaw being anxious to get home because Jean was in her ninth month and already had her hands full with one baby.

"I was concerned about them," noted Dottie. "These were

all friends of mine. Patsy could see the way I felt as I really tried to persuade her to change her mind and ride with us. But she had decided. And that was that! In a way, I guess, it was loyalty to Randy."

"I'm just gonna be worried about y'all," Dottie told Patsy. "I don't want y'all riding in that small plane. It might crash in this weather. Please don't let Randy take off if it's bad!"

"Don't fret," Patsy told her

"I can't help it. I'm gonna be worried."

"Don't worry about me 'cause when it comes my time to go, I'm just gonna go. Hoss, if that little bird goes down, I guess I'll go down with it."

"Are you sure you won't change your mind?"

"Hoss, it's time for you to leave!"

Dottie and Patsy gave each other a hug and kiss.

"And that's the way we said goodbye," sighed Dottie.

Later that morning as Peebles prepared to return to his home in Wichita, he ran into Patsy, Randy, Hawkshaw, and Cowboy leaving the hotel with their luggage.

"Where y'all going? I thought you were grounded."

"Haven't you looked out?" Randy shot back. "It's stopped raining and starting to clear. We're going on out to the field so we can take off as soon as the airport opens."

"We walked to the parking lot together," said Peebles. "I told them how much Anne Call appreciated what they had done, how she had cried at the benefit. And I thanked them for coming.

" 'Hell, Hap, we been friends and working together a long time,' Randy admonished me. 'If we can't help our friends, who do we help? Cactus Jack was always on the bandwagon for Ferlin, Billy and Patsy.'

" 'Hap, when you coming to Nashville?' Patsy asked me. I told her, 'Oh, hon, I don't know. I'll definitely have to be there for the D.J. Convention.'

" 'Hell, don't wait that long!' replied Patsy. 'Why don't you just pick up and come on back with us now?'

" 'What? Oh, that'd be real nice! Who's gonna put on the shows with Hap Peebles in Nashville? I can't go anyway. What would I do with my car?'

" 'Just leave it in the lot. They know you here!'

" 'Young lady, where am I gonna sit. That plane of Randy's only holds four!'

" 'Hap, you can sit in my lap!"

" 'Oh, honey, if the little lady ever found out about that she'd take a rolling pin to my head!' "

The group exchanged farewells. Peebles got in his car and headed for Wichita. Randy and his passengers got in the rental car and drove to the airfield.

At the charter and flight service adjacent to the airport Eddie Fisher, the owner, apprised them of the weather bureau bulletins that warned small craft against flying.

"Hughes looked over the weather advisories," explained Fisher, "and talked back and forth with the others. I thought for a minute he was going to attempt to fly in that weather. In the end they decided against it and headed back to the hotel."

The quartet seemed down. They had wanted to get on their way. Patsy, for one, became a nervous wreck when she had nothing to do and nowhere to do it. She would take to smoking a lot in situations such as these.

At the Town House the party was checked in again. Each went to their room to call respective families. Patsy spoke with Charlie and Julie. She asked her husband if Randy was any better. Charlie told her the boy still had a fever and was crying a lot.

"He misses his Mommie!" he advised

"His Mommie misses him, too. We're gonna get out of here as soon as the weather clears. I'll let you know what we do. If the baby gets any worse, call a doctor." Patsy ended the conversation as she always did, "Well, I'll get back to you later."

Later in the evening Patsy and Randy spoke about her scheduling. "Hon, I'm gonna have to slow down. Here I am making the dough and not having a goddamn minute to enjoy any of it. The baby's at home sick right now and I'm stuck here in Kansas City."

"But, Patsy, now's the time to work. You're riding high—we're demanding big money and getting it, by God. 'Leavin' on Your Mind' is climbing the charts, and you're gonna have two, maybe three, singles from the session you just finished. We're raking it in!"

"Yeah, but there's no time to spend it! I'm working a lot more than I should be, and feeling the worse for it. And I miss the kids. Every time I leave that house for the road I feel guilty."

"Honey, you worry too much. Let me handle everything."

"You have been—and look at the damn mess you've got us in!"

"Even I can't predict the weather!"

"Well, I'll be! We have finally found something you can't do! Glory be! I didn't think you could, but I never thought I'd live to see the day you'd admit it!"

"Stop worrying! It'll all come out in the wash. Now, let's go find Hawk and Cowboy and do something."

Tuesday, March 5

Patsy decided to call her mother, Hilda Hensley, in Winchester, Virginia.

"Hi! Here I am still fogbound in Kansas City," Patsy told her mom. "It seems that every time I stick my neck out, I get my foot into something else." They discussed Sunday night's benefit and the pittance that was raised. "Billy says there should've been more. But nobody knows what happened. We worked for nothing but expenses and it looks like the wrong person got helped!"

Patsy told Hilda that Randy was having another bronchitis attack when she had to leave home for the weekend, and that he was running a fever.

"For goodness' sake, now don't you go worrying about the kids!"

"Mama, I can't help it!"

"I know, but Charlie will make sure everything's fine."

"Charlie!"

"No matter what, when it comes to the children you can depend on him. He loves them as much as you."

Patsy told her mother she wasn't feeling too well but that the worst of her flu was gone.

"Is it clearing there? That's what I want to know? Or do you think you're gonna be there all day?"

"I hope not! It's pretty bad, though. Randy says we might be able to leave about two o'clock."

The two exchanged idle conversation. Mrs. Hensley even remembers Patsy cracking a couple of jokes.

"Be careful. Don't y'all take any chances, hon."

"We won't, Mama. I just want to get back to my babies. The next date is a big show March sixteenth in Baltimore. Thank goodness I don't have to work anymore till then. I'll have some time to rest."

"Now, you call me before you leave," requested Mrs. Hensley. "If I don't hear from you, I'll know you're still there."

"Well, I'll get back to you later."

The group checked out of the Town House about noon and once more made the trek to Fisher's flying service.

"Hughes talked to the weather bureau for a long time by telephone," Fisher reported. "There had been a clearing in our area but the bureau showed bad weather at Springfield, the river and lake region south of Vichy, and along the Mississippi from St. Louis down.

"We got the plane ready. They got in. It was tiny and the window kept fogging up from their breath. Hughes couldn't see a thing. They tried again later, but the moisture from their breath kept fogging the window."

"Okay, everybody," cracked Patsy. "There's one way we can make it home. You gotta hold your breath!"

"Well, Patsy," Hawkshaw quipped, "if we go and do that we won't be in any condition to enjoy the bumpy ride!"

The four left the plane, went to Fisher's office, sat, and talked. "They were full of life and appeared to be nice, down-to-earth people. Hawkins and Copas kidded around and asked if I had any parachutes.

"I told them, 'Yeah, but they're old ones and y'all better not fly into anything where one'll be needed.' It cleared and Hughes said, 'This is it!' I warned him that if the weather got bad near Vichy, he should turn around. 'We don't want another casualty like the one Sunday,' I told him. 'Someone crashed into the side of a bluff between St. Joseph and Omaha.' "

Hawkshaw phoned his wife to let her know they were leaving. Randy called Kathy and informed her, "We're on the way."

"Hughes seemed level-headed and assured me that he would avoid foul weather. 'We won't fly into anything bad,' he yelled to me just before they taxied. 'We'll come back and fly west or go some place else.' Everyone seemed happy to finally be getting underway."

The takeoff at 1:30 went smoothly. Randy kept in radio contact with weather stations as he traveled across Missouri and down into Arkansas. He followed a storm all the way.

"Randy would land, wait for the front to get sufficiently ahead of him, then go on," Kathy Huges noted. "At Little Rock they ran into rain and sleet, and had to wait that out. Randy called again to let me know they were preparing to leave and would stop to refuel in Dyersburg [Tennessee]."

The flight distance to Nashville from Kansas City is approximately 500 statute miles. Hughes' single-engine plane could clock about 120 miles an hour. The expected arrival time in Nashville was 6:00. When Hughes landed his plane at the Dyersburg Airport at 5:20, he was surprisingly not far behind schedule, considering his stop in Little Rock.

The Dyersburg field, two miles south of the city, was the fifth heaviest traveled in the state. It was serviced commercially then only by Southern Airways.

Bill Braese, who now builds utility trailers, was the airport manager. "Hughes told me he had followed a storm all day and that they had to land three or four times to let the front pass.

" 'Well, the news I have for you is not much better.' I said. 'We've had thunderstorms off and on all day. There's been some flooding in some parts. We're getting all this precipitation because of a front hanging over Kentucky Lake at Camden and over the Tennessee River.' "

"I'm familiar with that area around the Lake and the Tennessee River," Hughes informed Braese. "I've flown over it several times."

"You're gonna have that storm right on your flight path," replied Braese. "Get on the horn to the Atlanta Weather Bureau for an update."

While the plane was refueled, Randy met with the weather station attendant at the airport. He was given a full briefing on the situation. Then he went to the restaurant to meet with the others.

There were few, if any, passengers in the airport coffee shop but it was populated with locals stopping by for a quick supper. No one could remember when there had been three big Grand Ole Opry stars in that restaurant at one time. Several people approached Patsy, Hawkshaw, and Cowboy for autographs on napkins. A woman gave Hawkshaw a matchbook and asked him to sign it.

"Hon, I don't sign matchbooks! Quick, grab a napkin."

The three were having coffee and Cokes when Randy joined them to discuss the weather and if they should go on and chance the flight or take the car the airport kept for emergencies.

"How much further do we have to go?" Hawkshaw asked.

"How long will it take us to get to Nashville in the car?" Patsy wanted to know.

Randy gave them the details and it was decided that they

would do whatever he thought would be best.

"Everyone was sober," Braese pointed out. "There was no fighting or arguments about whether to go or stay. All of them were nice and very polite.

"The fact that Hughes was not an instrument-rated pilot never came up in our conversations. But I surmised he wasn't because of what he told me about staying behind the storm. I just knew he hadn't filed a flight plan."

Randy decided they would go on in the plane. He called his wife.

"It wasn't much before six o'clock," remembered Kathy. "Randy asked me about the weather in Nashville. 'Hey, honey, go check and see if it's still raining,' he told me. I did and told him it was not at that time.

"Part of our conversation had to do with the fact that Sleepy McDaniel, who had worked with Hank Snow for years, had died. The family called me and asked if Dad could be one of the pallbearers at the funeral the next day.

"Randy asked me to call Cornelia Field so they would turn on the runway lights. He told me they would be leaving within a few minutes so I would know when to expect them. I called Charlie Dick to let him know they were on the way; then Jean Shepard, Hawk's wife, and told her 'Our boys are on the way!' Jeanie exclaimed, 'Thank God!' Then I left for the airport with my mother to await their arrival. It would take them about 50 minutes."

Braese recalls that after Hughes got off the phone he came back to him and said, "Everything's gonna be all right. My wife says you can see the moon and the stars in Nashville. It's all clear."

"She's seeing the eye [calm] of the storm," countered Braese. "You shouldn't go. I don't recommend that you attempt it in this weather. You're gonna be fighting high winds all the way. Why don't you stay the night?"

"Naw. Hell, I've already come this far. It's only another 90 miles. We'll be there before you know it."

"I don't know. I think you're taking a chance. Why don't you take the airport car. It's a Plymouth station wagon, nineteen-sixty-one. But it'll get you there. I'll bring your plane to you tomorrow and pick up my car."

"That's nice of you but we're going on. I'm gonna take care of it and if I can't handle the situation, I'm gonna come back."

"The car'll be waiting."

Hughes signed the receipt for the gasoline and took his copy, folded it, and put it in his money bag. The plane had enough fuel to stay in the air three and a half hours.

They taxied off at 6:07 P.M.

The weather in the area was described as "extremely turbulent." According to the Federal Aviation Authority, at least one commercial liner saw fit to change course.

Randy Hughes' Piper Comanche 250 crashed at approximately 7:00. There were no survivors.

a fan remembers:

Starring in a Better Land

*by Dorsey Dixon**

The world stood still and trembled,
When the news was flashed around,
That a fatal aeroplane failed to fly,
And came crashing to the ground.

Cowboy Copas, Hawkshaw Hawkins,
Patsy Cline and Hughes
Never dreamed when they took off,
That they were going to lose.

Their plane roared out from Kansas,
And headed for Tennessee.
Flying back to dear old Nashville,
And the Grand Ole Opry.

No one will ever know just why,
That fatal plane went wrong,
Carrying our wonderful singers,
To that wonderful land of song.

*Dixon was a successful regional (The Carolinas) singer and songwriter. His forte was traditional mountain music.

The country music loving world,
And that's including me,
Will miss those Grand Ole Opry stars
That sang for you and me.

Let not your heart be troubled,
For God can give and take.
Ever since He made this world,
He's not made one mistake.

In closing my sad story
About these happy four,
Now singing in a better land
With loved ones gone before,

I want to add there's peace and hope
In trusting in the Lord.
Just keep on trusting, doing good,
And you won't lose your reward.

There'll come a time when everyone
That's living here below
Will understand the reason why
Our singers had to go.

Don't say goodbye forever,
For there will be a change.
Just keep the hope that in a better land
We'll hear them play and sing.

Cowboy Copas, Hawkshaw Hawkins,
Patsy Cline and Hughes,
We'll meet you in a better land
Where we can never lose.

(*K-Bar-T Country Roundup* newsletter; April 1, 1963)

2
"Gotta Lot of Rhythm in My Soul"

Patsy Cline: **"Mama, we got company."**

Hilda Hensley: **"Virginia, it's eleven o'clock!"**

Patsy Cline: **"It's Wally Fowler!"**

Hilda Hensley: **"I nearly dropped dead!"**

"Everybody asks how Patsy got interested in country music," began Mrs. Hilda Hensley, Patsy Cline's mother, who still lives in Patsy's home town of Winchester, Virginia. "All I can say is that it must have been in her blood. She certainly didn't take after me or her daddy."

Virginia Patterson Hensley was born September 8, 1932, in the hamlet of Gore, some fifteen miles outside of Winchester on Highway 50. The small country house in which she lived stands today, rundown and overrun with weeds.

"As a child Patsy idolized Shirley Temple. She would come home from the movies after seeing the pictures twice and say, 'Mama, I want to be a dancer like her.'

"I'd say, 'What! Now listen, Virginia. . .' but it didn't do any good. It wasn't too long before she was tap dancing all over the house. I'd stand there and watch her and shake my head. But I couldn't help but smile or laugh. She was something!

"We entered Patsy in a dance competition when she was four. To our utter amazement she won! She took first prize! And Patsy had never had any formal training. At first, I figured she was just going through a phase, but then I began to wonder. But I was right! Because then came the music. Not singing, but playing the piano."

Patsy had a half-brother, Randolph, and a half-sister, Tempie Glenn, from Mr. Hensley's previous marriage.

"Tempie Glenn was an accomplished pianist," Mrs. Hensley related. "Whenever Virginia visited her, she would be in ecstasy. She'd even come home on a cloud. Virginia loved to just sit and listen to Tempie Glenn play for hours. When she got home she'd tell me, 'I'm gonna play like that one day!' I'd say, 'What! Now, listen, Virginia. . .' I explained to her that we couldn't afford to give her lessons.

"But, Virginia being Virginia, she finally drove us so crazy about having to play the piano that her father and I gave her one for her seventh birthday. Now she could play the piano at home, at least.

"Oh, she'd already been playing the piano—any piano she could find—even though she never had a lesson. Virginia could play by ear. Once I arranged to give her instructions. The teacher asked Virginia to sit at the piano and play something. In the middle of the composition the teacher looked at me and said, 'She's got a natural gift. You'll be wasting your money. She's terrific playing by ear. I don't think I could ever teach her to play the hard (correct) way.'

"So I've always felt it must have been Patsy's love of music that made her want—that drove her so—to become a Country singer. That was the one thing Patsy longed to achieve more than anything else. From the time she was about ten, Patsy was living, eating, and sleeping Country music. I know she never wanted anything so badly as to be a star on the Grand Ole Opry.

"Patsy loved all the Country stars—she didn't have one particular favorite. She adored them all. And she could tell you about each and every one of them. If she could help it, she'd never miss the Opry broadcasts."

Mrs. Hensley discovered early on that when Patsy set her mind to doing something, it was not long before she achieved that goal. Even Patsy's friends took her seriously when she spoke of being a Country star. Sometimes kids laugh when you speak of future aspirations, but it seems the kids in Gore realized Patsy meant business.

"The way I looked at it, if I wanted to go to Nashville and be on the Grand Ole Opry, the earlier I got started the better. So I used to sing or hum along with just about every song I'd hear on the Opry shows."

While Patsy was in grammar school the Hensleys moved into town. Their new house, on South Kent Street between Monmouth and Germain, only a few blocks from downtown and the Winchester City Hall, was a wide, two-story house with shuttered windows, a porch, and oak trees in front. Being in town put Patsy in closer proximity to the local radio stations and achieving another goal.

"The one thing I wanted to do more than anything was sing Country music. One day I got real brave and decided it was time for me to do what I wanted to do."

At the ripe old age of fourteen Patsy had paid enough dues.

His Saturday morning live show had become a tradition with Patsy, so it was natural she would single out Joltin' Jim McCoy to introduce the phenomenon that was to become Patsy Cline.

"She came to see me at WINC," laughed McCoy. "I was one of the disk jockeys there who had a band and did live broadcasts. Someone buzzed me to say this girl was waiting to see me."

Patsy described her meeting with McCoy: "I found the musicians and asked who the leader was. This big fellow came out and looked at me and replied, 'I'm the leader. What can I do for you?'

"You're Joltin' Jim McCoy?"

"Yes," McCoy answered. "Who are you?"

"Virginia Hensley from here in Winchester. I listen to your show all the time. I'm a singer and I want to sing on your show."

McCoy explained that Patsy was as cocky as anything he had ever seen, "But I was impressed with her naïveté and determination— and nerve. I was polite and listened to what she had to say."

"If you give me a chance to sing with you on the radio, I'll never ask for pay."

"Honey, you think you're good enough to sing with us live on the radio?"

"Yes, sir."

"Well, if you got nerve enough to stand before that mike, I've got nerve enough to let you do it."

McCoy noted that, even then, "I should have known to whom I was speaking. Nobody needed to have warned me. I should have seen it right away. Nothing scared Patsy, least of all a mere microphone in a radio station that broadcast to thousands of people.

"She did a bit for me, and as soon as I heard Patsy I realized this girl meant business. I thought to myself, 'Someday this gal is gonna be a star.' "

Patsy became a Saturday morning regular with McCoy and his band, the Melody Playboys. She began practicing long, hard hours to develop her natural gifts.

"And they were many," McCoy said. "Here was this young child from Winchester who walked in off the street one day and none of us knew what a find we had or what she was capable of doing. How she would impress and thrill us. She wanted to be a star and nothing was going to stand in her way. But Patsy just didn't want to be a star, she knew she had to work hard and she didn't mind that one bit."

Mrs. Hensley concurred. "Patsy was really dedicated to becoming a serious singer and worked at that goal without let up. She had to. The only place she'd ever sung was in the Gore Baptist Church choir where she'd do duets with me. Patsy had a lovely voice and people always enjoyed listening to her and made comments on her singing. She especially loved gospel and religious songs.

"Patsy always knew what she wanted! She was determined from her teens to get it. Everybody she spoke to about becoming a singer told her how tough it would be for a woman to go into country music. But that didn't faze Patsy! Knowing her, it probably made her all the more determined.

"I knew there was no way of talking Patsy down, but I'd say, 'What! Now, listen, Virginia. . .' It didn't do any good. She had made her mind up. It was going to be a struggle. In those days it was difficult for a woman anywhere—no matter what she wanted to do. It wasn't just in Country music."

Mrs. Hensley decided that if Patsy was going to do it, she might as well do it right. It was time to do something positive to help her along. Hilda took Patsy by the Melody Lane Club on the Martinsburg, West Virginia, Pike and introduced her to Jumbo Rinker, a young pianist from Winchester.

William R. Rinker, 60, still living, playing the piano and organ, and working in Winchester, "was awfully robust as a child and that's how I got that nickname Jumbo. Even after I grew up and became quite skinny, the name stuck."

"Patsy's mom brought her to see me and asked me if I would back her on local dates whenever possible. Patsy was about fourteen or fifteen, but just as pretty as could be and, at first, I thought she was older. I found out how young she was when I asked her for a date, but we still went out though I was eleven or twelve years older than she was. It didn't matter to her, she told me."

Rinker not only dated Patsy off and on for 11 years but also was to play a very important part in introducing Patsy to her first professional job.

On the home front, while Patsy was in the throes of establishing herself locally, Hilda's marriage to Sam Hensley, a master blacksmith at the Norfolk, Virginia, Navy Yard, who was several years her senior, was deteriorating. Hensley had the two children from his earlier marriage and, with Hilda, another daughter, Sylvia Mae, and a younger son, Samuel, Jr.

Mrs. Hensley does not discuss what circumstances led to problems in her marriage, but acquaintances and friends of Patsy's from the area said, to quote one source, "from the way Patsy talked, Mr. Hensley's heavy drinking might have contributed to the matter."

Patsy's early homelife in Winchester has often been described as an unhappy one. It was far from it. She had a beautiful relationship with her mother, whom she turned to time and time again for support and found it.

"If I made a list of the people I admire," Patsy said once, "mom would probably fill up half of it. She could do anything and everything. And she'd do it for me. She was the one person I could depend upon. She never once let me down. I would never have gone anywhere if it hadn't been for Mother's faith and support."

In 1947, just after Patsy turned 15 and Hilda was 31, Sam Hensley, for whatever reasons, deserted Mrs. Hensley. The burden fell on Patsy to help support the family. "This is going to sound like a mother talking," explained Mrs. Hensley, "but I could never have asked for a better daughter than Patsy. After her father left, and with Sylvia and Sam in grammar school, Patsy quit Handley High School early in her sophomore year and went to work at Gaunt's Drug Store downtown as a clerk and fountain attendant. I don't know what we would have done if it hadn't been for Patsy. It was terrible that she had to leave school, but there was no other way we could have made ends meet. Patsy considered it her family obligation.

"We had long talks about it. Patsy was born when I was sixteen so, even as she got older, we were more like sisters than mother and daughter. We had the type of relationship where I could go to her and she could come to me and discuss very personal things. In spite of her enthusiasm for becoming a Country singer, she was really level-headed and realistic. Patsy had a head on her shoulders.

"If I never let her down, I can turn around and truthfully say she never let us down. And, when she went to work, neither did her employers, the Gaunts. They proved to be true, understanding friends.

"The Gaunts treated Patsy more like a daughter than an employee," Mrs. Hensley noted. "When she got singing dates they let her off early so she could come home and change. With any extra money saved after Patsy and I took care of the bills, I would buy material and make outfits for her to wear."

Years later, Patsy remembered those bleak days of working all day and night, and laughed heartily about them: "Mother would come and pick me up at work and take me wherever I could get a job. We only had the one car, so Mom either had to stay with me the whole night or drop me off and come back and get me later. Jumbo Rinker and Kenneth Windle played for me then, but Mother didn't trust anybody with me. Usually we'd get home about three in the morning—totally exhausted. A few hours later I was up getting ready for work and Mom was fixing breakfast for the kids. And, you know something, we loved every minute of it!"

Winchester photographer Ralph Grubbs met Patsy at Gaunt's Drug Store. "I like to think I played at least a small part in helping Patsy get started. I was older, about thirty-six, and very much interested in her when others didn't seem to care, and she rather depended on me for advice. I was a good listener. We met at the Gaunt's soda fountain. I went in almost every afternoon for a milkshake. I didn't know Patsy had quit school. She looked older than her sixteen years.

"The main topic of conversation was Patsy's burning desire to become a singer on the Grand Ole Opry. The first time I heard her sing—she was, of course, Virginia Hensley—was in an amateur contest sponsored by the Winchester Forty and Eight [a civic organization]. I was on one of the committees.

She and a girlfriend, Virginia Taylor, put together a song-and-dance routine. I tried to get Patsy to do a solo after I heard her sing. I felt she'd have a better chance of winning.

"Patsy refused. 'I can't break up the act,' she told me, 'and I don't want to make Virginia mad and lose her friendship. It's gonna be a team.' They had costumes that I believe Patsy's mother made. She didn't take first prize, but she and Virginia were runners-up. This made her only more determined to get on the Opry. She had had a taste.

"One afternoon at the drugstore Patsy showed me a letter she had written to the Opry to ask for a chance to audition. She said everybody made fun of her for even thinking she'd be able to sing in Nashville. 'A friend told me I'd be crazy to send it,' she told me. 'What do you think?' I said, 'By all means, do it. You've got everything to gain and nothing to lose.'

"I was not a musician or a judge of musical talent. I only knew what I liked to hear, and to me Patsy's voice was much better than some of those singing with the Grand Ole Opry at the time. About a week later Patsy received an answer from the Opry asking for pictures and a recording of her voice. She asked me, 'Could you take my picture and let me pay you something each week when I come back from Nashville?'

"She admitted she scarcely had enough money saved to even make the trip. 'I don't know what my mother is going to say about all this!' she worried. Patsy said she didn't know what she was going to do about getting a recording 'cause she certainly didn't have that kind of money. Recordings were expensive then. There was no tape. They were made on wire reels [a spool of guitar string-type wire was fed over a magnetized head. These machines were not always reliable and never became popular].

"I spoke to Bob Gaines, a partner in the G&M Music Store, and he agreed to make Patsy's recording in their studio. When Patsy and I selected the pictures from the proofs, I told her, 'This is a gift, so you don't have to worry about paying me. It's my contribution to getting you started on your singing career.' Bob didn't charge Patsy for the recording either. A couple of weeks later Patsy told me she would soon be going to Nashville and the Grand Ole Opry. I don't know whether the audition was a result of her letters or Wally Fowler's visit to Winchester."

Wally Fowler and his Oak Ridge Quartet came to the Palace

Theatre in Winchester for a performance in 1948. Through his old-fashioned country and gospel All-Night Sings, broadcast live on WSM Friday nights from the Grand Ole Opry's Ryman Auditorium, Fowler had become a country music institution (in 1964 he took gospel music to Carnegie Hall). Today he is one of the all-but-forgotten pioneers of that staple of Country called the gospel caravans.

He was a big enough star for his appearance in Winchester to be considered a major event—at least among Country fans. Fowler's visit is surely something Mrs. Hensley has never been able to forget.

"How in the world could I ever forget that incident? One day while I was preparing supper, Patsy came into the kitchen. She put her arm around me. I thought to myself, 'Something's up! What's she got up her sleeve now?'

"Patsy said, 'Mama, Wally Fowler's at the Palace and I'm going down to the theater and see if I can get on the show.'

"I looked at her and said, 'What! You're going to do what?' But by then Patsy was good and used to that."

"Mother, you heard me. I'm going down to the Palace and try and catch Mr. Fowler and talk him into letting me be on his show."

"Well, I knew the decision had been made so there was no use trying to talk to her. No force on earth could have stopped her when Patsy was determined.

"Patsy went to the stage door of the Palace and asked to see Mr. Fowler. The man on the door just laughed. He told her 'Nothing doing.' Mr. Fowler was a star and he couldn't have people bothering him before the show.

"But, ha, they didn't know Patsy. With her, where there was a will there was a way. Even if there hadn't been, Patsy would have found one!

"She knew one of the ushers. Patsy asked for her at the lobby. When she told her friend her scheme, she managed to sneak Patsy by the ticket taker. As soon as she got into the theater, Patsy made her way backstage just as if she was working there. She waited in the hallways and dark corners as she made the rounds looking for Mr. Fowler. When Patsy found him, she went up to him and stopped him cold in his tracks."

" 'Mr. Fowler, can I audition for your show?' she bubbled enthusiastically.

" 'Who's this girl' boiled an obviously vexed Fowler, who was surrounded by his entourage.

" 'My name's Virginia Hensley.'
" 'What do you want? What do you do?'
" 'I sing—'
" 'Oh, is that right? Boys, she sings!'
" 'Mr. Fowler—'
" 'So you think you can sing?'
" 'Yes, sir. I think so. I know so. I'd like you to listen and tell me what you think.'
" 'Oh, you would, would you!'
" 'Why, yes. Yes, sir!'
" 'Okay, young lady, you sing.'
" 'You mean it?'
" 'You sing. I'll listen.'
" 'Just like this?'
" 'Just like this'
" 'But. . .'
" 'But what? You wanna back down now that I'm giving you your big chance?'
" 'Well, you—'
" 'Young lady, are you gonna sing for me? I've got a show to do.'
" 'I just. . . Okay.' "

Patsy sang, Fowler listened. He stood there mesmerized by what he was hearing—and that very night at the Palace Theatre in Winchester, Virginia, little Miss Virginia Hensley made her theatrical debut.

It would be a night to remember.

When Fowler introduced Patsy to the audience as his new discovery right from Winchester, it came as a big surprise. As Patsy came out on stage there was a wild burst of proud applause for this home-town girl.

Patsy sang and captivated the audience. She went off stage to thunderous applause.

"This little girl is really something," thought Fowler. "She might have the potential to be groomed for bigger and better things."

"When Patsy got home I was already in bed," Mrs. Hensley said. "She came into my room very quietly and told me, 'Mama, we got company.' I said, 'What! Virginia, it's eleven o'clock.' She told me what she had done. 'It's Wally Fowler.' I replied, 'Wally Fowler! You've got to be kidding.' I got up and put a robe on. I went into the living room not knowing what I was going to find. But sure enough, there was Wally Fowler, big as life. I nearly dropped dead!"

" 'Now, don't let me interrupt anything, ma'am,' Fowler told me.

"I don't know what he thought I'd be doing at that hour of night!"

" 'I just wanted to talk to you about Virginia. She wants to be a singer on the Grand Ole Opry.'

" 'That's right.'

" 'She has an amazing voice. I'd like to arrange an audition for her in Nashville with WSM Radio.'

"Mr. Fowler went on and on and Patsy got more and more excited until I capitulated and finally agreed to the audition. He left that night and I, honestly, never expected we'd hear from him again. But Patsy sure hoped so. That's all that was on her mind for days. She was optimistic, so I didn't want to see her let down.

"Patsy kept telling me over and over, 'If Wally Fowler came over here from the theater, he must have liked the way I sing.' I kept praying over and over, 'Please, God, in your eternal wisdom, let Wally Fowler call so we can get some peace around here.' "

Of course, Mrs. Hensley did not know that Wally Fowler had an infamous reputation of "discovering" young girl singers in the various towns he played. He'd audition them and they'd never hear from him again.

Either Fowler had method to his madness or he was sincere because as Mrs. Hensley relates, "I have to say, Mr. Fowler was a man of his word. He had taken a genuine interest in Patsy. He called us a few weeks later and asked, 'Can you bring Virginia to Nashville for an audition at WSM with Jim Denny, the general manager of the Grand Ole Opry?' "

"Oh, Mama," enthused Patsy, "I knew Mr. Fowler wouldn't let me down! I just knew it."

"Well," says Mrs. Hensley, "as excited as Patsy was, I knew I'd be a goner if I said no, so I agreed to bring her to Nashville. He told me he'd call me back with the arrangements."

Fowler set the Nashville audition with Denny for a Friday morning.

"The trip was nearly eight hundred miles and our old car could not make it," smiled Mrs. Hensley. "But I asked a friend and she offered to take us to Nashville. The Gaunts gave Patsy a Friday off. I had no one to leave Sylvia Mae and Sammy with so we had to take them with us. We didn't have money for a motel, so we drove all Thursday night. Oh, dear, what a mess it was! Patsy was fidgety, the kids were fidgety, I was fidgety, and we probably all drove our friend fidgety!

"We reached the outskirts of Nashville just as the sun was coming up. We pulled into a rest area east of town to stretch. Patsy saw these concrete picnic tables and said, 'I'm tired, Mama. I'm gonna take a little nap.' I have no idea what the poor people passing by at that hour of the morning must have thought. Looking back, however, it was funny. Then it was a mess! A real mess!

"Driving into town a little later, we stopped at an Esso station so everyone could wash up. That's also something I'll never forget! There I was with the kids and Patsy in the ladies' room—all of us in this cubicle doing one thing and then another. And if that wasn't bad enough, Patsy was trying to change into her good dress and put on her makeup!"

In later years, Patsy, backstage at the Ryman Auditorium in what was called the "girl singers' dressing room"—nothing more than a cubicle in the ladies' room—used to joke that "before I ever came to the Grand Ole Opry, I had a better dressing room than this. And it was a crapper, too!"

The Grand Ole Opry is and always has been a revered institution. And since its inception on November 28, 1925, it has become a show business phenomenon.

More than a month before, on October 5, the National Life and Accident Insurance Company's radio station WSM—its call letters reflecting the firm's insurance goals: "We Shield Millions"—began broadcasting.

WSM began as a 1,000-watt station, then one of only two in the South. The station's signal was twice as strong as 85 percent of the radio broadcast operators in the United States.

The idea for a live Country music program came from George D. Hay, who on radio called himself "the solemn old judge." As chief announcer at WLS in Chicago he originated the WLS Barn Dance. When he joined WSM as station director he launched the WSM Barn Dance. Two years later, in a moment of jest, Hay gave that program a name that has stuck ever since.

As an affiliate of the National Broadcasting Company radio

network, WSM carried an hour program called "The Music Appreciation Hour" hosted by Dr. Walter Damrosch, the composer and Metropolitan Opera conductor. WSM followed that with three hours of country music that ranged from an 80-year-old fiddler, Uncle Jimmy Thompson, who boasted "I can fiddle the taters off the vine," to string bands and minstrels.

Had Dr. Damrosch been touring in the Deep South with his Damrosch Opera Company and tuned into the barn dance broadcast he probably would have choked on his baton.

As Hay once said, "We must confess that the change in pace, when we hit the air with our mountain clans and vocal trapeze performers, and quality was immense. But that is part of America—fine lace and homespun cloth."

Dr. Damrosch signed off his "Music Appreciation Hour" with some dignified comments but one particular night—for some unexplained reason—he presented a young composer from Iowa who, with symphony backing, depicted the onrush of a locomotive.

Judge Hay, not to be outdone by a Yankee, said upon signing on, "Dr. Damrosch told us it is generally agreed that there is no place in the classics for realism. However, for the next three hours we will present nothing but realism. It will be down-to-earth for the earthy."

At the close of a solo by DeFord Bailey, a black harmonica player who was considered a wizard of the instrument, Hay intoned, "For the past hour we have been listening to music taken largely from grand opera, but from now on we will present the grand ole opry."

It did not take long for crowds from throughout Tennessee and the South to clog the corridors of WSM at Seventh Avenue and Union Street in downtown Nashville. The popularity of the Grand Ole Opry led to the construction of Studio C, an acoustically designed auditorium that held 500 fans.

When WSM could no longer accommodate the throngs, a move to the southwest section of the city was made, and the old Hillsboro movie theater was rented. The next home was a large tabernacle across the Cumberland River in east Nashville. The setting here, splintery benches and sawdust on the floor, was perfect but within two years the Opry outgrew this location. The show moved to the new War Memorial Auditorium near the state capitol and, in an effort to curb the ever-growing crowds, an admission of 25¢ was charged. This was no deterrent. The weekly Opry fans averaged more than 3,000 and many in the overflow crowd had traveled long distances. In 1943 the Grand Ole Opry relocated on Fourth Avenue near lower Broadway in the Ryman Auditorium.

Riverboat captain Tom Ryman built the auditorium in 1831 as a tabernacle for a preacher who he had heckled in a tent revival meeting and who subsequently brought Ryman to the Lord.

The Grand Ole Opry quickly became the most popular, loudest, and strongest single voice for the propagation of Country music. (In 1974 the Opry moved to a magnificent 4,400-seat facility in the National Life Opryland complex.)

So it was with much trepidation that Patsy Cline came to audition for "what was not some little Winchester show but the Grand Ole Opry, the biggest country music program in all of the United States."

Patsy had tuned in weekly to hear such personalities as Whitey Ford, "the Duke of Paducah"; comedienne Minnie Pearl; Texas Ruby and the Fox Hunters; Roy Acuff; Lester Flatt and Earl Scruggs; Mother Maybelle of the famed Carter family; and Lonzo and Oscar.

When she arrived at the station with her mother, Patsy was a bundle of exploding energy. "But if she was nervous," her mother said, "you could have fooled me."

At the stroke of nine, Mrs. Hensley asked for Jim Denny whose reputation as one of the shrewdest spotters of Country talent had only recently been tainted by the fact that he had passed by Hank Williams, who was recommended to him by Ernest Tubb. Williams signed with the competition, the Louisiana Hayride in Shreveport. (Later when he came to the Opry Denny also had the distinction of firing him in 1952.)

A receptionist informed Mrs. Hensley that Denny would be detained for a while on business that suddenly came up. Patsy and her mom went over what she was going to perform. They both were disappointed that Fowler could not be there.

Denny came to meet them and was very matter-of-fact, as if he was doing the audition because of an obligation to Fowler. He and Patsy talked and she won him over with her enthusiasm. Patsy told Denny how much appearing on the Grand Ole Opry would mean—how she had grown up wanting to pattern her life after so many of the stars. Soon Denny had his arm around Patsy and was ushering her into one of the small studios where bands would perform live on the radio.

He introduced Patsy to Moon Mullican and Patsy nearly went into shock. Denny was general manager of the Opry but an unknown entity to her, but "Oh, my God, Moon Mullican!" He was a star.

It was a moment she would never forget.

Audrey Mullican was a Texas farmer who became a showman's showman. Since he was from Moscow, Texas, Mullican was often chidingly called "the Russian." Because of his deftness on the piano at playing authentic blues sounds and adapting them to suit the country beat, it was said Mullican "could play the moon around anyone."

The nickname "Moon" stuck for a lifetime.

Mullican used the tag "King of the Hillbilly Piano Players."

"And that he was," asserted Ernest Tubb. "Moon was a character and a fine, fine artist. Owen Bradley, who was the leader of the WSM orchestra and eventually head of the Decca label in Nashville, modeled his playing on Moon's.

"Owen produced my sessions and used to play piano on the duets Red Foley and I did. Owen's an accomplished pianist but he's a pop musician. He'd keep it down when he was playing. And that wasn't good.

"I recall once he was playing real precise—you know, pop fashion—and I hollered, 'Owen, boy, loosen up. Play it hillbilly!' And he did.

"Then he asked, 'E.T., how was that?' I know he was expecting a compliment but I shot back 'Oh, it was all right but you need to play it like Moon Mullican.'

"When we finished, he asked, 'E.T., was that okay?' I replied, 'Well, yes, but it was about half as good as Moon would do so I'm gonna start calling you Half-Moon!'

"On the actual take I cued Owen, 'Okay, come in, Half-Moon.' Not long ago out in Montana a customer who'd been drinking too much asked, 'Hey, where's Half-Moon Bradley?' What a memory!"

By his death in 1967 Mullican had written such best-sellers as "New Jole Blon" (with Lou Wayne) and, he claimed, "I'll Sail My Ship Alone" (no credit given), which Patsy later recorded. He had over 600 releases.

Denny conferred with Mullican for his opinion after the

audition. They were so pleased with what they had heard that Denny asked Patsy and Hilda to stay over in Nashville at least another day so he could arrange for other WSM and Grand Ole Opry executives to come and hear Patsy sing.

Patsy had celebrated a birthday since she met Fowler, but had Denny signed her she would have been one of the youngest performers ever to appear on the Opry.

Remaining in Nashville proved to be the true obstacle. If Patsy was to stay over, that meant that Mrs. Hensley and the children, not to mention the family friend, would also have to remain. Either Denny did not state the situation in a positive enough manner or the Hensleys were too embarrassed to ask for assistance.

"It was not an easy decision to make," according to Mrs. Hensley. "I felt like I was holding Patsy's future in my hands. But I didn't know what to do. We simply did not have the money to stay in town."

Then there was an interruption.

Roy Acuff was in the adjacent studio preparing to guest host the popular "Noon- Time Neighbors," a farm news and country variety program that went on the air daily as a big dinner bell was rung. He came into the studio where Patsy and Hilda were talking to Mullican. Acuff asked Mullican, a "Noon-Time Neighbors" regular, who it was that he had heard singing.

"Roy, I want you to meet Miss Virginia Hensley from Winchester, Virginia," drawled Mullican. "And this is her mother. Y'all, this is Roy Acuff!"

"Well, we nearly dropped!" Patsy told entertainer Del Wood sometime later. "It was hard to believe. There we were talking to Roy Acuff!"

Miss Wood added, "From the way Patsy carried on, you could tell she still got her blood pressure up when she spoke of that moment and how exciting it must have been for her."

Acuff told Patsy, "Virginia, that's one of the sweetest voices I've ever heard!"

"He was so considerate and polite," explained Mrs. Hensley. "Quite the gentleman. He asked Patsy if she would honor him by singing on the 'Noon-Time Neighbors' broadcast. It was all too much! We had not been prepared for this type of reaction and response."

Patsy's guest spot over WSM with Mullican playing piano for her went off without a hitch, and Acuff again congratulated her and wished her luck. "We hope you'll be working with us real soon," he told her. "Don't let all these big shots running around here scare you. They're just like me and you. Stay calm and just be sincere!"

After the program Denny and Mrs. Hensley spoke. He told her he needed more time.

"I was standing there attempting to sort out in my mind how Patsy might be able to stay the night so Mr. Denny would have the time to do what he needed to do. Everything looked so positive. It also looked like that whatever Mr. Denny wanted to do would take a while. Things began to drag into the afternoon and still there was no definite word. It just did not appear possible for us to stay.

"I had Sylvia Mae and Sammy. My friend had to get back home. Patsy had her job. And we didn't have enough money to let the others go back and then return home on the bus. When it got late and we had not heard anything, it looked as if we would be left in Nashville without a way back. More than anyone, I knew how much Patsy had her heart set on all this, but we had just money enough for the gas to get us back to Winchester. I decided we would leave and see what would happen.

"Nothing happened. No one volunteered to do anything. I took Patsy aside and explained we could always come back again. She took the news, as disappointing as it was, better than I expected. That showed me what a big girl she was."

The group returned to Winchester. Patsy and Hilda's gambol did not pay off.

"We never heard from anyone," piped Mrs. Hensley. "Not a letter or call from Mr. Denny or anyone. I really thought that was a shame. They let us down. I guess we expected better treatment than that.

"Back home Patsy went back to work at Gaunt's Drug Store and back to doing singing dates with the local bands. She was determined more than ever. I knew she would never give up trying to make her dream come true."

Patsy waited. She just knew that one day WSM or Jim Denny or someone would call, and that her contract to appear with the Grand Ole Opry would be ready for her to sign.

It was not to be.

Nine years of ups and downs—both in Patsy Cline's personal life and career—followed.

But Patsy was undaunted.

"After all, Mama," she told Hilda. "Wally Fowler, Moon Mullican, and Roy Acuff thought I was great!"

She was, but only a handful of people knew it at the time.

3
"Crazy Dreams"

Patsy Hensley: **"My, you're a big man!"**

Gerald Cline: **"Yeah, and I got a fast car."**

Patsy Hensley: **"Which of you is fastest?"**

Gerald Cline: **"Want me to show you?"**

Like most Country artists starting out, Patsy Cline played rough places—taverns, beer joints, racetracks. Like any female singer, or any female, the least bit attractive, Patsy had her share of men chasing her.

"Those rough spots didn't bother her," laughed Mrs. Hensley. "Patsy did the family clubs, too, but she would go anywhere there were people willing to listen. Anyone who bothered her soon discovered she could take care of herself."

Men literally fell at Patsy's feet, but she was chasing rainbows and steady-dating Jumbo Rinker, her accompanist.

"Patsy could smile and the guys would be hog-tied," commented Rinker. "We had a thing going, but we were just romantic friends and not heading for any altars."

Besides working with Jumbo, Patsy joined Gene Shiner's Metronomes band as lead vocalist. Besides Gene on electric guitar, there was John Anderson playing bass, Bruce Van Kuern on piano, and Johnny Naid playing saxophone and violin.

"Patsy and I were neighbors on Kent Street. She and her mother lived in a big, old brick house. I knew she had been working with Jumbo, and I told her I had an opening. Sorry to say, the Metronomes didn't last but about four months, but we were a good solid group. We didn't do country, but were more or less a popular music band. Patsy sang torch songs. We played locally at the Winchester Armory, V.F.W., and the dance hall at the Winchester Airport."

Though Bill Peer is virtually uncredited, except for a mention occasionally that Patsy worked for him, he—in spite of several rivals who say they did—gave Patsy her first professional break and was responsible for making one of her dreams come true, that of becoming a recording artist.

Peer was an area disk jockey and musician, well known locally and in Nashville circles. He had been playing since age 13 when he joined the Log Cabin Boys on station WFMD in Frederick, Maryland. After performing with others for the next 10 years, Peer organized his own group, the Melody Boys and Girls, in 1941. Throughout the Forties and Fifties, Peer and band were regulars at the Joe Turner Arena in Washington, on the Mount Vernon Showboat, which cruised the Potomac, the Charles Town Racetrack in West Virginia, and the tri-state Moose Lodge circuit.

There are three reliable accounts of how Patsy Cline met Bill Peer. Each holds merit because of the source from which it emanates.

Mrs. Dolly Spiker of Kearneysville, West Virginia, the second wife and widow of Peer, recalls, "On numerous occasions after Patsy became successful, Bill told me how she came to the studio at WEPM in Martinsburg [West Virginia] in the early summer of nineteen fifty-two and introduced herself. She asked, 'Can't I sing with your band?' She and Bill discussed her aspirations and what she was doing to achieve them.

"Bill advised her, 'Okay, young lady, if you want to get to Nashville, I'll help you. First you get some material ready and then we'll get serious.' "

Mrs. Jenny Yontz of Charles Town, the first Mrs. Peer, reported, "Patsy came to Bill when she was just a young thing. She looked him up here at the Goode Brothers Garage, where Bill worked as parts manager. He was away in Michigan, so Patsy left word that she wanted to see him about auditioning for his band. When he returned, Bill contacted Patsy and she came back to the garage to meet with him."

Jumbo Rinker remembers that in late summer, 1952, he introduced Patsy to the steel-guitar player in Peer's band, Bobby Carper, a friend who ran a Winchester automobile body repair shop. Weeks later Rinker, while Patsy sat in the car, put more pressure on Carper, "Hey, Bobby, she's driving me nuts! When you gonna set Patsy up with Bill?"

Carper spoke to Peer that weekend and Peer told him, "Sure if she's ready, bring her over."

Whatever the route, Patsy did arrive at the Brunswick, Maryland, Moose Club September 27, 1952, before the 9:00 program of music was set to begin.

She walked up to Peer. "Hey, there, you remember me?"

"I sure do."

"Well, I'm ready."

"We'll see about that."

Patsy auditioned and "impressed the hell out of Bill." He hired her that Saturday night as lead vocalist for the Melody Boys and Girls. Bill was immediately smitten by Patsy's voice and although eleven years her senior, her charms. He began a relationship that would haunt him until the day he died and that caused him, and those close to him, heartache, bitterness, and regret.

"The first thing we gotta do," Peer told Patsy, "is change your name. Virginia just isn't right for a singer. Got any ideas?"

"Let me think about it."

"Your middle name's Patricia—"

"No, Patterson."

"It'll still work. How about Patsy Hensley?"

"Okay."

Peer told more than one person, "God, she's fantastic. A bundle of talent! She's got a voice that is gonna take her places." He rehearsed regularly with Patsy to improve her musical styling. In addition to his radio and garage jobs, Peer worked part-time selling Buicks and working for Fritt's Appliances in Frederick.

"Bill saved up everything he could and even went into debt spending to help Patsy," said Mrs. Yontz, with a tinge of anger in her voice. "He bought her clothes and attempted to get her a record contract. People in this area knew Patsy and her reputation. The first time I saw her I knew there was trouble ahead for me. She was definitely a person any man would take a second look at. I told Bill when she came along, 'Be careful. She's just going to use you. She'll stay with you until the opportunity she wants comes along.' But, of course, he didn't listen. He just fell in love. And love is blind!"

Besides Rinker, Patsy had been dating Elias Blanchfield of Martinsburg, to whom she was briefly engaged when she was 17, and Ray Horner of Le Gore, Maryland. She also continued to date Jumbo off and on. So whether Patsy was ever in love with Peer is a matter of conjecture. Some say, yes; an equal number say, no. Certainly she respected him, appreciated what he did for her career, and even grew to be very fond of him.

"Patsy was a rough person and, yet, tender-hearted, too," said Mrs. Yontz. "When I think back, I know she was never in love with Bill. It was one-sided. But he wouldn't let her alone, and she wanted to get ahead. And she took the opportunity."

Suddenly Patsy decided in December 1952, to mend her evil ways and settle down. It was not to be Patsy Hensley much longer. She shocked her mother with the news that she was getting married—and to the most unlikely candidate of all.

Gerald Cline, from all indications, was by sheer dint of the luxury of his grandiose bravado a big shot.

"Or so he said," pinpointed a former pal to a friend's query about Cline's persona. "If what you mean is was Gerald a bullshit artist, yes, he was that—and more!"

Gerald Cline was, perhaps, the most fascinating man to enter Patsy's life. He was definitely unique. Reviewing his life and their life together, one can only be puzzled at Patsy's attraction to him, especially at a time when she was vigorously pursuing a relationship with Bill Peer.

"When it all boiled down," asserted Fay Crutchley of Frederick, a long-time friend of Patsy and Gerald's "you just had to like Gerald. He was a truly likeable person. There was only one problem. You never knew when he was telling the truth. He'd be talking and carrying on, and I'd be laughing at him and calling him a lie bag."

Said Mr. Crutchley, "He was a lot of bull, but a really nice guy."

Reflected Mrs. Yontz, "Gerald Cline? Oh, my goodness! I always liked Gerald. I think everybody did. I really never got to know him too well—only from the Brunswick Moose Club. He was a braggart, but a lot of fun. Maybe he made Patsy laugh."

Cline's brother Nevin said, "Gerald liked flashy cars and bragged about money all the time—money he was supposed to have. When Patsy married him she found out Dad had the money."

Gerald Cline was born in 1925, the son of Earl Hezekiah and Lettie Viola Cline. Mr. Cline operated a general contracting and excavating firm under the name Earl H. Cline & Sons in Frederick, Maryland.

"My brother, whom I haven't seen in years," noted Nevin Cline, "gave everyone the impression he had plenty of money and that he owned the family company. In fact, he never had any money until Dad died. Gerald was never any kind of wealthy, except Saturday-night rich—after payday—and then Monday poor. He could only take the girls out one night a week. That's all he could afford.

"He never lifted a finger to help in the business unless he was forced. He was supposed to drive one of the trucks, but he'd only do that if you made him. Dad finally gave up on him and, in the end, had to make him secretary of the company, but I don't know what he ever did even in that position!"

Gerald Cline was definitely a ladies' man—his description will come later. He had sealed the bonds of matrimony several times—"and, I think," says Nevin, "each time with invisible glue."

In 1943, Gerald marched Ruth Moser up the aisle only because he was forced to by both families. She was three months pregnant. According to Nevin, Cline immediately went to live on the Moser farm to avoid the draft (farm exemption). Gerald and Ruth were divorced in late 1947—"after the war, please note!" Ruth Cline took Gerald to court a few months later, suing him for nonsupport of the couple's son, Ronnie.

"Dad never paid much attention to me when I was growing up," explained the 38-year-old Ronnie, "Hardly anybody knew he was my father. I haven't seen or heard from him in the last ten years."

Gerald began dating the late Evelyn Lenhart before his divorce from Ruth was final. Shortly after, his brother Nevin married his wife, Dorothy, that year, Gerald and Evelyn moved to the second floor of their two-family house in Braddock Heights, Maryland.

"My brother and I are total opposites," Nevin Cline pointed out. "I was more like my mother, he was more like my father. But Dad did have drive and ambition. Gerald would have been right at home in the time of the hippie movement. He never liked to stay in one place very long, or with any one person. I guess you could say he was what you'd now call a swinger."

The relationship between Gerald and Evelyn was shaky, at best. They were "together" nearly four years, and when they split he played the field, which was exactly what he was doing the night he came to join friends at the Brunswick Moose Club and heard Patsy Hensley singing.

Several of their friends have "no idea on earth what Patsy saw in Gerald." But, as Nevin put it, "as far as Gerald being attracted to Patsy, that's easy. She was a woman, attractive enough, and had a nice build."

On October ll, 1952, the five-foot-eight, 220-pound Gerald arrived for the Moose dance. There was no admission charge to hear Bill Peer and the Melody Boys and Girls, who had a contract to appear each Saturday night. No liquor was served, only setups. The crowd was family-oriented and many couples brought their children.

"It may not have been love at first sight when Patsy saw me," laughed Cline, "but it was for me. I walked into the party, the band came on, and there she was. She knocked me out!

"Patsy was just starting to appear with Bill Peer and do one-nighters with his band. The show began at nine o'clock, and during the first break I went up to meet Patsy and see if she'd join me for a drink."

Gerald introduced himself to Patsy when he was finally able to get her to one side. Bill Peer, who managed to hang on to Patsy, was right behind them.

"Hi, I'm Gerald Cline. I think you're fantastic."

"My, you're quite a big man!" Patsy was said to have replied.

"Yeah, and I got a fast car."

"Which of you is fastest?"

"Want me to show you?" Gerald was said to have shot back.

Patsy did have several drinks that evening with Gerald, but whether she left with him friends cannot recall. She probably did not, since it was not at all unusual for Patsy to have a date bring her to Brunswick and sit at a table with party regulars she met. Following their meeting, Gerald and Patsy began seeing each other regularly. Often he would drive to Winchester and pick Patsy up and bring her to work in Brunswick.

The couple applied for a marriage license on the morning of Friday, February 27, 1953, before Ellis Watcher, the Circuit Court clerk for Frederick County, Maryland, in Frederick. Gerald gave his age as 29 and his occupation as contractor. Under marital status, it was noted that he was divorced. Patsy listed her age as 20. Cline gave his parents'address at 436 East Patrick Street in Frederick as his local residence.

On Saturday afternoon, March 7, the Reverend Paul L. Althouse presided at the marriage of Patsy and Gerald in the Frederick Evangelical Reformed Church (United Church of Christ). Afterward they posed for photographs on the steps of the church. It was a small, simple wedding. Cline had not even invited his family.

"They were married and had an apartment before Nevin and I even knew about it," said Mrs. Dorothy Cline.

That evening Fay and Harry Crutchley attended the Brunswick Moose party and were seated at the same table with Gerald.

"We hadn't been to the club in several weekends and when Pat came on I poked Harry and said, 'Hey, this gal is fantastic! Where did Bill find her?' I asked Gerald, 'Who is that fantastic singer? You always know everyone—at least, all the pretty girls.' "

"That's Patsy Cline," Gerald told Fay.

"Patsy Cline? Is she related to you?"

"She's my wife!"

"Oh, Gerald, you're crazy. Come on, now. Who is she?"

"I told you! She's my wife. We just got married."

"You're crazy. I can't ever believe anything you ever say. I don't know if you're telling me the truth or not!"

"Well, you can believe me this time if you never believed me before. That's my wife."

Fay turned to Harry and asked, "Do you think that ole Gerald is telling the truth?"

"With him you never know! But he sure seems to be set on it. Must be."

"Gerald, if that's your wife, congratulations! I'd like to get to know her. She's a doll and a real terrific singer."

Later that night when Gerald introduced Patsy to Fay "was the first time I really and truly believed what he had been saying."

Patsy and Fay Crutchley began a friendship that evening

which lasted "until the day she died."

Says Fay, "Although I didn't see too much of Pat after she became really big, we had a strong bond between us that neither one of us could ever let loose of. We had some times together. Patsy and I shared a lot of confidences. Doris Fritts of Charles Town and I were two of Pat's closest friends. We were buddies, the girls she ran around with.

"I really never asked Pat what she saw in Gerald. As cocky and boastful as he was—you know, always acting like a big shot— he was a lot of fun. But, just like Harry said, he was full of it! Some people thought of Pat as a hard woman, but not me. We got along great. She had a marvelous sense of humor. For that time period—the fifties—I guess Pat, as far as the way men looked at women, was a bit on the brassy side. She liked colorful clothes, dangly earrings, make-up. But, from the standpoint of a friend, she was lovely, warm, and generous.

"I can sit right here in my living room and look across to the couch and still see Pat sitting there laughing and doing all sorts of crazy things. Besides our friendship, I must say that I idolized her way of singing. I guess I was one of her biggest fans.

"I never got tired of being with her or listening to her sing. On Saturdays we used to spend almost the entire day together. I'd leave Frederick about twelve-thirty and meet Pat at the Brunswick Moose about one, then just sit with her and the band while they rehearsed. I'd bring some clothes with me, go to a girlfriend's and change, then go back to the Moose that evening. Harry would join me and we'd have a long table near the stage where all the regulars sat. Pat would be with us off and on throughout the night. On special occasions, like New Year's Eve or someone's anniversary, Harry and I and Pat and Gerald would get together and have dinner before the show."

According to Mrs. Hensley, "Patsy seemed to have no misconceptions about marriage slowing down her career goals or sidetracking them completely. We all liked Gerald. Not only was he a very nice person but he was also quite considerate. We were all just a bit surprised at their marrying. I would have thought that with her career drive, marriage would have been the furthest thing from Patsy's mind."

It was not long, given Patsy's determination to become a star and Gerald's personality and mode of living, that problems developed in the marriage.

"Pat was the type of person who liked to travel and get around," explained Mrs. Crutchley. "And she never lost sight of her goal to become a big singer. She knew she was good and knew she was going to make it. She told me many times, 'I'm going to the top. I'm going to the top.' I don't think anything in the world could have stopped Pat from reaching for that star of hers. It wasn't even that far away, as far as she was concerned.

"It was obvious that Gerald wanted a wife, someone to take care of him. It didn't seem that Pat's working bothered him at first. He would even travel with her from date to date with the band for a while. It didn't take long before he got tired of that, and Pat didn't seem to mind. But, on the other hand, you had Bill Peer coming into the picture. It gets complicated from then on and some of the things that went on were absolutely ridiculous and hilarious."

According to one of the musicians in Peer's group, "Gerald never did help Patsy that much with her career. It was always Bill who was putting out the money to help her along."

To get away from his family, Patsy and Gerald took an apartment at 824 East Patrick Street in Frederick. It was only a block away from the impressive Cline family home. They lived in the second floor unit of the two-family house, which was owned by Harry Newton, one of Cline's employees.

Bill Peer was good at his promise to help Patsy get to Nashville and the Grand Ole Opry. On April 10, 1953, Bill and his wife, Jenny, drove Gerald and Patsy to Music City.

"We had adjoining rooms at the Colonial Motel. The main purpose of the trip was to go to the Opry, but Bill also planned to try and introduce Patsy around. He knew Ernest Tubb from his appearances in our area, especially at the Charles Town Racetrack. Bill would either be playing that same date or sometimes even providing backup for Mr. Tubb or one of the other acts.

"It was Mr. Tubb, I believe, who invited Bill to come down to Nashville and WSM radio. We went to the Grand Ole Opry and, courtesy of Mr. Tubb, got to go backstage and stand just off the stage and watch the broadcast."

Peer's son Larry remembers his dad speaking of the trip to Nashville, "Dad told me he was there just before Elvis Presley became really famous and that he got to see him sing on the Opry. And he told me of how the people in the audience didn't like Elvis. Dad said Elvis came off the stage in tears and that

Ernest Tubb took him aside, put his arm around him, and consoled him, 'Don't you worry about that now, boy. You did a fine job. They don't know.'

"Dad told me Elvis replied, 'Well, I'm gonna show 'em. I'm gonna make 'em eat all those words!' "

After the Opry, the Clines and the Peers went around the corner from the Ryman Auditorium, across Broadway, to the Ernest Tubb Record Shop.

Tubb had come to Nashville out of Crisp, Texas. He was quickly dubbed "the Father of Country Music." He had a massive following who adored his Western swing music and hillbilly vocals. Tubb is given credit for experimenting with and popularizing the electric guitar. He was the first Country performer to play New York's Carnegie Hall, where he uttered the oft-quoted remark, "My, my! This place sure could hold a lot of hay!" He came to the Opry in 1932, via two forgettable Durango Kid Westerns, after his smash "I'm Walking the Floor Over You." Tubb was nicknamed "The Texas Troubadour," had countless hits on Decca/MCA Records, and was a Country music staple both on the Opry and in his annual tours until his death in 1984.

During the fifties, prior to the onslaught of the record clubs, mail-ordering Country and gospel records, promoted over radio airways, was big business. Tubb's huge shop virtually monopolized Country products through its Grand Ole Opry advertisments and constant plugs on his very own radio show, "The Ernest Tubb MidNite Jamboree," broadcast live after the Opry on Saturday nights.

It was tradition for the Country stars to make periodic visits to be on the show. Tubb would introduce them with great fanfare, making sure to note their latest release was in stock "in a record bin right here before my eyes." It was also customary for Tubb to receive promising newcomers and let them do a quick number with his band.

That Saturday night the Peers and Clines visited Tubb they were treated as old friends. Tubb brought Patsy on the broadcast and had her sing two songs and paid Peer and his band several compliments. After the program, while the ladies stargazed, Peer and Gerald, spoke with Tubb about what direction to go in with Patsy.

Upon their return to Maryland the couples became good friends. "I'd only get to the dances at the Brunswick Moose once in a while. My children were youngsters and I had to be at home most of the time. But whenever I'd go, it was like a party—Gerald and his jokes and big talk, Patsy singing, and Bill's band, which was really quite a good one. There were times when I'd go out on the one-nighters with them, but this was rare. Gerald enjoyed going with them. He probably acted like a big shot and told everyone he was Bill and Patsy's manager or that it was his band!

"But soon Gerald was staying at home and suddenly a lot of funny things were going on. I had a feeling that I knew what it was, but then I wasn't positive. Bill was always making excuses. He'd tell me one thing, and often Patsy would say something else. I didn't believe Bill, and I didn't know whether or not I could believe Patsy. After a while I wouldn't believe anything either one of them would tell me."

What was going on was an increasingly torrid romance between Peer and Patsy. They would go off together, then he'd return to Jenny, and Patsy would go home to Gerald. Patsy evidently felt comfortable enough with the situation of considering Jenny her friend because she invited her to the twenty-first birthday party Mrs. Hensley gave for Patsy in September 1953.

"Whatever happened between Patsy and Bill Peer," indicated Nevin Cline, "Gerald allowed to happen. Patsy would ask him to take her to the different places where Bill was working and stay with her through the show. He did that a few times, but soon he got to where he refused.

"He told Patsy, 'I want you to stay home! I want you to be my wife!' She'd tell him, 'Well, I ain't gonna. I have to sing!' Dad spoke to Gerald and asked him, 'Son, why don't you take your wife where she needs to go when she's working? Don't use coming in on time [to the contracting firm] as an excuse, 'cause you sure ain't doing a damn thing around here.' "

Of the Cline marriage, Fay Crutchley noted, "I don't think there was any one major problem. Pat simply just liked music, and Gerald kept telling her he had a business to run—at least, he was supposed to be working with his family. Pat wanted to go, go, go. Gerald figured she should be home at night with him.

"But, as far as any romance between Pat and Bill, at that time, they fooled me. When we all would go out, it was like Pat and Gerald were one big happy family. After the shows Saturday nights, when Bill got everything packed away, Pat, Gerald, Bill, Harry, sometimes our son Harry Lee, and myself would all go over to Hagerstown [Maryland] to a Chinese restaurant that stayed open all night. We'd either get chow mein to take out or we'd sit there and eat and just have a royal good time.

"When Gerald was at the Brunswick Moose, he and Pat would occasionally dance together, and I don't think it was something she really enjoyed doing.

"They seemed to have a marriage just about like anyone else's, except Pat was in show business. They didn't have children, and I don't know if they wanted any. Pat was certainly not one of these women who went around talking constantly about wanting to have kids. She was more concerned at that time about making a career for herself as a singer. Harry and I never even remember Pat saying that she and Gerald had fights."

Fay told of a time Patsy expressed what she thought of Gerald's bragging and showing off. "It was Pat, Gerald, and Bill and they were coming back from somewhere late at night. Gerald was speeding, as always, and Pat said, 'Babe, you better slow down. The cops patrol this area all the time.' He got real puffy and exploded, 'Cops! Screw them. I ain't scared of any cops. They know who I am and how important my family is. Ain't no cop gonna give me a ticket!'

"Pat told me, 'And then it happened, just like clockwork. The cops were coming after us with sirens blaring. Gerald pulled over and we waited for the officer. He asked Gerald for his driver's license and wanted to know if Gerald knew he was way over the speed limit. 'I wasn't speeding, was I?' he meekly asked. I wanted to laugh. Then Gerald just sat there, scared to death to open his mouth. He didn't say a damn word! Bill did all the talking.'

"It seems Bill might have known the patrolman or vice versa. But it was Bill's smooth talking that got them off with only a warning. When they started up again, Gerald said out loud, 'You see, it was just like I said. I guess we showed him!' Then Pat yelled, 'Pull over! I think I'm going to puke!' "

On a Saturday night in June 1954, Gerald was not with Patsy when she needed him. She was at the Brunswick Moose Club that afternoon for rehearsal and complained of not feeling well. Fay Crutchley noticed it right away and tried to get Patsy to go back home and rest.

"Nah, hoss, it ain't that bad," Patsy told Fay. "I can't miss a night's work and let my public down."

"Listen, Pat, your public can do without you for one night. Bill can always get another singer, but I'll never find a friend like you. You better get off your feet and take it easy."

"Now, you quit worrying. It's only some little kind of virus."

According to Mrs. Crutchley, "Pat did go on that night with the band at nine o'clock, but she was not her normal self. When she was up on stage, she would just move all over the place. She was full of life. But not that night. She looked all pale and drawn."

Patsy had terrible stomach cramps and spent a good deal of the evening in the bathroom. Finally the pain got so bad, she asked Elias Blanchfield, her former fiancé, if he would please take her home to Frederick. Elias was at a table with the Crutchleys and Fay's sister, Frances, whom he was dating. He helped Patsy to his car and they left. In her apartment on East Patrick Street, Patsy had a miscarriage.

"Elias and Patsy had been friends from childhood," said Mrs. Crutchley. "They remained good friends after her marriage, but Elias and Patsy were positively not dating or anything like that. He was someone she felt she could trust."

No one ever spoke of the incident. It was, as a friend put it, "very hush-hush." Those close to Patsy said there was no talk of her going to the hospital for a checkup, or taking any type of medication—it was all taken care of that night at her apartment. Patsy stayed off her feet that week, but was back at work at the Brunswick Moose Club the following Saturday night.

"I thought it was unusual that Pat didn't go to the hospital," Mrs. Crutchley explained, "but this was just one of the many things happening that were unusual. Patsy was pregnant. I don't think she was that far gone, but she was having problems because she had consulted various doctors in Frederick and still couldn't get to the bottom of what was bothering her."

Patsy was determined that she would not have any more "accidents" after that. She told Gerald he would have to be more careful. This predicament may have caused the first problems in the Cline marriage, because, from all accounts, Gerald began being far from faithful to Patsy.

With the help of Bill Peer and her appearances with the

Melody Boys and Girls—at ten dollars a performance, Patsy Cline was beginning to make it as a celebrity on a regional basis. She certainly was a plus to the Peer band and always drew a rousing response from audiences. Patsy had not, however, achieved the national stardom she wanted so badly. Peer advised her that to accomplish this, she would need a record deal.

In late 1953 he made a demonstration tape with Patsy and, through his label contacts at WEPM in Martinsburg, West Virginia, began pursuing a Nashville contact. It did not come.

But Peer did hear from William A. McCall, the president of the Pasadena, California-based Four-Star Records, the independent label once owned by Gene Autry.

Bill McCall saw potential in Patsy Cline and, it is quite obvious, he only planned to make use of Bill Peer to capture what he thought to be a big prize package. He had signed Jimmy Dean to Four-Star and made many plans, but Jimmy managed, the first opportunity he could, to slip right through McCall's hands and went on to sign with Columbia. Now McCall could envision the Jimmy Dean buildup for Patsy Cline.

On September 30, 1954, in the presence of Bill Peer, who witnessed the proceedings, Patsy signed a two-year contract with Four-Star Records.

It was probably the single biggest mistake Patsy had ever made in her professional life.

4
"Just Out of Reach"

Patsy Cline: **"Goddamn It! Can't you guys ever get the beat on this song right?"**

Grover Shroyer: **"Step all over us. You can do it now! After you got what you wanted. You don't need us anymore!"**

Bill McCall, it could be politely put, is not the most popular man in Nashville's music annals. By no means.

"He was a bastard!" claimed Patsy's second husband, Charlie Dick of Nashville.

"He was a first-class, son-of-a-bitch." declaimed singer-songwriter Doyle Wilburn.

"He was an honest, hard-working businessman, who was always there when you needed him," orchestrated songwriter Donn Hecht. "There are two sides to every story."

"He was a tough little guy who worried the crap out of everyone," burst former Decca Records A&R chief Milt Gabler.

"He was a goddamn con artist," growled veteran recording star Faron Young.

"So I don't have to elaborate on the reputation of Bill McCall!" exuded recording/television star and businessman

Jimmy Dean. "Bill McCall was, in all probability, the smoothest operator you'd ever seen in your entire life."

According to Gabler, "McCall operated just this side of the law. You would never be able to prove in court that he was conducting shady dealings. As far as Patsy was concerned, McCall had her signed to a bona-fide contract. Sometimes it took longer, but sooner or later the artist would get wise to what was going on."

The contract Patsy Cline signed with Four-Star Records and Bill McCall was the standard American Federation of Musicians form. The terms specified "a minimum of 16 (sixteen) 78 r.p.m. record sides, or the equivalent thereof. . .and additional recordings shall be made at our election. The musical compositions to be recorded shall be mutually agreed upon between you and us, and each recording shall be subject to our approval as satisfactory."

Four-Star offered Patsy a royalty of 2.34 percent of the retail list price on A.F. of M.-mandated 90 percent of all records sold in the United States. Overseas sales would be computed on yet another scale. Patsy's services would be exclusive with Four-Star for two years with a one-year option renewal (the fact that the contract lasted six years remains unexplained. Patsy may have later signed a contract extending her services). Any recordings Patsy made for the company would remain their property.

There was the standard paragraph on session musicians being paid within 14 days of services being rendered and this paragraph specified that such payments, at scale, would be deducted against Patsy's royalties when earned (except for Patsy's share of royalty monies, these terms are standard). Another paragraph stated that Four-Star could not transfer or assign control over the contract or Patsy's services without the consent of the A.F. of M.

Making records had been such a long-time goal of Patsy's, "she went into this new phase of her professional life with guns a-blazin'," according to Roy Deyton who played upright bass, lead guitar, and fiddle in Bill Peer's band. "From all I understood, and the way the band thought it was to be, Patsy was to do the singing, Bill would produce her, the band would provide backing, and there was to be publishing for any songs we wrote for Patsy. In the end, though, we never got *officially* involved. We were just simply used.

"I don't mean this in a negative sort of way, but it will point out where Bill's interest was. He did everything for Patsy. He was working with her on a daily basis, really priming her for the record session that was to come. Patsy did whatever Bill told her to. She'd say, 'Well, I guess, I better. He's my manager.' "

Within weeks of the contract signing, McCall set out to divest himself, but not Four-Star Records, of the problems of dealing with Patsy and Bill Peer.

In late October, or early November 1954, Bill Peer and Patsy made a trip to New York—a part of Patsy's professional life where all the pieces of the puzzle do not fit. This trip was filled with tension, intrigue, and behind-the-scenes wheeling and dealing. Some details and sequences of the New York visit make no logical sense, but, at one time or another, it appears that Patsy may have been using Peer and that Peer may have been using Patsy. Twenty-six years later, bitterness and accusations still exist among members of the band Peer used.

According to Mrs. Yontz, the first Mrs. Peer, the purpose of the trip was to audition for Arthur Godfrey's CBS-TV half-hour, prime-time "Talent Scouts" program, which since 1948 had become an enormous showcase for introducing undiscovered professionals from across the nation.

But, musicians Peer hired note that while an audition did take place for the Godfrey show, the purpose of the visit was to secure a record-leasing deal for Patsy and Four-Star with Decca.

Bill McCall arranged for Patsy to be seen and heard by Paul Cohen, assistant A&R chief and head of the Country division. Cohen, as part of his functions, made quarterly trips to Nashville, staying up to six weeks at the Andrew Jackson Hotel. He supervised recording sessions and signed new talent. Since he was credited with the production of the first commercial Country recording session in Music City—with Red Foley in March 1945 at WSM's Studio B—Cohen had become a respected industry pioneer.

Decca had an array of impressive stars: Bing Crosby, Ella Fitzgerald, Judy Garland, Al Jolson, Peggy Lee. Cohen was attempting to have as strong a lineup in the Country arena. He worked closely with Owen Bradley and went into partnership with Bradley and his brother Harold in their studio operation.

(Paul Cohen was elected to the Country Music Hall of Fame in 1976 and was a former president of the Country Music Association. He resigned from Decca in the early sixties on "conflict of interest" charges when it was discovered that, like many another A&R executive, Cohen had set up a publishing company and was placing songs he was licensing on B-sides of hit or prospective hit records, thus collecting handsome royalties in the process.)

Next, McCall stepped in to seduce Cohen with Patsy Cline's talent. He knew Decca was top-heavy with male Country vocalists but had only one best-selling female, Kitty Wells, who was establishing a solid reputation for herself. McCall set out to prove that Decca needed Patsy.

McCall had heard Peer's group, the Melody Boys, and told Bill to put together a more experienced, pop-oriented band for New York. Peer made the Godfrey arrangements and set up some dates the band could play over the 11 days they were to be in town. Pete O'Brien, a former Melody Boy who formed the group the Legionaires was asked to come along, all expenses paid. Peer's brother-in-law, Gene Shiner, formerly of the Metronomes, and Legionaire Leo Miller completed the musical team.

Patsy, Peer, and group traveled to New York in two cars, arriving on Tuesday afternoon. They checked into the Dixie Hotel, on Forty-second Street in the heart of Times Square. Peer immediately took Patsy shopping in the early evening, for two new dresses for the audition, which was set for the following Monday.

An incident on the trip—a considerate gesture by the management and concierge—was the first solid clue Mrs. Bill Peer was to have of an affair between her husband and Patsy.

The audition for "Talent Scouts" was on the sixteenth floor of the CBS building. Jeanette Davis, an "Arthur Godfrey Time" regular and the host's administrative right hand, presided. Shiner recalls everyone being concerned that they may lose out because of a child, a girl, all dressed in petticoats and a white ruffled dress, who was a virtuoso violinist playing on a prized Stradivarius.

Shiner, now 51 and living in Mocks Corner, South Carolina, gave up his musical ambitions in 1960 "when I found out I had to work for a living to support my family." He has gone back on a full-time basis to what was only a part-time job, automobile body repair work. He vividly recalls the audition and what followed.

"Miss Davis was polite and considerate, but it was obvious she was not too taken. She sat down with Bill and the rest of us and said she would be happy to book Patsy on the program but only as a solo act. The band would not fit in. She told Bill that she felt Patsy transcended Country and was more of a blues singer.

"I had once tried to tell Bill this myself, based on my experiences with Patsy in the Metronomes, but neither one of them would listen. All they knew and wanted was Country and, frankly, I had to admire that. Well, the whole reason for coming up was to try to get the band and Patsy on the show, but we all knew getting Patsy on was the number one reason. We all talked it over and decided that if that's the way it was and if Patsy had it, as we all thought she did, that she should go ahead and accept.

"But—and I will never forget this—Patsy refused. She said we had all been working together and that we were a package or it was no deal at all. So it was no deal. And that little gal with the Stradivarius went on that night and won.

"Miss Davis did take Bill and Patsy aside to talk with them. She made a commitment that if ever Patsy wanted to come back and audition, she would personally see that it was done. And, I believe, that Patsy, with or without Bill, did go back at some point before the time she was on in 1957 and won."

According to Shiner, following the audition, Miss Davis phoned manager Richard Lisell, who had Teresa Brewer under contract, and suggested that he meet Peer, Patsy, and the band.

"Miss Davis was especially taken with Patsy," said Shiner, "and felt she had major potential. She told Richie that the band was good, too, and that he might be able to use us on some local bookings. Lisell contacted Bill and invited us all to come visit him at his apartment in the midtown area."

After hearing Patsy, Lisell may have had it in mind, asserted Miller and O'Brien, to snatch Patsy from Peer and become her manager.

"Bill's always touting Patsy as the second greatest singer in the whole U.S.A.," Shiner noted, "may have backfired on him."

The band went to work playing Country, a novelty in New York then and popular music—whatever music the date required—and one evening they did one-hour sets at four different nightclubs, including the popular Latin Quarter.

"It is one night I won't ever forget," said O'Brien, "because I got tired of putting up music stands, sheet music, and instruments, and tearing them down."

O'Brien and Leo Miller recall some of the cloak-and-dagger goings-on surrounding the auditions and demonstration sessions at Decca and Coral.

"One thing became clear immediately," explained Miller, who played piano and the vox [organ], "and that was Bill Peer was out for Patsy and the rest of us didn't seem to matter. Bill was representing Patsy as her manager to both the Godfrey people and the folks over at Decca and Coral. We were not being offered as a group until a couple of us had a few words with Bill. I mean, that was the idea behind my guys and me taking off two weeks to go with Bill. We were after a record deal."

McCall had given Peer Four-Star copyrighted songs for Patsy and the band to learn for the demo sessions. These were at the Decca/Coral studios on West 57th Street and West 70th Street at Broadway in a former Knights of Pythias temple. Among the tunes Patsy and the musicians cut were "Turn the Cards Slowly," "Three Cigarettes (In an Ashtray)," and "Crazy Arms."

The sessions did not go as smoothly as Peer and Lisell had thought. The group had to record "This Ole House" 27 times before it proved acceptable. In addition, Miller said that the band and Patsy had disagreements, and that she and Lisell had a falling-out of some kind. Patsy did not show for one of the club engagements Lisell had booked and he was, reportedly, quite upset with her.

Decca was supposedly impressed enough with the band's efforts that the label was prepared to offer them a year's contract, but, because of jobs and families at home and the fact they would have to spend a good deal of time in New York, the musicians did not pursue the deal.

"Finally," said O'Brien, "because of commitments we all had back home, at the end of the eleven days, I told Bill, 'We just can't stay here any longer. We're heading out in the morning.' "

When the "Bill Peers" checked out of the Dixie, they did not check thoroughly enough for personal belongings. The maid found Patsy's coat still hanging in the room's closet, turned it over to the manager, who returned the clothing to Mrs. Bill Peer, Brunswick Moose Club, Brunswick, Maryland, with a courtesy note: "Dear Mrs. Peer, We are happy to inform you that the coat you and Mr. Peer left behind in your room has been turned over to this office. We are returning it herewith. Sorry if your oversight caused you any inconvenience. It was a pleasure to serve you."

When Mrs. Peer opened the package she wondered what on earth the hotel was sending her Patsy Cline's coat for. It took her exactly three minutes to put two and two together. When she confronted Bill with the situation, "he lied to me the way he had been lying to me about everything else."

Pete O'Brien and Leo Miller would not forget the sessions they recorded at Decca. Both claim that when the songs were eventually released with Patsy as featured vocalist, it was they and their musicians providing the backup instrumentals.

Patsy returned to Frederick to Gerald and his early Christmas present, a sporty 1955 Buick Roadmaster. She took to wearing a most flattering coiffure by pulling her hair up and over her head. Besides the outfits Mrs. Hensley had made, Patsy shocked rather staid Brunswick Moose regulars with her New York purchases.

The most flattering item of apparel was a two-piece black gown with silver highlights that Patsy tied with a chiffon sash. The sequined bodice had a sexy, semi-strapless effect since only a minimum amount of fabric draped her left shoulder.

Now that Cohen had had the opportunity to review the New York tapes, McCall called on him. Cohen also saw Patsy's potential to the label and attempted to buy her contract outright from Four-Star.

"No," McCall informed him. "That's not what I'm looking for. You can't buy her outright. What I'm offering is a leasing and distribution deal with Four-Star. We will retain all artist and publishing rights."

Cohen was rightly suspect of such an arrangement, whereby Decca would do all the work and Four-Star would retain a majority of the profit and all artist and publishing rights. By agreeing to McCall's demand that only Four-Star Music copyrights be used for Patsy, Cohen knew Decca would be severely limited in song selectivity.

Four-Star was simply to supply Patsy Cline to Decca under a lucrative new contract, but only pay her according to her existing contract. No matter how much money Four-Star made if Patsy proved to be a success, Patsy was to see little of it. In addition, the leased material from Four-Star Music would always be the property of Four-Star. Decca was to have no long-term rights. Cohen discussed the matter with Gabler, who said that Cohen did not cotton to McCall.

Ultimately, though they had reservations, Cohen and Gabler acquiesced to the Four-Star terms. Having observed Patsy in New York, Cohen told Peer, "She seems to have a mind of her own. Can you keep her under control?" McCall replied, "Oh, don't worry about her. I'll take care of it." He was good at his word, though none of his methods have ever been revealed; no doubt, McCall's rapidly thinning hair was a result of his run-ins with Patsy.

Patsy's first session took place in Nashville January 5, 1955. It should be noted for its results—or lack of them. Four tunes were recorded: "I Cried All the Way to the Altar," "I Don't Wanta," "I Love You Honey," and "Come on In." Cohen and Gabler were less than happy with the product and none of the cuts were immediately released.

"I Don't Wanta," co-written by D. Haddock, W.S. Stevenson, and Eddie Miller, who would later pen "Release Me" and have a long-term writing relation with Patsy, is not a bad tune at all. It has a rockabilly arrangement in the Elvis Presley tradition, and Patsy's vocal was very much in the style of Kay Starr. It was rerecorded and released in late 1957.

From the quality of the songs from Patsy's session, it is possible to understand the quandary in which Paul Cohen found himself. He had an artist with a pop voice and the commitment to make her a Country star.

"I Cried All the Way to the Altar" is not a great song, but it showed the raw element of Patsy's voice—with its growling, or yodel, effect on the high notes. The song did not see the light of day until after Patsy's death when it was packaged in a budget album by Four-Star.

"I Love You Honey" was a typical hillbilly ballad. "Come on In," on the other hand, was a standout. A bouncy, uptempo number with Paul Jones-type fiddling as the predominant background, it was able to capture the essence of the Patsy Cline who, recording-wise, would not emerge for five years.

The latter songs were marketed as a back-to-back single on February 5, 1956. "Come on In" was not only well received but also became Patsy's theme song on her tour dates.

Cohen had on his hands an artist who did not fit well in either category. Patsy's voice was not the problem; it was the material being forced upon her to record. Cohen felt he should have taken a heavier hand in the sessions. He and McCall had words. Decca wanted more than a mere marketing and production role. If the label was only able to choose from Four-Star copyrights, McCall had better get a wider selection of material that, hopefully, would show Patsy off at her best, or start looking for better songwriters.

Within weeks McCall gave Patsy some new songs to learn. He also asked Peer if he couldn't get his Melody Boys in good enough shape to back Patsy on the session. Roy Deyton recollected, "Bill got us all together one night and Patsy said, 'Mr. McCall has given me some new songs to learn and I'd like to ask y'all to help me out.' Bill asked us to rehearse with Patsy. We ran through the songs a few times with Patsy and she even performed one or two of them at the Moose to test response.

"Not long after that Bill asked us to keep a Saturday free, and he booked a whole day at a radio station, the only facility with decent equipment, in Fredericksburg, Virginia. Patsy was really primed for the occasion and was in good form. We recorded four songs—'Turn the Cards Slowly,' 'Honky Tonk Merry-Go-Round,' 'Hidin' Out,' and 'A Church, A Courtroom and Then Goodbye'—as backup band for Patsy. Bill's plan was to send these to McCall and, I believe, someone either in New York or Nashville. We may have been paid something, but I think we all did it to help Bill and Patsy. She was his Number One project. It seemed to us that Bill would not rest until he had helped make Patsy a star."

The following weekend, as the Melody Boys gathered for the Saturday afternoon rehearsal, Patsy got angry and yelled, "Goddamn it, can't you guys ever get the beat on this song right? Bill, can't you do something? They're awful!"

"Grover Shroyer, the drummer, might have had a couple of drinks," recalled Deyton, "but he wasn't high. He got really angry and told Patsy, 'That's right, honey, just step all over us. Yeah, you can do it now! After you got what you wanted—the trip to New York, the record session. Treat us like dirt! You don't need us anymore!'

"You could hear a pin drop. No one else said anything, but Bill could see most of us felt the same way but hadn't said anything because we didn't want to upset him. We had to keep talking to Grover to console him and smooth his feathers. Before the show, Patsy came over and spoke to him. Oh, she didn't mean anything. There was pressure on everyone. It became evident to Bill that his interest in Patsy was splitting the band."

And it was splitting the Peer and Cline marriages.

"I could see that Patsy was playing Bill along," said Jenny Yontz, "but I figured she'd move along after she got what she wanted and he'd come to his senses. I had two childeren so I was busy raising them. Just like you hear people say, I was trying to keep us together for the sake of the kids."

Bill and Patsy were having a discreet and sometimes indiscreet relationship. Patsy would go to Fay Crutchley's and Bill would pick her up there and they would go off to "rehearse. . .be interviewed. . .look for new sheet music. . . see a prospective promoter."

"I was Pat's friend," explained Fay, "but I didn't ask a lot of questions and she did not, thankfully, bring me into the middle of things. We spent a lot of time together, even ran around shopping, you know, things like that. All I knew was that she was married to Gerald at the time, but they were not always together. She and Bill were going to this one-nighter and that one-nighter. They probably saw more of each other working than Pat and Gerald did of each other married.

"Pat would be with Gerald one week and then they would separate. The next thing you'd know, they'd be back together —or, at least, living under the same roof. When they split, I don't know where Pat went—back to her mother's house in Winchester or where—but she didn't come here. Pat and Bill might have been fooling around, but Gerald was not any bargain either!"

Gerald was openly dating, on one occasion, even bringing his "cousin" to the Brunswick Moose Saturday night dance party. "Well, now," said Nevin Cline, "this just might have been my brother's way of trying to make Patsy come to her senses!" One of the table regulars revealed that Gerald's attitude was, what's good for the goose is good for the gander.

Bill and Patsy booked a flight in late May to Nashville to turn over the tapes to Cohen and McCall. Peer was not a drinker. According to members of his band, he would take a drink, at most, twice a year. The flight to Nashville was to be one of those days.

This was Bill and Patsy's first plane ride. She was a bit apprehensive; Bill was scared out of his wits. He later told a friend, "I was as white as a ghost, holding on to the armrests for dear life." Both had taken a couple of drinks before the flight, and, during the ride, were consuming more than their fair share. It didn't take too long before Bill and Patsy were enjoying sailing through the skies to the roar of engines.

Patsy was friendly to the crew and even offered to help in their duties. Bill recalled this hilarious incident as the plane approached the Nashville airport.

"The light above went on and so did a little lighted sign at the front of the plane. The stewardess came on the speaker and said, 'Ladies and gentlemen, the captain has lighted the fasten seat belts sign.' Suddenly Patsy jumped out into the aisle, straddled her legs across it, and yelled, 'All right, ladies, you don't want to ignore the captain! Fasten your sanitary belts!' At first there was shocked silence, then everyone broke out laughing. I grabbed Patsy and pulled her back into the seat."

The idea behind the recent session with the Melody Boys was that, hopefully, Four-Star and Decca would release these tracks. "That's the impression we all had going into the recording," Deyton noted. "It was to be a package. I told Bill it was okay with me, but privately I didn't think that it would ever come to be. I knew, and Bill knew, how things worked in Nashville. McCall was approaching the arrangement as a master deal, you know, where he would provide the company with ready-to-release material.

"I only know what Bill told me later, that no one would listen to the tapes or that they were unacceptable. They told him Nashville had its own studio musicians and that even big stars couldn't bring in their bands to back them."

McCall, through Paul Cohen, was to have set up a session for Patsy. Cohen consulted every artist on Decca, save Miss Wells, about what to do with Patsy, and still had not made up his mind. Then Ernest Tubb asked if Decca had signed Patsy. Cohen told him, "No, we've got her under a Four-Star deal. E.T., do you know her?" Tubb replied, "Yeah, From Bill Peer's band."

"We've hit a snag. Patsy's got potential for an even broader appeal than Kitty. She's got a pop sound. It's there. I just know it."

"Well, heck, Paul, if she's got a pop sound, why don't you get Owen Bradley to work with her?"

"Patsy kept popping into my life," touted Ernest Tubb. "Of course I knew her from Bill Peer's band and then on the

Connie B. Gay circuit. Sometime in the middle of nineteen fifty-four, the late Jack Drake my fiddle player came running up to me backstage some place in the Washington, D.C. area and said, 'E.T., I want you to say hello to a really fine singer.'

"I looked up and there was this pretty gal all decked out in cowgirl clothes. I said, 'Well, howdy do. Nice to meet ya,' and went about my business.

"At least, I tried to. Jack got me aside, 'E.T., you remember Patsy from Bill Peer's band.' I looked up and said, 'Patsy? Well, why didn't you say so! Hello, Patsy, honey, how are you? It's nice to see you again. How's ole Bill?' I hugged her neck and she hugged mine.

"Jack came over to me again and lowered his voice. 'I kind of promised Patsy I'd arrange for her to sing a song with us. Don't make me look bad!' I think Jack mighta been kinda sweet on Patsy, but I looked him in the eye and told him, 'You shouldn't have done that. It's still my show!'

"Of course, I didn't mind letting Patsy sing. She was darn good, but those things have a way of getting out of control. I went to Patsy and said, 'Patsy, honey, I sure am glad you've come to visit us. Hey, do me a favor and sing a song with us tonight.'

"Why she got so excited, she just threw her arms around me and thanked me with a big kiss. When she got up to do her song, I gave her a nice introduction and the crowd loved her. We left town and her name didn't come up for a while.

"Then, not too long after that, Patsy, God bless her, came to see us in Maryland. Jack came in and said, 'E.T., look who's here. Patsy came down to see us.' She gave me a big hug and we talked. She told me she was having a real hard time, that things hadn't been going well.

"I told her, 'I'm sorry to hear that.' She said, 'It don't matter, but it sure would mean a lot if I could sing just one song with you today.' I replied, 'My God, honey, of course, you can!' "

Owen Bradley was a WSM personality—a capable pianist, guitarist, and arranger—whom many artists felt was more suitable to popular music than Country.

In fact, Bradley was at home in either field. As a businessman, with ethics yet, he became one of Nashville's wealthiest. Musically, since he was unafraid to be innovative at a time when Country had become static, he was years ahead of his rivals.

He developed countless hitmakers for Decca Records and became one of Music City's most respected figures. In 1974 he was elected to the Country Music Hall of Fame. While others may have dabbled in song publishing, Bradley chose real estate and recording studios.

By 1955 recording studios in Nashville were not a novelty, but neither were they taken for granted. The first studio of consequence was the Castle in the now-razed Tulane Hotel. Next came the Brown Brothers (Charles and Bill) Studio at Fourth Avenue and Union Street. Downtown was still alive with the Ryman Auditorium and the Grand Ole Opry, but, farther out, toward the West End, what has come to be known as Music Row was taking shape. One of its prime forces was Owen Bradley.

Bradley was the first individual to have any longevity with recording operations, beginning with his studio on Twenty-first Avenue South behind McClure's Department Store. Then Bradley moved to a house on Sixteenth Avenue South (now Music Square East). Later, at this location, he built an annex in an adjacent quonset hut that was dubbed Bradley's Barn.

After several years as a television studio for "The Stars of the Grand Ole Opry" series and a facility for producing kinescopes (the film forerunner to videotape) of musical programs for the Armed Forces Network, Bradley created one of the most technically advanced studios in the industry here. The hut still stands, now a part of CBS Records. Bradley has moved his base to outlying Mount Juliet in a building constructed to actually resemble a barn.

The recording sessions took place June 1, 1955, at Bradley's studio. Peer told Deyton and Harry Crutchley, but not his own wife, that he had to lay out $1,500 in front money for musicians' payments. This was an outright violation of Patsy's contract with Four-Star, which stipulated that the record company (Four-Star, not Decca) was responsible for the fees and that later these would be deducted from Patsy's royalties when earned.

"Bill had been spending pretty freely on Patsy," said Deyton. "He had come into an inheritance as a result of his mother's death and this was the bankroll he was using to launch Patsy."

Harry Crutchley noted, "But, certainly, Bill never planned on laying out that kind of money. He told me he was standing there in Bradley's studio waiting for things to get going when someone came out of the office or control room and asked, 'Hey, Bill, who's going to make the financial arrangements for this? We have to pay the musicians.'

"Bill told them, 'The contract says that Four-Star will pay the musicians.' The studio spokesman said, 'Well, Four-Star has made no arrangements with us.' "

Peer asked Owen Bradley to phone McCall, who is supposedly to have stated, "Bill will have to lay out the money himself, because we're in no position to do it right now." A very angry Peer got on the phone with McCall, "What the hell is going on? If we had known this, we could have stayed home. Now that we're here, you're screwing around and trying to walk all over us."

McCall calmed Peer down and told him if he would lay the money for the musicians out, he would be reimbursed within a couple of weeks. Patsy was equally upset. She said to Peer, "Well, if you've got the money and want to go ahead, let's do it as long as he says he'll pay you back."

Bill is reportedly to have pulled out a roll of hundred-dollar bills and paid Bradley. "And don't forget my receipt!"

"We talked about that occasion several times," reflected Deyton, "and a lot of good that receipt did Bill. But the first time I heard about it, I thought to myself, 'Somebody's gonna take a shellacking out of this.' And it was Bill. So when it is said that Bill Peer was instrumental in Patsy Cline's career, you can believe it. Patsy didn't have it at the time, but, to my knowledge, she never made any attempt to pay Bill back."

Fay Crutchley says that, "In the beginning Gerald helped Pat some, but it was minimal. Bill was the one who laid out the money that got Pat to New York and Nashville and into the studio with Owen Bradley. And, as far as Harry and I know, Bill was never paid back by anyone."

Bill often spoke to friends of the interest that Ernest Tubb had taken in Patsy and the session. "Bill was just being nice," commented Tubb. "All I did was sit down with Paul, Owen, Bill, and those Four-Star folk and pick out the best four songs they had to offer."

While they were looking over material, Bill told Deyton, that Decca's chart-topping star Webb Pierce dropped by and offered to review the songs also. "You may have some good ones here," he told Peer, "but you ain't got nothing that can beat out ole Webb."

Boastful Webb Pierce, as he swaggered off into the sunset, probably did not realize the impact of what he was saying—or that he hit the nail right on the head.

The four tunes recorded were "Turn the Cards Slowly" by Sammy Masters, "Honky Tonk Merry-Go-Round" by Stan Gardner and Frank Simon, "Hidin' Out" by W.S. Stevenson (McCall) and Eddie Miller, and "A Church, a Courtroom and Then Goodbye," also by Miller.

Cohen had been attempting to build a strong roster of Country artists on Coral. He decided this was to be Patsy's label. The release date of Patsy's first single, "A Church, a Courtroom and Then Goodbye" backed with "Honky Tonk Merry-Go-Round," was to be July 20, 1955.

McCall sent out a pitch on Four-Star letterhead—dated June 1, 1955, the same day of the session in Nashville—from his Pasadena, California, office to radio station disk jockeys. In part, it read: "We think Patsy Cline sings better than any female vocalist we have heard. Her diction, sense of timing, and phrasings are exceptionally good. We hope that you will agree with us and will give her first record a chance to be heard. . . ."

According to Bradley, "Of course, McCall was correct in what he wrote. Patsy was exceptional, but it didn't happen right away. Paul did not mind waiting. He had patience. He'd say again and again, 'Owen, she's got it. She's special! We're gonna hit it. It may take some time, but we'll do it. All we need is the right combination.'

"And that was the hardest thing to come by. What made the situation a cross to bear was that we were limited in the material Patsy could record. We couldn't just do a song we thought was right for her. All her numbers had to be Four-Star copyrights. It is difficult enough breaking in a new artist, but with restrictions like we had, well it was really a burden."

Tubb says, "From that session, my favorite was 'A Church, a Courtroom and Then Goodbye.' I think Paul wanted to put something else out, but I talked with him and said, 'You oughta go with this one.' Paul tried to give Patsy a good shot, but it was the timing and the material. She had a fine voice, but it just wasn't there in the songs. The record got Patsy started, even if sales were mediocre. Patsy had that itch. She couldn't wait. But Nashville wasn't built in a day."

Listening to "A Church, a Courtroom and Then Goodbye," it is puzzling why anyone would release it as an artist's debut product. The song is a slow, mournful ballad with twangy guitar and crying-fiddle effects, the latter courtesy of famed session musician Tommy Jackson. It is the type of song you play on a tavern jukebox while crying in your beer, and was not at all suited to Patsy Cline's talents and potential.

Something could be said for it, however. It was a Four-Star Music copyright.

A Church, a Courtroom and Then Goodbye

Words and Music by
Eddie Miller

The first scene was the church,
Then the altar
Where we claimed each other
With tears of joy we cried.
Our friends wished us luck there forever,
As we walked from the church
Side by side.

My next scene was a crowded courtroom,
And like strangers we sat side by side.
Then I heard the judge make his decision,
And no longer were we man and wife.

I hate the sight of that courtroom,
Where man-made laws pushed God's laws aside.
Then the clerk wrote our story in the record,
A church, a courtroom and then goodbye.

We walked from that courtroom together,
We shook hands and once again we cried,
Then it was the end of our story,
A church, a courtroom and then goodbye.

Patsy and Bill left for home immediately after the session. Now it was a matter of waiting. Patsy walked on air. "I'm beginning to realize my dreams," she informed a friend. "I've been taking things one step at a time and it's finally going to happen!"

Bob Gaines, the partner in Winchester's G&M Music Store who made Patsy's recording for her Opry audition, related that after the trip to Nashville for the first session Patsy began coming by the shop to practice and try and learn more about the techniques of recording.

"She would come several times a week," said Gaines, "go into one of the soundproof booths and spend hours recording and listening to the playbacks. Then she would rerecord a number until she would finally get a song the way she wanted it."

Patsy and Bill returned to Nashville June 27. Bill introduced Patsy to as many music people as possible, even taking Eddy Arnold to lunch in the hope he would take notice of Patsy. She was very much in Bill's corner. If anyone talked to Patsy about business, she'd say, "Talk to Bill. He's my manager."

Fay and Harry Crutchley, Elias Blanchfield, and Fay's sister Frances Null joined Patsy and Bill Friday, July 1, at the Drake Hotel Courts on Murfreesboro Road, about four miles south of downtown.

"Bill drove us all by Bradley's Studio," recalled Mrs. Crutchley, "took us sightseeing, and backstage at the Grand Ole Opry. I remember we just pulled up at the back entrance and went right in. It was quite a thrill. All that, and Pat getting to sing on the broadcast."

Ernest Tubb hosted the Ralston-Purina portion of the Opry and he brought Patsy on with a flourish: "Here's a little lady with a powerful voice. I've been predicting big things for her. Make welcome Coral Records newest star singing her debut recording, 'A Church, a Courtroom and Then Goodbye.' " As Patsy walked out, Tubb threw his hands in the air and, as is customary, motioned the audience to keep the applause coming.

"She was nervous," Tubb revealed. "Maybe because she was new and this was a first. She told me she had a chance to be on the Opry when she was just sixteen, so I guess it was real special. But I hadn't seen her that way before. She was always so sure of herself. So it could have been the song and not her.

It wasn't exactly uptempo! But Patsy, God bless her, did a terrific job."

"I remember there wasn't much applause after Pat finished," Mrs. Crutchley said, "and Mr. Tubb rushed out and put his arm around her and leaned into the microphone to say, 'Folks, Miss Patsy Cline, isn't she terrific!' As she was walking off, he called her back, 'Patsy, honey, come on. Take another bow!'

"There wasn't anything in the world that could have brought Pat down that night. She was in ecstasy! She ran off crying right into Bill's arms, saying how appearing on the Grand Ole Opry was one of her biggest dreams come true. Pat was in fine voice. It was the song that was the problem. It would bring a pall over an Irish wake! It was downbeat and just didn't go over too well. That song was one problem Pat should not have had to contend with that early on in her career. It had the effect of stopping her before she got started."

Patsy and Bill took their guests around backstage and introduced them to many of the artists. They met Kitty Wells, Cowboy Copas, Jean Shepard, Hawkshaw Hawkins, Roy Acuff, Curly Fox, Texas Ruby, Whitey Ford, and Minnie Pearl. Patsy had her camera taking pictures and, right along with the others, asked for autographs. She posed with Tubb and Acuff.

"Bill had been a musician a long time," Harry Crutchley indicated. "and was a popular regional disk jockey. A lot of the stars had used Bill to play backup for them when they were up our way. He had a lot of contacts. At one point there we were all talking to Ernest Tubb, Roy Acuff, and Minnie Pearl, and standing right beside Carl Smith and his wife Goldie Hill, who was a big singer at that time. It was something Fay and I have never forgotten."

Tubb's manager, Gabe Tucker, now of Houston, Texas, grabbed the star and excitedly told him,"E.T., I think we've found us a female Red Foley. This girl sounds like nobody'll believe! Everybody's talking about her voice."

After the Opry Tubb and Tucker invited Bill and Patsy to Tubb's record shop. Patsy was quickly scheduled to perform her new single on the "Mid-Nite Jamboree" radio broadcast there. Following the program Tubb and Tucker spoke at length with Bill and Patsy, then Tucker directed Patsy into a record audition booth where she made several acetates, singing a cappella.

Tucker played them back and then played them for Tubb, who exclaimed, "Gabe, you're right. That gal can reach out and get it. This stuff is great."

"I'd love to manage her, E.T.," said Tucker, "but I can't talk to her without that guy butting in."

"That guy," replied Tubb, "is Bill Peer, the bandleader from West Virginia. And he's already her manager."

Tucker says he knew from the way Bill and Patsy were talking that they were low on money. "I was a booking agent, also, and handled Roy Acuff's park in Clarksville. So I asked Patsy and Bill if she'd be interested in playing there later that same Sunday. They were agreeable. I booked Patsy for fifty dollars for the show."

The Crutchleys recalled, "It was quite a July Fourth weekend. That day, after we got a few hours sleep, we all journeyed the fifty miles to Roy Acuff's Country music park, Dunbar Cave, Patsy sang on the afternoon show.

"The next day, Monday, the holiday, Bill and Patsy decided to continue on to Memphis where Ernest Tubb and Faron Young were appearing at the ballpark. Patsy's idea was to go backstage and visit with Tubb and get him to let her sing a song on his part of the show. But the temperature was over the one-hundred degree mark and we decided to get an early start for home."

Both Tubb and Young remember Patsy and Bill's visit with them in Memphis. Here is Tubb's recollection. "Patsy came backstage with Bill and Jack Drake [Tubb's fiddle player]. She told me she'd like to sing on the show—not for pay, but for free—just for the exposure and to be with the Sheriff [Young] and me. Of course, I let her and gave her a big introduction. There must have been fourteen thousand people there and they loved Patsy.

"Afterwards, Patsy was crying on Jack's shoulder and telling us how tough times were, that nothing was happening. When it was time to go, she just started bawling and none of us knew what to do. She said she wanted to stay and go out on the road with us. I told her it would be nice, but we didn't have any room in the cars. So she kissed and hugged all of us, and she and Bill were on their way."

"That Saturday night Bill and Patsy were back performing at the Brunswick Moose," Fay Crutchley said. "But something was different, it seemed, especially with Bill. He was subdued and it looked like he was straining whenever he smiled."

No doubt Bill Peer's condition was a result of the surprise he found waiting when he returned home to wife Jenny. Mrs. Peer informed her husband that he had made her the laughing stock of the area for the last time, that she was going home with the couple's children to live with her mother, and filing for divorce on the grounds of adultery.

Mrs. Peer filed her action Monday, July 11, 1955, at the Chancellory Court of Jefferson County, West Virginia, in Charles Town. The clerk assigned a date of September 22 for the case, slugged Virginia M. Peer vs. William Peer, to be heard.

"I don't want to give the impression it was all Patsy's fault," asserted Jenny Yontz. "Bill was older; she was only 22. And he was a persistent and insistent fellow. I blame him as much as I do her. She's dead. He's dead. They can't defend themselves.

"I knew what was going on, but I had no solid evidence. I could not go around saying things I couldn't prove. When you talk, you have to be able to back it up. As far as lying goes, they certainly did that—about everything. I didn't know about them going to Nashville. I forget what they told me. They probably lied about that, too. I was hurt and terribly scarred by it all."

Did Patsy Cline break up Jenny Peer's marriage to Bill? "She was a contributing factor. When I went into the divorce proceedings, I felt sure Bill would marry Patsy as soon as the final decree was granted."

With Mrs. Peer's filing for divorce on grounds of adultery, Patsy and Bill put distance between themselves. The only time friends saw them together was on band dates. Patsy was again being squired around by Gerald "and they seemed as happy and in love as two peas in a pod." Patsy even showed the wallet photo of her and Gerald on the steps of Frederick Reformed Church on their wedding day. Friends laughed and snickered, nevertheless. Everyone knew the truth. Some even saw Bill's car parked late in the afternoon across from the five-and-dime store.

One of the town's dime stores burned and the city allowed it to relocate during the rebuilding process to an exhibition hall at the fairgrounds on East Patrick Street at Monroe Avenue. Patsy and Gerald's apartment was just across the way. For their clandestine rendezvous, Bill would park in front of the five and dime as if to go shopping, stand on the corner to await

Patsy's prearranged signal that the coast was clear, then hurry across Patrick and up the shaky flight of stairs to the Cline's one-bedroom apartment.

Gerald, whose working hours were unpredictable—depending on his tolerance and indebtedness, surprised Bill and Patsy one day. Bill was about to leave when they heard Gerald's car drive up. In an instant they were scrambling around trying to decide what to do. At first, Bill was going to hide in the closet, but Patsy thought better of that and had him get under the bed. As soon as Gerald came in he would head for the kitchen and the refrigerator for a beer. And then Bill could jettison himself into the living room, through the screened door, and back to the fairgrounds.

By the end of July radio stations had Patsy Cline's debut single, but they were not giving it the chance Bill McCall had pleaded for.

"McCall's letter was the only promotion the record got," Roy Deyton noted. "It was downbeat, but the worse thing was that there was no publicity or promotion. There was no hope for it. Bill was ticked off about the way Four-Star and Decca/Coral just let it die."

"A Church, a Courtroom and Then Goodbye" did not even receive much notice at the Brunswick Moose Club from Bill Peer and the Melody Boys featuring Patsy Cline.

But on that moot point no explanation was necessary.

Side Two

"I'm hungry for love,
Like a hobo for food,
Like the devil hunts for bad,
Like the angel looks for good..."

—"Hungry for Love," recorded by
Patsy Cline, written by W.S. Stevenson
and Eddie Miller. • 1957 by Four-Star
Music Co., Inc.

5
"Ain't No Wheels on This Ship"

Patsy Cline: **"Mr. Dean, I want to sing for you."**

Jimmy Dean: **"She came out in full western regalia. I thought, 'What the shit!' Then she sang. . .and knocked everybody's hat in the creek."**

Patsy's fortunes increased when she entered the annual National Championship Country Music Contest at Warrenton, Virginia, in 1954.

"This was staged as a fundraiser for the Jaycees (Junior Chamber of Commerce)," reported Connie B. Gay, the Virginia entrepreneur who sponsored the contest. "Patsy entered the female vocalist category and won the first prize of one hundred dollars, which was a lot of money back then. But I was so impressed with her singing ability that I asked her to come to work on my afternoon 'Town and Country Time' radio show on WARL in Arlington, Virginia."

Besides her work with Peer and WARL, Patsy did "Town and Country Time" transcriptions (sent out on disks) for Gay at WARL in Washington under his contract with the Department of Defense for the Army's recruiting campaign. This program was regularly heard on 1,800 stations.

Shortly after the release of Patsy's first single, Lee Burrows of Nashville met Patsy in Washington. "I was plugging songs and promoting records. I was at WMAL on Connecticut Avenue where Patsy was working for Connie B. Gay. One of the disk jockeys introduced me to her and we hit it off right away.

"Patsy asked me what I did and I told her and I also let her know I was a writer just in case she might be looking for some material. 'Let me hear something,' she requested. So I played a couple of demos for her. Patsy said she really liked the songs but told me. 'It's no use. I can't do any song unless Bill McCall and Four-Star have the publishing rights.'

"Patsy talked to me about Gerald," continued Burrows. "The first time I met him, I would have quite easily mistaken him for Patsy's uncle as opposed to her husband. Things have been rough, she said, and she spoke of how mixed up she was.

" 'I don't want to hurt Gerald,' Patsy told me. 'I don't want to leave him. I haven't fallen out of love with him. He's been a good husband.'

"I don't think he would have cared if Patsy wanted to sing. What seemed to get him was her running here and there. He had money, or so I thought, from his family's business and maybe he knew how hard show business could be. As much as Patsy appeared to love him, she just had to sing. She'd tell me that over and over. When it came to her career, she and Gerald would really go at it."

" 'A woman should be where her husband makes his living!' Gerald would tell her.

" 'I can't quit now!' was Patsy's loud response. 'I've got to have my music. I'd just die if I couldn't sing!'

" 'I'm not asking you to give it up! Just to stay at home and be with me sometimes.'

" 'But what about my dates?'

" 'I want you to have a good life. Running around all over three states and back and forth to Nashville ain't no way to live.' "

Patsy confided later to Lee Burrows, "Oh, Gerald's real thoughtful. He's not the type who goes out and buys you surprises all the time, but anything I ask for or want, he'll try to get for me."

Back in Charles Town, on September 22, 1955, Jenny Peer was awarded her freedom "upon consideration of all the evidence it appears to the court from the proceedings and proof presented herewith that the cause of the divorce in the case of Virginia M. Peer vs. William Peer is granted on the grounds of adultery."

"After the divorce, when he was free to marry Patsy," said Mrs. Yontz, "everything I told Bill about her came back to haunt him. He found out I was right all along."

Patsy and Bill were seeing each other, for sure, but whenever Bill would talk about Patsy's divorcing Gerald and marrying him, he encountered stalling tactics.

"Bill, you know I love you," Patsy would say, "but it will take some time with Gerald. Right now, he's got the upper hand."

In point of fact, Patsy was cooling on Bill Peer, not so much because she never loved or was fond of him, but because she was enjoying her D. C. fling. She was in the big city and having a blast playing the field.

"Things were especially tense Saturday nights at the Brunswick Moose when Gerald would come around," Roy Deyton revealed. "Tense between Gerald and Bill, Bill and Patsy, and all of us. We had known for a long time that Bill was after Patsy and we knew that would eventually break up both marriages and, as far as we could see, tear up the band. We were all good Southern boys and we didn't go for the sort of stuff that was going on.

"I guess ole Bill had it all figured out, but the plan sure backfired on him. After he was divorced from Jenny and found out Patsy wasn't really serious about marrying him, well, he almost had a nervous breakdown. It seemed to us he had really gone off the deep end.

"One night after we had played in Washington, we stopped in a restaurant to eat. Bill began talking about Patsy and what she was doing to him. It was kind of embarrassing. Then he broke down and cried like a baby right at the table. He just went to pieces. Grover [Shroyer, the drummer] turned to my brother and I and said, 'Hey, Bill's taking this thing hard. We're gonna have to do something to take care of him or he's gonna destroy himself.'

"We tried to talk to him, but it didn't do any good. He was sitting there with his head down, sobbing, and shaking. I told him, 'Now, Bill, if you don't stop this and come around, you're gonna make yourself awfully sick. We're gonna have to take you to the hospital. You can't let this get to you or you're gonna do yourself harm.' But, poor Bill, didn't hear a word I said. He was gone."

Fay Crutchley laughed and said, "Some people might get the impression our tri-state area is a Peyton Place within a Peyton Place! And, well, they'd be just about right. I guess Pat might have had the reputation of being a little loose and on the wild side, but, as far as I know, the women never considered her a threat or were openly hostile to her.

"The funny thing was that Pat was no standout at what she was doing. It was going on all over the place. A lot of people were running around with each other's husband and wife and we didn't even know anything about it! That's no lie.

"And we had some very close friends at the table. They were all breaking up and going their separate ways, but all of them remained friendly afterward. Even Bill and Jenny were friendly after it was all over. So no one could single out Pat and throw stones at her."

Patsy's last date as part of Bill Peer's Melody Boys and Girls was Saturday evening, October 1, when they played for the opening of a Chevrolet dealership in Martinsburg, West Virginia.

"When Patsy told Bill she was leaving the group—and him—she really shook him up," Deyton remembered. "It was sad, the type of thing you didn't want to see. We all kept an eye on him because we were afraid he might do something stupid. Patsy and I talked some.

"She told me, 'Well, Roy, it's time I started moving on. I'm going to miss you. Staying on is not going to help matters any or help my career.' From the way Patsy talked, you could tell she was desperate to get to the top as quickly as she could. It was almost as if she knew she didn't have that much time. We were both about the same age, twenty-three, so there I was figuring I had years ahead of me and there was Patsy talking as if she *had* to get it done by tomorrow.

"Patsy had played the game as best she could—probably no worse than anyone else would have done it. She did hurt Bill, there's no doubt about that. And maybe he asked for it. I don't think she ever intended to hurt him. Patsy went to great lengths to get where she wanted to go. I can't fault her for that, but, I guess, she was more than a bit deceptive and used people.

"I certainly didn't like a lot of the things she did and the way she did them but I can't say that I disliked her or hold any ill feelings against her. We were as close friends as she had back then. And Patsy was responsible for me marrying my wife. I was being pulled between taking my music seriously, you know, going to Nashville with my brother Ray and everything—or settling down and getting married. One night on the way to some date, Patsy asked me, 'Well, hoss, how's every little thing in your life?'

"Not very good," I told her.

"What's the matter?"

Deyton explained what was going on in his mind.

"Playing music makes you happy?"

"Yeah, it sure does."

"Does it make you happier than she makes you?"

"No, it don't."

"Then, there, you've just solved your own problem. Can't think of how much money I saved you! Hoss, you do what's gonna make you happy. If you really love her, marrry her. With me, you see, it's different. I don't love nothing more than music."

"Patsy was right," noted Deyton, "because no career goal could have ever brought me the joy and fulfillment that my marriage has."

The words "Town and Country" became a lucrative service mark for Connie B. Gay. In addition to the Army transcriptions and "Town and Country Time" daily on radio from noon to 3 p.m., there was the "Town and Country Time" half-hour nightly television show, emceed by Jimmy Dean. This latter show was generated from across the Potomac from Arlington on WMAL, Channel 7 (now WJLA), in Washington, D.C.

Gay also produced a "Town and Country Barn Dance" (modeled after the WLS Barn Dance in Chicago), "Town and Country Time" package shows, and the "Town and Country Jamboree." The latter because America's first late-night musical variety television program, and was to be another stepping stone in Patsy Cline's career.

"Town and Country Jamboree" went on the air live from 10 P.M. to 1 A.M. Saturdays, but what made the show an event were the 15,000 customers at the Capitol Arena in downtown Washington, who enjoyed music and dancing from nine to two. The show became a regional institution—not for the same reason the Grand Ole Opry had, but because it was the one place in town you could be assured of a good-time, party atmosphere. There was beer and hot dogs, and lots of single women and lots of single men.

The television portion was carried on the—yes, you guessed it—Town and Country Network, Gay's regional lineup of stations in Baltimore, Richmond, and Salisbury (Maryland).

When Patsy was added to the Jimmy Dean shows in October 1955, she became quite the busy commuter. She would do the radio show five mornings a week, then "Town and Country Time" on TV plus the weekend "Jamboree," and all for just a bit over sideman's scale.

"Union scale for radio was sixty dollars and eighteen cents a week," says Gay, "which was damn little, but those were the rates. Nineteen fifty-five was not nineteen eighty. The rate was about double for television. Jimmy was making twice as much. I paid everyone a bit more than scale so Patsy and the rest of the cast made an average of fifty dollars a day for a six day week."

Jimmy Dean has not forgotten the first time he met Patsy. "I was working in a D.C. club and had Roy [Clark] on that date with me. During one of the breaks, this gal packing one of those clothing bags came up to me. She said, 'Hi, Mr. Dean. I'm Patsy Cline. And I want to sing with you.'

"I looked her over. She was downright good-looking. I figured, 'If she can sing, too—great!' I said, 'All right. You go and change and we'll go over some music.' When she came out in full western regalia, Roy looked at me and I looked at Roy. I thought, 'Holy cow!' Then, after a second when I looked around the club, I thought, 'What the shit! Nothing but a bunch of drunks. What will they care?'

" 'Okay, lady' I told Patsy, 'let's mosey over to the piano and see what you can do.' We went over some sheet music, then she sang and when she did Patsy just knocked everybody's hat in the creek.

"Yes, sir, Patsy Cline was something else! She was as cocky as hell about her ability. She knew she could sing and she loved to sing. She thoroughly enjoyed listening to herself, too—as opposed to me. I can't stand to hear my own voice. But Patsy loved it.

"Aside from that aspect of her, Patsy was brash—very brash—in other ways. Brash to the point where, if you did not know her, you would say that Patsy Cline was a callous, arrogant person. She really wasn't. Far, far from it. Also, Patsy had a way with words. She was not exactly what you'd construe as a polished lady at any time. This is not to say she could not be ladylike. She could be as warm and sweet as you'd want. But she had a mouth on her that would embarrass a truck driver."

It is interesting how few people on the "Town and Country Time" shows knew Patsy was married. Most of her acquaintances remember Charley well, but had only a vague knowledge of Gerald. Patsy was not the type to go on about what a wonderful guy she was married to. Dean recalls that Gerald came around occasionally on the package shows. "I just remember he was short and heavyset."

Others said it was not much of a marriage from the way it hardly came up. It did not seem, from the way Patsy carried on and did what she wanted to do, that she let her marriage vows stand in the way of having a good time.

One of her "Town and Country Time" co-workers related, "Patsy flirted with anything in pants. Sometimes you had to pull her off you. There was one particular member of the band that she had her eye on. She flirted with him incessantly and, finally, decided she was going to have him. He talked about the way she was in bed for days, until one of us had to shut him up.

"He said that after they finished Patsy looked him straight in the eye and asked, 'Now, hoss, wasn't that the best fuck you ever had?' He couldn't get over that—the way she visualized it as the type of thing you should get a testimonial about."

Gerald did not give up trying to persuade Patsy to cut down. but headstrong Patsy could not fathom giving up any portion of her singing career. When she was home, Gerald would be working or doing whatever he did. When he was home, Patsy would be working the Jamboree or on the road with one-nighters with Dean and his troupe.

Bill Peer was back in Patsy's life, but, according to Peer's son, Larry, this time it was solely on a professional basis. "It was my impression that Dad was constantly going up and down the road working with Patsy as her manager or periodically going to Washington to see her."

Jenny Peer explained that "Bill was not so much a bitter man about what Patsy had done as he was hurt and disappointed. He and I became good friends again, and I even took him back. We married a second time. I was alone with two children, and I did love Bill. I thought—again—that he'd straighten up now that Patsy was once and for all out of his life, but, no, he didn't. There was another woman, and we divorced again."

Though his marriage to Patsy had long ago deteriorated, Gerald did attempt to make some semblance of trying to hold on to Patsy. He finally came to the realization that Patsy was never going to be an everyday housewife and he rid himself of such illusions. Gerald even took to reaccompanying Patsy on some of her "Town and County Time" package dates.

"Connie booked Patsy on a lot of shows," Gerald said. "I couldn't always go because I had to get up early the next day to operate my business. But, whenever I could, I'd usually take Patsy and stay with her. And I'll tell you something, everywhere we'd go—anywhere Patsy'd sing—everybody would come up to me and tell me, 'Hey, you've got some wife! We've never heard anybody like her.'

"The reason they didn't is because there wasn't. In my mind, Patsy was unique. She became real popular—a name—in the area and she was always in demand. Of course, Patsy was not completely happy because none of her records had made it. But, live and in person, no one could come close to touching Patsy."

"Like Connie B. Gay," says Billy Grammer, "I recognized from the very beginning that Patsy was unique. From the very first, Connie saw a big potential in her. I knew she was married to Gerald, but it was a relationship that I was not acquainted with. I only saw them together a few times, and I was not the type of friend to Patsy that she would dicuss her married life or problems with. I liked her very much. She liked me. But we were not confidants. She always impressed me as being a loner and the type of person who didn't trust too many people.

"Don't get me wrong, now. Patsy would not reject your friendship or throw you out of her dressing room—just the opposite. She loved to hold court! But she had something standoffish about her. She wasn't cold-hearted, but there was a certain warmth lacking. And she could shock some folks. Oh, yes! Patsy could be rough-house when she wanted, but she never embarrassed me. But, then, I never took anything she said seriously or to heart. If I had to point out one trait, other than her singing, that to me made Patsy Cline special, I would say it was her sense of humor. She had a wonderful, devilish laugh. She often made me laugh. And I made her laugh. I always considered that a compliment when I did."

George Hamilton IV remembers Patsy: "I met her when I joined the 'Town and Country Jamboree' in nineteen fifty-six. She came on strong and I said to myself, 'Who is this woman?' My first impression of her, all decked out in a cowgirl outfit—hat, boots, skirt with sequins and rhinestones—the works—was that she was a tough lady. And she was.

"Suddenly, at nineteen and having just finished my freshman year at the University of North Carolina at Chapel Hill, I was confronted by this brassy lady from Winchester, Virginia, who fairly frequently used words I had never heard before. With her salty language, Patsy struck me as being more truck driver than Country singer. She did shock me at first, which was what she set out to do.

"I was six foot to her five-foot, six-inches, but Patsy was much more formidable than I. She had an overpowering presence. I always felt intimidated by her. I went to Washington more than a bit naive, and the first thing I encounter is initiation by fire from Patsy. She was sort of bemused by me, this lanky kid from the sticks. She knew I was bashful and wet behind the ears, yet she took great delight in embarrassing me.

"Jan Gay, a Duke University student, heard my record of 'A Rose and a Baby Ruth,' made locally by the label Andy Griffith began with [Colonial]. He told me his dad, whom everyone in that area knew of, was looking for another act for the TV show starring Jimmy Dean. I got a call to guest on the Jamboree. I arrived wide-eyed and bushy-tailed. I wanted to be a Country singer all my life, so doing the show was a thrill. I grew up idolizing the Grand Ole Orpy stars.

"My appearance turned out to be an audition for a permanent spot, so I saw quite a bit of Patsy. When I was around her, I blushed most of the time. Jimmy told me later, 'Heck, she throws out words she never even uses when you're in the dressing room because Patsy knows it'll make you blush. She likes to count and see how long it takes you to turn red!' Patsy always succeeded in a hurry.

"What I didn't know was that Patsy was putting me to the Patsy Cline Worthy-of-My-Friendship Test. I must have failed I don't know how many times before I finally passed.

"It wasn't long before I realized that Patsy liked people to stand up to her, and I never did. I don't know if Patsy liked me so much as she tolerated me. I was the youngest of the group, which was made up mostly of seasoned players. But Patsy and

I did hit it off on a friendly basis eventually.

"Patsy was outspoken, but she never put me down or poked fun at me to the point of hurting me in front of others.

"In private, it was quite another thing! She'd find me backstage—usually hiding from her—and come up to me and hit me across the back and say, 'Hey, hoss, I'm gonna have to light a fire under your goddamn ass! You're gonna have to learn to get out there in front of those cameras and hold your head up. Take charge when you're singing!'

" 'Yes, ma'am,' I would reply.

" 'You walk out there like you're embarrassed to be on that stage. Are you ashamed to be singing with us?'

" 'No, ma'am."

" 'What kind of singer are you? Ain't gonna go nowhere with that kind of attitude. That's not humility! That's a weakness. You gotta get up there and show 'em!' Patsy would throw up her hand and outstretch her palm. 'You gotta get 'em to eat right outta your hands. You're the star. When you're doing your songs, take command, hoss'. "

Laughs George today, "Of course, it was good advice. And Patsy helped me a lot. It was just the way she told me. She'd jab me and say, 'Hey, chief' or 'Hey, hoss, let me tell you something.' And she'd sprinkle in more than a few four-letter words for emphasis.

"It didn't take me too long to see that Patsy Cline had a rough, tough, I've-lived-a bit exterior, which concealed a very warm heart and a fantastic personality."

Dean expresses a similiar view. "I'll tell you this much, if Patsy Cline was your friend you didn't have a worry in the world. She was your friend to the end. She'd go to the wall for you!"

Jimmy discussed the uniqueness that was Patsy's. "When Patsy worked for me—actually Connie B. Gay—she was not a great showman. She couldn't talk. But she could sing! She really ripped up a lyric. Patsy sung her butt completely off! She was a huge fan of Kay Starr's. You could see a lot of that style there.

"Patsy was a pretty girl, and a lot of people thought she was the sexiest thing they'd ever seen. I really don't know why, because I could never see it. We were both in our twenties and at our peaks, you might say. But to me Patsy was totally void of sex appeal. And still I loved her to death! But there was just no sex appeal—no physical attraction—there for me.

"We became the closest of friends. I was already married [to Sue], so there was no hanky-panky behind the scenes between us. I may have been one of the few people Patsy did not have an affair with at that time. She got around.

"I'm not that easily shocked, but one time we were working a date somewhere in Canada and were checking into the hotel. Patsy and I were together and she looked around and saw this big guy—a Canadian Mountie.

"Right out loud she said, 'He's a big, good-looking son-of-a-bitch! I want him! I'm screwing the boots off him tonight.' And she took off across that lobby for him, made contact, *and* did what she said she was going to do."

Dean explained that, being a country boy himself, he liked most of all Patsy's down-homeness and plain talk. "You always knew where you stood with Patsy—no b.s., no hustle, just the facts.

"Patsy was obsessed with becoming a star. I don't know if I ever saw anyone that wanted it more. Maybe Dottie West. Dottie was always that way, too. She *was* gonna make it.

"With Patsy, all she could think of was getting away from Winchester and making it big—getting away from anything that she felt might be holding her back. She knew she was good. Oh, yeah! You betcha! She was gonna make it and that was it. I don't think anything in the world would have stood in the way of that. Nothing! In Patsy's mind, there was no price too big to pay for it. She wanted it that bad. And professionally, there was very little I could ever find wrong with Patsy.

"She had two things that if you're going go be associated with me in any way, you must have: punctuality and professionalism. She could do what she was paid to do, and she did it damn well. I've always said that time is a man's most valuable asset and that it would be terribly presumptuous and rude of me to think I was privileged to waste that. I will not waste your time nor will you mine.

"Patsy laughed a lot and she had a good time. That was important to me, too. But when it came to career time, no one could have been more deadly serious or deliver the goods the way she did."

Dale Turner of Nashville recalls the night in Washington she first encountered Patsy: "She literally upstaged me! I was working a little club called Strick's , where I was sort of the belle of the ball. There was a stir—the kind you have when someone well known in the business visits—and I look to see which celebrity it is, but all I saw was this girl in a big, white western hat, red cowgirl outfit with white fringe, and white boots. And I thought, 'Well, who on earth is that?' As soon as I heard her name, I realized I had heard people in the area speak of her, that she was out of Winchester, Virginia, and supposed to be darn good. She was! Everybody got excited when she agreed to get up and sing. Agreed? I don't think there was any way anyone could have stopped her!

"When Patsy finished the song she whipped off that cowboy hat and held it up in the air. I mean, she *did* know how to end a song. She really did. I said, 'You can learn a few things from this gal.' I didn't meet Patsy that night. When I came to work on the 'Town and Country Jamboree,' I was under the impression I was to be the only girl singer. And there was Patsy, and I said to myself, 'Well, now, that's really all you need!' But we became friends immediately, and I still think the world of her."

Back on the Nashville front, Paul Cohen set another Patsy Cline release, "Hidin' Out," backed with "Turn the Cards Slowly," for November on Coral. This would coincide with the annual WSM Birthday Celebration and disk jockey convention.

Connie B. Gay Enterprises set up a hospitality suite in the Andrew Jackson Hotel. "Patsy had Gay's office send me a hospitality suite invitation," reflected Lee Burrows, pulling the folded and engraved parchment from a box of mementoes. "That Connie had a way with words. He's got his stations listed—WTCR, KITE, WFTC, WYFE, WGAY, WSHO—and his offices—San Antonio, New Orleans, Huntington (West Virginia), Ashland. My favorite is the way he defines country music:

" 'The prayer of a sinner
The dream of a lover
The lament of the weary
The tears of the forsaken
The story of a vagabond
The remorse of a cheater
The blessing of friendship
The praise of a divine God'

"That covers all the bases! Anyway, Patsy and Gerald came down for the November 1955, convention."

Gay, like many of the label executives, attempted to make the convention of country d.j.s something it is not. The annual event does have value and merit, but stacked against this are a bunch of drunks—jocks and artists alike. There are label showcases to present veteran acts and new faces. There are award dinners of all kinds, interview sessions with the stars for the d.j.s to broadcast back home over their respective stations, special performances of the Opry, promises of more support on the stations for whichever label is giving the bash, and [beginning in 1967] The Country Music Association Awards.

Then, as now, the main interest is seeing how much liquor can be consumed in as many visits as possible to hospitality suites. The Grand Ole Opry is, with so many acts in town, crammed full of names.

"I think," recalled Lee Burrows, "Patsy came down to the convention for Connie so she could go to the Opry. That's the way it seemed. I picked her and Gerald up at their motel and drove them around. We had dinner at some little out of the way spot on Murfreesboro Road, and Gerald picked up the tab. Patsy and Gerald were lovely. He was at his most charming, which was not hard for him to do. Gerald really was a nice man.

"I wasn't that big in town, but I had a few connections and was able to get backstage passes for the Opry. Patsy literally could not wait to get to the Ryman. Backstage she told me excitedly, 'This is such a thrill being here. When I stop and think of all the great names that have played on this stage. Oh, my! It just makes me so proud to be a part of it.'

"What tickled me was that Patsy was the biggest fan of Country music. From working with Gay she knew many of the artists and she was having a big time with her camera and getting autographs. Patsy was like a kid with a new toy." There is, even in the new house, no awe or solemnity for the institution that is the Grand Ole Opry. The artists mingle with the guests, they mill around slapping each other on the backs, and the Coke bottles roll across the floor.

More than anything else, the purpose of the Opry is for everyone—in the auditorium and the radio audience—to have a good time. For the artists it is a social occasion—few do it for the money—when they visit friends they don't see, since one act will often be on the road when another is home. Out front, the fans continually run to the front of the stage and snap away with their Kodaks and flash cubes.

"That night Patsy was just like one of the fans," Burrows laughed. "She was a big admirer of Del Wood [who had a ragtime piano hit with "Down Yonder"], who has to be one of the most outgoing people you'd ever hope to meet. When I introduced them, Patsy bubbled over, gave me her camera, and said, 'Here, Lee, take one of us together.' She got autographs by the dozens and pictures of the Wilburn Brothers, Roy Acuff, her friend Ernest Tubb, Stringbean [David Akeman, the famed Opry banjo player and later co-star of TV's "Hee Haw," and who was murdered in 1973], and Faron Young.

"When I took Patsy and Gerald to the motel that night after we stopped at Tootsie's [Orchid Lounge, the musician's hangout on lower Broadway], Patsy said, 'Lee, it's a night we'll never forget.' Looking back, it's one I've never forgotten."

On her January 1956 visit Patsy stayed with Lee Burrows [then Lee Rosenberg] and her family in their home on Murphy Road and West End Avenue [the present location of the restaurant Ruby Tuesday's].

"At the house my room was a huge front space that was formerly a den. I had a combination home recording studio and living quarters—two couches that converted to beds—in there.

"There is one memory of Patsy's visits that is vivid in my mind: Patsy standing in the middle of that room singing. I loved to hear Patsy sing because she really lived every word of the lyrics. You'd have to say that Patsy was a writer's singer because of the way she treated the lyrics—like an actress would treat dialogue.

"I had shown Patsy this song, 'If I Tell What I Know,' and she liked it immediately and said she wanted to record it. I don't know if she saw something of her own life in it or not, but it was the kind of torch song she could really sink her teeth into.

"Patsy idolized singers such as Kitty Wells and some of the old timers. She said 'If I Tell What I Know' was the type of song Kitty might do, à la her hit 'It Wasn't God Who Made Honky-Tonk Angels.'

"Anyway I left the song with her and the next morning there she was singing it exactly the way I intended it to be sung. She couldn't have looked it over but about once or twice and there she was doing like she was in a session.

"I showed the song to Owen and told him how much Patsy liked it. Owen and I worked well together and I'd take him material for his artists. But when it came to Patsy, he said to me, 'Lee, hon, I like it and Patsy likes it but now we gotta get Bill McCall to like it? My hands are tied. He's only leasing her and his songs to us.' "

In March 1956, the Sunday magazine of the *Washington Star* ran a cover story on Patsy being in the "Jimmy Dean Town and Country Jamboree." The writer slugged her "the hillbilly with oomph."

At the Ozark Jubilee show in Missouri Patsy spoke with Red Foley, the resident star, about her career. He told her, "Well gal, you sure got it. Just keep singing and you're gonna get there."

On April 22, 1956, Patsy was back in Nashville for her third session. The songs recorded were "Stop, Look, Listen," "I've Loved and Lost Again" by Eddie Miller, and two gospel numbers, "He Will Do for You (What He's Done for Me)" and "Dear God." The first two were released July 8, 1956, becoming Patsy's first Decca single. Cohen had put aside the plan to make Coral a premier country label. The last two songs remained unreleased until after Patsy's death.

Patsy was a recording and regional television star, yet that right combination Paul Cohen had spoken to Owen Bradley of did not materialize. Patsy's records had not become hits nor had the public or the country disk jockeys paid them much notice.

Mrs. Hensley remembers Patsy speaking often of the fact that the national recognition she had long coveted seemed farther and farther away the closer and closer she got.

"Something's wrong somewhere," she told her mother, "and I don't think it's me. I'm trying to run forward, and they seem to be holding me back. It's time I took the initiative."

"Patsy was serious," intoned Mrs. Hensley. "She meant business! I knew what she was like when backed into a corner. Somebody had better watch out."

Patsy got her records together and sent them along with photos to Jeanette Davis at the Arthur Godfrey office in New York with a note: "Are you still interested? I am."

6
"I'm Moving Along"

Patsy Cline: **"Daddy, I've been accepted on 'Arthur Godfrey's Talent Scouts' in New York."**

Sam Hensley: **"I don't want you going off to New York. It's too big and it's not safe."**

Patsy Cline: **"After being out of my life for seven years, it's a fine time to start showing concern. I'm going. And you or no one else is gonna stop me!"**

Connie B. Gay has his admirers and detractors, but he was responsible for giving Jimmy Dean, Patsy Cline, Roy Clark, George Hamilton IV, and many others their first taste of the big time. There were hours of hard work: three hours of radio and a half hour of live television five days a week and three hours of live TV Saturday nights

"It amazed me that we looked so good," Dean exclaimed, 'cause it was a gigantic mess! Talk about doing things assembly-line style! I'd get with the gang to set the show and just fill in tunes to pace the allotted time. I'd ask Patsy, 'What you gonna sing, doll?' She'd tell me, 'Hoss, I'm gonna do this, this, and this.'

"I'd say, 'Great. What key you gonna do them in?' Patsy'd reply, 'Hell, I don't know.' So I'd jump in with the guys and say, 'Okay, let's try this one. You know all the words?

Good...Sounds like it might be conducive to a fiddle kick in... Buck [Ryan], hey, pardner, you wanna try that? Do da do doom, do da do doom... Yeah! Okay. Let's run it down once...You missed a chord, Herbie [Jones, on rhythm guitar]. That goes chunk. Chunk, got it? Okay. Let's use a diminished chord there...' "

"Town and Country Jamboree" audiences were diversified. Some came for the music, others to party, still others out of curiosity. There was everything from pickup trucks to Corvettes and Cadillacs in the parking lot. It was an event. The sponsors were Gunther Beer, Briggs Hot Dogs and Ice Cream, L & M, and, among others, Otha Williams Buick.

There were local bands and singers and guests from the Grand Ole Opry. The house cast included Roy Clark on banjo; Quincy Snodgrass, bass and rube comedy; Mary Klick, rhythm guitar bass and vocals; Dale Turner, vocals; Marvin Carroll, steel guitar; ventriloquist Alec Houston; Grammer; Hamilton; and, of course, Patsy.

"That wasn't all!" said Dean, letting out a modified yell. "We had Tiny Jenkins, and, oh, my God, Texas Jim Robertson. You had to see him to believe him. Texas Jim was a fine singer who wore cowboy outfits topped by this big, white Stetson. Under the hat was a real bad rug, in a pompadour style yet! He'd come to the microphone and cock the hat back of that pompadour and just sing away. But it was very hot in the arena. We were using three cameras and many more lights than they do today. My God, it was hot! Jim used to sweat down two, maybe three outfits a night. Once when he was singing, the sweat melted the stick 'em he used on his rug. Everything started to go. I went into a tailspin of shock! Texas Jim's rug and hat slowly just started to slide. He was singing and at the same time giving it a shot to get it back in place. And the more he tried, the worse it came down. Ah, live TV! I took a flying leap to the [video] truck out in the street and shouted, 'Shoot the crowd. Shoot the crowd, dammit! Whatever you do get off Jim.' Poor Jim!

"On a given Saturday night there must have been twenty dozen cups of coffee on that stage if there was one cup. A cup of coffee could be all the way across the stage and it would somehow work its way over to get spilled on me. By two o'clock I was a big stain. I had it spilled on my sleeves, on my pockets, on my pants leg. I've even got it spilled on my crotch. There I was playing the piano and smiling into the camera and at the same time grimacing in pain. Oh, but those were the good times!"

Dale Turner and Billy Grammer agree. "We were on superpower Channel Seven," says Turner, "so word had drifted everywhere we were the one guaranteed place to come and have a good time. Any musician working the area would come to the arena at midnight when the D.C. bars closed. At one time or another there was Johnny Cash, Carl Smith, Ferlin Husky, Faron Young, Bob Wills, Mac Wiseman, Hank Thompson, and the Wilburn Brothers, who were backing Webb Pierce. Washington had become as big a country music entity, minus the recording, of course, as Nashville and Jimmy [Dean] was the big cheese. He was as popular as anyone at that time. But it was Connie B. Gay's empire, and he was at the center of anything involving country.

"When I came to the Jamboree, things were in a state of transition. Roy Clark was leaving and Billy Grammer was coming. Mary Klick needed some time off to have a baby. She did the duet and trio work with the guys. I thought I was going to be the only girl singer and then in walks Patsy. I said to myself, 'Oh, no! What did I do to deserve this?' The first time I heard her sing I nearly died and sighed, 'Lord, who can stand up to that?' And now here I was on the same show with her. I just knew she was going to make me look bad.

"Patsy was a big name in our area. Washington, D.C., may be small but the area around it is not. You never heard the name Patsy Cline, even in the outlying counties of Virginia and into parts of Pennsylvania, that you didn't know who she was. On the other hand, I was very inexperienced. I got on the show strictly through a prayer! I had known some of the guys —Jimmy, when he was working a little club called the Harmony behind Union Station—because I had sung locally. I was from Washington.

"When she came to the Jamboree, Patsy was a star, but she had no big money. In those days a secretary was paid sixty-five dollars a week, so we were making decent money. Money wasn't a big thing to us. We weren't aware of what 'stars' could make, so whatever we had seemed big to us. Patsy was even making records, but nothing was happening. Four-Star had a bad reputation for not paying, but if you had a label then you praised the Lord. That meant you could work personal appearances, get recognition, and get on the Grand Ole Opry.

"Patsy not only wanted records, she wanted hit records. The most important thing to her was her career. Everything else revolved around it. It did with most of our whole group. They might have been married and had families, but their careers were more than livelihoods."

"And with Patsy around there was never a dull minute!" says Grammer. "She was a true blithe spirit. Patsy'd march back and forth in her star-spangled outfits causing all kinds of fun. When she wasn't telling somebody off and where to go, she was driving the Opry guest stars crazy for autographs. We also had a Mother Superior in Dale Turner! Dale's Granddad had once owned the Capitol Arena. Dale was a sweet girl and quite a singer herself. She was old-fashioned and gave poor Jimmy a hard time. Patsy and I had to conspire to get the best of ole Connie. But Dale would say, 'Connie says we have to do this. When Connie says do something, we should do it.'

"They did call me, in jest, 'Your highness, Mother Superior.' Patsy might be telling a joke and she'd see me coming and yell, 'Hush, here she comes, her highness the Mother Superior!" smiled Dale.

"When I used to fuss at Jimmy or Patsy, they'd say, 'God, do we really need a nun here?' At particularly rough moments in run-throughs or what-have-you, Jimmy would look over at me and say, 'Dale, honey, please stop praying for me! Everything's going badly enough. I don't want you to make it worse!'

"Patsy had great faith in me as a singer, and she'd get a little upset with me from time to time because I didn't get too excited. But for me, it was a job not a career. You'd watch her and say to yourself, 'My goodness, she's giving it her all.' But, in fact, she always was holding something back. When she got to the last note, you'd know it."

As the success of the "Town and Country Time" shows grew larger, Patsy's following throughout the area also increased. It was time for Connie B. Gay to review her salary. As far as she was concerned, she was being underpaid. She went to Mr. Gay and asked him for a raise and he informed her she was being paid more than enough for a woman in the business.

"For our package show dates," said Jimmy Dean, "Connie really broke down and spent some money. He bought what Patsy and I referred to as the 'kidney buster,' an old bus with springs so shot it was more like a damn produce truck. There were lots of times we'd be traveling eighty-five to a hundred miles in an evening, work until two A.M., and then drive home, and then go and do a damn afternoon [television] show. That thing was the worst. It was just a tough thing to ride in. You couldn't sleep, and you couldn't relax. The only reward you got was a sore butt. But that's what we did. It was a living. Two hundred and fifty a week."

Gerald and Patsy Cline fell out of love—whatever type of love they had fallen into. Cline claims he and Patsy "lived together" until the end of March 1957.

"Well, that might have been the case," said brother Nevin Cline, "but if it was that's all you could call it—living together. He was playing around, and so was she."

According to Roy Deyton, "Patsy and Gerald weren't getting along worth a plug nickel. It all boiled down to the fact he didn't have the money or desire necessary to promote or push her. His family had it—plenty of it—but they wouldn't turn it loose. By as early as nineteen fifty-five Gerald was almost totally out of the picture, except for appearance's sake, although he and Patsy were still saying they were married and lived in the same house."

Fay Crutchley noted that "at one point after Jenny filed for divorce, Pat and Gerald were back together. They moved from East Patrick Street into a mobile home in Dutrow's Trailer Park on Bowers Road. But the coming and going of Pat and Gerald was an ongoing thing. A month they were hot, a month later they were cold. A month they were on, a month later they were off. You needed a scorecard to keep up. Before the divorce mess, one month Pat and Gerald would be separated and she'd be with Bill and then the next month she'd be back living with Gerald. Sometimes when she'd tell me she was going home, I wondered just where she meant.

"After the divorce when Jenny left Bill, Pat was back with Gerald. Bill couldn't get over that. He was very sad and he'd keep saying, 'Why is she treating me so cold? Why is she doing me the way she is?' He told me, 'I've given up my wife for her and Patsy doesn't seem to care.' "

Patsy later described her marriage to Gerald in this way to pianist Del Wood, "Oh,hoss, it was like a bad dream with no tunes in it. Gerald and I had a good marriage, as marriages go, in the beginning. My problem was that when I got married I don't think I knew what love was."

Said Wood, "Patsy told me she had mixed up love and companionship. It's hard enough making it in the business, but finding a man who'll understand, well, that's another story.

"It's a hurting business. I don't think he wanted to bring up a family in that kind of atmosphere. When you're a big star, you're miserable because you have no privacy and have to hide. When you start to decline, you're called a has-been. There's nothing worse than someone coming up to you and saying 'Oh, yeah, I remember you. What's your name again?' after you've been on top. Maybe he knew all that. My impression was that Gerald never realized how much stardom meant to Patsy."

"Patsy and Gerald were quite a pair," said Lee Burrows. "Patsy was five-six or five- seven and Gerald couldn't have been more than an inch taller. He weighed about two hundred pounds, though. I was impressed at how he seemed to adore the ground Patsy walked on. Who's to say he didn't sweep her off her feet?

"I know Gerald was trying to make Patsy happy. She'd say, 'Oh, Gerald's real nice. He wants to take care of me, give me this and give me that.' He was some nine years older than Patsy, but she had affection for him. The age difference might have been one reason for the attraction. Her father left when she was quite young. She looked up to Gerald in that way. Later, I'm sure, she discovered she married anything but a father figure."

Love was in the air in early 1956.

Bill Peer, Gerald Cline, Mrs. Hensley, Dale Turner, even Patsy herself had quite a surprise in store. Patsy met a boy her own age and fell head over heels in love—"And *this* time," she later confided to Del Wood, "it was for *real!*"

Prior to going to Nashville in April 1956, for her fourth recording session (the third with Owen Bradley) and less than a year after coming to the "Town and Country Jamboree," Patsy met Charlie Dick. It was Friday, April 13. Superstitious or not, Patsy's life was never to be the same after that.

"I grew up in Winchester, but I never really knew Patsy," said Charlie. "I had seen her in a school play of some kind but I didn't know who she was. I dropped out of school at the end of the tenth grade and, eventually, started working at the Winchester Star as a linotype operator.

"On Friday nights I used to go to Berryville, about twenty miles from Winchester, to the armory dances. My friend Bud Armel, who still plays in that area, had a band called the Kountry Krackers. They were a good time band. The dances were good, clean fun. This particular Friday night I was just hanging out and I saw this gal go up on stage.

"Bud introduced her as Patsy Cline. I thought she looked familiar but the last name threw me. I would have known her had he said Hensley, probably. This was the first time I had heard her singing and she literally bowled me over! Patsy sang every kind of song imaginable and really wowed me. Nobody could belt out a song like Patsy. I still don't think there's anyone who can compare to her. Man, how she moved. Patsy couldn't stand still and sing. She was all over the place. Patsy put everything she had into her act—lots of motion and emotion. I think, looking back, that's what made her so great and created the impact she had on the industry.

"During the first break I went over to Bud and asked him who this Patsy Cline was. He told me she was one of the regulars on the Connie B. Gay 'Town and Country Jamboree' in Washington on Saturday nights with Jimmy Dean. She was going to be working with him on Fridays.

"I got him to introduce us, but Patsy was playing it cool. I tried talking to her and she just didn't seem too interested. But I didn't let that deter me. I decided the moment I saw her that I was going to make my move. She not only sang well, but she was also a knockout. Then I found out she was married and I said to myself, 'Well, that explains the way she's acting.' But I decided to give it another shot. When I asked her for a date, I thought she'd say no, *but* she didn't."

Although they continued to live together, hardly seeing each other, all vestiges of a relationship disappeared in Patsy and Gerald's marriage. From that April 13 weekend on, Patsy and Charlie were a magic twosome—well, call it semi-magical, anyway, because in addition to seeing Charlie, Patsy was back dating her former accompanist Jumbo Rinker. Gerald did not let any grass grow under his feet—he never did. He began dating others.

Patsy was dating, but there was, according to what she told friends, only one man in her life and that was Charlie.

"There's quite a bit of life in my man," said Patsy. "He's a man, all man!" Charlie told a friend what being in love with Patsy was like: "When I'm with Patsy, she takes me halfway to heaven!"

"In nineteen fifty-six" recalled Donn Hecht, "I think I wore out four pairs of shoes carrying my song folder to every music publisher in Hollywood. In those days Coffee-Dan's, near the corner of Sunset and Vine, teemed with every would-be songwriter and singer in the world. I remember the Country artists who gathered there were never considered part of 'the family,' and usually were described as 'hicks who couldn't read music and sang through their noses.'

"It was there that I first saw Patsy Cline. Not often, but enough to remember her without knowing her name. Not beautiful, not plain, she walked like a dancer, and something played off her that made her stand out from the crowd. Later on I was thin and broke and sitting before Bill McCall at Four-Star Records in Pasadena. 'You're a comer, boy,' he told me. 'I think you've got real talent, and I'm gonna gamble on you, *but...*'

"That 'but' meant signing a seven-year writing contract, guaranteeing a six-hundred-dollar monthly draw against my royalties. It further said he could fire me anytime, *but* that I could not quit! My car was up for repossession, my rent past due, and I had less than three dollars in my pocket. I signed. Two weeks later, I was set to produce material for Country artists. I groaned, 'Me?' A writer of semi-classical music?' I took home demonstration tapes and listened to hundreds of singers. My assignment was to pick a star and write a hit.

"I told McCall, 'Sorry. I need the money, but I'm afraid I can't write this stuff.' He glared at me and said, 'You've heard the worst, now listen to this, and listen good.' He put on the phono and before the record made ten revolutions, I almost fell off my chair. I was hypnotized by a girl's voice that reached out and penetrated me in a way I'll never forget.

" 'Who is she?' I asked. 'Her name is Patsy Cline,' he replied, 'but there is a problem. I've already spent a fortune releasing her stuff and she's bombed out every time. Can you tell me why?'

" 'Hell, that's easy!' I said. 'She's not a Country singer.' McCall told me, 'I don't agree. She's got the same tear in her voice that you have in your material. But if she bombs out one more time, I've got to drop her.' I told Bill that I'd give it some thought. I went home and went through a stack of unpublished material until I came across a yellowed lead sheet of a song nobody wanted called 'Walkin' After Midnight.' I had written it with Alan Block, an electronic engineer, who wrote mainly as a hobby.

"It was written for Kay Starr, but her A&R department wouldn't let her do it. It was pure B-flat blues and, with Patsy's voice still surging through my brain, I put the two together. I performed some minor surgery, called a recording session, and redid it with another singer. When Bill heard it, he was very pleased and called Patsy in Virginia. She hated the title, but said she'd listen over the phone. She hated the song! Then Bill told her to come out, at his expense, so they could talk about it.

"At our meeting in Hollywood the next week we all clashed. McCall played the song over and over and this force-feeding made Patsy angrier and angrier. He told her he had spent a fortune on her and that she would, like it or not, do as he said. She yelled, 'But it's nothin' but a little ole pop song!' I countered, 'And you're nothin' but a little ole pop singer who lives in the country!'

"Bill left us alone. We gave each other the silent treatment. Then I broke out laughing and Patsy did, too. She apologized, I apologized. She said, 'Two years of singing what everybody else wants, and when it flops, who gets the blame? Me! It just ain't fair.' I told Patsy to ask Bill if she could pick a side, if he had to pick one.

"'Look, Mr. Heck,' Patsy began and I interrupted to say, 'It's pronounced like Hector without the "or,"' and she went on, 'Look, Mr. Hector without the "or," don't you think I've been through this before? He never lets me pick a song.' I told her, 'I'll back you on it.' She told me she still hated the song, but that she *did* like me. I considered this a compliment, coming as it did from one tough little lady, but I told her that it wouldn't do and that her singing a song she didn't like would come over to the audience.

"Bill returned with coffee and doughnuts and Patsy told him point blank, 'Mr. Hecht and I have decided to do one side I really like along with this one and release them back to back.' Bill arched his eyebrows and studied us both with surprise. 'Then, if your side sells,' added Patsy, 'I'll never argue about material again. *But* if my side sells . . . '

"Bill had the last word, saying, 'Okay, but if neither side sells, what then?' And Patsy shot back, 'Then you just get yourself another singer. Is it a deal?' Bill bit into his doughnut and sipped his coffee and finally muttered, 'It's a deal.' "

Patsy returned to Virginia and Bill McCall set about planning her next recording session with Paul Cohen.

Patsy took her new romance in stride and continued doing business as usual. She returned to Nashville the week of November 4, 1956, for her fourth recording session and to attend, for Connie B. Gay Enterprises, the WSM Birthday Celebration and disk jockey convention. Decca also kept Patsy busy in the hospitality suite and at the WSM studios meeting and posing for photographs with the visiting d.j.s.

"This is the period when my brother Doyle and I got to know Patsy on more than just a passing acquaintance," indicated Teddy Wilburn of the Wilburn Brothers. "We first met Patsy on the 'Town and Country Jamboree' in Washington not long after she came on.

"She was more of a fan than she felt she was a good singer or someone with star potential. Patsy was very insecure. To the degree that you might have thought she was putting you on a bit, but it was real as it turned out.

"Patsy'd come to our personal appearances whenever we were in the Virginia-Maryland area and, best that I can remember, she would ask to sing a song on the show. And we'd get Webb to put her to work. If we were anywhere close to where Patsy was, you could bet she'd show up backstage to say 'hello.' She was extremely well-meaning and you just couldn't help but like her. I mean, we loved Country music, and to look at her and see how much it meant to her and how badly she wanted to make it—well, that did something to us."

The Wilburns, on several occasions, saw Patsy's temper flare.

"The one time I won't forget," laughed Doyle, "was at the DJ Convention in 1956. We always took rooms at the old Andrew Jackson Hotel to be near the Decca hospitality suite and the center of things. We'd work around the clock visiting the d.j.s. By the end of each day our hands would be sore from shaking so many people's hands, and you just wouldn't want to see another highball for a week—and that's something coming from me! Our voices would be shot from lack of rest and too much talking over the crowds. Around the second night of the convention I decided I needed to take a break and all the handgrabbing and go up to the room for a catnap.

"On the way to the room I ran into Patsy in the hall. She was real upset, so I invited her to come in and talk for a minute. Patsy sat on the bed and just started to cry.

"I asked, 'Patsy, what's the matter?,' but she was crying so bad she couldn't even answer me.

"Well, Patsy was angrier than all get out at McCall because he was making her record a song called 'Walkin' After Midnight.' She hollered, 'I hate the goddamn song. It's awful. I just can't stand it.'

"So I said to her, 'Patsy, just tell him you don't want to do it.'

" 'I've told him 'til I'm blue in the face,' she answered. 'It looks like I don't have a choice.'

"One of the stipulations of Patsy's contract with Four-Star stated she could record songs only from Four-Star Publishing."

(The Four-Star contract Patsy signed actually stated only that songs to be recorded be "mutually agreed upon between you and us.")

The song "Walkin' After Midnight" along with "The Heart You Break May Be Your Own," "Pick Me Up on Your Way Down," and "A Poor Man's Roses (Or a Rich Man's Gold)," was recorded on November 8, 1956.

(Of the material, "A Poor Man's Roses" was not Four-Star. It was a Shapiro-Bernstein Music copyright recorded because of a promotional inducement from the publisher. "The Heart You Break May Be Your Own" appeared on several budget album releases only after Patsy's death. "Pick Me Up on Your Way Down," by Glenn Reeves, Burt Levy, and Mae Axton [not to be confused with Harlan Howard's song of the same name published in 1958], was backed with a later recording, "Crazy Arms," and released as a single, also after Patsy passed away. This cut was packaged in a budget LP offering, too.)

"Patsy and I talked a lot over the phone while she was preparing for the session," said Hecht. "She told me about her Blue Ridge Mountains in Virginia and how she loved to go fishing and hunting. She was very fond of her mother and was upset because she wasn't able to do a lot for her. She got to me. Here was a girl, attractive but plain, simple but complicated, with a heart as big as the mountains that made her eyes shine each time she spoke of them.

"During the sessions I heard Patsy was never completely

happy with anything she recorded. 'Please, let me try it one more time' was her classic statement to Owen. She was always eager to do better no matter how close she came to perfection. She did not even treat demo sessions in L.A. lightly. Patsy once told me, 'It's like writing in your diary when you sing a song. I want to get it just right so that when other people see it, they see how it was and how you really felt.'

"A very serious Patsy Cline existed at such times, and the pressure, the strain, and enormous stress, Patsy said, would cause her to lose between five and six pounds over two days of recording. Patsy was stubborn in that any material performed by her under any circumstances had to be pure Country, 'or else,' she said, 'I would feel like a whore.'

"She was finally convinced she was not a majority of one, that none of the songs she recorded had sold, but the only reasons she recorded 'Walkin' After Midnight' was because everyone was pointing a finger at it. Maybe she felt she could have been wrong. But I doubt it!"

When the session work was complete and Patsy had recorded the song she hated, she returned home to Winchester. The shows and one-nighters she had lined up would keep her busy through Thanksgiving and Christmas.

One morning on a day Patsy planned to stay home and rest, a long-distance call came. Mrs. Hensley answered the phone.

"Patsy it's the Godfrey people!"

"Who?"

"It's the Godfrey show. They want to talk to you."

When Mrs. Hensley recalled the occasion she laughed, "Here, a major television show was calling. But, oh, that girl was cool."

Patsy whispered to her mother, "Let them wait a few minutes. They let me wait a few weeks. Tell them I'm next door."

"What? Patsy, you come to the phone! Are you crazy?"

Patsy had decided to play too available would be a mistake, so she got up from where she was sitting and went through an elaborate charade. She opened the front door and then slammed it. When she came to the telephone, she took the receiver from her mother and started to talk as if she was out of breath.

"Hello . . . Yes . . . Oh, it's the Arthur Godfrey folks. . . . Hi, how are y'all doing?"

Godfrey's spokesman told her they wanted her on the show. "What about the band?"

"Oh, no problem. I'm not with them any longer."

"Then you'll come up and do the show?"

"Well, okay." They discussed the program, asking each other questions.

"Who will be your talent scout [sponsor]?" the spokesman wanted to know.

"My mother—"

"Oh, no, you can't do that."

"How come?"

"Well, it might prejudice the audience. Look around and see if you can find someone to bring to New York with you. We'd like to have you on the show next month."

After the call Patsy and her mother huddled to think of someone they could ask. As far as Mrs. Hensley was concerned, there didn't seem to be any way around the Godfrey program's ruling.

"But, of course, I should have known I could depend on Patsy to come up with a scheme! She suddenly lit up and grabbed me. 'Patsy, what's running through your head?' I asked her. She exclaimed, 'Mama, I'm Patsy Cline and you're Mrs. Hilda Hensley of Winchester, Virginia. You'll be my talent scout—not my mother!' "

Patsy mapped out her conspiracy and when the show had someone call back the next day she informed them she had found a talent scout and gave the name.

"Is she a friend?" asked the Godfrey representative.

"Yes, my best," Patsy told them. "She's known me all my life."

Patsy and Charlie were hotter than the coals on a fire and because of that Patsy was in hot water yet again.

Charlie Dick will be the first to admit he is "one hell of a partying man." He was a connoisseur of booze and he gave Patsy an appreciation of it. He and Patsy would often date after her Friday shows at Berryville, Virginia, and the Town and Country Jamboree in Washington.

"Ah, the up-and-down saga of Patsy and Charlie," sighed Jimmy Dean.

"Patsy and me were more than just business acquaintances. We were friends. She would listen to me when I told her things. She didn't have a father complex. Don't get me wrong.

Hell, I was only about four years older than she was, anyway. It was like we were peers and, I think, she respected me professionally because I respected her. When she had something bothering her, Patsy wasn't bashful. She'd come up to me and say, 'Hoss, come over here. I need to speak to you.'

"Mostly Patsy would come to me around work when we'd be sitting in a dressing room or something like that. Rarely did she discuss anything professionally. We had a good team, and there were no problems or star egos. The topic was usually Charlie. She was always calling him names.

"They'd be happy as a barrel of monkeys one day and then on the outs the next. But then they'd make up. She'd kick him out of her life 'once and for all' and the next time you saw them together, you'd never know there was anything wrong. That's the way it was—up and down."

Billy Grammer recalled, "Ole roustabout Charlie was somthing else. I was there when he started dating Patsy. I think she was still tangled up with Gerald, but it was all but over. I called Charlie 'ole loudmouth' because he had something to say about everything. He wasn't a bad guy. I loved him. I still do. But when he got to drinking he could be pretty well uncontrollable, and he really lived up to my nickname for him. If he wasn't ole loudmouth Charlie, he wouldn't be Charlie to me. I know he'd be sick or that something was wrong. He's a very likeable guy. You betcha! We were all buddies—it was like a big family. And, in spite of their problems, nothing in the world could have convinced me Patsy and Charlie were not in love."

Reminiscing about the time Patsy and Charlie began dating, Dale Turner said, "When Charlie and Patsy started, he didn't so much hang out with us at the Arena as he was just there with Patsy. Whoever was with you was with you. And Charlie was always with Patsy. There weren't a lot of questions. She wasn't abusive to him and didn't order him around. They were boyfriend and girlfriend."

Patsy never talked to Dale about Charlie getting drunk and beating on her. "But it was standard knowledge that they battled. They'd be riding around in the car in Winchester and he'd be drinking or do something and she'd kick him out of the car. I mean, really kick him out of the car. I don't think he always went voluntarily, because Patsy'd have a black eye sometimes. I'm not trying to smear either one of them. It was just always funny the way Patsy reacted.

"She'd kick Charlie out for fighting with her and then she'd have him arrested. And guess what she'd do? She'd mourn and carry on about it for a night, and go and get him out the next day. They had that type of relationship from the time I met them.

"Patsy would stand up to Charlie if she thought she should. She said whatever she felt like saying, but to me she didn't say it in a dirty sort of way. It kind of came out as vernacular with her! When things got bad between Patsy and Charlie, she would go to Jimmy and cry on his shoulder and tell him how miserable she was. She was in love with Charlie, but they battled. They'd break up and then get back together again. Jimmy said to Patsy, 'Hey, will you make up your mind about that guy!'

"Patsy and Charlie were just rough on each other. Sometimes that can be a form of love. Patsy could take anything he dished out. She was a tough lady."

For someone determined to make it to the big time, Patsy killed one of her biggest opportunities for stardom by overindulging in drinking and keeping late hours. Jimmy Dean had always maintained that, for anyone who worked with him, "time is a man's most valuable asset." He considered punctuality first before all other considerations.

Patsy began continually defying Gay and Dean and upsetting the harmony of the family-like group. She also refused to do the dance segment of the Town and Country Jamboree.

"I was the baby of the show," Dale Turner explained. "I didn't have the experience or power base the others had, so I did what I was told. Patsy hated to go out and do those Paul Jones dances—you know, the square dances where the boys are on the outside and the girls are on the inside, the boys go one way and the girls go the other, and then they blow a whistle and you turn everything around.

"Whoever stopped in front of you was your partner and you danced with that person, then got back in a circle, and started it all over. Patsy didn't much like to dance, but the reason she finally refused to do the dances was because of her outfits. She wore white boots with her western costumes and she told Connie that people stepped all over them and got them filthy.

"Patsy loved to be on stage singing, but she couldn't stand having to 'prostitute myself,' as she said, by going out and dancing with a rowdy bunch of men. Whereas the rest of us simply had to get out there and do as we were instructed, Patsy just refused to do them at all."

The straw that broke the camel's back for Gay and Dean was Saturday morning, January 5, 1957, when Patsy phoned the Capitol Arena to say she would be late for rehearsal. She had already upset Gay by requesting time off to go to New York to do the Godfrey show.

That Friday night, Winchester photographer Ralph Grubbs was at Deb Siberts Service Station on the corner of National and Berryville Avenues. Patsy and Charlie drove in and while Charlie was inside with Siberts, Grubbs went over to the car and spoke with his friend from Gaunt's Drug Store.

"I asked Patsy to let me sponsor her in her attempt to get on the 'Arthur Godfrey Talent Scouts' show," remembered Grubbs. "We had been talking about this for some time. But Patsy told me, 'Well, Whitey [his nickname], you're a little too late. I'm all set to go up to New York and be on the show. Mother is going to be my talent scout, but, for God's sake, don't tell anyone as you're supposed to have a friend and not a relative do it.'

"Needless to say, I was thrilled for Patsy. She told me all the necessary arrangements were being made and that she would be on the show within the next couple of weeks. I wished her a lot of luck in case I didn't see her again before she went to New York. Then Charlie came out and they drove off in the direction of Berryville."

Patsy and Charlie did an extensive evening of partying—into the wee hours, as a matter of fact. Patsy was separated from Gerald and staying with Hilda. But she would often stay at 333 National Avenue, not far from downtown Winchester and the Hensleys' at the house Charlie shared with his mother and younger brother (his dad and another brother were deceased).

Mrs. Dick did not know to wake Patsy and she overslept. By the time she got up, it was past the start of rehearsal for the Saturday show at the arena. The Dicks had no telephone, so Patsy and Charlie went four doors down the street to

Grayson's, a neighborhood grocery, to call Jimmy Dean.

Patsy stood at a small desk in the store, waiting for Dean to come to the phone. "Jimmy, I'm awfully sorry. I had to work real late last night and I just got up. The alarm didn't go off. I'll be there as soon as I can. I'm leaving right now."

"Hold on a minute there, girl!" an incensed Dean yelled. "Just go right back to sleep. Don't bother to come, you hear? If you can't make it on time for the rehearsal there's no need for you to come down for the show because there won't be a spot to put you in. Consider yourself fired!"

Ralph Grubbs, Charlie's neighbor, was in the store at the time, and said, "I will never forget the expression that came over Patsy's face. She was so upset she turned as white as a ghost. I could hear some faint noise coming over the receiver and then she told Charlie, 'Jimmy just fired me!' Patsy looked like she was in a state of shock. She couldn't believe it."

In a recent heated argument with Patsy, Connie B. Gay told Patsy, "People who start at the top, young lady, usually end up at the bottom, so I advise you to watch your step." Now it was Dean's turn to get digs in. On that evening's telecast, while he did not mention her by name—he left little doubt as to whom he was talking about—Jimmy said, "People on the way up should be especially nice to those they pass, because they might need them when they come tumbling down. I'd like to dedicate this song to a girl you all used to see a lot of."

Dean went into the song "Pick Me Up on Your Way Down," Patsy's still unreleased recording from 1956. At the finish he said, "On my way up, I'll pass you on your way down."

It was arranged for Patsy and Mrs. Hensley to go to New York at the end of January. In the meantime, Patsy's father had become ill and his family had him admitted to West Virginia's Veterans Administration Hospital. It was a serious illness and a member of his family called Mrs. Hensley to inform her.

"Patsy told me she'd like to visit her dad in spite of everything," said Mrs. Hensley. "Since it appeared he was real sick, I told her it was a good idea and that I'd go along."

After she had been in the hospital room for a while, Patsy told Sam, "Daddy, I've been accepted to appear on 'Arthur Godfrey's Talent Scouts' in New York."

Hensley took his daughter's hand and sternly admonished

her, "Now, I don't want you going off to New York, Virginia. It's too big and it's not safe. You don't need to be running off up there. You stay right at home."

Patsy did not tell her father that she had been to New York for two weeks with Bill Peer to audition for the Godfrey program and to make club appearances and the demo session for Decca/Coral.

She stressed the importance of being on the show to her dad and told him how much it could do for her singing career.

"I still don't want you going up there."

Patsy looked at her father and said angrily, "Daddy, after being out of my life for seven years, it's a fine time to start showing concern. I'm going. And you or no one else is gonna stop me!"

Her decision was a milestone in her life.

Sam Hensley was not even able to try and stop his daughter, who at 24 was rarely frightened of anything much less New York City. He passed away a week later.

As soon as Patsy's appearance on "Talent Scouts" was set and confirmed, she called Nashville to tell Owen Bradley and Paul Cohen. They would get with Bill McCall to select material for her to sing on the program.

In Nashville to pick up tapes and music lead sheets of her songs, Patsy spoke with Donn Hecht, in Los Angeles.

"God! New York! That town scared me to death."

Hecht tried to allay her fears, "It's just another town with a few more people. You'll do fine."

"It's the people I'm worried about!"

"People are alike the world over."

"Maybe, but New York people aren't like country people. They dare to make you like them."

"I'm not country—and I like you."

"Oh, maybe you're right," Patsy laughed, "but those New Yorkers still scare me."

Music publisher Al Gallico, who calls Patsy Cline "the greatest country singer in my forty years in the business," had become friends with Patsy on trips to Nashville and Washington. He was then general manager for Shapiro and Bernstein Music Company.

"When Patsy told me the news about Godfrey, I was as excited as she was," Gallico indicated. "I knew that 'Talent Scouts' wasn't paying for too many things so I told Patsy, 'Make sure you call and let me know where you're staying.'

"Patsy said Godfrey was only paying for one ticket and

sighed, 'I really don't want to come up alone.' I answered that I thought she was bringing her mother.

" 'Well Mom wants to come,' she replied, 'but it's going to be very expensive.' So I told her. 'Heck honey, if that's the problem, don't worry about it. I'll get a ticket for your mother.' "

Gallico had a stake in the proceedings since one of the songs in Patsy's Godfrey portfolio was Shapiro-Bernstein's "A Poor Man's Roses" from Patsy's November session.

Patsy and her "talent scout" arrived in New York on Friday, January 18.

"I assumed that Arthur Godfrey, though he wasn't famous for being a big spender, was sending a car to meet Patsy and taking care of their hotel," said Gallico, "but that was not the case.

"They arrived at LaGuardia Airport and took the airport bus into Manhattan. No matter how much you tried to teach Patsy, she was basically a country girl at heart. There was no changing that. When she and Hilda arrived, Patsy decided to stay at the hotel from her previous visit.

"Late that Friday when I hadn't heard from her, I started calling the hotels. I thought I had called every one and still I couldn't find her. I figured maybe they missed their flight and would be in later, but there was no call. I sent one of my song pluggers [promotion staff] to the Godfrey office to see if they knew where Patsy was. And then I got a call from her."

"Hello, Al. We're here."

"Hey, where the hell are you staying? I've called every hotel in town and I couldn't find you registered."

"You didn't call the Dixie [now the Carter]."

"On Forty-second Street in Times Square?"

"Yes—"

"That's a dump!"

"No. I'm at a very nice hotel."

"You shouldn't be there! It's not for you."

"I like it. It's my kind of people. And, furthermore, it's cheap. Only thirteen dollars a night."

Gallico drove to the hotel to meet Patsy and her mom. Forty second Street in 1957 was not the three-ring circus of drugs, pimps, prostitutes, and erotic book shops with peep shows that it has become today. Nevertheless, it was not considered the most desirable neighborhood in town. The Dixie was, more or less, a budget establishment, catering to large tour groups and senior-class trips.

Patsy and Hilda met Gallico in the lobby and he took them on a guided tour of town.

"It seemed to me that Patsy was really on edge, but I took it for nervousness," Gallico noted. "She seemed to relax over dinner, but we didn't make too long a night of it."

According to Hilda, "Patsy was on needles and pins the whole weekend in anticipation of appearing on Mr. Godfrey's program."

On Monday Patsy went to the CBS studio on Broadway between Fifty-third and Fifty-fourth Streets [now christened the Ed Sullivan Theatre], and met with Jeanette Davis, a regular from the star's 60-minute daily morning show and his Wednesday evening special "Arthur Godfrey and His Friends." They picked out material that would best exhibit Patsy's talent from the lead sheets she brought with her.

"We went over thirty songs, I bet," Patsy told Hecht on the phone, "and still Jeanette asked me if I had any others!"

Davis believed Patsy's voice had wide appeal and she told her, "You're not just another hillbilly singer."

"What's wrong with being hillbilly?" Patsy demanded.

"Oh, my goodness, nothing, Patsy!" soothed Davis. "But, look at it this way, you've got the potential to reach a far vaster audience."

Explained one of the arrangers who worked on the Godfrey staff, "Patsy was cocky, assertive, and sure of herself, but not that sure of or secure about her material. She'd like one song more than another, and a few minutes later would change her mind pick out something entirely different.

"We were trying to reach for the broadest possible appeal to please a large segment of the audience, but Patsy was thinking in terms of what was and was not Country. As far as Jeanette could tell from listening to Patsy's tapes and to her when we met Patsy, it didn't matter what she sang."

Jeanette Davis told conductor Bert Farber, "What makes this girl special is the magic her voice weaves. It really is unique."

When Davis returned to ask Patsy for more material to select from, Patsy threw her arms into the air and, for lack of having any other material on hand, showed Jeanette "Walkin' After Midnight" and "A Poor Man's Roses."

"Ah! Now we're getting somewhere," sighed Jeanette. "Where have you been hiding these?"

Davis and Farber went over the new songs and they liked them both.

"Well, thank God!" Patsy exclaimed.

"If we have to choose," Jeanette told her, "let's go with 'Walkin' After Midnight,' The blues sound fits your voice and style perfectly."

Patsy was disappointed, that, with no prompting from anyone, the song she disliked always seemed to be everyone's favorite.

"Let's go with 'A Poor Man's Roses,' " snapped Patsy.

" 'Walkin' After Midnight' would be much better, I think."

"Then let's not use either one."

"What?"

"You'll get me in trouble."

"Trouble? How?"

"You see neither one has been released, and it's Decca policy not to allow their artists to publicly perform songs before release."

"That's a technicality that can easily be gotten around. Now sing this ["Walkin' After Midnight"] for me. . . ." Patsy complied, reluctantly. When she finished, Jeanette said, "Now sing it again as if you mean it!" When the music ended, Jeanette said, "That's it! That's the one you've got to do on the show!"

"But it's nothin' but a little ole pop song!"

"Maybe so, young lady," replied Jeanette Davis, "but don't be surprised if it just might make you famous!"

Patsy called Hecht in Los Angeles and told him, "Guess what they want me to sing?"

He enthused, " 'Walkin' After Midnight'?"

"What else?"

"Oh, wow! Hey, that's fantastic!"

"For you, but not for me!"

"Come on, Patsy!"

"Okay, I give up! I surrender! It's four against one now."

"What do you mean?" Hecht wanted to know. "What's this about four against one?"

"Sure," laughed Patsy. "There's Paul, Owen, Jeanette Davis, and you. First thing I'm gonna do when I get back to Nashville is record that song again!"

"Why?"

"Because I like it. I really like it now! And we're gonna win with it."

Mrs. Hensley recites the excitement of Patsy's appearance on "Talent Scouts" as if it were yesterday: "That afternoon,

Monday, January twenty-first, we all ran through what we were supposed to do. Mr. Godfrey was not there. He never met the performers before going on the air. But they used a stand-in for him. Patsy, who was used to television, was at ease and her rehearsal of the song went fine.

"As the time for the live broadcast approached, however, both Patsy and I became nervous wrecks! Besides hoping the show would go well, we had to worry about whether or not our little play-acting was working. Oh, my, it nearly killed me, having to keep quiet! And, I have to say, I felt a bit guilty about being deceptive—or only telling half the truth. Whenever Patsy would want me, she'd have to call out, 'Oh, Mrs. Hensley.' I'd look to see who it was. I wasn't use to Patsy calling me anthing but 'Mama.' I must have looked awfully suspicious!

"The time *finally* came for the show to begin. The theatre was filled with people. They called Patsy and then positioned me on stage to introduce her. I really didn't know if I was going to make it."

The program went on the air at 8:30 P.M., and toward the end Godfrey brought on Mrs. Hensley who told of her find from Winchester, Virginia, and Nashville, Tennessee. Then he announced, "Ladies and gentlemen, Miss Patsy Cline."

"Patsy walked out on stage so nonchalantly and took her place before the cameras. Her eyes darted to where Mr. Godfrey was sitting. They smiled. The orchestra began to play. I was back standing off stage now, wringing my hands, and watching Patsy on a monitor.

"When she started to sing 'Walkin' After Midnight,' Patsy sang her heart out for a little over two minutes. What happened after that was just unbelievable. There was an eternity of applause. The people in the audience were standing and yelling for more. The applause meters froze.

"Patsy cried, and I cried. I wanted to run out and throw my arms around her, but I knew I couldn't. This moment was everything Patsy had ever dreamed of—the recognition and receiving such fantastic exposure over national television. And the response.

"Later Patsy told me she had a strong impulse to holler out 'Mama!' but she thought better of that and got control of herself."

Godfrey finally had to calm the audience.

"Well, little lady, you sure know how to sing! Will you do another song for us?"

The crowd went wild with applause again as Patsy broke into "Your Cheatin' Heart," the Hank Williams classic.

Mrs. Hensley said, "And when she finished, the audience went crazy again. That certainly had to be one of the most memorable occasions of my life, not to mention Patsy's!"

Walkin' After Midnight

Words and music by
Donn Hecht and Alan Block

I go out walkin' after midnight,
Out in the moonlight,
Just like we used to do.
I'm always walkin' after midnight,
Searching for you.

I walk for miles along the highway,
Well, that's just my way
Of saying I love you.
I'm always walkin' after midnight,
Searching for you.

I stop to see a weeping willow,
Crying on his pillow.
Maybe he's crying for me,
And as the skies turn gloomy,
Night will whisper to me.
I'm lonesome as I can be.

I go out walkin' after midnight,
Out in the moonlight,
Just hopin' you may be
Somewhere walkin' after midnight,
Searching for me.

Patsy may have been the most unexcited participant—or she knew she was going to win. That night she wrote in her diary, "Went on the Godfrey Talent Show...Won."

"The next day when we went to see Mr. Godfrey, we made up our minds to tell him the truth," said Mrs. Hensley. "After he exchanged pleasantries with us, Patsy started to say, 'Mr. Godfrey, Mrs. Hensley is really...'

"But Mr. Godfrey smiled and we realized he already knew. I guess we were right, there are some things you just cannot hide. He looked at Patsy and scolded her, 'My God, girl, I'd be ashamed to show my face back in Winchester if I had my mother with me and didn't introduce her to everybody watching!"

Patsy went to interrupt Godfrey to tell him that she wanted to bring her mother, but she held herself in tow. Maybe he didn't know what his staff told people over the phone.

Godfrey told Patsy, "You may not always be the wide-eyed little country girl you are now but, for goodness' sake, don't you ever change from the girl that you really are because no one will ever love or respect you."

The surprise was that Godfrey offered Patsy a job on his morning show, " Arthur Godfrey Time," and scheduled Patsy on the "Talent Scouts" program for the following Monday, January 28 [the date that has generally been given for her debut appearance on "Talent Scouts"]. Mrs. Hensley returned to Winchester. Patsy moved from the Dixie—but not far from it. She found another, more residential hotel on Forty-fourth Street between Seventh Avenue and the Avenue of the Americas.

No one expected the type of response Patsy elicited. Or were they quite prepared for it? There were rumors that the entire "Talent Scouts" contest was rigged, that Patsy was to be the winner all along, that it had been arranged.

But if there was any rigging, certainly Mrs. Hensley was not in on it. Her recollections of the event in Patsy's life never gave any inkling of fraud. Donn Hecht says the allegations of a fixed "Talent Scouts" are unfounded and absolutely false.

Winchester went wild over its native daughter. "Her appearances on Mr. Godfrey's show were really something for the people here, "Mrs. Hensley noted. "It was quite a big day for the town right after she went on. The city sent Mr. Godfrey a bushel of our famous Winchester red apples. They wanted to plan a welcoming reception and a Patsy Cline Day.

"She may have been a celebrity elsewhere, but at home they were all used to her, so right afterwards everything was the same. They saw her walking up and down the streets with her hair in rollers and never paid any mind to Patsy or made a fuss. But they were mighty proud. I always thought it was funny that when she needed them, they never knew she was there. Suddenly there was everybody taking credit for her success. In fact, Patsy worked hard and did it herself."

Patsy began on "Arthur Godfrey Time" on Wednesday morning, January 23. Introducing her to his audience of ten million, Godfrey exclaimed, "Now, ladies and gentlemen, I want you to meet one of the finest country-western-blues singers in the world. Here's a gal that can sing just about any kind of song that was ever written and make you love it. We think she's got everything—sincerity in the delivery of a song, poise, finesse. Welcome Miss Patsy Cline."

There was a loud burst of applause which Godfrey interrupted. He asked his new performer, "By the way, Patsy, just what do you contribute your success to?"

Patsy hesitated a moment, then answered, "I don't know. I guess that's just me!"

"Well, just leave it like it is!" replied the host. "Don't ever change it."

After the program that morning Patsy went to the Decca Records offices. She was elated when, during her meeting with Paul Cohen, she was told the label was caught with an unreleased hit on its hands. Patsy told Paul she was broke and asked for an advance of twenty-five dollars.

Cohen told her, "Is that all? Most stars with a hit record would come in here demanding two hundred and fifty or twenty-five hundred dollars."

"Well, that's all I need to get by on 'til Mr. Godfrey pays me."

Since Patsy was not a Decca artist—her royalties would come from Four-Star—Cohen gave her the money out of his own pocket.

Following her meeting with Cohen, Patsy returned to the Godfrey offices to see her new boss.

"Mr. Godfrey," she said, "I've given it some thought—you know, about what you asked me this morning—what I contribute to my success—and I owe it all to the wonderful people who have given me a helping hand along the way."

"It's great, Patsy, never to forget that," replied Godfrey,

"but hon, don't sell yourself short. You've evidently done some work, too."

Godfrey told several friends he was "thoroughly taken by Patsy and her marvelous talent. She's really something, and a very nice girl to boot."

In a few days he would fire her.

And Gerald fired a salvo of his own that week. On January 23 he filed a bill of complaint for divorce with the courthouse in Frederick, Maryland.

Charlie Dick was the straw that broke the camel's back as far as Gerald was concerned.

"I came home one night and there Gerald was," Patsy revealed. "He was all red-faced and just angrier than all get out. I asked him, 'What's the matter? What the hell has got you so upset?' "

Gerald allegedly went to slap Patsy and she warned him, "Don't you dare!" Then he calmed down and they talked. "Patsy, honey," Gerald told her, "I can't go on like this. It's driving me crazy. I want a divorce."

"When it came time for Pat and Gerald to get a divorce," indicated Fay Crutchley, "we weren't shocked, just a little taken by surprise. We honestly never heard Pat or Gerald ever speak of any problems in their marriage. The obvious one about Bill Peer never came up, but everyone knew. When it got out that Pat and Gerald were getting a divorce, most of the people who knew them just assumed that the reason was because Bill had come between them—again.

"I wouldn't go so far as to say Pat was the only reason that Bill Peer ended up divorced from Jenny the first time, but I guess it could have had something to do with it. Bill and Pat were together for a time after his divorce, but then she went back to Gerald. As far as I knew Bill was completely out of the picture by now.

"After Pat left Bill's band, we didn't keep in touch as much as we had. We weren't sure of what the main problem was, but we counted Bill out. I think that Gerald, once and for all—and, perhaps, Pat, too—just realized that it wasn't going to work. They sure had done it the trial-and-error method enough times to know what the answer was."

Roy Deyton explained, "After Patsy left the band, we hardly ever saw her. Oh, Bill was seeing her off and on, but their relationship had changed. For a while there he was trying to be her manager, but that even came to an end. When we heard about the divorce, some of us who had heard Patsy talk about her childhood figured it was this Winchester boy she always spoke of.

"Late in nineteen fifty-eight when I met Charlie, I assumed that he was the sweetheart from her school years that Patsy had mentioned often. She used to say that he was the only boy she really ever loved and that it was too bad things hadn't worked out. When I heard the news about Patsy and Gerald, I imagined that Patsy had gone back to Winchester after he got rid of everybody he didn't want and went back to him [the sweetheart]."

An acquaintance said, "I never could understand Patsy's attraction to Charlie. She could have had a very comfortable life with Gerald. Instead, she chose to date Charlie right under his nose. Gerald was bitter. In a way, he had a right to be—not that he was any angel—because of the way Patsy rubbed it in.

"Charlie was not an especially attractive guy, but after I got to know him I found him to be a truly nice person and he literally adored Patsy. The feeling must have been mutual because Patsy would look at Charlie and say, 'That's my man!' "

The relationship between Patsy and Charlie was definitely a physical one—romantic, torrid and satisfying, according to what she told Brunswick friends. There were extreme highs and depressing lows and, as it grew, mutual abuse.

7
"Hungry for Love"

Arthur Godfrey: **"I heard you got married."**

Patsy Cline: **"Yes, I did."**

Arthur Godfrey: **"Are you happy?"**

Patsy Cline: **"As happy as if I had good sense."**

Patsy Cline was heralded an "overnight sensation."

Mail poured into Decca's New York headquarters and Godfrey's offices. The public was clamoring for copies of "Walkin' After Midnight"—there were none yet—and information on Godfrey's new star.

On the next "Talent Scouts" Patsy made an unusual encore appearance, performing the in-demand "Walkin' After Midnight" and "A Poor Man's Roses." At the end of the latter, Godfrey called out to Patsy, "Hey, how's your mother? Before she could even answer, he cracked, "There, that'll let the world know who that nice Mrs. Hensley was last week!"

The "Arthur Godfrey Time" studio was located at 49 East Fifty-second Street, between Madison and Park Avenues, the location where Patsy on her trip with Bill Peer had auditioned. There was a run-through of the day's program from 8 A.M. to 9:30.

Godfrey never participated in rehearsals. Jeanette Davis pinch-hit for him.

"Patsy was only on with us for about two weeks," noted Remo Palmier, a guitarist with Godfrey's orchestra, "and then I believe she made occasional guest spots on Mr. Godfrey's Wednesday night special, 'Arthur Godfrey and His Friends.' In spite of that I remember her quite well. She was not someone you could ignore. Patsy demanded your attention. Just looking at her, you could tell she had lots of color and was full of gusto. She had a magnificent voice. She was the type of singer you could just hear once and you know she had big things in store."

Members of the Godfrey staff told Patsy that she was "wasting your time recording in Nashville. That's just the wrong place for you. New York is where it's happening." The feeling was that Patsy's talent and appeal was too broad to be limited to only Country music. Patsy, with her love for the Grand Ole Opry and country roots, was not easily swayed.

"Patsy loved Country music," said Lee Burrows. "I don't think she would have ever wanted to be a pop star. She wouldn't have minded the money from the crossover success, but she definitely would have wanted to remain Country. When I saw her during her stay in New York, Patsy was miserable. Anybody else would have been happy on the Godfrey show.

" 'I hate every minute of it, Lee,' she cried to me one night in her hotel room. 'I want the Grand Ole Opry, not Arthur Godfrey.' But Godfrey was thrilled with Patsy. She was pretty, had a good figure, sang like a pro. And Jeanette Davis, who was Arthur's right hand, loved Patsy. She could have had quite a future on television in New York with Godfrey and CBS. They'd never found anybody like her.

"What made Patsy angry was the MOR [middle of the road] material they had her singing. She was being leaned toward pop, and Patsy wanted Country. Patsy bugged Jeanette and Arthur to let her wear some of the western outfits her mother had made. But they kept saying no. Patsy was most unhappy and they could tell. Finally, because Patsy was driving him crazy, Arthur relented and agreed to a show with a western theme. I won't forget seeing them do that one because Pat Boone, who was on the show then, was on that program with Patsy. They wore white western everything.

"Some people would have given anything to be in Patsy's spot, but, I guess, she was different. Certainly her choice was unique. Most singers would have wished for New York and

Broadway. Patsy wanted Nashville and the Grand Ole Opry."

Ralph Grubbs also remembers Patsy's unhappiness while on the Godfrey programs. "When Patsy returned from New York she told me, as I'm sure she told everyone else, that Arthur wanted her to sing popular music instead of Country. She bucked him every time he brought it up. Finally, when she was adamant about making the switch, he let her go."

Back on the Town and Country Jamboree, Connie B. Gay was "ticked off that Patsy left us to do those extended appearances with Arthur Godfrey," said Jimmy Dean [Patsy Cline was fired from the Jamboree by Dean and/or Gay, wasn't she?]. "He fed us a lot of malarkey and, for a while, he even got through to me and I was irritated with Patsy. Connie said, 'She deserted us—the very ones who helped make her.'

"He felt he was getting the short end of the stick when he should have been reaping the benefits of Patsy's newfound success with increased bookings on his "Town and Country" circuit.

After the dust settled from her Godfrey work, Patsy sat down with Gay and Dean for "a long little talk." She humbled herself, needing money, and promised to turn a new leaf. She was rehired.

As star of the "Town and Country Time" shows, Dean found himself becoming a regional phenomenon who was ever broadening his base of popularity. CBS-TV in New York heard from their Washington affiliate what was going on, and the network began careful consideration of making Connie B. Gay an offer he couldn't refuse.

Word leaked that CBS was terminating its 7 A.M. "Will Rogers Jr. Show" and was considering replacing it with a Country program. It would certainly be a gamble. Network brass were not at all sure if coast-to-coast America was ready for Country music that early in the morning. As CBS vacillated on whether or not to make the plunge, the competition for the slot grew fiercer and fiercer.

Everybody wanted in the act. WLS and the "National Barn Dance" in Chicago, KWKH and the "Louisiana Hayride" in Shreveport, the "Ozark Jubilee" in Springfield, which was already being syndicated under the title "Jubilee, U.S.A.," and the Grand Ole Opry set forth to audition for the network.

Town and Country Jamboree was set to do a live audition for CBS on Saturday, February 2. Patsy had been scheduled to appear but did not. She also missed the Jamboree show that night at the Capitol Arena. In her diary, the entry for Sunday, February 3, simply reads, "Stayed home."

The following Friday night Patsy left Winchester for Springfield. The next evening she appeared on the "Ozark Jubilee." singing "Walkin' After Midnight."

Decca was finally able to rush release a single of "Walkin' After Midnight" on February 11. It became an immediate across the boards—Country and pop—smash. The record was on the Billboard Country charts 19 weeks and, on February 20, hit the Number three position. It was on that magazine's pop charts 16 weeks and went to Number 16. "Walkin' After Midnight" is Patsy Cline's third best-selling record.

Patsy was netting the national recognition she had long desired. She realized yet another goal when, on Saturday night, February 16, 1957, she was invited to guest star on the "Grand Ole Opry" and sing her hit.

"This is the crowning moment in my career," Patsy throbbed to Roy Acuff before her segment. "It took me almost nine years but I'm here!" (Perhaps Patsy meant to say she had finally arrived, or had she forgotten her appearance with Ernest Tubb on the Opry in 1955 when she sang "A Church, a Courtroom and Then Goodbye.")

Friends Lee Burrows and Del Wood along with Ernest Tubb were in the wings to give Patsy enthusiastic support. Patsy also saw the Wilburn Brothers and Faron Young, and met for the first time Cowboy Copas and Pee Wee King (the writer, with Redd Stewart, of "The Tennessee Waltz," which in King and Patti Page's versions became one of the best-selling records of all time).

Patsy received a thunderous ovation before she uttered a sound. At the end of her song there was deafening applause. She was genuinely moved and, as she thanked the audience, tears rolled down her face. When she came off stage, artists hugged and kissed her. Ernest Tubb, who long believed in her talents, and Moon Mullican offered congratulations. For once in her life, Patsy Cline was speechless. It was when she looked up and found herself in the arms of the great Opry comedienne Minnie Pearl.

Jim Denny, the Opry general manager, took Patsy's hand. He had watched from the sidelines, no doubt with egg on his face for letting this star slip through his hands in 1948 when she came to town to audition for the Grand Ole Opry with Wally Fowler as her mentor. "Patsy, you were terrific, "he praised. "Come back and see us real soon."

"Mr. Denny," gushed Patsy with a modicum of modesty, "this has been unbelievable. And definitely worth the wait! I've never seen anything like it. There ain't no place like the Opry!"

That night, as she and Jim Denny went off into a corner behind the famed Martha White Flour oleo to talk, Patsy Cline may have made a costly mistake.

At the height of her popularity, Patsy returned to New York, not for more Godfrey shows, which she was to do from time to time, but to appear on the "Alan Freed Show."

"Patsy took me along on that trip," said Dale Turner, "and then got mad because I was so excited about being in New York. I was running off in all different directions to see the sights. She'd say, 'Dale, for Christ's sake, would you please be a lady!' Patsy could be rough, but she also wanted everything to be ladylike at the proper time.

"Since Freed was the kingpin of rock 'n' roll, I wasn't so sure Patsy would go over. But his rock background didn't bother Patsy any. The show was very well staged and Patsy got out there and did whatever they told her to do. She wasn't like me, scared. She'd just go out and throw it at 'em! She was powerful.

The return to the "Town and Country Jamboree" was, at first, triumphant. "Everyone was a bit surprised at the turn of events," Patsy told Lee Burrows, "but no one was more surprised than me. Whoever would have believed all this could have happened?"

It was to be a short-lived honeymoon. Patsy was painting her clouds with sunshine, but stormy weather brewed on the horizon.

Patsy had a competitor for Charlie's affection—Uncle Sam. At the end of March 1957, when Gerald Cline was granted his divorce from Virginia P. Hensley Cline *a vinculo matrimonii* (free of all obligations and released from all matrimonial vows), Charlie was drafted.

The childhood sweetheart Patsy had often spoken to Roy Deyton and Fay Crutchley about was none other than Jumbo Rinker, her piano accompanist. He was back in Patsy's life playing another role—substitute for Charlie Dick. On weekdays, at any rate.

"I guess, you could call Patsy and me music buddies, you

know," said Rinker, who was 12 years older than his former protégé. "I had moved from Winchester to try and find work in Baltimore. I ran into Patsy one weekend at home and she told me she and Gerald had broken up and said, 'Maybe we can go out sometimes.' So I started coming down weekends, and we'd go up in this little single-engine plane I flew. She loved it. Patsy was sort of a daredevil. Nothing scared her. A lot had changed in her life, but Patsy was the same. She still had a great sense of humor and loved to laugh. We talked of the old days and just had a good time. It was never anything serious."

Charlie was the pivotal object in Patsy's life and she was totally enamored. Dick was two years younger than Patsy. He had dropped out of school at the end of the tenth grade and gone to work at various jobs—selling newpapers, working in the mailroom of the local paper, the Winchester *Evening Star*—to help support his family.

Before going into the service, Charlie graduated to the composing room of the *Evening Star*, owned by Harry F. Byrd, the former Virginia governor and Democratic senator (1933-1965).

Charlie did his Army basic training at Ft. Benning near Columbus, Georgia. Later, when he was interviewed by officers to determine what specific field work he was best suited for, "the damn idiot who spoke with me didn't know what the hell a linotype operator was. I told him, 'I set printing type for newspapers.' He answered, 'Great, then you can operate a printing press.' I knew better than to try any further explanation."

He was transferred to Ft. Bragg, near Fayetteville, North Carolina, and assigned to the lst L&L—for loudspeakers and leaflets—a branch under the jurisdiction of the Special Warfare Center attached to the Radio Broadcast and Leaflet Battalion of STRAC (the Strategic Army Corps). The mission of the lst L&L, the only branch of its kind in the continental United States, was the planning and carrying out of the techniques of psychological warfare. Like the 101st Airborne, the lst L&L had to be ready to jump into action anytime the controversial Green Berets special units or Marines were called into wartime action. Their job was to broadcast propaganda and drop leaflets on foreign troops.

"When I found out what I was going to be doing, I said, 'Hell, I don't know anything about psychological warfare. I'm a linotype operator! These guys are making a big mistake.' But I got in there and found out I could do that as well as anything. And, once you are assigned something in the Army, you learn you might as well adapt because to get transferred or anything there is nothing but miles of red tape."

Lawrence van Gelder, a cultural news writer and editor at the New York *Times*, was stationed with Charlie. "I was one of those rare born-and-bred native New Yorkers, so being in the South was a new experience. Charlie came into our unit, and right away he hit it off with everyone. It was impossible not to like him.

"There wasn't much to do with no imminent threats to world peace, so we all appreciated Charlie's sense of humor. If he wasn't around, the days got boring. Charlie was a good ole boy, and I don't mean that in a derogative way. He did his work, liked to have a good time, and enjoyed a drink. He introduced me to more kinds of Southern bourbon than I ever knew could exist."

Whenever he could, Charlie commuted the approximate 350 miles to Winchester to be with Patsy, who, though madly in love with Charlie, had work commitments to fulfill. She began burning her candle at both ends—again.

At Connie B. Gay Enterprises the competition for the new early-morning CBS spot caused quite a bit of tension. In the eye of the hurricane was Patsy Cline.

"More than anything," indicated Billy Grammer, "it was the circumstances that Patsy came back to that hooked her. Jimmy was Connie's ace in the hole for moving up, but, for sure, Patsy was his trump card. Everything he had going, when you got down to it, hinged on the two of them. They were the shining stars."

It is alleged that Patsy saw an opportunity to move forward and played both sides against the middle. Gay has his version of what transpired, and there are other recollections. Elements of fact surface in each treatise.

It is not rare to find differing opinions about a particular person. In the instances of Connie B. Gay, Charlie Dick, and Patsy Cline, however there are countless impressions. In the case of Patsy, and to lesser degrees with Gay and Dick, the examples lead to a belief that these individuals were extraordinarily complex.

"Connie wasn't simply the producer of the many 'Town and Country Time' operations," explained Billy Grammer. "He was the man with the money and, thusly, the man with the clout. Connie had the last word. Jimmy was the star, but he never had any say as to who was doing what. Connie had Jimmy under contract and, more than that, he had his thumb on the whole thing. As the western cliché goes, Connie was the bossman."

Gay came from Lizard Lick, North Carolina, and a respected, but poor family. He educated himself by working his way through the University of North Carolina, then went to work in Washington in the Forties on a government-sponsored radio network program called "The Farm Hour."

"Connie once joked that Washington, D.C., was the biggest city in North Carolina," noted Grammer. "What he meant was that more people from there had come to Washington and to work for the government.

"With his country raising and love of Country music, it soon dawned on him that they weren't being played—catered—to. They weren't getting what they love—good, old-fashioned Country music."

Gay went from "The Farm Hour" to WARL, a 1,000-watt station at Arlington. He started spinning Country records as a disk jockey, but soon was producing and promoting local shows, using the Grand Ole Opry as his source for artists. He had all the prevailing stars of Country, from Little Jimmy Dickens to Eddy Arnold, working for him at one time or another.

He was an astute businessman, and it did not take Gay long to amass quite a fortune. This is when he began buying his own stations. From all but a few sources, it is said that Gay was a fair, honest, and good man to work for. From all but a few sources.

"We were busy, always on the move," George Hamilton IV says. "But I never felt cheated or overworked during my time with Connie. He became my manager, and I never had the feeling he was a crook. I was being directed to the rock 'n' roll camp with my teeny-bopper songs—you know, 'High School Romance' backed with 'Teen Age Quarrel.' I was getting great exposure, doing the 'Dick Clark American Bandstand Show' and the Alan Freed shows in New York at the Brooklyn Fox. I felt like I was part of an era.

"But I was not happy. In November nineteen fifty-nine, I came to Nashville with Connie for the annual WSM-sponsored

Grand Ole Opry Birthday Celebration and Country Disk Jockey Convention. At the Ryman I saw Ernest Tubb, one of my heroes, perform and I got tears in my eyes. 'This is where I belong,' I thought. Under my high school yearbook picture one of my friends wrote, 'Grand Ole Opry here I come!' I told Connie I wanted to go to Nashville and try to make it as a Country singer.

"No one who's established themselves in the pop field has ever done that, he informed me.

" 'Yeah, I know, but I want to try.' And Connie said, 'If that's what you want, I can't help you in Washington.' Then he tore up my contract. Jimmy and Patsy had their differences with Connie, so I guess they look at him in a different light. But that's their business."

Behind his polished desk at Jimmy Dean Enterprises in Dallas, Dean pronounced, "Connie was just one of those guys. I'll give you some for instances. He once had me sign something. He said, 'Hey, Jimmy, this is just a form, a simple formality. Nothing important. Doesn't mean anything. You gotta sign this.' I forget when it was, but I signed. That's how much blind faith I had in Connie B. Gay.

"That piece of paper I signed tied me up tighter than a drum to him. I was his! I was getting ready to go into the studio and do the radio show. I didn't have time to look it over—let that be a lesson to everyone!—and like a fool I signed it. But I trusted the man.

"I once knocked a guy at a service station on his ass for saying Connie was a crook. I looked at him like a father figure. 'How's that crook you're working for?' that guy said to me. 'I know how he is!' I hauled off and knocked him on his back.

"When I went to work for Connie at WARL, Sy Bloomenthal, who owned the station at that time, tried to put me wise to Connie B. Gay. He pulled me aside one day and told me, 'Jimmy, watch out for him!' But did I listen?"

In 1980, Gay was named to the Country Music Hall of Fame. His citation plaque reads that he was a man who "brought Country music to the 'big city' and made it a multimillion dollar industry. Advisor to the five U.S. presidents, he was a broadcasting entrepreneur who pioneered commercial Country radio. Gay started the first Country show aimed at a major city, 'Town and Country.' He was founding president of the Country Music Association, and is a past president of the Country Music Foundation."

The Hall of Fame makes no mention of the fact, but, besides Gay's ability to make money, he also had a pretty shrewd eye for talent.

Connie and Patsy always had disagreements. The biggest irritation to Gay was that Patsy stood up to him. He was the tsar of Country in the capital. He was used to respect. Gay had drawn the lines with Patsy and there was only so much he could take. Her downfall came when, as Billy Grammer describes it, "Patsy pulled a boo-boo. She knew that WSM and the Opry was the center of things and she just figured she ought to be in the Mainstream since, probably, the Grand Ole Opry would automatically get the CBS spot. Patsy either volunteered or was asked to audition with WSM's Nashville forces. But the Opry made a mistake, one they have made time and time again. They filmed their show and they went for the big stars.

"Instead of turning the camera on the artists and getting a 'live' presentation of the Grand Ole Opry, they made a Z-class movie. After we got the nod from CBS, Connie and I saw their film. There was Xs on the floor to mark blocking positions [where the artists stand to be picked up by the spotlights and to be within camera range], the quality was poor, and it was terribly stilted.

"They were trying to be so so-so. If they caught the *real* Grand Ole Opry—with all its spontaneity and excitement—no doubt about it, WSM would have gotten the CBS network spot hands down.

"What Patsy did was considered a double-cross by Connie and Jimmy. We loved Patsy, and Connie's heart was broke. He was bitter because he was always loyal to his people. Connie had helped make Patsy well-known on the home front. Until Godfrey, she had not jumped off on a national basis. He knew the value of her appearance of 'Talent Scouts' and the recognition accorded Patsy by Godfrey."

"Connie was angling to get that CBS morning spot and WSM was really going after it, too," commented George Hamilton IV. "When Connie found out Patsy—part of the Jimmy Dean troupe—was on the WSM pilot he probably felt, 'That's our girl. What's she down there helping them for?'

"There I was sort of amazed at all the sudden success Patsy was having. I don't know all that happened. I wasn't privy to a lot of things that went on. I think what Connie didn't like was

Patsy going to Nashville after the record ['Walkin' After Midnight'] starting to happen instead of headquartering in the Washington area and letting some of her success rub off on the 'Jimmy Dean Show.' In spite of all that Connie stuck with Patsy."

Gay remembers the incident differently: "WSM, myself, and everybody in the United States who had an organized Country show was trying to get on CBS. Patsy Cline was the best damn singer I had ever heard in my life—then or now! So I considered her a major asset to the show and I didn't want to loose her. These are the facts. Patsy was not on the WSM audition film. Somebody's memory is faulty. I don't know what the hell Patsy was doing when she went to Nashville, but she was not on the Opry's audition.

"Jim Denny, who was in charge of WSM's Artist Service Bureau, was, perhaps, my best friend, so he would not have put Patsy on their film. He knew she was working for me. I also had a relationship with the Bureau whereby WSM would furnish all talent from the Nashville area for my shows. Jim would not have cut his own throat. I had nothing to do with Patsy's firing. She has only herself to blame."

Since there was no videotape—only film kinescopes—and Gay wanted to stress quality to the CBS executives in New York, he fed them a live, closed-circuit telecast of the "Town and Country Time" show. Gay purchased time "at the huge sum of a hundred and fifty dollars," according to Grammer, on the AT&T cables.

"Connie came around telling us how much money he had expended to let CBS get a look at us in action," said Grammer. "Maybe a hundred and fifty was a lot of money then, but he did it the most inexpensive way and still we came off looking the best because CBS went for it."

Dean recalls Gay spending "next to nothing, about two hundred and fifty dollars, to cut a kinescope to send to New York. But, whatever way it was done, we got it. A lot of the shows had spent a ton of money down in Nashville doing the audition films and the bargain-basement brand ended up on the top shelf. I always credited our getting that CBS morning show strictly to the ignorance of the network's top brass. Because they didn't know Eddy Arnold from Ernest Tubb, it didn't make any difference to them that I was a nobody. They sat down and looked at our show and said, 'We'll take this one—you know, the one with the big-eared fellow with the toothy smile.' "

When CBS decided to go with Connie B. Gay and the "Jimmy Dean Show" they made the deal contingent on seeing how the situation would progress. The network still wanted to protect themselves with an out clause.

"This was a whole new ballgame for the network," says Gay. "It was a new show, a new format, and since it was untried, a new thing for CBS. Not only were they worried about projecting a hayseed image, but here they were faced with doing a daily live variety program from Washington. They sent their geniuses down here from New York to 'help' us get the damn thing ready. They came in hoardes, like an invading army, and every time you turned around there was one looking over your shoulder. And, sorry to say, just when I was counting on her most, Patsy Cline let us down. Maybe the chain of events was uncontrollable, nevertheless she did let us down.

I knew Jimmy would appeal to CBS.
He was a natural with audiences and they soon found out what he was capable of doing and how much people liked and responded to him. But Patsy was also a bright hope for me as far as securing that network morning spot. Her talent was unique. Patsy had star potential. She was capable of big things. I knew I had a magic combination. I thought she'd be a standout."

Jimmy was planning to carry Patsy and Mary over to the network show. He made Gay promise him that much. Mary Klick was a talented guitarist, and he had worked up many harmony numbers with her as vocalist. Dean admired Patsy's talent and felt she would be making a major contribution to the new program.

But Patsy hardly impressed the powers-that-be at CBS. Their headhunters were searching every closet to look for skeletons. Patsy gave them reports full.

Rehearsals were scheduled for 7 A.M., but when the show went on the air showtime was to be 7:00 with a 4:30 A.M. call. Patsy was again chronically late, and, according to sources close to the production, showed up for work with the heavy smell of liquor on her breath. Perhaps from being out partying all night, Patsy was not her usual exuberant self and appeared to be exhausted and tired. The consequences showed glaringly in her performances.

CBS liked Patsy and thought she had much potential for star grooming but, as Gay reported, "they did not want to muck around with this sort of thing. If she can't be on time now, they kept telling me, what the hell is going to happen when we go on the air and she's got a live spot to fill? We may not always be prepared to cover for her."

Network officials gave Connie B. Gay an ultimatum—"Either she's on time or she goes."

The "Jimmy Dean Show" was produced at the CBS-affiliate WTOP. It became the first network show, other than news broadcasts, to originate from Washington. The program aired on a Monday-through-Friday basis, premiering April 8, 1957—without Patsy Cline.

Connie B. Gay asserts that there was never any bad blood between him and Patsy. "None whatsoever! Not one drop. Never was—when Patsy was sober. Drinking and work don't mix. It was one of the things I insisted upon. I'm an alcoholic, so I ought to know. I've been in AA for twenty-four years. A person cannot do their work and drink at the same time. What Patsy did when she was not working didn't make a damn bit of difference to me. You drink and do what you want, but you can't be fit as a fiddle and tight as a drum, as the old saying goes. Those were the only problems Patsy and I had.

"The Godfrey shows had nothing to do with it. You might say her appearances helped me. Every little bit helped in those days. Any time you could get one of your artists or your own name mentioned on radio or TV it was good. Patsy and I were business acquaintances. I never got involved with any of the cast as a father figure. I ran like hell from that type of situation. It was not in the purveyance of Country music. That was in the purview of domestic problems. To my knowledge, Patsy's domestic problems never interfered with her work. The only problem that ever raised its head had to do with booze. As far as Patsy not wanting to do the dance segment of the Jamboree, I never heard her complain.

"I was quite disappointed to lose Patsy, but she ended up being edged out not by my decision but by CBS and her own volition. She would have been sensational. But when Patsy started having her 'can't get up and get there problems,' well, CBS just didn't want any part of it. They kept telling me, 'You have to have dependable people.' Patsy said she couldn't make it a couple of times, so CBS said 'bye bye.' "

Thanks to her celebrity from "Talent Scouts" and the Arthur Godfrey shows, Patsy's hit record, and her regional popularity on the "Town and Country Jamboree," she did not have to want for work. She made several appearances on the "Don Owens Show" in Washington, Richmond's "Old Dominion Barn Dance," and, on August 10 and December 5, was seen on the Ozark Jubilee telecasts.

Free again on Saturday nights, Patsy paid a surprise visit one weekend with Charlie to the Brunswick Moose Club. "Bill seemed glad to see Patsy," remembered Fay Crutchley. "And he asked her to come up and sing her hit 'Walkin' After Midnight.' I don't think it was a matter of his wanting to have Patsy back, just that the audience wanted to hear her. He was pretty big about not letting his feelings show."

That night it is said that Gerald Cline was there with his fiancé, Geraldine Hottle. "Well, I wouldn't have been the least bit surprised," laughed Fay. "Even after the divorce from Patsy, Gerald didn't show any feelings one way or the other. He was just a happy-go-lucky person. It was just another experience to chalk up."

Of Gerald and Geraldine, it might be noted that he took her for his third wife. "Gerry was what Gerald always tried to be and never could achieve," said Cline's brother Nevin. "She had looks and she had class. She was somebody. The only problem, I believe, was that she went into the marriage with a big misconception. She thought Gerald had money. She didn't find out her engagement and wedding rings were not paid for until after the wedding. Gerry got so angry she got all of Gerald's clothes and threw them out of the windows and doors. And then she threw him out, too! I know because he called me that night and asked me to come pick him up."

Gerald eventually divorced Miss Hottle and remarried yet again.

On her return to the Brunswick Moose, Patsy sang her song and then tried to hush the audience. "Thank you all very much. You know, it all started right here, and I'd rather be right here singing for you all than running all over the place doing this TV show and that one. If I had my choice, I'd choose being at home."

According to Joseph Shewbridge, the fiddle player who had joined Bill Peer's band, "The people there that night didn't believe that for a minute and some of them made some loud and rude comments, you know, things like, 'You don't expect us to believe that, do you, Patsy?' A couple of the ladies booed.

"That was my first time to hear Patsy live. She came back several times and Bill let her get up and sing, mostly because the people at the club bugged him, 'Why don't you invite Patsy up?' Patsy didn't have a real smooth voice, but she could really drive a song home. She could take a tune and keep it moving. We might be dragging along and Patsy'd come up and set everything on fire. She'd turn around and say, 'Now, you got it, boys! That's it! Keep it going.' Patsy really moved. She did know how to keep things going. When she was on stage there was no way you didn't know it!

"What made Patsy stand out to me was the way she dressed. The things she picked to wear—now, I'm not talking about her cowgirl outfits and white boots—were the type of things a—well—a loose woman would wear. Her lips would stand out because of the way she used to paint her mouth red. She wore tight-fitting dresses and dangly earrings. Patsy wasn't that tall so it seemed she liked those shoes with the spiked heels. I didn't know Patsy except when she'd come by the club, but a lot of the men and women thought of her as a sexy lady. I guess you might say she tried to give that appearance."

Charlie was drafted in March 1957 and joined Patsy in Winchester and on the road on as many weekend leaves as he could muster.

On the Nashville front, Paul Cohen and Owen Bradley were keeping Patsy busy in the studio in an attempt to build enough good cuts for an album. She was in town for session work April 24 and 25.

Patsy was a hot enough property, but she still considered herself a Winchester native. So she was thrilled when the city fathers asked her to ride in their event of the year, the Apple Blossom Festival Parade on Friday, May 3, 1957. Patsy shared honors on her convertible perch with none other than her former mentor Bill Peer.

That same night she left for Dubuque, Iowa, on the Wisconsin-Illinois state lines, for a sellout appearance the next evening. This was Patsy's first big-paying one-nighter thanks to the success of "Walkin' After Midnight." She noted in her diary: "Plane ticket $120...[got] Paid $700."

Her success on the charts led to other things, such as a series of radio commercials that she recorded in Washington on May 15. Eight days later she was in Bradley's Studio again. On the three sessions, Patsy laid down a total of 14 tracks.

Patsy returned to Winchester the very next day after that latter session, May 24, to celebrate Charlie's birthday. The day ended on a low note as she saw him off to Ft. Bragg. She and her mother spent the evening working on new outfits and packing.

The following morning Patsy left on her first personal appearance tour, sharing billing with her new friend Brenda Lee and Porter Wagoner. The stars traveled in a cavalcade of two Cadillacs, a station wagon for the band, and a trailer for the instruments and equipment. During this tour Patsy and Brenda were to lay the roots for a long and endearing friendship. As far as Porter was concerned, the veteran star who was famous for wearing those spectacular nudie-sequined-and-frilled costumes noted that he and Patsy "had what you might describe as a brief road fling."

"Patsy was working a lot as a result of 'Walkin' After Midnight,' " old friend Roy Deyton said. "And she had another single out that May [the 27th], 'Today, Tomorrow and Forever' and 'Try Again.' But she still didn't have anything to show for it in the way of money. I don't know where the royalty money was going, or if there really had been any. You don't get it right away, even when you do have a big hit.

"When I saw Patsy that July at the park in Warrenton, Virginia, where she had won the National Championship Country Music Contest back in the Fifties, and asked her, 'Are you happy?' she told me she was. Then she asked, 'Hey, hoss, did you ever get married?' I told her I did.

" 'Are you happy?' she wanted to know. I told her I was. We talked about how things were going. She said, 'I'm a star and got a big hit, yet here I am still struggling. I gotta get me a follow-up hit now. It never stops! It's a vicious circle.'

"We talked about her contract with Four-Star Records and Patsy said that financially, things were pretty bleak. 'In spite of a hit record, I haven't made any money to speak of. Not many royalties and lots of deductions!' "

On August 12, Decca marketed that long-awaited follow-up, "A Stranger in My Arms" backed with "Three Cigarettes (In an Ashtray)," and released Patsy's first album, "Patsy Cline." Both were only modest Country successes.

The wait would be longer than Patsy ever imagined.

Gerald was out of her life so that summer, with things seemingly climbing upward in her professional life, Patsy told Hilda, "It's time I put my personal life in order. I'm all set to make married life compatible with my career goals." Patsy and Charlie set the wedding date for September 15, 1957.

"That Saturday before they got married, we were out partying," reported Dale Turner. "Everyone was in high spirits, celebrating the marriage and Patsy's twenty-fifth birthday [September 8]. That evening I got an indication of the games success plays. At this club amidst the toasts and goings on they asked Patsy to sing. She was furious. She said, 'You'd think they'd leave me alone, and let me have some fun in my own home town.'

"To Patsy this was an invasion of her privacy. It was that way whenever we'd congregate in Winchester. She was a home-town girl, but she was also a star. When the band called Patsy up that night, she went but she told them off—and she told the audience off, too. She knew most of them well, but Patsy never hesitated. I told her, 'Calm down. Don't get angry. You know when you're well known you don't have any privacy. That's one of the prices you have to pay.' "

Sunday afternoon about 50 friends and family members gathered at Mrs. Hensley's on South Kent Street for the ceremony. "After Patsy got to working," Dale recalled, "she moved her mom, sister, and brother on down the street to this big brick house. It wasn't a mansion, but just comfortable and elegant in a quiet sort of way.

"Patsy was proud that she moved her mom into it, and that's where she got married. Mrs. Hensley, or Patsy at that point, didn't have a lot of money, and neither did Charlie, so it wasn't a fancy affair. Patsy's mother was as smart as a tack and she had the living room fixed up nice."

A minister friend of Hilda's performed the ceremony. Patsy wore a pink two-piece knit suit, pearl earrings, an inverted bowl hat with attached feathers, high-heel shoes with a paisley print, and a large corsage. Charlie was on leave and out of uniform. He wore a beige suit, suede shoes, and chain-smoked before and after the service. Rice was strewn everywhere and Mrs. Hensley followed the couple with a broom sweeping up. A small reception was held in the upper hall of the local Moose Club. Since both were working, there was no immediate honeymoon.

A few days after her marriage Patsy was in New York to appear with Arthur Godfrey. During an afternoon rehearsal at the CBS Studio, Godfrey passed through and stopped to speak.

"Hello, you pretty thing!"

"Oh, Mr. Godfrey, how are you?"

"Fine. Fine! Hey, I just heard you got married."

"Well, yes, I did."

"Are you happy?"

"I sure am! Just as happy as if I had good sense."

Those who knew Patsy well indicated that she was always hungry for love. People have tended to forget that, in spite of her close relationship with her mother, Patsy was a lonely child. With Charlie, she found what she had long been looking for.

It was another new beginning for Patsy—one filled with more surprises and career highs, not to mention bouts of great depression and sadness. Over and over again, until her death, Patsy was to redefine the term "wedded bliss." Her marriage to Charlie might have been "made in heaven," as Patsy like to tell her friends, *but* it was full of hell.

Side Three

". . . And I knew right then from God
I'd never roam.
When I get my summons on the
judgment day,
I hope I can hear my Savior say
Come on in
And sit right down,
And make yourself at home."

—"Come on In" recorded by Patsy Cline,
written by Eddie Miller.

8

"Stop, Look and Listen"

> *Musician:* **"Hey Grandpa [Jones], do you think that Patsy is pretty?"**
>
> *Grandpa:* **"Well, she's got all the men running after her!"**
>
> *Musician:* **"You're avoiding the question!"**
>
> *Grandpa:* **"She's really got it. Just like the stink off an old hog!"**

Whenever things got especially trying career-wise, Patsy would sigh, "Oh, God, don't let me die an unknown." She had found a man she truly loved in Charlie, but as yet Patsy's dream of national stardom had been elusive. "So far," she would say, "it's been hit and miss, hit and miss." It was a situation Patsy would have to live with. Stardom in the true sense of the word was three years away.

It was not as if all the forces in her life weren't trying. Patsy went on the road to help beat the drums. Paul Cohen and Owen Bradley took her into the studio again and again. Records were released, the disk jockeys played them, but the public did not respond. If the public was the problem, certainly the material—difficult for anyone to identify with—was at fault. Patsy and Bradley pleaded with Bill Mc-

Call to open the door to a wider variety of material, but he remained steadfast in his resolve that Patsy record only Four-Star Music copyrights.

By the time Charlie had completed basic training at Ft. Benning in Georgia and was transferred to Ft. Bragg in North Carolina, Patsy was in semi-retirement and moved to Fayetteville to be near her husband. They rented an off-base house on Pool Drive. While Charlie became deeply enmeshed in the top secrets of the 1st L & L, Patsy uncrated wedding gifts, bought furniture and drapery, and busied herself redecorating.

Patsy told Hilda and friends she was "taking this marriage seriously, putting supper on the table, making friends with the neighbors, and working on having a healthy baby instead of hit records."

Lee Burrows remembers meeting Charlie the first time during the D.J. Convention in Nashville in November 1957, "If Gerald looked like Patsy's uncle, it certainly was altogether different with Charlie. He looked like a kid, especially in his Army uniform. I believe he was a couple of years younger than Patsy, but, I think, Patsy had just turned twenty-six.

"I was in the lobby of the Andrew Jackson Hotel and we passed. I said, 'Well, hello, Patsy! How are you doing, girl?' She had this handsome soldier on her arm. 'Lee!' she hollered. 'Good to see you. I'm doing just fine. In fact, I've gotten married since I last saw you. Lee, this is my husband, Charlie.'

"I told him, 'It's nice to meet you.' I don't think I was too enthusiastic, and Patsy looked up at me as if she was surprised. It was as if I was disappointed, or did not approve. Knowing Patsy, she wanted a good reaction. In fact, I guess, I was disappointed. Maybe it was just the stigma of a man in uniform. But I could only wish Patsy well. I didn't know Charlie, and from all she told me later, they were perfectly suited. 'Lee,' she said, 'I'm really in love this time. It's the real thing!' "

At the 1957 WSM Birthday Celebration and disk jockey convention in November, Patsy listed among her "Walkin' After Midnight" awards citations such as *Billboard* Magazine's "Most Promising Country Female Artist" and Music Vendor Magazine's award for the "Greatest Achievement in Records in 1957."

Old friend Dale Turner was often in touch with Patsy in North Carolina. "After Patsy and Charlie married, I didn't want to lose contact. I was married to a serviceman and stationed in Florida, but Patsy and I spoke on the phone and corresponded.

"She was not having it easy. Patsy told me about making all the records and I knew she had a hit with 'Walkin' After Midnight,' but she said that she had nothing in the way of money. 'How long does it take to see a few bucks from a hit? she asked. I laughed and told her, 'Don't hold your breath! No one gets paid, didn't you know that? The labels figure you owe them, since they're giving you the opportunity to work the road by virtue of being a star.'

"In one conversation, Patsy told me she was going to retire when she got pregnant. I just laughed. She must have been down to be talking like that. I don't think anyone like Patsy wants to retire. In her case, what happened was she moved to the South and the same sort of thing that happened to me happened to her. There was no money down there. Great, Patsy and I had been on the 'Jimmy Dean Show' in Washington, D.C. They weren't too impressed in places like Mississippi, where I was at first, and North Carolina because they hadn't seen the show."

On November 18, 1957, the single 'Then You'll know"/"I Don't Wanta" from the May sessions was released. Patsy and Charlie, who managed some leave, drove to Nashville for another studio set on Friday, December 13, 1957—"Stop the World (And Let Me Off)," "Walkin' Dream," "Cry Not for Me," and "What a Wonderful World."

The Dicks had quite a delightful Christmas surprise. Patsy returned home from a physical to greet Charlie with the news that she was pregnant. This new situation exposed the two faces of the Patsy Cline that were emerging from the charming, aggressive, yet precocious Shenendoah Valley girl cum roughshod tomboy who had hit the music big time.

"Patsy was as happy as you might expect, having a baby after the miscarriage while married to Gerald," a friend noted, "but at the same time she was concerned that, just when she was starting to gain ground professionally, having a baby might affect her career. She talked of a lot of things, but that was just Patsy rambling on hoping you'd help her find the answer. I think when she saw how excited Charlie was she put all other thoughts out of her mind. Patsy suddenly became the most devoted mother-to-be you'd ever seen! That was Patsy, though. Just when you thought you had her figured out, she'd do the reverse and fool you. She never did anything half-way.

'Half-way is half-assed,' she used to say, 'and that ain't for me!'"

In January yet another single, "Walkin' Dream," backed with "Stop the World," came on the market. In spite of the fact that Patsy had suddenly become a cold artist, was only on lease to the label, and that their stake in her sales potential and future was limited, Decca—Paul Cohen and Owen Bradley—was not giving up. Patsy was showered with the kind of attention even few artists signed directly to the company received. Cohen believed wholeheartedly he had unearthed a star capable of achieving the heights of a Kay Starr and Patti Page— who were, after Kitty Wells, two of Patsy's idols and influences—and Teresa Brewer.

On the same level with her love for Charlie and her mother, Patsy had a great fondness and respect for Country music and its stars. She often turned to Ernest Tubb and Faron Young for advice, and learned many of the dos and don'ts of the business from Jimmy Dean, the Wilburn Brothers, and Del Wood. Now that Patsy was only occasionally working the road, she looked forward to going on the Grand Ole Opry to plug her records and see her good friends.

"You could always find Patsy and me back in the ladies' dressing room," reminisced Del Wood. "Back when Patsy was married to Gerald she was telling me that he would give her anything she wanted if she would quit the business. But she was so in love with it—consumed with it like the rest of us—that she didn't care whether she made a living at it or not.

"It was something she had to do. Patsy wanted recognition, and, I guess, the money that goes along with that. Here she was with a hit under her belt and now making records that were going nowhere.

"This is one of the frustrating things about the business, you know, to have that burning desire to accomplish something and the talent and opportunity to make it happen, and yet you still feel cast aside. That's the way Patsy seemed, the way she was talking now that she was about to have a baby. I told her, 'Heck, women have had babies and lived to sing again!' I suggested what she needed was to move to Nashville, where she could see and be seen. 'But, whatever, girl,' I said, 'don't throw in the towel! You've got a few good years left.' It just wasn't like Patsy to be talking of quitting."

Patsy returned to Nashville and Bradley's Studio on February 13, 1958, to record six more songs. Four of these were shelved until after her death. "Come on In," a remake of the 1955 tune she used on dates as her theme, coupled with "Let the Teardrops Fall" was issued as a single in April. On Saturday, the twenty-sixth of that month, Patsy did the Ozark Jubilee. Instead of plugging "Come on In," Patsy sang the B-sides of her current and last releases.

On this "Jubilee" appearance, especially with Patsy in her fourth month and starting to show, her up-and-down struggle with her weight was more than obvious. She had gained considerably. Over the next months, Patsy ballooned so, many people predicted she and Charlie would be the parents of twins.

Perhaps being stuck all those months in an Army town and her doubt about her career was partly responsible, but Patsy began turning more and more to drink—some say it came about as one method of "keeping company with Charlie" and his continual round of parties with fellow GIs.

The pregnancy scared Patsy from all indications. She was debating the merits and demerits of "retiring" to be a model mother. But, as singer Jean Shepard pointed out, "Patsy never could have retired. She had this damn business in her blood. And when it gets you, it gets you. There weren't no way!"

"Walkin' After Midnight" remained a solid seller with good radio airplay throughout the summer. And Patsy was making bigger bucks on the one-nighter trail and appearing regularly on the Grand Ole Opry.

"Patsy came into the ladies' room at the Opry—I believe it was in January 1958—and she was madder than hell," reflected Jean Shepard. "She was stomping and raving, and just a-cussing. Patsy was in no mood to be cajoled or kidded with."

"Goddamn it, Jeanie!"

"What's the matter, kid?"

"I'm pregnant!"

"Well, honey, that's great! I'm thrilled for you. Is this your first?"

"Yeah."

"What are you so upset about? I think it's wonderful."

"Wonderful? It's horrible! Damn it! It's not great."

"You've got to be kidding, Patsy. Everything's going great guns for you."

"Yeah, here I am just coming off a big record and I go and get pregnant. I won't be able to go out on the road. This is really gonna tie me down. No road and no TV appearances."

Patsy was furious, almost "frothing at the mouth."

"Well, if you behaved yourself," kidded Jean, "things like this wouldn't happen! Oh, honey, everything's gonna be alright."

"No, it's not. Everything's gonna be awful!"

In June, Patsy and Jean met up again in the Opry girls' dressing room. Patsy was beyond the showing stage. She came rushing into the room.

"Jeanie, give me a hand!"

Patsy had an old-fashioned waist-cincher corset in her hand.

"What are you gonna do with that, honey?"

"I need your help. I can't do this alone."

"Patsy, you can't put that on in your condition!"

"I've got to!"

"No, you don't!"

"Oh, yeah!"

"Honey, you can't!"

"Yes, I can. I just need you to lace it up for me."

"No, honey, I'm sorry. I just can't."

"Jeanie, goddamn it!"

"Patsy! Oh, my God, don't! You will kill that baby."

"I don't give a goddamn!"

"I'm sorry, honey, but I can't help you. I won't help you do harm to that baby and also to yourself. You don't know what you're doing!"

Patsy slammed that cincher down on the basin counter.

"Well, damn you, Jeanie!"

"I don't care, Patsy. I'm not gonna help you."

Patsy stormed out of the dressing room. A few minutes later she returned with Essie, the much beloved black woman who was a Opry backstage veteran.

"Get in here, Essie!"

"What you want, Miss Patsy?"

She handed Essie the cincher.

"Here. Lace me up as tight as you can."

"Oh, no, Miss Patsy!"

"Goddamn it, Essie! Do as I tell you!"

Jean looked on in disbelief as Patsy had Essie lace her up.

"Patsy, you've got to be out of your mind!" Jean told her.
"I know what I'm doing!"
"I hope so. I hope so."
A much "pulled-in" Patsy Cline performed on the Opry that night.
"I was concerned about Patsy and the baby for the next few weeks," related Jean. "Then, at the end of August or in early September, I heard that she had a baby girl—a healthy baby girl. I was relieved."

In the middle of August, Patsy went to Winchester from North Carolina to await the baby. Charlie came home on emergency leave. On August 25, 1958, Patsy delivered her "bundle of joy." She told friends when they wrote or called, "We have decided on the name Julia. I think it's a beautiful name for an absolutely beautiful, precious baby. I am so proud I could shout her name from the rooftops! I had some rough going near the end, but when I hold my Julie I can forget everything. All I have to do is gaze upon her gorgeous face."

An elated Charlie returned to Fort Bragg to celebrate his new status with his outfit and a few rounds of bourbon. When Patsy decided to remain with Julie and her mother in Winchester, Charlie gave up the Fayetteville house and moved on base.

Hilda indicated that Patsy became the epitome of a doting mother. "Her entire life centered around that baby. Even I was surprised." Patsy seemed to relegate all thoughts of her career to the background and concentrated on marriage and motherhood for a few months, anyway.

She went on a strict diet and was making plans, much to Charlie's dismay, for a full-time comeback. "I've just got to sing," she told Charlie. "Sitting around the house playing the wife and mother is driving me crazy."

Roy Deyton, Patsy's musician friend from the Bill Peer band, met Charlie Dick and saw Patsy for the first time in three years in October 1958, at the Agricultural Exposition Center show at Gaithersburg, Maryland, said, "I couldn't believe what I was seeing. Patsy introduced me to Charlie, and thinking this was the boy she had often talked about—her childhood sweetheart—all I could say was wow! I didn't get to talk to him much because he was in no condition, but I didn't like what he was doing to himself and to Patsy.

"Charlie was stumbling around and Patsy was high. They were having an argument. She seemed embarrassed that we had to witness something like this and we were. Charlie kept telling her he didn't want her to go on for the show. Patsy told him, 'But, honey, we're here and I've got to go on or I don't get paid.'

"He yelled, 'Well, don't worry about that, damn it! I don't want you in this business. I can support you! You ought to be home like other wives taking care of your baby.' When Patsy got up from the table where we sat red-faced, Charlie grabbed her and said, 'I told you I didn't want you to go on!' Patsy replied, 'I heard you, but I'm a going.'

"Charlie shot up and grabbed Patsy. When she pulled away, he took a drink from the table and poured it all over her. If he thought that was going to stop Patsy from getting up on that stage, he didn't know her as well as I did. She just went and changed, and got up there and sang for her money."

Charlie has admitted he was not taking home a terrific salary on a soldier's pay and since he was thought of as the breadwinner it hurt to see Patsy go out and work. But it was a fact of life he gradually came to accept. Certainly in the early stages of their marriage, Patsy never threw this back at him as she was later to do. She was a singer who loved to sing, and if people were willing to pay her for doing something she loved, all the better.

In Nashville on January 8 and 9, 1959, Patsy recorded new Four-Star Music copyrights. The results were the worst yet. Owen Bradley and Paul Cohen didn't know if there would be anything salvageable. Owen, Paul, and Patsy were fed up with the selection of material from Bill McCall. Patsy's career, with the constant flow of back-to-back singles, was in a dead-in spin because the songs being released were of no consequence. Her debut album had created not a stir.

Cohen wanted Patsy signed to the Decca label, so that in the studio there would be freedom to record what they wanted. This idea was quickly shot down by Decca vice president of sales in New York, Sidney Goldberg, who pointed out the disastrous trend of downhill going after the high of "Walkin' After Midnight."

The complete details of Four-Star's lease arrangement with Decca have never been made public, but McCall did get Patsy to sign renewals on March 30, July 2, and November 29, 1956.

In addition, there is an amazing legal embryo of contracts, leasing agreements, claims, and counterclaims with Liberty Records of Los Angeles (June 9, 1954; term of three years), Federal Records (June 24, 1959, and January 29, 1960), and King Records.

Bradley and Cohen's sought-after goal was to, somehow, work magic in the recording studio and turn Patsy's career around so that she could eventually be signed to Decca.

Charlie was costed out of the service one month early, in February 1959. He and Patsy found a small house on Route 7 outside of Winchester. Patsy was working a full schedule, besides commuting back and forth to Nashville.

Two singles resulted from January sessions. In February "Yes, I Understand" became the B-side to "Cry Not for Me," which was recorded in 1957. On April 4, Patsy appeared once again on the Ozark Jubilee to promote the release. During this period there were frequent guest spots on the Grand Ole Opry. In July "I'm Blue Again" and "Gotta Lot of Rhythm in My Soul" came out as a 45 r.p.m. Three other of the January tunes were packaged by Four-Star for budget albums throughout the mid- and late Sixties.

That July, much against Owen's opposition, Patsy did two spirituals, "Life's Railway to Heaven" and "Just a Closer Walk With Thee." Her performance on the latter is a shattering listening experience, but for market reasons Bradley and Cohen held the record back. After her death, McCall was happy to license them.

Patsy took advantage of every opportunity to be near the Country artists performing in the Virginia-West Virginia-Maryland area. It was one way of keeping up with what was happening.

Teddy Wilburn recalls that "once when we worked Watermelon Park near Berryville, Virginia, Patsy and Charlie came to see the show. She told Doyle, Don Helms, our steel guitarist [who played with Hank Williams 11 years], and myself that she had been cooking all day and that we had to come to the house and eat."

"I told Patsy, 'You don't have to bribe us to sing a number on the show!'" Doyle added. "Then she lit into me, 'Y'all better take me serious. Charlie'll tell you, I've been cooking since morning and you're coming to eat.'"

Teddy answered, "It would be nice, Patsy, but we've

checked into the motel. We're going to Pennsylvania and New York State from here."

"Well, you can just check out of that damn motel!" Patsy exclaimed. "Teddy, you don't understand! I've got this big ham in the oven that I fixed just for y'all! You can't let it go to waste."

"Teddy, why are we standing her arguing with her," said Doyle, shaking his head. "We ought to know better. Ain't nothing gonna do her until we check out of the motel and go have supper with them. Okay, Patsy! Okay."

The Wilburns and Helms followed Patsy and Charlie home to Winchester after the show. "It must have been about 40-50 miles," remembered Teddy. "She wasn't bluffing. Patsy had plenty to eat and it was good. We sat up all night talking and singing. I'd written a song called 'Dakota Lil' and did it for Patsy on my guitar. It was an outlaw song, done in the first person.

"It went:

'I wore my guns so proudly
I'd kill for just a thrill
No man could ever back me down
Not me, Dakota Lil'

"There were a couple of stanzas and then it finished up,

'I wore my guns so proudly
No more I ever will
Though I must die no one will ever forget
The name Dakota Lil'

"Patsy had me do it over and over for her. She loved it. 'I've gotta record that,' she said. 'I've gotta do it. Get me the lead sheets as soon as you can.' But the song was never recorded. I was told later that Patsy cried and cried because Owen Bradley and Bill McCall wouldn't let her cut it. That was a shame, because I can't think of a song that really fit someone to a tee the way 'Dakota Lil' fit Patsy."

Patsy was not seeing any positive financial results from her success and often she called on old friends for help. Don Owens had her on his music variety television show in Washington and Winchester disk jockey and bandleader Jim McCoy, whom Patsy had first sung for as a child, put together shows with Patsy and his band for the home area drive-in-theater circuit.

Patsy kept hearing, "Move to Nashville. That's where it's at," whenever she'd complain of how tough the going was becoming. If Patsy could achieve membership on the Opry, at least there would be an outlet for much-needed exposure and some money, little as it was. She told friends, "I keep hearing I'm too far away, so I'm gonna have to pick up and move here. I can always be on the Opry even if I never sell another record because I've been finally established as a star! Owen Bradley'll see so much of me he'll be sick."

At home in Winchester, Patsy told Charlie it was time she relocated to Music City. It wouldn't be a problem with his references from the Winchester *Evening Star* to get work in Nashville with a newspaper or printing plant. Charlie knew not to argue with Patsy once she made her mind up.

When she came to town, in an effort to achieve her Opry membership, Patsy lent her services to many Opry-sponsored benefits. On December 21, 1959, for example, Patsy starred with Roy Drusky and Porter Wagoner, another veteran of the "Ozark Jubilee," in an Elks-sponsored show for the Tennessee Vocational School. Patsy helped serve ice cream, cake, and candy to over 750 underprivileged children and assisted in handing each a new dollar bill.

As far as Bradley was concerned, he never got literally "sick" of Patsy Cline, but there were days when he surely regretted she ever moved to town.

"I swear," laughed Bradley, "I think Patsy set about on a calculated effort to drive me crazy!"

Pearl and Carl Butler are two of the greats of old-fashioned Country music. They summed up the dreams and attraction of youngsters wanting to come to Nashville in their 1969 recording of "Sundown in Nashville," written by Dwayne Warrick.

Outfits such as this became Patsy's trademark while on the Town and Country Jamboree, Washington, D.C. Photo by Rush Studio, Winchester, around 1956.

Patsy, circa 1957, by Winchester's Rush Studio. *Photo/collection of Jimmy Dean*

The sign says welcome to Nashville
From whatever road you've been down
It seems like the first of the milestones
For here is the city, the town

It's a quaint, old, mystical city
Where idols and legends have stood
Port city where dreams come to harbor
A country boy's Hollywood

But it's lonely at sundown in Nashville
That's when beaten souls start to weep
Each evening at sundown in Nashville
They sweep broken dreams off the street

You walk down Sixteenth to Broadway
You walk pass the new Hall of Fame
And the record man with the big cigar
He never once asked me my name

You'll find some discarded love songs
And visions of fame on the ground
And pieces of dreams that's been shattered
They drift to the outskirts of town

Bob Allen, in the Nashville *Gazette* in 1980, probably summed up the changes wrought by progress in downtown Music City: "There was a time when all roads led to Lower Broadway, a time when the music of the Grand Ole Opry shook the shaky walls of the Ryman Auditorium every Friday and Saturday nights. . . . But that's all gone now—the excitement, the vitality, the spirit—all gone. Now it's a forlorn, tawdry strip of everything it wasn't. . . . You, too, may be overcome with a sense of loss, a vague feeling of sadness for the musical history that has been misplaced somewhere among the pallid neon glow of the dirty-movie theaters and the dark shadows."

Almost every large city or metropolitan area has an area downtown similar to Nashville's Lower Broadway. It is lyrical, almost magical, however, to think back on what it once was.

As Patsy Cline climbed the ladder of stardom, she shared her exuberance about the Country music business with such new friends and peers as Dottie West, Roger Miller, Loretta Lynn, Jan Howard, Brenda Lee, and Barbara Mandrell: "If you want to know what Country music is all about, I'll tell you. It's singing in clubs and sleazy joints, traveling on dusty, rutted roads, and staying in motels that have seen better days. It's signing autographs, doing the very best job you can, and meaning something special to a whole bunch of strangers who suddenly become like family to you."

It is but a memory now, but to attempt an understanding of the Country music phenomenon that has gone on to sweep the nation all one had to do was journey to Nashville and roam the hilly streets downtown where the Grand Ole Opry held forth at the Ryman Auditorium. The lower depths of Broadway where the Opry stars and fans mixed at Tootsie's Orchid Lounge at the rear of the Ryman, Linebaugh's Cafeteria, the Ernest Tubb Record Shop and home of the Mid-Nite Jamboree, and where every joint blaring with the music of a guitar picker was a hillbilly palace was, until recently, the bustling center of Country music commerce.

The facades still stand, and decades of ghosts haunt the remains but the guts of a unique world have all but disappeared. The warehouses in the shadow of the Cumberland River that symbolized Nashville as the leading furniture, printing, and publishing center of the Southeast are vacant or being recycled. The Grand Ole Opry has relocated to glorious new quarters at Opryland and taken the pizzazz and zest of old with it.

There are still bus tours of the stars homes, souvenir shops, western wear shops—some featuring junk at $15.98 and others featuring junk at $5,000; musical instrument stores; and pawn shops. In addition, there is now sex, pornography, cocaine, and marijuana on sale at every turn. Tootsie's is open, dark, dank, and shabbier than ever but, alas, Tootsie and famed Maggie the Cook are gone. The beer joint's unpainted, dirty walls are plastered with hundreds of faded 8 by 10 glossies of memorable and unmemorable stars, has-beens, and might-have-beens.

Hank Williams, Stonewall Jackson, George Jones, Johnny

Cash, Eddy Arnold, Faron Young, Webb Pierce, Porter Wagoner, Jack Greene, Patsy Cline, Willie Nelson, Roger Miller, Johnny Paycheck, Charlie Rich, Loretta Lynn, Waylon Jennings, Buck Owens, Dottie West, Merle Haggard, Tammy Wynette, Bobby Bare, Kris Kristofferson, and Glen Campbell—to name but a few—once upon a time sat in Tootsie's and drank, ate, smoked, and/or wrote. If an occasional star drops in these days, it is more out of a respect for things past and a shrine that was one hell of a watering hole.

Still, as Allen wrote, "in its own peculiar way—as Willie might have said—Lower Broad maintains a semblance of its old image: the pimps wear cowboy hats."

Throughout the city, today as yesterday, on the dark side streets, in parking lots, or in roadside parks, you see the immensely loyal, tough breed of Country music fan eating canned goods and wax-paper-wrapped sandwiches from home. They sleep in their cars or pickup trucks because they cannot afford the price of a hotel or motel. The greasy spoons, such as the bus station coffee shops and cafés specializing in home cooking, and boarding houses are filled with young and not-so-young struggling musicians from points north, south, east, and west who want to make their mark in country.

Patsy Cline could appreciate these folk, more than the executives along Music Row and the stars in their fabled mansions. She traveled the same road into town they did. Patsy had come from humble beginnings and deep inside—despite the sometimes harsh exterior of wigs, makeup, painted lips, and dangly earrings—she had not changed.

"Carl and I had met Patsy a couple of times," reflected singer Pearl Butler. "She had this black address book she carried around with her. We first encountered Patsy—I say it that way because it was a time I will never forget—at the Town and Country Jamboree in Washington. There she was all decked out in one of the cutest cowgirl outfits I had ever seen. She just came up and said, 'Hi, Pearl, I'm Patsy Cline.' It was love at first sight for both Carl and myself.

"She took down our name and address and said, 'Someday I'm gonna be coming to Nashville and I'm gonna look y'all up.' I told her, 'Why, Patsy, if you don't, we'll be mighty hurt.' And she knew we meant it. Right after Patsy and Charlie came here in September or October nineteen fifty-nine they found our house on Twenty-seventh Avenue, and knocked on the door. I went to open it and there was Patsy, Charlie, and their little girl, Julie.

"I yelled, 'Why, my God! Oh, my gosh. Carl, it's Patsy and Charlie! Y'all come on in here out of the cold.'

" 'You mean you're gonna invite us in?' Patsy asked.

" 'What do you mean, am I gonna invite you in?' I replied 'Y'all know y'all can stay right here if y'all want to. Our home is your home.'

" 'Well,' Patsy noted, 'we've been to see a lot of people who told us to look 'em up if we ever came to Nashville and not a one of them has invited us in.'

" 'Honey,' I hooted, 'we ain't nobody else!'

" 'It sure is nice of you.'

" 'Nice? Why what's so nice about it? You're our friends, aren't you?'

" 'Patsy and Charlie rented a two-story house on Marthona Drive in Nashville's Madison suburb, just across from Hank Snow's home. But they were staying in a motel because not all their furniture had arrived from Winchester.

" 'We spent the whole day together," continued Pearl, "Had supper and all, then sat around talking. We walked them out to their car that night. After they drove off, I noticed that Patsy had dropped her address book. I saw her again three weeks later at the D.J. Convention and I asked, 'Did you lose something?' "

" 'Yes, I did,' replied Patsy.

" 'Well, I've got it." Pearl went to give Patsy her book.

" 'Now that we know you and Carl,' Patsy told her, 'we don't need this anymore.'

"I guess that welcome to our home sealed the bond between us," reflected Pearl. "But though we were friends with Patsy and Charlie, I don't want to give the impression we were intimates. Whenever we saw each other backstage at the Opry it was like old home week, exchanging stories on what had happened to the other and talking about the children and so on. Patsy was to make several show trips with Carl and myself. Usually, since she had no band or instruments to worry with, Patsy would fly to her dates. But if we were all on the same package, as was the case many times, Patsy'd go with us in the car.

"Carl would do the driving and Patsy and me would stretch out in the back seat and talk about the business. It was rough on everyone back in those days, but the women had it especially bad and Patsy and I would commiserate with each other."

Patsy had no hit records and wasn't making any money from her Four-Star deal.

According to Charlie, "Patsy should have been a wealthy woman from the way everything was going on 'Walkin' After Midnight.' But she had a deal with Four-Star and not with Decca. During the whole time, Patsy only earned nine hundred dollars from 'Walkin' After Midnight,' a Country and pop hit, and all the other sales royalties combined.

"It was a disgrace. Four-Star and McCall had Patsy coming and going! It was really sad how they took advantage of her. God, if anybody worked to earn a living, Patsy certainly did. She never stopped. I used to wonder where on earth she got the strength. The TV shows Patsy did paid very little, that's the way it was back then. Television did not yet have the power it enjoys today. And she got damn little for her road dates. Since I was not making a hell of a lot at the Nashville Newspaper Printing Corporation [the Nashville *Tennessean* and Nashville *Banner*] as a linotype operator, every bit helped.

"The reason Patsy got the short end was because Four-Star deducted every conceivable expense, such as her trip to California, hotels meals, and phone calls from her royalty money. She was left with virtually nothing. To make it worse, the company controlled everything she did in the studio."

Whatever else you find to say about Bill McCall, you have to put him right up there with the fascinating characters in Patsy's life. He was of Scotch-German background. Prior to World War II he developed a serious heart condition while living in the heat of the California desert searching for precious metals in order to establish mine claims. When the war began, McCall entered a partnership with a man who had a formula for synthetic plastic that he could not market. McCall saw exploiting it for use in the record industry, which had no material because of war priorities. He made a fortune.

Eventually, McCall bought the partner out and began establishing sales agreements with smaller record companies. Four-Star was one. When the business faltered, and was about to go into receivership, McCall stepped forward with an offer to take over, in consideration for the large debt owed him for the synthetics. When this venture was made public, the industry laughed that a man who knew absolutely nothing about music was the president of a record and publishing company.

In the early stages, whenever a song was offered, he checked it out with his chief A&R executive, Truly, the night cleaning woman. His theory, according to Donn Hecht, was, "This woman mops my floors for a living, works hard for her money, and knows as much as I do about the song business. But you can bet your ass I've got to be interested in any song she likes well enough to go out and buy."

Hecht, noting McCall's appearance, recounted, "He had steel-gray eyes, but a speaker he was. And his delivery, tone, and emphasis could charm a grape from the vine, and made one wonder why he was not sitting in some governor's chair or an important seat in Washington. He possessed instincts which I have never witnessed the equal of in a man then or since.

"A cheat? A thief? Perhaps. From my own experience and from what I witnessed, I cannot say he was. Do I believe I should have made more money than he paid me? Yes. He told me that from time to time he might have to deduct monies from my royalty account which I might not agree with, but that this was necessary because of his considerable investment.

"This led to the now-famous clause in all of McCall's contracts which stated, 'all monies due the artist or writer should be paid out of funds received and actually retained by the company.' This meant expenditures for recording sessions, arrangements, studio facilities, musicians, promo pressings, trade advertising, and so on, could be deducted from royalty accounts.

"The misunderstanding about Patsy's profit picture comes about because neither she nor those close to her admit the staggering number of failures together with the total losses that were deducted from her account on 'Walkin' After Midnight.' I recall a figure of nine hundred and fifty dollars looked pitifully small, indeed, for such a hit, but there were considerable losses and considerable costs over a long period of time.

"Now, as far as Bill buying up rights to songs from the writers, they did come to him. He did not go to them. I can remember many times when a writer left, small check in hand, and Bill would sit back in his chair and sulk, 'What the hell is the matter with you people? That stupid bastard just signed away everything!' And Bill would reach back into his drawer and extract the just-signed agreement and tear it into shreds, saying, 'A genius of a man pissing his money away on booze, destroying his liver!'

"When I asked why he would offer to buy all rights to songs by a writer, he replied, 'What the hell do you expect me to do? If I don't, they will go sell their goddamn songs for pennies to a competitor! And they'll have him add six or seven copyrights to the agreement for the same money!' Of course, Bill *did not* tear up all such agreements, but there is another side to him.

"I certainly don't want to suggest that everyone's heart start bleeding for Bill McCall," moved Donn Hecht. "No one loved Patsy or knew her better than I, except for Charlie, of course. She and I were like brother and sister. But, listen, things have really been exaggerated. I never saw actual statements, but I happened to be present when Patsy was in California or called Bill collect from Nashville and asked for cash advances for herself and Charlie—to make car payments, for the rent, you name it—and also for Patsy's mom.

"Patsy was always calling Bill and asking for advances on her royalties. I remember once she told us that her mother was not satisfied with a four-year-old car and wanted a new Cadillac.

"Also, Patsy had only one hit up to 'I Fall to Pieces.' There were a lot of sessions and singles in between. None of those releases did anything big, so where does the money come from to pay for those sessions and those costs? Out of her royalty fund on 'Walkin' After Midnight.'

"Listen, all these years, I've kept in touch with Bill, who now lives out in Hawaii, and I can honestly say he did not cheat Patsy."

Owen Bradley told of how Patsy "would often come to me and cry about the selection of songs that were being forced on us. But there was nothing anyone of us could do until her five years [at that point] were up. Patsy was always getting down and depressed and she'd ask, 'Hoss, can't you do something? I feel like a prisoner.' I tried, but the only thing I could do was talk with Paul and see about signing her direct to Decca, which he wanted to do all along, when her Four-Star contracts expired."

Patsy went to work on the road fronting shows for Ferlin Husky and Faron Young. Husky was 33 years old and had been through two aliases. Ferlin Husky was his real name, but he felt it sounded unreal and adopted the monickers Terry Preston and Simon Crum. His recording of "Gone" was a flop as recorded by Preston, but a big smash when released by Ferlin Husky.

On stage Husky was outrageous. He wore foppish three-piece silk suits and lavender-and-ruffled-lace evening shirts. However, when he sang he could transfix and audience.

Women meant everything to Ferlin and he had four marriages to prove it—six to date. In 1953 he and Jean Shepard (later Mrs. Hawkshaw Hawkins) recorded the hit, and now Country classic, "Dear John Letter." In 1958, Husky and Faron Young made what may be one of the worst movies in the history of cinema, *Country Music Holiday.* Their co-star was none other than the unlikely Zsa Zsa Gabor. Don't ask what she was doing in a Western!

Then there was Young, himself, in Patsy's career and life. He was born in Shreveport, Louisiana, home of the Louisiana Hayride, which he became a member of before going to the Opry. Faron has been one of the country's consistent hit-makers and has enjoyed amazing longevity on the personal appearance circuit.

With his crooner-type voice, Young was an early crossover to the pop market and thus established a broad appeal base. He has had many Number One Country hits, such as "Hello, Walls" in 1961. This was an early Willie Nelson tune and helped establish him as a sought-after writer. Young was asked by a young Nashville bellhop for a job in his band as drummer. He gave this budding musician, Roger Miller, an audition and Miller worked, played, and wrote for two years.

Faron Young was one of the first to give Patsy Cline an assist.

"Of all the people who say they knew Patsy well," touted Young, "I probably met her the earliest and knew her best. I knew Patsy and Charlie, their ups and all their downs. I was a friend Patsy could count on when she needed a shoulder to cry on.

"At first I was very attracted to Patsy. She was built like a brick shit house. When she moved, the earth shaked. I couldn't take my eyes off her body. Oh, she knew what I was thinking and once when I tried to get into her pants she hauled off and told me, 'Hoss, what are you up to? No!' "

Patsy, very much in love with Charlie, felt her association with Charlie should be merely professional.

"Patsy had come to Nashville back in nineteen fifty-five," said Feron," and, of course, I saw her that time, at the ballpark show in Memphis. By the time Patsy came down to guest on the Opry after Arthur Godfrey and 'Walkin' After Midnight,' things had changed.

"You could have pricked Patsy a thousand times and still not bust her bubble. Since we knew each other, it was natural for us to hang out together even on that trip. I kinda took Patsy under my wing and made sure she knew all the ropes.

"Back in those days, we did things like that. Country folk were a lot tighter then. Today it's dog-eat-dog. When we were coming up, we all looked after one another. When Patsy needed help, people like me and E.T. [Ernest Tubb] tried to provide it. If we didn't have money, we, at least, gave encouragement.

"When Patsy and Charlie first moved to Nashville in fifty-nine, he came to see me," informed Young. " 'Well, Sheriff,' he said, 'times are tough. Can't you put Patsy on some of your fair and road dates?' I replied, 'Hell, yeah, I can. We gotta have a girl singer. Will Patsy work for the right price?' He told me, 'Oh, yeah. I'd just like to get her out there so the public can see her. The records just ain't making it.'

"That was the main reason Patsy was willing to work for me. Exposure. I was hotter than hell at the time. Patsy never minded getting out in front of folks and strutting her stuff, and the crowds reacted fantastically to her. She was an asset. She worked for me on and off for three years. She was terrific.

"Nobody got paid a helluva lot in those days. I paid Patsy fifty dollars a night and then up to about five hundred and took care of the hotel bills. She rode on dates in the car with me. I traveled in a Cadillac limousine and had a station wagon following with my band. They pulled an instrument trailer. Then nobody was even talking damn buses. Only the gospel groups had them. Hank Thompson and Bob Wills out West and Ray Price here in Nashville were the first artists to get 'em."

"People in the business back then," says Brenda Lee, "tended to take advantage of you more than today. It was, for instance, a common thing not to get paid or for a promoter to run off with the proceeds. That's actually how I met Patsy. I didn't get paid one night. The promoter skipped.

"It was nineteen fifty-seven and I was almost thirteen. I had been signed by Paul Cohen on Decca since I was nine. I'd had some records but it was before I had any big ones [two later hits were 'Sweet Nothings' and 'I'm Sorry'. We had done a show in this tiny Texas town. I don't remember who else was on the bill other than Patsy, and it's best that I don't.

"The ones on the show who went to the front before the performance got paid, the ones who didn't got left out. The promoter ran out on us. I didn't have a manager at the time. My mom traveled with me. We didn't know any of the ropes. We were left stranded—we didn't have a dime to call home. That's when I had my first contact with Patsy. She heard about what happened from someone and came to the back of the hall to see us. She was boiling mad that something like this could have happened. Patsy took me by the hand and said, 'Don't you ever let this happen again. Always make sure you get your money before the show and in cash no matter what the promoter's excuses are. You tell him, no money, no show, you hear?'

"My mother told Patsy that we were depending on the money from that date—I think it was somewhere between Amarillo and Lubbock—to get to the next town. Patsy came to the rescue. She fed us and took us back to Nashville in this big white car of hers. I think Hilda, her mother, might have been with her. It was a wonderful gesture that I've never forgotten.

"How many people would have done what she did? There were several other artists on that show and nobody else offered to do anything. And, don't forget, this was before Patsy started making any real big money herself. It was something that really drew me to her and, in spite of the differences in our ages, we became fast and very close friends.

"On the way home I told Patsy how happy I was that 'Walkin' After Midnight' was such a hit. Her answer surprised me, 'Well, thanks, but damn it, it ain't doing me no good. I'm not making anything off it.' I thought, 'Gosh, what's she talking about? She's on Decca. They've been honest with me. She's got a big hit. She must be doing all right.' Then Patsy told me about Four-Star and Bill McCall. It sounded terrible."

"Many artists were taken advantage of," said Faron Young. "When Nashville was exploding there were only about five major labels. They weren't able to take on all the acts.

"So here come Patsy and some others. They had someone like Bill Peer, who didn't know the angles, guiding them and wanting to be their manager. They'd do anything to get a record. If you had records, you worked. They'd sign with anybody. They didn't think down the road. They let someone take it all away from them without even thinking what might happen. And when you signed a contract with McCall, it was like signing everything away.

"It all happened too quick for Nashville to absorb. Most of us didn't know better. Within a two-year period in the early fifties there were all sorts of publishing companies and artists coming in here and the labels weren't growing fast enough Folks began signing with the small labels, but just when a record or artist would start to hitting real good, they couldn't handle it and they'd lease them over to one of the majors. Patsy signed a two percent deal with Four-Star and McCall was probably leasing her to Decca for eight percent.

"They had no morals. You couldn't go to someone like McCall and say, 'Look, that girl's a hit. You're making a lot of money off her. Why don't you halve the goddamn royalties with her?' They'd tell you in a minute, 'Oh, nah!' They'd always tell you they had a contract. Poor Randy went through hell with McCall.

"I even went and had a talk with Bill and told him, 'It ain't a question of you having a contract, it's a question of your morals! Legally, you are right. Morally, you are wrong, wrong, wrong.' It didn't do no good.

"Slim Willet, the boy who wrote and cut 'Don't Let the Stars Get in Your Eyes,' was owed over a hundred thousand dollars in nineteen fifty-three and received only fifteen hundred dollars. If you got in McCall's office past his ten secretaries, he was such a smoothie he could talk you out of killing him. God knows, enough of us tried! But Slim just walked in there, reached over McCall's desk, grabbed him by the neck, and like to beat the shit out of him. He left with a check for sixty thousand dollars in his pocket."

Patsy Cline met Randy Hughes when they worked for Ferlin Husky. Hughes played guitar and was Ferlin's road manager. When he and Patsy became friends and she told him of her McCall problems he said, "What you need is a manager. One who knows how the hell this town operates. Someone who'll fight for you." Patsy spoke to Charlie and Owen Bradley and the consensus was that it certainly couldn't hurt any.

Lightnin' (Floyd Taylor) Chance, the Mississippi country boy who was so fast with a football and at boxing that the city kids gave him a nickname, indicated, "As soon as Patsy signed with Randy he went to the goal for her. He didn't have much luck at first. He and McCall were constantly at each other's throat. Because Randy was naturally all for Patsy and McCall was always trying to dip into the gravy for his share.

"I remember Charlie telling Randy and I that McCall and Four-Star deducted everything but the kitchen sink from Patsy's royalties. Randy kept harping to McCall about it. But McCall would just harp right back. Poor Randy used to say, 'God, I wish he'd give us a break!' As I understood it, Patsy got very little."

Chance not only was a fantastic bass fiddle player who was in on the development of the Nashville Sound but he also played on session and Opry dates for Patsy and was Hughes' business partner. Randy handled artist management, with an assist from entrepreneur Hubert Long, and Chance ran the insurance and stock brokerage end.

"We were just doing some little things and turning the stock commissions back into buying more stock. Randy liked artist management and went in with Hubert. When Ferlin was running real hot, Hubert wanted to take over his career. He kept telling Ferlin, 'You need someone who knows how to do things.' Hubert was established, but Ferlin said, 'If I go, you gotta take my boy.'

"Ferlin was quite loyal. As much as he probably realized he needed Hubert, he didn't want to let Randy down. Hubert took Randy under his arm and really taught him about management. And Randy was to take some of the load off Hubert."

Patsy's last Four-Star session was on January 27, 1960. It was, ironically, the only Four-Star session with a good array of material. The songs recorded were "Lovesick Blues," "How Can I Face Tomorrow?," "There He Goes," and "Crazy Dreams." The latter three were "co-written" by W.S. Stevenson.

Singer Billy Walker, who was also managed by Randy Hughes, recollected, "Patsy used to tell me how McCall would hold her to the fire whenever she wanted to record anything other than a Four-Star copyright or when she brought up wanting more money.

"She told me, 'He don't want anybody else to do nothing for me—unless he gets part of the action.'

"I want to show you how McCall was. After Patsy had a hit with 'Walkin' After Midnight,' McCall went into the studio and took Patsy singing the song at forty-five r.p.m. and slowed it to thirty-three-and-a-third. It sounded like a man's voice and he released it on another label!"

Actually, in fairness to McCall, the authentic story should be told. He did go into the studio and cut a 45 r.p.m. single of Patsy singing "Walkin' After Midnight," and he pressed the record at the speed of 33 1/3 r.p.m.

"Bill sent the record out as a joke," related Donn Hecht. "He slugged the record with an artist's name of Calvin Coolidge. I think, all total, he made about two hundred and fifty of them. After he sent them out to d.j. friends he called them to ask what they thought of the record and when would they be getting on it [playing it on the radio].

"He told them, 'This is a hot record and this is the first male vocalist version.' The d.j.s told him the record was terrible. 'So you think it's terrible, huh?' McCall said. 'Well, yes,' they replied. 'It's nothing like Patsy Cline's version.' 'Oh, it's not,' Bill said hotly. He told what he had done and everyone would crack up. Bill really enjoyed that little prank."

It should be noted the name W.S. Stevenson was—or was thought to be—none other than the pseudonym Bill McCall used on many Four-Star copyrights. In fact, W.S.—for William Shakespeare—Stevenson encompassed many Four-Star regular house writers, such as Donn Hecht, Alan Block (the co-writers of "Walkin' After Midnight"), Eddie Miller, and Slim Willet.

"It was a gimmick," says Hecht, "to make some extra money that started with Bill but later carried over to a lot of us. It usually came about when Bill was able to buy all rights to a song and/or if a purchased song needed fixing by one of the writers. Not everyone that walked in off the street in those days was a Hank Williams.

"Bill once told me, 'Well, son, one thing for certain, if we ever go broke or if Four-Star is ever sold from under me, we'll have one hundred thousand dollars or so a year coming in from the most prolific writer in town, W.S. Stevenson."

It might be pointed out that, at this time in Nashville, this was not an unusual practice among publishers or artists who were approached by newly signed writers who had no power base and who were hungry for financial assistance.

"I remember Bill telling me when I first met him in California," said Hecht, "all about his costs and all that sort of thing. Then, as an afterthought, he added, 'Son, I'm gonna have to tell you that I'll be expecting you to hand back some money from time to time.' "

Ralph Emery, WSM radio and television personality, was country music's premier disk jockey at the time Patsy was coming up the ranks. He had WSM's Dawn Patrol show and was an announcer at the Grand Ole Opry. He reflects on the business aspect of artists and their record labels.

"As far as Bill McCall is concerned, I don't know if Bill McCall was the pseudonym and W.S. Stevenson was the real man or vice versa. McCall and label owners, such as Pappy Daley of Musicor, were often badmouthed. Now these artists can bitch a lot but they were on records and that's what they wanted. They may have sold their souls to get on, I don't know, but no one pushed them into these deals.

"When you're a singer and you're not making records and you want to be so badly, you'll do damn near anything to get it. Then if you have a few hits and become successful, you get pissed about the deal you made. But it's a two-way street. It's hard if not impossible to have it both ways.

"A lot of the big shots took publishing, writing, everything they could get their hands on in those days. And they could justify it by saying that if it wasn't for them putting up the money for the sessions and the costs, no one would have been making records. It was their way of getting back their money, in some cases, which is the purpose of business. Exxon does that every day.

"I've heard that Patsy was taken advantage of, but, well, you have to remember nobody knew Patsy was going to become such a giant. She came here after 'Walkin' After Midnight' and the Godfrey shows, but she couldn't get it together and the records didn't happen. At that time I was married to Skeeter Davis, who you might say was a rival of Patsy and Jean Shepard's. She was on 'Country Style, U.S.A,' the Armed Services recruiting series. Faron was the host, and Patsy was looking so down and forlorn.

"Skeeter and I went to speak to her and said 'Usually you're the life of the party.' She told us her career was going nowhere since 'Walkin' After Midnight.' She was a damn good singer and I'm sure she knew it. She could outsing most of the people here today. But Patsy hadn't been proving it. You always need proof. Where she came from, she was held in esteem because of Jimmy Dean, and now she was just a nobody. She got here and she was still a rookie. Patsy desperately needed a record. McCall served her purpose. I'm sure he made money in the process, but he surely must have spent a lot, too."

Lee Burrows remembers the time she took Patsy by Owen Bradley's studio and stood, at Patsy's urging, singing to Bill McCall the words to a song, "The Wrong Kind of Woman," that Patsy liked.

"Anyway I sang the song and he said, 'If Patsy likes it, I'll just have to get it for her.' I sent it to him later, but he never gave it to Patsy. It was always like that."

Charlie Dick summed up McCall by saying, "He's the type of guy no one will miss. He was despicable."

On January 9, 1960, while in Music City to make an Opry appearance, Patsy was accorded regular cast membership in the "Grand Ole Opry." This meant that she would have to set aside two-thirds of her weekends annually to perform on the Saturday Opry broadcasts and WSM's "Friday Night Frolics," which many people took as simply another Opry broadcast. This meant commuting back and forth to town, but she was to be guaranteed massive air wave exposure for her new records.

Grampa (Marshall Louis) Jones, the Country banjoist-guitarist and comic (and now star of "Hee Haw"), was an Opry regular and he remembers the sensation Patsy created whenever she was at the Ryman Auditorium.

"I was always standing around or in the wings and you just couldn't miss ole Patsy when she'd come in," Jones laughed. "She was a good-looking gal with a nice figure and used to really turn the guys' heads with the way she wiggled when she walked. I recall one night, not long after Patsy joined us as a regular, she flew past a bunch of us near the back alley to the Ryman [Auditorium].

A musician asked, 'Hey, Grandpa, do you think that Patsy is pretty?' I replied, 'Well, she's got all the men running or looking after her!'

" 'Now, Grandpa, you're avoiding the question!' this musician told me. 'Do you think she's pretty, that she's sexy?'

"I blurted out, 'Yes, sir, I do. She's really got it. Just like the stink off an old hog!'

"And in the same category with looks and sex appeal, Patsy had a marvelous talent. It was always fascinating to watch her go out and perform for the audience. She knew how to stop a show. I knew Patsy from the time she worked for Connie B. Gay. I liked her the first time I heard her—and she was quite some yodeler, then. Later we appeared on lots of the same dates together—one memorable occasion was the Grand Ole Opry show at Carnegie Hall in New York. She was a fine singer, I'll tell you that. I think, she may have been ahead of her time.

"Patsy was also one tough lady. People didn't mess with Miss Patsy. They knew better! That's what I always called her, Miss Patsy. 'Grandpa,' she used to tell me, 'are you gonna try and make a damn lady out of this girl?'

"She wasn't always the very model of patience, but I had to give her credit. She knew how to get things moving when they bogged down. Right after Patsy came to the Opry we were over at WSIX-TV in Nashville for a special of some kind. We got there early and we were still there at noon and going nowhere.

"We waited 'til we was blue in the face. Finally, I got mad and went up to Patsy and said, 'Well, they better hurry up 'cause I got a date in July.' She told me, 'Damn right, Grandpa, I gotta get home, too.' Patsy strutted over to whoever was in charge and started to raise hell. You could hear a pin drop. Then, suddenly, everything fell into place and we got to work.

"Maybe Jimmy Dean told you how he and Connie used to preach to everyone about not wasting valuable time. That must have sunk in on Patsy. She didn't cotton to those hurry up and wait situations. 'Don't waste my time' was her attitude. I could talk more about her, but it wouldn't help to know her better. You really would have had to be around her. Patsy Cline was one of a kind."

Patsy's membership on the Opry was prestigous to both sides. She could now mention she was a star of the Grand Ole

Opry, which automatically would net her more bookings. At the same time Opry press releases made much ado about Patsy's background: the Godfrey television experience, Jimmy Dean, TV's "Jubilee, U.S.A." (the "Ozark Jubilee"), the "Town Hall Party" in Compton, California; the "Bob Crosby Show," "Alan Freed Show," and appearances with such co-headliners as Pat Boone, the McGuire Sisters (both on the Godfrey Shows), Tex Ritter, Ferlin Husky, and Faron Young.

In late April 1960, Patsy excitedly brought Charlie the news she was pregnant again. The couple, whose daughter Julie was 20 months old, hoped for a boy. This time Patsy did not go into "retirement," but continued a hectic schedule of appearances on the Opry and with Faron Young. She was allowing time to lapse for the expiration of her Four-Star contract and planning on signing with Decca in a big-money deal. As much as Patsy would have liked to take time off, she couldn't afford it.

"She had asked Randy to keep her working as much as possible because Patsy and Charlie needed the money," said Kathy Hughes, who was Randy's wife. "They had absolutely nothing—and when I say nothing, I mean nothing. Patsy and Charlie had more than their share of ups and downs, personally and financially. They struggled to meet the rent on their house and the car payments. Patsy had had a long career, but a short period of stardom. In other words, she hadn't started to see any money yet.

"As husband and wife, Patsy and Charlie, just like any other married couple, had some rocky roads. She always leaned on Randy when anything went wrong or happened between her and Charlie. He had to be her soothsayer. But we were used to that since we had gone through the same thing with Ferlin.

"Patsy threatened to leave Charlie frequently, but that got to sound like a broken record. They'd go through a struggle and then everything would be okay again. We'd get calls at all hours of the morning. Patsy wanted Randy to come over and help, but when you get calls like that—made in heated moments—you really don't know what's going on in the other person's house because sometimes the person calling makes the situation worse than it is. Patsy and Charlie were in love and married. That in itself brings lots of joys and lots of problems."

Jean Shepard, until Patsy, was Kitty Wells' hottest rival for top female vocalist honors. Jean noted, "Oh, my, Patsy and Charlie had ups and downs. Plenty of them. But there had to be some love there. Patsy was no angel. I don't think that comes out too often. Usually, it's ole Charlie that gets it. Don't get me wrong, he wasn't no angel either. I don't know which of them was the biggest burden! Maybe they both deserved medals.

"I loved Patsy. I got along well with her because, just like me, she was quite plain spoken. She had a great sense of humor and was on the brassy side. I don't think, though some might disagree, that I was quite as brassy as she. But that was Patsy and I liked her as she was. You either liked her or didn't and she either liked you or didn't. There weren't too many people that met Patsy who didn't like her. She could be mean as hell, but she could also be as adorable as they come.

"You might say the same for Charlie. I love Charlie Dick to death, but he had and has his problems. However, that does not take away from the fact that he is one hell of a nice guy."

The Dicks' marriage was not all smooth going, but baby Julie helped add a stabilizing force, and "Patsy felt this force would increase," as a friend said, "by leaps and bounds with another child."

It was not to be. During the summer Patsy suffered her second miscarriage. She had flown to California in mid-July for an appearance on the popular "Town Hall Party." She was the guest of Jane Deren, Tex Ritter's niece and the associate producer of the Compton live and televised show.

"Patsy was the delight of my life the week she stayed here," said Mrs. Deren. "She was always so full of pep. I asked her, 'Patsy, honey, where do you get all that energy?' She was a star, but the most down-to earth person you've ever hope to meet. Everybody fortunate enough to get to know her just fell in love with Patsy."

After her performance on "Town Hall Party," Patsy did several dates in southern California. "I booked her, kept her, and cherished her," exclaimed Mrs. Deren. "Patsy had come out alone. I never had the pleasure of meeting her husband. My brother took Patsy to her various dates in his car.

"Near the end of the week, Patsy woke up in the middle of the night. She was pretty sick and in acute pain. She told me she was three months' pregnant. I was totally shocked. I had no idea, since Patsy had said nothing. We felt horrible, having driven her around all over the place. She should not have been doing all that riding in her condition. I called my doctor, a man whom many of the artists used when they were in California, immediately and he advised that we get Patsy to a hospital as soon as possible. We rushed her to the Queen of Angels and he was there waiting.

"When we heard the news about her losing the baby we all cried. The next morning Patsy called Charlie. He was more worried about how she was taking it. Patsy was in good spirits. All the staff at the hospital, including my doctor, fell in love with her. Even in the hospital, her energy was abundant. And what a sense of humor!

"I have heard people say that Patsy had a filthy mouth and that she drank a lot, but, of all the times I was around her, I never recall her talking dirty. She was always very lady-like. She knew who she could be. I would not have been shocked, as I had heard it all backstage. But I never heard it from Patsy. I had a young daughter, who Patsy adored, and I'm sure she took that into consideration. However, I do think that aspect of Patsy has been exaggerated."

Owen Bradley, who eventually became Patsy's full-time producer—in fact, he always was—reminisced about Patsy Cline, her attitudes, her troubles, and her musical outlook.

"Patsy's voice was multi-textured. It was the type you wanted to reach out and touch. To me, there was a velvety feel that could brush the heart and soul. Patsy had a great torchy quality. I thought of her as the Helen Morgan of country."

Bradley and his brother had been partners with Paul Cohen so he had already established connections with Decca. The producer has said that he had never heard of Patsy Cline when Cohen asked him to be musical supervisor of her sessions "except for the fact that she was reputedly a little hard to get along with."

The reputation that preceded her to town was unjust, Bradley added. "She did prove to be a problem, but not temperamentally. Patsy's problem was a unique one—she was too good! You don't hear that too often.

"She was one of the greatest singer/stylists—male or female—to come along in the entertainment business. If she had wanted to, Patsy could have done blues, jazz, pop—anything! She was petite and could be very feminine, purring like a cat, and lady-like, *but* she could turn around a moment later and be tough and tom-boyish. She was far more attractive than she photographed. Her pictures never did her justice. Sometimes I looked at them and said, 'Why can't it look like the real Patsy Cline?'

"Mind you, I don't know how possible that would have been! She was a complex soul. But, often, in her photographs she wore wigs and jewelry and clothing that masked the person she was underneath the veneer.

"As that person, Patsy was lovable, sensitive, sweet. But that softly accented voice of hers could fool you. She could show a fierce temper if the need arose, sometimes even if it didn't. And she had her salty moments. Yes, Oh yes!

"I don't believe I can recall a time in the studio when I didn't see Patsy without a cigarette. [Many others interviewed could never recall Patsy ever smoking a cigarette.] Now, she never inhaled as a result of something to do with rheumatic fever as a child, but, oh, how Patsy could smoke up the air.

"It sometimes got so hazy in the studio that I'd say, 'Patsy, hon, if you're trying to kill us, please wait till we've finished the session.' But she'd keep on puffing away. When I asked her why she smoked so much, she'd say, 'I like the taste of tobacco, and it gives me something to do.' " Bradley also remembers that when it came to drinking, Patsy could hold her own against any man. "But, I will say this, she was never out of control or went too far when she was working—either in the studio or on the road. Patsy liked taking a drink at home and after a performance."

Patsy's reputation for being a heavy drinker gained a considerable foothold in Nashville circles, but Charlie asserts, "The stories are just untrue. Patsy enjoyed a drink now and then, but she was not a drinker and certainly never a drunk. We'd go to Tootsie's [Orchid Lounge] after the Opry and have a beer, but that was about it. We partied and had a good time, but I was the one who raised hell and did the drinking, usually with Mooney Lynn, Loretta's husband, after we met them."

Patsy was now signed direct to Decca, and Owen became firmly in control. He was free at last to choose what Patsy could record and big plans were being made.

"When we began working together in nineteen fifty-five," said Bradley, "it was hard to sell a silky smooth voice like Patsy's to Country audiences or get the Country stations to play the kind of records we could have made. We did some things in the studio that might make you ask, when you listen today, 'What did you do that for?'

"It was to rough up the recordings so they'd be considered more up the traditional vein of Country for that time and place. Decca officials in New York felt Patsy had crossover appeal and kept after me. I kept telling them, 'It won't work, especially with the Four-Star material. Leave her be.' At one point I feared if they kept it up Patsy might go to another label when her Four-Star contract and our deal expired."

Patsy was in financial hot water when she joined Decca "in the red." The label showed their faith in her ability whenever she was in difficulty, and Bradley would arrange to advance Patsy money on unearned royalties. However, Decca's brass in New York had method to their madness. The assumption was that "if we were nice to her, she'd be nice to us and record the way we saw fit."

For sure, Patsy didn't see it that way! Bradley continued to get pressure from New York to push Patsy into recording more in a pop vein. "They told me, 'That's what the public wants. That's when she's at her best. As it is, she's only selling ten to fifteen thousand on each single. We can *always* go back to that.'

"When I told Patsy what Sidney Goldberg [sales] and Milt Gabler [A&R] said, she had a good laugh. In those days fifteen was considered great for Country. 'What the hell do they think I am, a machine! What the hell do they want from me?' "

Ironically, in the first session under the Decca banner, there was one particular song, "I Fall to Pieces," which proved Decca/New York had the right idea and that Decca/Nashville knew what they were doing. It was another turning point in the career of Patsy Cline.

9
"Fooling 'Round"

> *Patsy Cline:* "Alright, little Sheriff, you always wanted to make out with me. Tonight you're gonna get some."
>
> *Faron Young:* "Get your ass outta here!"

Hank Williams died in 1953, leaving behind a heritage of unforgettable songs. He was at the height of his career, on the road doing personal appearances. Williams was the greatest hillbilly singer of them all, but what has made his name and his music a permanent fixture on the entertainment horizon is the fact that his songs and records gave the first clear indication that Country could become a dominant factor in the mainstream of pop.

Even after Williams' impact on pop—with songs that ranged the spectrum from tearjerkers and rockabilly to hilarious novelty numbers—the Country scene remained still a relatively self-contained culture. Country records sold in Country markets and the Country artists, for the most part, were unknown to pop fans. But Williams' songs emphasized the fact that the right song could broach the gap and achieve sales in the broader popular music field.

What is generally not noted is that pop did not so much accept Country as Country accepted many of the avant-garde pop trends. This became known as the Nashville Sound and Owen Bradley was at the forefront of the movement—and Patsy Cline was the one artist who, in the initial stages, was more responsible for lowering the barriers and widening the listening tastes of die-hard Country fans.

When Patsy came along there was only one female star, and that was the Queen of Country Music, Miss Kitty Wells. The title Queen of Country was quite a transient one until Kitty's tremor was felt on the field. It went to whomever was hot at the time. Miss Wells stayed hot for so long the title simply became hers—and no one has dared tried to take it away even though Miss Wells no longer records. However, her hits are well remembered and she and her husband Johnny Wright still tour extensively.

Until the advent of Kitty—or Miss Kitty, as she is often referred to—there was no real place in Country for women singers. The male vocalists were the superstars and the Nashville recording companies were lorded over by men, and still are today. Women singers were considered window dressing—or as Patsy described it, "extra baggage"—to bring along on the road to give the husbands in the audience a charge.

Since it was assumed that women were the ones going out and buying the records, it was also assumed that no woman would go out and buy a woman vocalist. Thus, few female vocalists were recorded.

Kitty Wells changed all that with her 1952 song "It Wasn't God Who Made Honky Tonk Angels," which was a slap at male attitudes of the day. Women identified and made it a massive hit. It began a trend that turned the industry on its ear.

There were, of course, other excellent singers: Texas Daisy, Maybelle Carter of the famed A.P. Carter Family, Molly O'Day, Louise Massey, Lulu Belle Watson, Cousin Emmy, Linda Parker, Barbara Allen, Texas Ruby—wife of renowned fiddler Curley Fox, Rosalie Allen, Patsy Montana, former Queen of Country Music Martha Lou Carson, Rose Maddox, and Rose Lee Maphis. These great women's voices opened the door for Kitty Wells, who in turn opened the door for Patsy Cline, Jean Shepard, Marion Worth, Skeeter Davis, Connie Hall, Wanda Jackson, Norma Jean, Loretta Lynn, Jan Howard, Dottie West, and Tammy Wynette.

Attitudes changed slowly. The labels discovered women singers had earning power. Patsy Cline, besides showing she could pack clubs and houses, was the first female singer to turn to the new breed of songwriter settling in Nashville. She was, perhaps, the first singer to come up the ranks who believed it was just as big a sin for a man to drink and be unfaithful as it was for a woman—and she didn't mind telling it like it was.

As is often the case, Patsy's professional life closely mirrored her personal life. To say her marriage to Charlie was rocky is only being polite. To say they both were guilty of "fooling around" is merely fact.

"When Patsy and I met," reminisced Del Wood, "and had our little meetings—or, as we referred to them, 'domestic discussions'—in the dressing room, you know, the ladies' bathroom, the conversation always came 'round to husbands. The layman sees you on stage, hears you on record, reads about you in the fan magazines, but he doesn't know split peas from popcorn about what your life is *really* like.

"One night she told me of a row she and Charlie had and said, 'Well, Del, I guess I jumped right from the frying pan into the fire.' From what she had told me, I got the impression that maybe Patsy had gone into her marriage with Gerald with her eyes closed. There was no communication between them.

"When I first met Charlie, I couldn't stand him! I wondered what attracted her to him. But, as any woman, including myself, will tell you, love is love. If it's blind, we often don't know it 'til we're totally in the dark. But the more I hung around Charlie, the more I liked him. You can't help but like him—when he's sober.

"I've heard a lot of tales out of school about Charlie beating on Patsy. Well, she never much spoke of anything like that. From all she said it seemed to be a problem of him neglecting her sexually. She asked me once on a road date if I'd had the same problem and I told her I did.

"Let me ask you to introduce me to a gal who hasn't! But a Mr. Patsy Cline, a Mr. Loretta Lynn, a Mr. Del Wood, or a Mr. Whomever is very jealous of a wife's success. And, I guess, it's not the, so-called, natural order of things. They don't love you enough.

"In many ways Charlie could be despicable. Sometimes Patsy would sigh and say, 'Oh, hoss, I was in a lot better shape when I was married to Gerald.' Since that marriage was not the best of all possible worlds, I can imagine how she was feeling. I don't think Charlie ever appreciated what type of wife Patsy was and really wanted to be. He surely didn't understand her drive. He used to bitch with her before she'd leave on dates, then he'd call and bitch with her on the road, usually when he was drinking, and he'd bitch with her when she got back. He had a job, so he couldn't come out on the road with Patsy and he wanted to know why she didn't stay home and let him support her. It went on and on. But the road was not the problem or the fact that Patsy was the star. If you have a tight marriage, the road or the temptation of other men, other women, is not going to disturb it.

"There were thirteen years' difference in our ages, but that didn't stop Patsy and me from being good buddies. Maybe in a way, she looked on me as a big sister. My being older than her and her being younger never occurred to either one of us.

"She said, 'Del, you know what keeps marriages together?' 'What?' I answered. 'Economics—and security,' Patsy told me. She went on, 'I don't think I could ever let Charlie go, especially since we've made it this far and lived to tell about it! I ain't no different from most other people. I need security. Charlie's mine and I'm his.'

"Patsy said she didn't know what she was going to do about the situation with Charlie. She was starved for affection. 'I got to be constantly reassured that *somebody* loves me,' she said. 'A lot of people say you've got all the loving in the world when you walk out on that stage and you feel the beat of that applause. But, hell, that goddamn applause don't help you any when you're laying in that bed at night being totally ignored.'

"I think Patsy would have given anything in the world for things to be different. She loved that Charlie. Sometimes she loved him so much in spite of himself, I said, 'Hon, you're a stickler for punishment, ain't you!' A happy home life would have given Patsy a fundamental security. She was one of the sweetest, warmest, kindest, most generous people I ever knew.

"She really hated to leave Charlie to go work the road, but she didn't have much of a choice. He wasn't a millionaire. She hated to leave her house, and, more than anything, she hated to go off and leave that precious little Julie at home. But the bills had to be paid. Patsy and I both had plenty of chances to go out, to cheat. But it was our unfortunate experience that anyone within our age group figured we had money to lavish on them, and anyone older wanted a place to crawl into and have someone wait on them. Patsy and I both agreed—to hell with them! At that stage of our lives we had no desire to be a waitress or a wet nurse either. Patsy and I both kept telling each other things were going to get better. But, they didn't. For two people who liked laying the cards straight on the table, we were very good at lying to ourselves."

Singer Billy Walker said, "Patsy was a warmhearted person who liked to have fun on her engagements. But there was a real serious side to her, too. She wanted her home and her husband to be a real, viable thing. I don't think she ever got the support out of Charlie that she deserved. She just wanted more than he could give, I guess."

An entertainer and sister-in-arms who knew Patsy as an Opry buddy and shared confidences with her explained, "Patsy could salt her conversations, but I never heard her use language that embarrassed me. She never got down to the nitty gritty around me. Patsy would get upset and say how Charlie accused her of being unfaithful when she was out working. But it was common knowledge that at home he was enjoying the status of being Mr. Patsy Cline. He was always out drinking and fooling around and when Patsy'd come home he neglected her."

Del Wood asserted, "You hear a lot about the way women were mistreated in that era of Country music, but it's all been exaggerated. The only women who got mistreated were us working gals and by our own men! The men in the business respected you if you demanded and merited respect. Patsy and I used to kid with some of the new gals coming up and say, 'Y'all are going to be all right. Just keep your chin up and your skirt down and it'll pay off.' The only man Patsy Cline ever wanted was the one she had at home. No one can explain these things, especially the ones most involved."

Ralph Emery noted, "You'd always hear that Patsy had a bad reputation and seemed set on working to keep it or make it worse. Well, that was not the Patsy Cline that Skeeter and I knew. From everything I ever saw, and what she told me, Patsy wanted to be a faithful wife.

"I know certain things did happen,but there were reasons that drove Patsy to this. For one thing, Charlie would call and badger the daylights out of her when she was working the road with Ferlin Husky, Porter Wagoner, and Faron Young. He'd berate her and say she should be at home with him and the baby. She'd break down and cry. He'd accuse her of being a—well, of being unfaithful. And she'd break down and cry.

"No matter how good their day started, it seemed that it would end in some terrible argument in which they would accuse each other of all kinds of things—usually because of Patsy's insecurities and Charlie's jealousy.

"If anything occurred between Patsy and anyone else, it was only because of Charlie throwing them closer and closer together."

When you talk of Nashville reputations, one name is always bound to surface. That of Faron Young. From all you hear about him, Young has got to be one of the most outrageous and contemptible characters in all of show business. Nothing could be further from the truth. It is impossible not to like him. However, he can embarrass a seasoned truck driver with his raunchy vocabulary.

Much has been said of Young—how much can be proved, however, is another story. Faron makes pronouncements that more than a few in Music City say are "total bullshit." He has been married to wife Hilda for 23 years and has four children. But to listen to Young carry on, you'd forget in a second he has a certain amount of distinction as a devoted family man and would only think that he has fooled around with every woman worth a second glance. Young is in a position to talk with authority about Patsy and Charlie. He was probably, at one point, their closest friend. And he knew them from the beginning and stuck with them through thick and thin. Since many of his comments were not prudent, what follows is a judicious transcript of his observations and experiences.

"Patsy was *so* pretty. Really. She did something to me. I had other motives outside of her talent being so fantastic. There was no doubt about what I was up to, but she never came across and gave me anything. I tried for well over a year!

"It was easy to see that Patsy and Charlie loved each other, though, sometimes, they had a funny way of showing it. I'll never forget Charlie telling me that the next day after he met Patsy he went to her house in Winchester to call on her. He got there and Patsy came to the door with her hair all rolled up and with no makeup on.

" 'Pardon me, ma'am,' Charlie said, thinking he was talking to her sister or maybe even her mother. 'Is Miss Cline in?' Patsy replied, 'Well, goddamn it, I am Miss Cline!' Charlie, Patsy, and me used to laugh about that incident. He'd say, 'Goddamn, I didn't know who the hell she was. Something had happened from the night before!'

"You're gonna find folks who'll say Patsy wasn't the prettiest girl in the world, but to me she was. Whatever she might have been lacking in the looks department, she more than made up for over the rest of her. Ah, she had quite an ass, and a figure like an hourglass. How can I say it? She had more curves than a highway! She just looked good. And if she looked great on the outside, she was double that on the inside. They didn't come any better than Patsy. She was a true friend."

Whenever Faron made a pass at his new co-headliner, Patsy would scold him. "No, you little mother, you ain't getting into the Cline's britches. You can just forget about all that stuff!" "So we ended up being like family. We liked to hang out together. Patsy cussed like I do, like a drunk sailor. Me and her could talk to each other and tell stories. No one ever got embarrassed or was shocked. We were on the same wave length, you might say," Faron remembered.

"When they first got married, Charlie treated Patsy like a dog. He'd get her up in front of a bunch of people and call her a no good whore, and everything else. He was drunk. Just drunk. And jealous. Charlie'd just go to pot when he'd see Patsy getting attention from somebody else or if some idiot called him 'Mr. Cline,' or introduced him as 'Patsy Cline's husband' instead of Charlie Dick. Now that got to him, especially when he was drinking. That's a natural ego thing to piss you off. But when you have someone—wife or husband—in this business, you're just gonna have to accept it.

"My sister came up here and told me, 'I never got so tired of anything as being introduced as Faron Young's sister. This was something Charlie could never adjust to. He only objected when he was drinking. They did need the money. Sometimes he would take a car and come with us. I used to play pool with him. One night I beat him for about fifty dollars and he gave me a check and said, 'Don't put it in the bank right away.'

"Later when I was with Patsy I said, 'I beat Charlie fair and square. This ain't a hot check, is it? That son-of-a-bitch is gonna pay me!' When he beats me, I hand over cash.' Patsy grabbed that damn check out of my hand. 'Hon, I'm only fooling. He'll pay me! She tore it up and reached in her bag and gave me the fifty dollars. 'Here goddamn you, go and take advantage of him again!' she hollered.

"Patsy went up to Charlie and turned him around and told him off. 'If you wanna bet on pool games, from now on bet with your own money. Now, you son-of-a-bitch, go across the street and get me a hamburger.' And ole Charlie started to run around, waiting on Patsy hand and foot.

"I said to myself, 'My goodness, the sleeping giant has awoken!' The tables had turned. 'Cause when she started coming out with me, Charlie used to tell Patsy to go get him things. After the way he had treated her, Patsy decided it was time to put the fire right back to his ass.

"The only time you'd see Patsy down and crying was when Charlie did something to her. She'd come in with money from a road gig. He'd take it and go blow it.

"You'd kinda wonder why they were together, married. You figured there had to be something there. I don't know if Patsy ever told me she loved Charlie. I know she told me she hated him! Sometimes hate can be love in an insane sort of way. I think she figured he'd help get her ass out of Virginia and get things going for her. This, that, and the other—no telling what all he done promised her about what he could do promoting her.

"Patsy used to get so frustrated with Charlie. One time when we were out on the road, I don't know what all was coming off between them. But before you could spit, Patsy was hauling off at Charlie. You know, it's funny, I got used to it but on the other hand, I never did. She tore into him, saying, 'Get the fuck outa here and go back to Nashville. We don't need you here anyway. You're just in everybody's goddamn way! I'm gonna fly back with Faron.' And Patsy put Charlie in the car with the band and he rode home with them. She told me, 'I'm not going to ride all the way back with that son-of-a-bitch!' I had learned not to interfere. I just got her a ticket and she came back with me the next morning.

"Probably by the time she saw him at home, Patsy had

forgotten all about whatever it was that Charlie had done and they were as lovey-dovey as can be. That's the way they were. Used to beat the shit outta me! They both put up with a lotta crap, really.

"I was over at their house one night with some guys from my band and Charlie borrowed one of the guitar players' car and went down the road after some whiskey. Would you believe he hit a bridge and demolished the car? The car wasn't worth more than eight or nine hundred dollars, that's all that guitar player owned. He had no insurance and Charlie never paid him a nickel. I don't know if Patsy took care of it or not. I only remember the car being towed off to the junkyard.

"Sober, I love Charlie. But, he can be so damn belligerent. Why, he used to walk up to promoters when Patsy was getting started and corner them about why they wouldn't book her. And at those d.j. conventions, he used to embarrass the hell out of me. Charlie would take those poor, unsuspecting d.j.s aside and tell 'em, 'I understand you haven't been playing her fucking records. Well, let's get on the ball!' Those disk jockeys would say, 'Fuck you, fella!' and walk away."

Faron talked about the two sides of Charlie and the strangeness of the couple's sometimes distant, sometimes intimate relationship. "When Charlie was sober, he'd love Patsy and that baby of theirs like there was no tomorrow. But he was just a Jekyll and a damn Hyde. Charlie is a good man, now—sober, like I said. They do not come any better. He's got a fantastic sense of humor and a loyalty. I know he really loved Patsy. There were times when he was drinking when he couldn't help himself. Charlie tried to do a lot for Patsy. He had his job at the newspaper [as a linotype operator], but he'd go out on the road with us. He'd go around to the Decca and Four-Star folk and talk with them and he'd write the disk jockeys and tell them about what Patsy was doing and give them the lowdown on her new record.

"Yeah, he loved her. He never lost his love for Patsy. They just had a bizarre way of doing things. Maybe things were happening no one knew about. I just don't know. I know that, usually, when Charlie looked around for another girl, he'd find another Patsy look-alike. That was true of his second wife, Jamey Ryan. She sang just like Patsy and everything."

Young has vivid, touching, hilarious memories of his relationship with Patsy Cline. "When Patsy got to where she was like a sister to me, I didn't try to fool around with her anymore. We got too close. But when Patsy was out on the road with me, Charlie'd get to drinking and call her wherever we'd be staying—or cut loose on Patsy when she called home to check on their baby Julie—and accuse her of all sorts of things. And he'd be the one, back in Nashville,doing just what he was accusing her of! He was telling her she ought to be at home, being a wife, instead of hauling ass all over the country singing and fooling around with every man, including me, she'd come in contact with. Truth was, Patsy was being quite the faithful little mama to ole Charlie.

"The only time Patsy and I were, how should I put this, you know, familiar was if we were on the road and the situation would present itself. And she would present it. Oh, yeah! I never went to her.

"One time, on a series of one-nighters, we ended up spending the night in Casper, Wyoming. She came up to my room, already about half snookered, with the pint of whiskey she kept in her purse. She told me she had been on the phone with Charlie and he gave her hell.

" 'All right, little Sheriff,' she said, 'you always wanted to make out with me. Well, tonight you're gonna get some!' I just laughed at her, 'Patsy, honey, are you crazy? Get your ass outta jere!' She said, 'No!' Patsy refused, began taking her clothes off and proceeded to get into bed with Faron.

When asked about this relationship with Patsy, Faron replied, "What the hell are you gonna do? She crawled in the sack with me!"

Did Patsy and Faron look at each other any differently after that? "Shit, naw. We laughed about it the next day." Faron said that Patsy was the type of woman who could laugh about such a situation.

It happened more than once according to Young but, after that first time, he remembers saying to himself, "Hell, this'll never work." He added, "She would present it. I never went to her."

Why did it happen? "Patsy's loneliness," Faron says, "and her spite against Charlie. She loved me like a brother—probably a little extra, too, because of the help I'd done for her." He commented that once Patsy got "to be big and had lost her love for Charlie—through his own doing—the only thing that concerned Patsy was her children."

"I can tell you this, Patsy wanted to be a good wife to Charlie. I'd say, the whole time she was married to Charlie, she didn't go out with but three or four different guys. But she did get to where she'd go out. But if she had a good home life she never woulda looked sideways at another man.

"Patsy just got to where she hated Charlie and what he had done to her. The tide changed and now she was bringing home the bacon. When she got popular and she and Randy [Hughes] hooked up [for management purposes], well, I knew damn well what was fixing to happen."

Faron Young also spoke of the qualities that endeared him to Patsy as a friend. "She had a talent that was bigger than anyone then or now. But Patsy had a heart that was bigger than she was. She'd do anything for anyone. She helped Loretta Lynn, Dottie West, Barbara Mandrell. She would see a girl singer and just knock 'em out with her supportiveness.

"When Patsy first came to the Opry, Margie Bowes, who was out of the Virginias and later married Doyle Wilburn [they are divorced], was on. She was a beauty and could sing real pretty. Patsy stood in the wings and told me, 'God, hoss, that little girl can sing. How can we help her?'

"Patsy was like a mother hen. She'd take all them girl singers under her wing—give 'em advice, tell 'em the facts about the men in the business, and tell 'em things about how to stage their shows.

"I remember that Patsy came on a little strong to a couple of the new girls—the ones from small towns and religious backgrounds. One night at the Opry this gal came up to Patsy and said, 'Why I don't know what I'm gonna do about so-and-so. He keeps bothering me. Honey, he's all hands!' Patsy shocked the shit out of this pretty little thing when she told her, 'Well, you tell him to keep his hands to himself or go fuck himself!' I thought that gal was gonna faint!

"Patsy said just what she thought. Never messed around, *and* it didn't pay to mess around with her. You couldn't get ahead of Patsy. Nope. If somebody farted, she'd just raise her ass and fart right back at 'em. I seen her do it! Didn't make no difference to her. She'd tell you to go fuck yourself in a minute. Let me tell ya, there was no pulling any shit on her! No, sir."

Faron remarked that his friendship with Patsy Cline is something he will always cherish. "As far as Patsy and I being close, we never tried to hide it. Patsy and I had a closeness that nothing could stand between. Everybody in this business is affectionate—at least to your face. It wasn't that way with Patsy and me. Whenever I'd see Patsy I didn't give a shit if Dick was there or who all, I just went right up and hugged and kissed her. It wasn't nothing to it. Oh, but ole Charlie didn't like people doing that with Patsy. I guess he got over it with me, though."

Dottie West observed, "I don't think Faron and Patsy could have ever fallen in love. But they were close. You can believe Faron when he tells you how beautiful Patsy was—on the inside and the outside. When she walked on stage anywhere, be it the Opry or some small club, she'd look so fantastic just about any man present would want to hold her in his arms. Maybe Faron tried, but how far he'd go, well, I really wonder."

"No! No!" said Dale Turner. "Patsy was never in love with any of them. Faron was famous for trying to get every girl to build his own ego. He was the type where you'd have to go and get married before he'd respect you. Patsy told both him and Ferlin, 'Keep your hands off!' She told me how she had to keep them in line. And it just wasn't Faron and Ferlin. Any girl singer that was young and looked half-way decent had to watch the men. It was habit, just a habit, you know. Most of us were silly and didn't take long to catch on to the games they played.

"Patsy certainly never fell for it. She would have a little crush that wouldn't last any time at all. It was always Charlie. Now, hey, that was it. Until they got back here to Nashville. They had their ups and downs. But she loved Charlie. Patsy didn't play around. If someone wanted to get wise or fresh with her on the road, she just didn't mince words. She'd tell them off in a hurry. She didn't play games. That kid didn't play games."

Musician Lightnin' Chance proclaimed, "It depresses me when I hear these stories of how Patsy played and would get so drunk and all this and the other. I don't know if I ever saw Patsy drunk in her life. Patsy was such a beautiful person. I never thought of her as being sexy. She was attractive, but a Bo Derek or Cheryl Tiegs she was not. Patsy was a good friend. I liked her especially because she was always for the underdog. She was a generous lady and she wanted to help people all the time—even when she didn't have a dime.

"You can't believe all you hear. I've been accused of being the wildest son-of-a-gun in the world and it just ain't so. If I had done or said a third of the stuff that I'm credited with, I'd be four hundred and eight. It would take me that long!"

Pearl Butler, the singer Patsy visited when she moved to Nashville, expounds on the legend of Faron Young. "Well, honey, you've never lived 'til you been on tour with the Sheriff! Oh, my! I guess you might say Faron is a ladies' man. If some of the young girls would come up to the hotel to see him after the shows, he'd never let himself get alone with one of them, and he'd always make sure to leave the door open.

"We had worked a date right outside of Chicago and there were about six girls on the show with us. Carl [Butler, her husband] and me had gone by one of the rooms to visit and all the girls were together. Faron came in and horsed around. You wouldn't have believed all what he did. He'd lay on the bed with one and then push her off and grab another one. He'd get up and ride around on their backs.

"When he got ready to leave, I asked 'What room you in, Faron?' He told me. I went back in and hatched a little plot. We chose this girl to go up to his room. She knocked on his door and he opened it. Faron looked out in the hall. He thought we'd be out there, too. As he did, the girl slipped in past him. You would have thought that door was coming off the hinges from the way Faron acted. Honey, when he realized she was inside he opened it so fast I thought it was gonna fly away and he flew out into the hall.

"Faron came hauling down that corridor and there we were waiting. I asked, 'What's wrong, Faron? You look like you done saw a ghost!' He replied, 'Nothin'. Nothin'! Ain't nothin' wrong. I just got lonesome and thought I'd come and stay with y'all for a while.'

"He went off and left that poor girl in his room! Faron likes to talk about it a lot—and he can turn you red when he does—

but his bark is much, much worse than his bite.

"Once this girl singer came for an interview. He told her, 'If you sing with me, you'll have to go to bed with me.' She told him, 'I don't need the job that bad!' And he shot back, 'Thank you. If you had said okay, you wouldn't have worked for me no way.' He wouldn't have hired her because he wouldn't have had no respect for her. That's Faron. All talk, no action. If Faron has got an audience, he will do and say anything in the world.

"On a tour in Canada, Faron had pulled jokes on everybody and I thought, 'How am I going to get even with him?' When we got to Buffalo, in the dead of winter, it was so cold Faron was sitting in his room with his feet propped on the radiator. I slipped into his room and closed the door. Now, when my husband Carl was walking toward you, you could always hear him coming. He has this way of clearing his throat that announces his approach. I waited 'til I heard him.

"Carl cried out, 'Pearl Lee! Oh, Pearl Lee, where are you, honey?' I yelled out, 'Wait a minute 'til I get my clothes on! I'll be right there.' He started banging on the door and Faron nearly jumped through the ceiling. He clean knocked that chair over and screamed, 'Oh, my God, Carl, come in here quick! Something's wrong with Pearl!' Carl busted in as we planned and grabbed Faron, 'Hey, Sheriff, what's going on here? I demand an explanation!' I kinda snuggled up to Faron and he pushed me away. 'I swear, Carl, I swear I didn't even know she was in the room.'

"Faron stood there in a cold sweat swearing his innocence. At nearly six foot, three inches, Carl towered over him. To Faron he was a brute. Then we broke out laughing and it took poor Faron about an hour to recover. It was wonderful. We really got him!"

Another entertainer explained, "It is true that Patsy and Faron were extremely close, and they certainly may have gone to bed together. But anyone that knows Faron and anyone that knew Patsy Cline knows that Patsy didn't have come begging for it. When any of the girl singers called his bluff, he didn't know what to do. Behind all that raunch, there is a pretty extraordinary man. If only he knew that!"

Porter Wagoner and Patsy worked several show dates. "I can truthfully say Patsy was a beautiful, great woman. She lived and breathed her music. As an artist, she was dedicated to the music business. Patsy and I had a lot of common ground. I was dedicated to making everything I was doing the very best I could, and so was she. We were both never satisfied with second best. Neither of us could live with knowing we didn't give something the best we had.

"Patsy enjoyed having a good time and so did I, so we always had fun on the road together. I have some great memories of Patsy. Lots of incidents became fun things when Patsy was around.

"Traveling to dates in the car with someone you liked to be around was nice, and it didn't happen that often. Usually, if there were three or four of us on the same dates, we'd travel along with the Cadillacs all in a row. You could always depend upon Patsy for entertainment. Nobody was a stranger around her. And she liked my band and became especially close to them.

"I knew Patsy for a long time, even when she was just breaking into the business, and liked and admired her. I also happened to be attracted to her. There was a great affinity between Patsy and me, and we enjoyed being together. More than a few times one thing led to another. It was beautiful and those moments were special to me. But I would not say that Patsy and I were in love, that we were lovers, or that we had any torrid romance. We were sharing what we felt for one another. It was just two people alone who had grown fond of each other, the communion of two spirits who found they had more in common than just plain friendship. In each other's arms it made a few lonely nights out there on the dismal road more bearable."

Plaque at Country Music Hall of Fame in Nashville. *Photo/Les Leverett*

Virginia Hensley (Patsy Cline), 16 (right), and Virginia Taylor, her partner, in Winchester, Virginia, amateur contest. *Photo/ Ralph Grubbs*

Patsy Cline and bandleader/mentor Bill Peer after riding in Winchester's Apple Blossom Parade, May, 1957. *Photo/collection of Mrs. Charles Spiker*

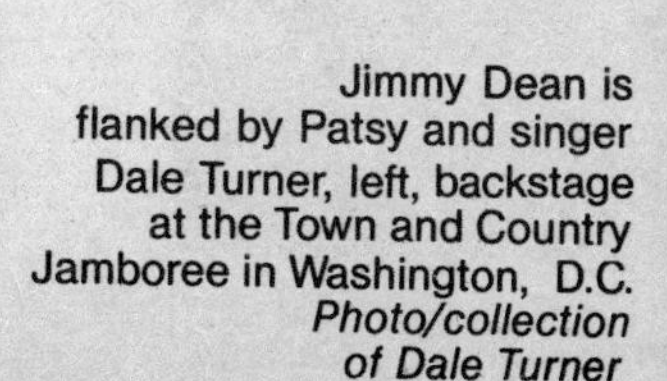

Jimmy Dean is flanked by Patsy and singer Dale Turner, left, backstage at the Town and Country Jamboree in Washington, D.C. *Photo/collection of Dale Turner*

Patsy and first husband Gerald Cline on visit to Nashville. *Photo/collection of Mrs. Mark Yontz*

The second-floor apartment of Patsy and Gerald on East Patrick Street, Frederick, Maryland. *Photo/Ellis Nassour*

Patsy marries Charlie Dick in Winchester, September 15, 1957. *Photo/collection of David Grimm*

Jean Shepard, who was married to Hawkshaw Hawkins, was one of Kitty Wells' rivals along with Patsy. She is still active on the road and the Grand Ole Opry. *Photo/Ellis Nassour*

Del Wood, Grand Ole Opry Star, met Patsy backstage in 1955 and continued life-long friendship with "domestic chats" in ladies "dressing room" and on tour. *Photo/WSM Photo/Les Leverett*

Two important men in Patsy's professional life: Paul Cohen, head of Decca's New York and Nashville A&R department (left), and Owen Bradley, Patsy's musical supervisor and later producer. *Photo/WSM Photo/Les Leverett*

Patsy Cline in Nashville, 1961. *Photo/WSM Photo/Les Leverett*

Patsy, backstage at the Grand Ole Opry, after recovering from near-fatal auto accident. Note crutches to left. *Photo/WSM Photo/Les Leverett*

Patsy, back on her feet after 1961 accident, at Tootsie's Orchid Lounge with singer Billy Walker, foreground. Manager Randy Hughes is standing in front of famed wall of autographs. Husband Charlie Dick is at left. *Photo/fan photograph from WSM Archives*

Singer Faron Young. *Photo/Ellis Nassour*

Singer Billy Walker and Patsy became close during her stay in hospital following auto accident. *Photo/Ellis Nassour*

Pearl Butler, shown with costumes Patsy gave her, and her husband Carl, who make up one of country's famed singing duos, was an early friend to Patsy and Charlie when they moved to Nashville. *Photo/Ellis Nassour*

The Wilburn Brothers, Teddy and Doyle Patsy often sought Teddy's opinion of her recording sessions. *Photo/Ellis Nassour*

WSM radio/TV personality Ralph Emery. *Photo/Ellis Nassour*

Brenda Lee discusses her friendship with Patsy Cline with author Ellis Nassour in Nashville. *Photo/Martha Haggard*

Singer Jan Howard was a good friend to Patsy Cline, and married to songwriter Harlan Howard, who co-wrote "I Fall To Pieces." *Photo/Ellis Nassour*

Patsy, center, arrives "uptown" for Grand Ole Opry gala at New York's Carnegie Hall. She's shown with clockwise, Grandpa Jones, Minnie Pearl, Jim Reeves, Faron Young, and Bill Monroe. *Photo/WSM Photo/Les Leverett*

Patsy and manager Randy Hughes, backstage at Carnegie Hall. *Photo/WSM Archives*

Patsy on the Grand Ole Opry with Lightnin' Chance, right, on bass fiddle, and, playing guitar, Randy Hughes, Patsy's manager. *Photo/WSM Photo/Les Leverett*

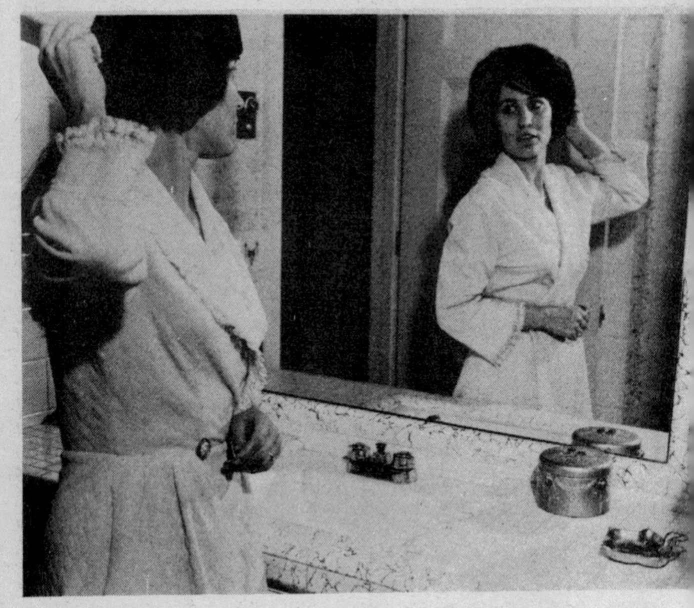

Loretta Lynn, in need of a nice "spread" for photo layout borrowed Patsy's "dream house," including her famous bathroom with real gold dust sprinkled into the marble tiles. *Photo /Les Leverett*

Patsy appears on WSM-TV's "Pet Milk Show" with friend and early supporter Ernest Tubb. *Photo/WSM Photo/Bev LeCroy*

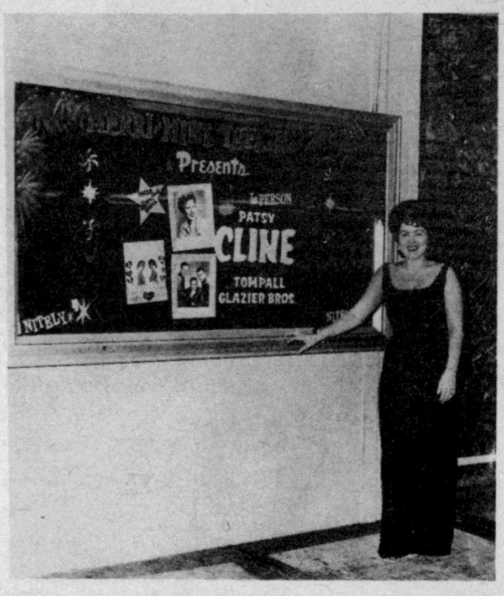

To help meet financial demands, Patsy played the Mint Casino in Las Vegas, November, 1962, with the Glaser Brothers (spelled incorrectly on display). *Photo/Mrs. Marvin Hughes*

1962 was Patsy's year: (left) accepting *Billboard's* "Favorite Female Artist" and (right) *Cash Box's* "Most Programmed Album" country awards were two among many Patsy received at the 11th Annual Country Music Festival. *Photo/WSM Photo /Les Leverett*

February, 1963. Patsy, hiding facial scars from auto crash with wig, meets D.J. Bob Clark of WEXL, Detroit, backstage at the Opry. *Photo/WSM Photo/Les Leverett*

Dottie West, at home in Nashville, reviews scrapbook Patsy gave her in late summer, 1962, because "I'll never live to see 30." *Photo/Les Leverett*

Patsy in session photos from album cover sittings in New York with Hal Buksbaum. *Photos/MCA Records*

Patsy singing "Bill Bailey" with WSM's Waking Crew Band for senior citizens group less than three weeks before fatal plane crash. *Photo/WSM Photo/Les Leverett*

Hawkshaw Hawkins, left, and Cowboy Copas, right, veteran country and Grand Ole Opry performers, were killed in the plane crash March 5, 1963, with Patsy and Randy. *Photos/ WSM Photos/Les Leverett*

Roger Miller amid crash debris and clothing of Hawkshaw Hawkins. *Photo/The Nashville Tennessean/ Gerald Holly*

Gaping hole marks impact site of Randy Hughes' plane carrying Patsy, Hawkshaw, and Copas (left). Patsy's body is removed (right). *Photos/The Nashville Tennessean/Gerald Holly*

Woodlawn Cemetery, Nashville, with curiosity-seekers and flower memorials following funerals of Hawkshaw Hawkins and Cowboy Copas. *Photo/Nashville Tennessean/Joe Rudis*

Opry memorial service was held Saturday, March 9, 1963, for Patsy, Hawkshaw, Copas, Randy, and singer Jack Anglin. Minnie Peal stands behind Opry manager Ott Devine. The Jordanaires, center, sang hymn. *Photo/WSM Photo/Les Leverett*

Patsy and Charlie's daughter Julie, age four, accepts Cash Box award from publisher Bob Austin in ceremonies at 12th Annual Country Music Festival in Nashville on November 1, 1963.
Photo/WSM
Photo/Les Leverett

Gateway erected at Shenandoah Memorial Park, Winchester, Virginia, by Patsy's husband Charlie Dick and family.
Photo/ Ellis Nassour

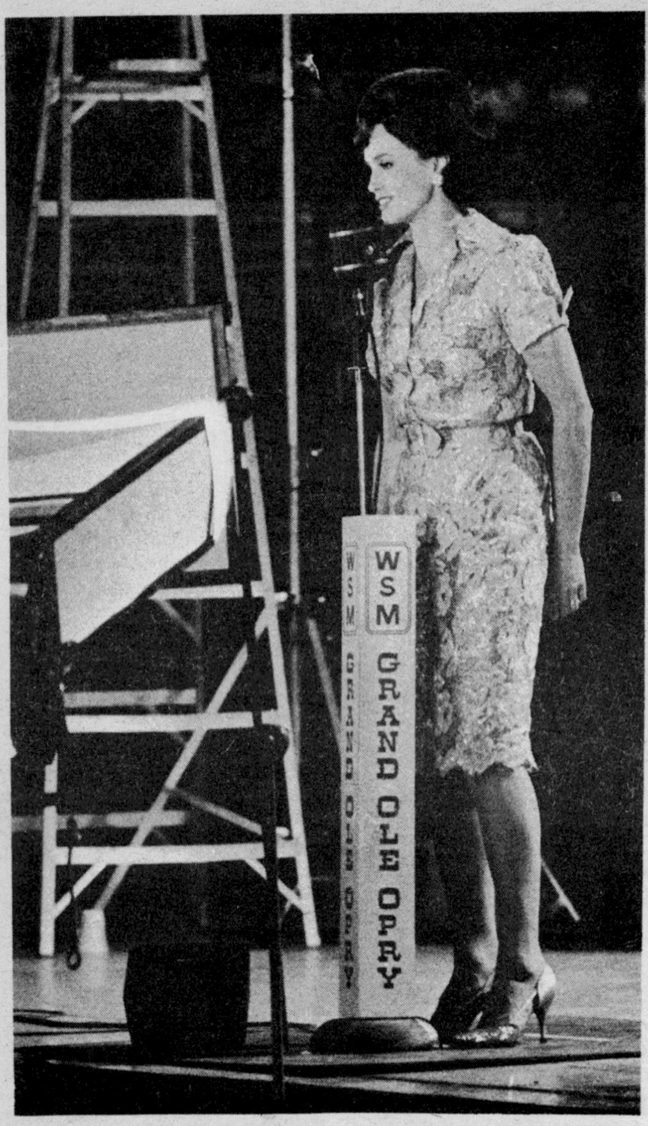

Jessica Lange as Patsy Cline onstage at the Grand Ole Opry in the film "Sweet Dreams." Photo/Kathleen Smith/*The Tennessean.*

10
"Come on In"

Patsy Cline: **"I don't know chords. Is that what you want?"**

Charlie Dick: **"No. A woman can't sing that note."**

Patsy Cline: **"Oh, Is that right? Let me try!"**

Charlie Dick: **"And she did it—probably just to spite me."**

At the end of May, 1960, Patsy had more good news for Charlie: She was pregnant again. They both hoped for a boy. Come August 25, daughter Julie would be two and she needed company in her playpen.

On Saturday, June 4, Patsy was in Springfield, Missouri, on ABC's "Ozark Jubilee" telecast. It was her first appearance since December 1959, when bagfuls of mail arrived after Patsy's duet with Ferlin Husky on "Let It Snow." This time around host Red Foley coupled Patsy with Country veteran Cowboy Copas for a duet on "I'm Hog-Tied Over You." In a moving tribute to Hilda and her newly discovered family way, Patsy sang "Mother, Mother" and was joined by an ensemble featuring Copas, Eddy Arnold, and June Valli.

Patsy was in her seventh month for her first recording session under the auspices of Decca on November 16, 1960. Three songs were recorded: "Lovin' in Vain," "Shoes," and "I Fall to Pieces," the tune that would reestablish Patsy in the pop field and recrown her "Queen of Country."

"The turning point, maybe the thing that saved us all, I guess, was 'I Fall to Pieces,' " indicated Owen Bradley. "Hank Cochran, besides being a young writer, was a song plugger for Pamper Music. He came by my office to go over some new material and told me about a song he'd written with Harlan Howard [who was married to singer Jan Howard]. I asked him to play it for me, and right away I liked it.

"But there was a problem. No one else did. By the time I got it to Patsy, six artists had turned it down. Roy Drusky was considering it, when, in my office, he decided that it was a woman's song. 'Owen, I really like it,' he told me. 'It's a beauty, but a man could never sing this. It would kill him!' Patsy was either nearby or within hearing distance and she said 'Well, heck, I'll record it.'

"The funny thing was that she didn't like it either. I don't think she ever did until it became a hit!"

Hank Cochran and Harlan Howard went on to become two of the most prolific writers in the music world. Both have indelible memories of Patsy.

"We were just real close friends," reminisced Cochran. "Oh, no, there was never any romance or any stuff like that. We kinda came from the same cotton. The bond started when we were both flat on the bottom and as we grew in stature—and financially—in the business, the friendship strengthened. It was something I was mighty proud of. Patsy was some kind of lady!

"I had quite strong feelings about Patsy. And it's still hard—after all this time—to get it out and talk about her. We just shared so much together. When I came to Nashville in nineteen sixty, Patsy helped pull me through a lot. We were both at the low end of the totem pole. We weren't starving, but we weren't eating high on the hog either. I think I was making fifty dollars a week and sending twenty-five of it back to California to my wife Shirley and the kids. I might have been living on about twenty-five dollars a week! It was possible in those days! And, hell, I was twenty-five and figured I had time.

"Patsy was doing no better. Though she had some records and had just come on the Decca label, the Four-Star people made all the money. She saw hardly anything.

"Near as I can remember, Darrell McCall, a Texas boy who was playing bass for Hank's wife, Audrey Williams, told me Patsy was looking for material and took me out to Patsy and Charlie's one night. It all started from there. I had begun writing back in Greenville, Mississippi, tried it in California, and was now trying to get it together in Nashville. I even had done some recording. I tried all the angles, but I hadn't had any success.

"There was a place in Nashville called Mom Upchurch's, where the half-starving musicians used to stay. Mom'd let us board for ten dollars a week at six-twenty Boscobel Street. Darrel stayed there along with Roger Miller, Johnny Paycheck, who was going under the name of Donnie Young then, one of several pseudonyms he used [his real name is Donald Lytle]; George McCormick, who was working for Wilma Lee and Stoney Cooper's Clinch Mountain Clan; and Shorty Lavender [now a top Nashville agent], who was playing fiddle for Ray Price. All of us were going down the up staircase.

"The first hit I ever had was by Patsy on 'I Fall to Pieces.' I didn't write it for her, but she ended up doing it—as I recall, kinda against her will. I had taken the song to Owen after it had been turned down by a whole bunch of people. When Roy Drusky at Decca turned it down, Owen tried to get him to change his mind but he wouldn't. Patsy said she wanted it and I don't know if she knew what the song even was 'cause she mighta just been trying to make sure nothing slipped by her.

"She wanted it and then didn't like it. She didn't say why or ask me to make any changes. She just didn't care for it. I've found, some people just don't like certain songs. I guess it was one of those situations. 'I Fall to Pieces' was written by Harlan and I in one of our many down periods, and it was tinged with just the right amount of, I guess you could say, hurt and despair."

Jan Howard cannot forget her initial meeting with Patsy or her impression of her [then] husband's new song. "Harlan and I hadn't been married too long when we decided Nashville was the place to be. I had a record out and was invited to be on the Opry.Some friends told me, 'If you do the Opry, the best way to stay out of trouble is to go down there, do your spot, and leave. Don't hang around.'

"I found that hard to do. I've been a member for over twelve years and I never tire of hearing the singers I admire. I'm not a fan-type person. I didn't get too excited about many singers, but I really enjoyed Patsy's style and I wanted to meet her. But I was shy, and to this day still am. I didn't want to go up to her and say, 'Hi, I'm Jan Howard.' I was afraid she'd say, 'Jan who? So what.'

"The only time that I would hang around was when Patsy was on. I'd come early just to see her, or stay late. I'd watch her and then go change. I didn't know that many people and had never met Patsy. Some of the Opry folks were nice, others were not so nice. Jean Shepard, Hawkshaw Hawkins, and Ray Price were among my friends.

"This particular night I met Patsy, I saw her come in with her fringe cowgirl outfit and hat and white western boots. I stood in the wings and listened to her sing and then went to the ladies room where we changed. There were a couple of dressing rooms off the stage but they were for the guys and the musicians. The girls rated last in those days.

"The door to the bathroom opened and in walked Patsy with her hands on her hips and she looked at me. I could tell from seeing the expression on her face she was fit to be tied. I thought, 'What a time to meet her!' And then she exploded—at me."

"Well," shot Patsy, "you're a conceited little son-of-a-bitch, aren't you!"

"What?"

"You heard me, stuck up! I've been watching you. You just come out here, do your spot, leave, and don't say hello to anyone. What's the matter? You think you're too good to talk to other folks around here? What are you so conceited for?"

Jan felt hurt, almost crushed that the singer she had come to idolize could talk to her in this way. "Now,you wait just a minute there, lady!" Jan's temper flared up. "Let me tell you something. Before I ever moved here from California, from the time I heard your first record, I've been a great fan of yours. I love to hear you sing. I was only following some advice I was given."

"Advice? What kind of advice?"

"That the best way to stay out of trouble is to do your spot and head out."

"So that's what I've been doing wrong!" exclaimed Patsy as she cracked up laughing.

"And that's exactly what I should've done tonight!"

"Why?"

"It would have been better. I stayed merely to hear you

sing! Where I was raised, when a stranger comes to town, it was the job of the people in that town to make that person feel at home. And, except for Jeanie, Hawk, and Ray, not a damn soul here has made me feel welcome. Including you!"

"Hold on!"

"I'm not finished! I think you're all a bunch of snobby bastards. I wish I hadn't stayed tonight. As a matter of fact, I'm sorry I did!"

Jan spun around and started to dart for the door. Patsy grabbed her arm. "You're all right, honey. You're all right! Anybody that'll stand there and talk back to the Cline like that is all right."

Patsy began laughing again and Jan's red face cooled and she joined in.

"Hi. I'm Patsy, Jan."
"Nice to meet you, Patsy."
"I can tell we are going to be friends!

"And," says Jan, "we were. Patsy was a fantastic person. That sounds so inane, I guess, especially when I am trying to describe someone I just absolutely thought the world of. I loved honesty. I take people for exactly what they are—what they are to me. Not what they are to anybody else. And if Patsy liked you, she loved you. If she didn't, she hated you. And she told you either way.

"On 'I Fall to Pieces,' after Harlan and Hank wrote it, I made the demo. They took it to Owen to get Brenda Lee to cut it, but Brenda didn't like it. Then Owen tried to get Roy to do it. And finally Owen made Patsy record it 'cause she didn't like it either. Let me be more definite. Patsy hated that song! She was adamant about not cutting it. There were some words flying between her and Owen. But he was just as adamant about her doing it.

" 'I hate that damn song!' she told me, knowing full well I was Harlan's wife. She said, 'I'm never gonna sing that thing.' Patsy liked the other side of the demo, 'Lovin' in Vain' by Freddie Hart.

"When I took it to Joe Johnson at Challenge Records, he

wouldn't let me record it. I told Freddie, 'Don't you worry. I'm gonna get you a record on this one.' I took it back to Patsy and she cut it. It was the B-side of 'I Fall to Pieces.'

"Patsy and Charlie came over to our house in Madison. She was pregnant with little Randy, but still working. They sat on one sofa talking to me, and Harlan and Hawkshaw sat on another sofa playing a hockey game in this big daylight basement our friends enjoyed hanging out in.

"She had just done the session and was going off to Louisville, Kentucky, for a fair date. She had not been singing 'I Fall to Pieces.' She was doing 'Lovin' in Vain.' Patsy said, 'Guess I'm going to have to get to work fast learning that damn song. I'm gonna have to start singing 'I Fall to Pieces.' I don't like it, so I never have even learned it. And now I got to do it tomorrow.'

"Harlan didn't bat an eye. He didn't care what she thought of the song, as long as she recorded it. When it started going up the charts, Harlan got excited one night when he was looking at Billboard and said, ' I bet Patsy'll start liking it now!' "

"Patsy was not always easy to get along with," laughed Owen Bradley. "No, sir. She was the high-strung type, constantly on guard and ready to show you who was boss. She was, of course! Well, to hear her tell it, anyway. You wouldn't have to tell Patsy anything about this women's lib business. I do believe she could have taught them a thing or two. I soon discovered that [in the studio] I had to place myself firmly in control or she'd just take right over.

"Oh, she could drive you nuts. No matter what I'd do, I couldn't please her. She'd start in on me and then have Charlie bug me. She'd tell me, 'Owen, I want to do it this way,' or she'd send Charlie over if she wasn't speaking, and he'd say, 'Owen, Patsy thinks it ought to be done like this.'

"But I never showed weakness. That would have been all she needed! Finally she'd listen to me. I kidded her that she was responsible for my first gray hairs. Patsy could be something else when she was trying to get her way.

"It was 'Owen, honey,' then 'Owen, please,' and when she got desperate it was 'Hoss, damn it!' But I had the same reply for her, 'No, Patsy! No!' Well, every once in a while I'd try and keep her happy by saying 'maybe.' After we got a hit with

'I Fall to Pieces' in April 1961, I said to her, 'I hope y'all will leave me alone for a while now!' And Patsy, Charlie, and me all laughed."

Don Helms, Hank Williams' steel guitarist who played on Patsy's sessions, does not ever "remember the situation between Patsy and Owen getting violent or belligerent. She was on the I-know-what-I-want side, but I respected that. Patsy was picky about what she wanted. She couldn't read music but she had her own ideas about tempos and arrangements.

"Patsy could be stubborn, especially when she had her mind made up on how she saw something. I'd have to say, and I guess it might be a bit embarrassing, but I think—personal opinion—she was usually right. However, no one envied Owen. He began as musical director but, more and more, Paul Cohen left things up to him and was in actuality the producer. Patsy and Owen had friendly disagreements.

"She'd just stop right in the middle of everything and say, 'What is this? What's he doing? Y'all wait a goddamn minute while I have a little *discussion* with *Mr.* Bradley!' But it was never anything that couldn't be ironed out."

Bass fiddler Lightnin' Chance recalls "Patsy giving Owen a hard time constantly. He stood up to her pretty well. Owen had this unique ability of doing it tactfully—until it got right down to the nitty-gritty, and then he let Patsy or whomever know who wore the pants in the studio.

"When it came to producing, Owen was smart. He kept Patsy selling records by keeping her mad. He must have known what he was doing. Whatever, it sure as hell worked. I'm talking voice control and the elements that make it up. That bitterness that came out in Patsy's voice because of inflection. Inflection comes over a mike, you know.

"I knew Patsy since before she came to Nashville. We met when I was working the road with Red Foley in Virginia. Later I did some freelance work for Ernest Tubb. I'll never forget Patsy following us around, always wanting to be on the shows. It seemed to me that Patsy was a hurt individual.

"She was hurting on the inside. This is not, you know, the Gospel but just what I observed from my roost. It seemed that Patsy had quite a guilt complex about leaving her first husband in order to be in the music business. And, maybe, some of it went back into her early childhood when her father deserted the family. We got into this minutely on occasions. It was amazing what we could end up talking about in those Cadillac and Chrysler Imperial caravans going from date to date.

"To me, the secret behind her—and later Tammy Wynette— selling so well was that Patsy seemed to have lived literally or figuratively every note and every word of those songs she recorded. I know it was that way when we cut one of her earliest tracks, 'A Church, a Courtroom and Then Goodbye.' There was one line in the song—it's really the only line I remember, and the reason I do is because Patsy made cold chills run over several of us—that told of how she hated the sight of that courtroom where man-made laws push God's aside. When Patsy said that line, you could absolutely feel the hate and bitterness. It just gave me the shivers the way she read it. [In fact, at the time of recording the song, Patsy had not yet divorced Gerald Cline.] Because Patsy was so expressive, I think there was a guilt complex there somewhere. Patsy had a story to tell and nobody really ever knew what it was. If there were parallels in her music, she had a way of identifying with them.

Patsy could get mighty uptight on the sessions. She would smoke a lot, especially when we'd be listening to playbacks of the material. When she was really into it, then and when she was recording, she could light them damn cigarettes. But Patsy was such a dynamic personality, you never tended to harp on idiosyncrasies.

"She was a hell of an artist. I really like Patsy very much, sometimes in spite of herself. She was a showman and could really sell out. I kidded her by calling her 'leather lungs.' She had to be at least two-thirds lungs. I told her it came from smoking so much.

"Patsy was terribly moody. I always told Randy [Hughes, her manager], who was my business partner and best friend, 'Man, I wouldn't put up with her for thirty seconds! That's the meanest witch I ever saw!' She could be mean to Charlie when he was at the sessions. I didn't know whether she liked having him there or not, but he was there and if he was there it must have meant Patsy wanted him there.

"Sometimes she'd do things that were a little out of context of the situation. But usually he let them roll right off. Quite frankly, since I loved Patsy as a person and showman, I formed a mental block against a lot of things that happened.

"If she really got going, I'd always bug her by telling her

off. Oh, I was always picking at Patsy. I'd say, 'You mean bitch, how the hell can you do that?' She'd just scowl at me and after a while she'd side up to me and say, 'Why the hell don't you let me be mad when I want to?'

"Patsy was a person I adored, but, God, I didn't envy Charlie Dick at all—or Owen. We marveled at Owen's knack of keeping Patsy in tow. I didn't cut many records with Patsy after she got big because Owen had his own group of musicians. I remember Patsy wanting to yodel on those early sessions the way she would do on her dates in her cowgirl regalia.

"Owen didn't think it was commercial and if anyone knew what was commercial, it was Owen. Jimmie Rodgers had his day, and I think that was wonderful. Patsy'd slip it in occasionally, for no other reason than just to say to herself, 'Well, my ass, Owen's not controlling me.' It was a cat-and-mouse game, and Owen always ended up being top cat!

"But let's render unto Caesar the things that are Caesar's. Bill McCall discovered Patsy's real potential after Bill Peer groomed her. He was the one who took a chance and put Patsy under his wing, and, oh yes, he and Paul Cohen had a work agreement. Paul was smart. He was the man who trained Owen in the basics. Owen was Paul's right hand. Paul Cohen got a lot of credit, but that don't mean he did everything. If you follow me, it's not easy to see where Paul and Bill [McCall] left off and Owen took over. But I can tell you, Owen was the creator, the innovator."

No one gave it much thought at the time, but Owen Bradley's innovations on the "I Fall to Pieces" session would be trendsetting and mark a milestone in Country music.

"When we began that particular session," notes Bradley, "that's when we started letting the strings creep in. And it wasn't even intentional. We just thought it sounded nice on 'I Fall to Pieces.' Patsy liked a big, full sound, and she didn't care if that meant a lush string arrangement. We were walking a fine line between Country and pop for that time in the industry—pretty far ahead of the way things were being done."

Patsy was later to worry if the lush arrangements and big sound she enjoyed were taking her too far afield of Country and making her a pop entity. In many ways, Patsy wanted it all and this led to problems. In the studio she became a real thorn in Owen's side—a superb singer and stylist but nonetheless a thorn.

Charlie confirmed that Patsy could often be difficult and

hardheaded, not only around the studio but also around the house. "You didn't argue with her. When she had her mind set on doing something a specific way, that was it. Patsy couldn't read music. She played the piano by ear. But she knew her music better than any musician.

"I especially remember one instance. A song called 'I Love You So Much (It Hurts Me)' came on the radio. We had gotten nice and cozy and I nonchalantly said, 'Honey, why don't you sing that in your act?' She said, 'Well, maybe I will.' She got up and went to the piano. I named a chord for her. Patsy told me, 'You know I don't know chords, but let me give you a little by ear.'

"She played and then stopped when she hit a particular note. 'This key? Is that what you want?' I replied, 'No, A woman can't sing that note. It's too low.' She got her dander up. 'Oh, is that right? Well let me try.' And she did it—probably just to spite me! [Patsy was evidently enamored of the song. She recorded it at her next session.]

"Patsy was strong-willed, and liked having things done a certain way, but on the other hand she could be easy-going and very flexible. I've heard a lot of people say that Patsy was moody. Well, hell, we all have moods or we just ain't human."

Faron Young contracted Patsy and Jerry Reed for a U.S.O. tour of Hawaiian bases in the Fall of 1960. Just prior to leaving for Hawaii, Patsy, very much pregnant, was back in the Winchester-Brunswick area. In Brunswick she paid a visit to the Moose Club where she had worked for three years.

"Patsy was sitting in the back of the hall with Charlie," said Joseph Shewbridge, bass fiddler in the Peer band, "and Bill was trying to ignore her. Bill and Jenny had remarried and divorced, and Bill was married to Dolly Huffmiester, who was now singing with the band. The folks at the dances would really bug Bill about getting Patsy up to sing, but he'd say, 'She's relaxing. We really shouldn't bother her when she's trying to enjoy herself.' "

In fact, whenever Dolly was not around Bill would grudgingly ask Patsy to sing a number, but when Mrs. Peer was at the club she would get upset at the thought and tell Bill, "No! How the hell can you invite her to sing with you? I just don't think she ought to get up there with the band after the way she did you. Where is your pride?"

Melody Boy fiddler Roy Deyton observed, "When Patsy

first returned to the area and Bill was back with Jenny, he would only get her up with the band if Jenny was not around. Bill went off the deep end over Patsy, and Jenny took him back. Patsy played both Gerald and Bill along and, in the end, only she got what she wanted. Now, whenever Patsy would come back, no one who knew any of them could blame Dolly. In a way, Patsy made fools of them all. We didn't see why they had to be reminded of it."

The second Mrs. Peer, now Mrs. Charles Spiker, explained, "I thought a lot of Patsy Cline. She had a hard trip up the road. Patsy and I were good friends and I had lots of wonderful times with her. The only thing she ever did that I didn't approve of was the way Patsy treated Bill and didn't credit him for what he did for her.

"I know Patsy had been singing before she ever came to Bill's band, but he was the one who believed in all the things she said she could do. As far as singers go, Bill didn't think anybody could come close to Patsy—and he was right. Often he put his own career goals aside to help her. I know Patsy appreciated what he did do, but later, when it counted, she never said anything. Everywhere you go, you'll find people claiming they gave Patsy her first break. It was Bill. She knew that, and everyone that really counted knew it, too.

"Eventually, Bill and Patsy had a falling-out. He had been guiding her career and all, and she decided she knew better. Patsy used Bill, then ditched him. She let him help her until she could feel her own way, then she left. At one time I do know that Patsy cared a lot for Bill. She told me. Age was a problem. She was much younger then. And, you know, you'd really have had to know Patsy to understand this, maybe Bill taught her too much."

For the trip to Hawaii, Young noted Patsy and Jerry Reed received their expenses and $50 a night. "It was a wonderful trip and we all had a great time. Patsy had to see a hula show while she was there. We didn't hear the end of that! We played Pearl Harbor and the Marine Corps Air Station at Kaneohe and then did a couple of concerts in Honolulu at Kaiser's Dome [a part of the Hilton Hawaiian Village].

"Patsy did the sightseeing bit and she loved the autographing and picture-taking after the shows. I don't think I can recall Patsy saying no, when circumstances presented itself, to a fan who'd ask to have a picture taken with her. She seemed to get off on that.

"There's an incident I can't forget because I never

remembered Patsy being down when she was on stage—and here she had hundreds of screaming, yelling, applauding GIs. But at the Marine Base, Patsy came off stage after a song, real depressed. She was in tears. I couldn't understand what had gotten to her.

"When she was introducing 'Walkin' After Midnight,' she said 'Back when I was playing with Arthur Godfrey . . . ' She was boiling. 'They wouldn't even let me finish the sentence before they all started laughing and jeering! I'm not going back out there. Those ignorant sons-of-a-bitches took what I said wrong! To hell with them.'

"I took her into my arms and soothed her, 'Honey, don't think anything of it. A bunch of gyrenes! Shit! They're just having a good time at your expense. They didn't mean anything.' It took a while, but she went back out. She didn't have much of a choice. I asked those guys, 'Hey, you want to hear another number from Miss Patsy Cline?' They went wild. Patsy came out and sang and forgot all about what had happened."

On Saturday, January 21, 1961, Patsy was missed at the Grand Ole Opry. She was in the hospital giving birth to a boy, whom the couple named Randy. (Many people have claimed this was given in honor of Randy Hughes, Patsy's manager and friend, but Charlie claims the name came from Patsy's half-brother Randolph.)

Patsy and Charlie's marriage was constantly "on the rocks," and Patsy confided to intimates that she hoped the arrival of baby Randy would provide a stabilizing force in the couple's relationship. Part of the problem with the marriage was Patsy's unquenchable thirst for superstardom. She became a workaholic.

Randy Hughes never had to beg bookings for Patsy and now with the release of "I Fall to Pieces" on January 30, 1961, Patsy was in demand more than ever. And away from home more often than not.

With Charlie's late hours in the typesetting room at the Nashville Newspaper Printing Corporation, he would be asleep when Patsy was home and the kids were up and about. His job prevented him from joining Patsy on road trips. Charlie accompanied Patsy on Opry appearances and, with their coterie of friends, they would always adjoin to Tootsie's across the alley from the Ryman.

After the birth of Randy, Patsy again had weight-control nightmares. This is particularly obvious in her performance February 9, 1961, on "Country Style, U.S.A.," a syndicated television series produced by Al Gannaway for the Armed Services recruiting program. The series was filmed at Owen Bradley's quonset hut studio on Sixteenth Avenue South in Nashville.

Faron Young was the guest host for the show, which featured Patsy in a country-store setting singing "Walking After Midnight." She was so overweight, she looked bloated.

"I did all those Army shows," says Lightnin' Chance. "I recall that one with Patsy well because they brought in bolts and bolts of material and stacked them on a countertop. They had Patsy in this pleated gingham dress [it was done in wraparound apron style with over-the-shoulder straps]. I almost got whacked in the head by Patsy with one of those bolts of fabric. She didn't like it when I said, 'Well, hello! You look like you just got back from town selling eggs and milk.'

"It was more the dress that gave the appearance Patsy had gained about thirty pounds. She wasn't that much heavier. It was the rage back then to show a country girl in a gingham dress. I can't forget that they were always bringing in bales of hay for the programs. I said, 'Someday they'll do a Country show without a hayseed image.' "

Patsy wore a short, page-boy hairstyle and was overly made up. As has been stated, Patsy Cline was no candidate for beauty contests, but her photographs—in bordello-style dresses, gaudy costume jewelry—always topped off by a pair of dangly earrings, cowgirl outfits, horrible wigs, and an abundance of cosmetics—belied a most beguiling smile and the natural beauty this still young Shenandoah Valley girl was beginning to exude. In the cause of show business theatrics, Patsy, overlooking her assets of piercing brown eyes and soft, wavy brown hair, made herself look ugly.

Country Song Roundup was an early supporter of Patsy Cline, even when she was not on the charts. Here, in typical fan-magazine rhetoric, is a delightful description of Patsy: "She has an extrememly fine wardrobe which includes quality rather than quantity, because according to her views, 'one good dress makes more of an impression, and lasts longer, than three of lesser value.' She is very fortunate in being able to wear the 'quality' she believes in, and could perhaps even have 'quantity,' because her mother makes so many of the clothes the songstress looks so well in.

"Miss Cline's choice of a gown for social occasions is one with sleek lines, and with an eye always on shades best suited to her coloring, she's frequently seen in blue, not the darker tones, but rather blues of the light, pastel variety. She loves to wear gloves and has them to match most of her dresses, all of elbow length. The final touch is a bracelet or two, which she wears over the glove, and with the stole she prefers for protection against cool weather, the lady looks like something from a band box when she steps out for an evening.

"As one of her hobbies, she collects earrings, then goes out of her way to find bracelets to match them, and exactly opposite from the rich, simple lines of her dresses, her jewelry is of the 'sparkly' type, but again, in excellent taste because she doesn't 'overdress' with it, usually wearing only the bracelet and earrings.

"The ensembles she wears on-stage depend on the occasion and location. She has something in her wardrobe to answer every requirement—fringed costumes, full-skirted dresses with tight bodice, formal-type wear, and skirts and blouses. Slacks and blouses answer most of her at-home requirements, and one of her major concerns always is that everything must have that 'just pressed' look.

"In the make-up department Patsy perhaps does more with lipstick than any other cosmetic. She limits her use of rouge, powder and eye make-up, because she has a very lovely complexion and looks always as though she's just come back from a morning walk in the cool, spring air. She accentuates this look by applying her lipstick brightly and liberally, and makes certain it remains that way with frequent retouches.

"Patsy wears her dark hair softly waved and curled, combed away from her face. She has no set rule for washing it, except to do it as frequently as needed. But one rule she does follow rigidly, is the hundred daily strokes, and it shows, because Miss Patsy's hair sparkles as brightly as her earrings.

"Shoes are one of her weaknesses, and there she goes overboard, possessing the kind with straps, without, backless, high heels, low heels, and any other types that appear as the current fashion. But there she's careful, too, by wearing shoes to match her ensemble."

"With 'I Fall to Pieces,' " pronounced Owen Bradley, "sales zoomed in both the Country and pop markets so, I guess, we were having our cake and eating it, too. It was a smash everywhere in the nation, with one glaring exception. It didn't do well in New York City. That was the funny thing. The Decca headquarters had their pop sound from Patsy and yet couldn't bring it in on their homeground. After that, Sidney Goldberg and the others left us alone.

"When we had finished the session in November nineteen-sixty, Patsy came to me and said, 'I think I've found out who I am and what we've been looking for.' I told her I didn't know what she was talking about. 'We don't have to search for my identity anymore,' she said. 'This is it! We're doing it right.' As she went to walk away, she turned and winked, then blurted a reference to what the New York office had said earlier, 'And, after all, if we don't do well, we can *always* go back to selling ten to fifteen thousand copies!'

"Around the time 'Pieces' was at the top of the charts, Patsy was overjoyed. 'Well, *we* finally did it!' I was thankful she included me—well, at least, I think she was. She was just a smiling from ear to ear. She told me, 'I never want to record again. I want to enjoy this one song forever!'

"When she sat down and we were reminiscing, Patsy fumbled around for a moment. I could tell she wanted to get something off her chest. 'You know something, Owen,' she said real solemnly, 'really I have to tell you the truth. I still don't care for "Pieces." It's the B-side I like.'

"Well, I decided if this was true-confessions time and she could still feel that way when the song was a smash, I'd level with her, too. I said, 'Hon, if I tell you something, will you promise not to throw anything at me?' She replied, 'Yeah, sure.' I told her, 'If you want to know the truth, after we started working with it, I really didn't like it either!' And we both just sat there and laughed."

"I Fall to Pieces" was slow to take off until Hal Smith, president of Pamper Music, for whom Hank Cochran and Harlan Howard worked, hired promotion man Pat Nelson to work the road and get the disk jockeys on it. Nelson pointed out what a radical departure the song was for Patsy, and to pop stations he noted what a radical departure the song was for a Country artist. It was the first time a record had been so pitched to the all-important radio stations. As a result, momentum built on two levels.

When the song reached the Top 40, Patsy placed an ad in which she stated: "I have tried and I have tried but I haven't yet found a way to thank so many wonderful people for so much." A writer, interviewing Patsy after a WSM-TV Country music program, was so impressed that he wrote, "Patsy Cline comes over like Ava Gardner, Marilyn Monroe, and Gina Lollabrigida all rolled up in one!"

Patsy was being termed one of the nation's leading recording artists and was ranked in popularity among young people with Jimmy Darren, Leroy Van Dyke, and Bobby Vee.

During the period "I Fall to Pieces" was at the top of the charts, Patsy returned home to appear live at the Winchester Drive-In Theatre on Route 11, north of town. Admission was 75 cents. She was accompanied by disk jockey "Joltin' Jim" McCoy and his group, the Melody Playboys. The highlight of the evening came when Patsy sang her big hit, but it seemed some portions of the house were stacked against her. Whereas there was a huge ovation of applause, there was a great deal of booing also.

"The mildew of envy permeated everywhere," said McCoy. "As in every town, you'll find jealousy. There were a lot of people in Winchester, sorry to say, who couldn't accept a hometown girl making it big. It was really sad. Way back when Patsy first came to see me at station WINC and did a little vocal bit for me, I knew, as soon as I heard her, that this gal meant business and that she was going to be a star. A year or two later, she had it. Patsy never forgot her roots. She always kept in touch, calling, writing. When times were tough she'd ask for just enough money to pay her expenses home so she could see her mother. We'd do shows at the Shenandoah County Fair at Mount Jackson and the drive-ins in Winchester and Harper's Ferry. The saddest thing about Patsy's success was that she never had a chance to enjoy the money she was beginning to make. She was killed when she was just starting to make the real big time."

A friend of Patsy's stated, "If the women booed Patsy at that drive-in appearance, it was because of a lot of things that had happened in town and in the area. It had gotten around about Patsy. There had been quite a few men in Patsy's life, and there were more than a few local women who didn't care one bit for her. So it wouldn't take me long to figure out who was doing the booing."

"I've never had a song that was a hit as long as 'I Fall to Pieces,' " remarked Harlan Howard. "It was Number One on the Country music trade charts on April ninth, nineteen sixty-one and it remained on the charts for thirty-nine weeks. It took a while, but by September Patsy had a Number 12 in the pop field, as well, and it remained on the trade magazine pop charts twenty weeks. That was unheard of for a Country tune.

"It was to have a great impact on my career, needless to say. From the songwriter's viewpoint, Patsy Cline was the greatest reader of lyrics that I've ever worked with. She understood that certain lines in a song are just there to be sung. They're not emotional lines. Patsy had the knack of being able to hold back on those lines, then when she got to the really juicy part of the song she would give it everything she had. Songwriters love that, because we know that, in order to write a song lyric, every word in the song can't be great. In every song you have certain lines that lead up to the best part. Patsy was the greatest at comprehending that. She really knew there was more to singing a song than just standing there and singing it.

"My favorite record by Patsy was a tune I didn't write. That was 'Crazy' by Willie Nelson. That song, in particular, proves what I'm talking about. It was unbelievable what Patsy did with it. Hank [Cochran], Willie, and I were Patsy's buddies. It wasn't like we were writers and she was just a singer we wanted to get to. There was a bond there. So we gave her the best songs we had. Every three months or so it was kinda dog-eat-dog among us as to which one of us would have the best song for her. She was quite demanding. Patsy wouldn't settle for just any ole song. Oh, no! It had to be your best shot."

Dottie West remembers the heated competition to come up with hits for Patsy. "I met Patsy backstage at the Opry just after I moved to Nashville in nineteen sixty-one. I went right up to her and said, 'Hello, I'm Dottie West.' She replied in that kind of high and mighty voice of hers, 'Oh, you are!'

" 'Yes,' I answered, 'and I want to thank you for that letter you wrote me.' Patsy looked at me and said, 'Well, you are welcome. What letter?' I told her that after I first heard 'Walkin' After Midnight' I wrote her telling what a big fan I was, and that she sent me back a real nice reply.

"I reminded Patsy that she wrote 'If you ever get to Winchester, I hope we can meet.' 'Well, here we are both in Nashville now,' I told her. 'Ain't it the truth,' she told me. 'Are you a singer, too?' I told her I was making records and she was very interested and supportive of me. In a matter of a few minutes, it was like we were old friends.

"Patsy invited me over to her house and before you knew it we were visiting and calling each other as soon as we'd come in off the road. I wasn't that busy, to say the least, in those days and sometimes I'd go out on the road dates with Patsy.

"I wasn't out singing with Patsy. I'd help her with her wardrobe. We enjoyed each other's company so much and, by watching her, I was able to learn so much. My ex-husband, Bill [West] worked with Patsy off and on, playing steel guitar, and Patsy would invite me to tag along. We'd go from date to date in this big Cadillac. Sometimes, when he could, Charlie would go with us and drive, but, oh, boy, could that Patsy drive that car. I remember on one tour, Roy Orbison was holding on for dear life in the back seat. Patsy was a daredevil behind the wheel.

"In Nashville, I was at Patsy and Charlie's in Madison a few times when Hank would come over after finishing a song that he thought was right for Patsy. He'd run in and throw his arms around Patsy and say, 'Hoss, forget those others. I've done it! I've done it again! I've written you a smash.' They'd go all through the house, upstairs, downstairs, as Hank would tell her about the new number.

"Hank would follow Patsy with his guitar as she'd be cleaning house or cooking and he'd be telling her, 'It's a great one! One of the best I've ever written.' She'd tell him, 'Well, cut the b.s., hoss, and let's hear the damn thing.'

"Sometimes Harlan and Willie would be breathing down their necks trying to get Patsy to listen to their material. A lot of people have forgotten, but with 'I Fall to Pieces,' Patsy became the premiere female Country vocalist after Kitty [Wells] and their recording styles were totally different so there was no heated competition between them for songs.

"Hank and Harlan knew a good Patsy Cline song when they finished one. They really liked Patsy and respected her talent, so they'd sit down—together and separately—and with her in mind, they'd write something really strong. The only time I can recall them disagreeing was on 'I Fall to Pieces.' She didn't want to record it until Roy Drusky turned it down. And Patsy might have said yes to Owen just so Roy couldn't have it if he changed his mind later."

"Patsy was never a selfish person with only her interests at heart," recollected Mrs. Hensley, "She did a song, 'Come on In,' that pretty well summed up her life. Patsy was a good-hearted soul and never knew the meaning of the word 'no.' As a child she'd bring friends home from school to play and insist that they stay and eat supper with us. Our doors were never closed. That's the type of home I believed in having and this certainly carried over into Patsy's life in Nashville."

Del Wood indicated that "Patsy and her sister and brother seemed to have had a normal, happy home life in spite of their father's absence. Patsy's mother was not an uneducated woman. She was also quite attractive, and I think Patsy favored her a lot. Not only in looks but also in outlook. She spoke of her mom always being ready to lend a helping hand whenever it was needed, whether they knew the people or not. This must have influenced Patsy a great deal.

"Patsy's heart, home, and wallet were always open. She especially wanted to do for her mom. She regretted that while her mother helped make her life such a good one, hers suffered. At that time Patsy and I were in the same boat, so to speak, as far as our marriages went, so we understood better what Mrs. Hensley had gone through raising Patsy, Sylvia, and Sam alone."

Pearl Butler laughed and then pointed out, "Honey, if you want to talk about what a thoughtful, compassionate person Patsy was we'll be here all day. To put it simply, she was an easy touch. No, people didn't take advantage of her. I would have like to have seen that. She'd know. But anyone in trouble or need—all they had to do was go see Patsy and she was there with either a good word or a helping hand.

"At home, nothing meant more to Patsy than those kids. She had two, and told me she thought that was enough. Patsy was always thinking of their future. She talked of setting up trust funds for them in case something happened to her. More than anything, it just killed her to leave Julie and Randy behind when she went on the road. They had to be the most spoiled babies in town. No matter where we'd be, Patsy'd go shopping to buy them something. She had her hands full at home, if you know what I mean, but, oh, she loved those babies. At night, driving from date to date, she'd make Carl pull over when she saw a phone. Patsy would say, 'I've got to call my babies and go the the bathroom—in that order!' "

Of Patsy's giving nature, Dottie West said, "I could not begin to relate the number of times Patsy helped people in and out of the business. Patsy loved fancy cars and one of the first things she did was get herself the biggest, whitest Cadillac she could order [actually, it was a used Cadillac]. She loved expensive clothes and jewelry, especially those dangling earrings. But Patsy did not think only of herself, and her generosity became fairly legend in Music City.

"She had a most generous temperament even in the period before she was really making any money. Patsy thought nothing of going to the supermarket and buying a couple of bagfuls of groceries and dropping them off to someone who needed them. If there were kids involved, she was especially thoughtful. And she was constantly giving away clothes. And money!

"None of us girl singers—Jan, Brenda, and, later on, Loretta—were working that much. Patsy was the hottest thing going with 'I Fall to Pieces.' She loved to cook. Patsy could make the greatest stuffing for pork chops, country ham, and fantastic mashed potatoes—just good country cooking. I used to ask her, 'How do you make your mashed potatoes taste so good?' She'd say, 'Well, kid, the secret is in how you mash 'em.'

"Patsy'd have us all over all the time. We'd have our little hen parties while the men gabbed and drank beer. I guess we thought of Brenda as more of a sister, but I looked up to her like a big star. The three or four of us would get together and talk shop. And laugh a lot. That Brenda was so cute and tiny—and, oh, what a personality! A youngster, but so grown-up."

Brenda Lee, Patsy's friend from the time she rescued Brenda and her mother when they were stranded in Texas, gives her impression of Patsy. "From the time Julie was about two, when Patsy and Charlie first moved to Nashville, I used to go over to their house in East Nashville, across the Cumberland River. It was real cute but tiny. Patsy was always saying, 'One of these days, hon, I'm gonna have me a real house.'

"Patsy had things everywhere. Not strewn around. She was neat. She just didn't have any room. It was like she was a pack rat waiting for the day she could move to bigger quarters. She'd get things and didn't have a place for them.

"If I must say so, Patsy had strange taste—to me, that is. She'd go out shopping and one day she'd bring back something that was as fine as could be. And another time she'd come back with something just as kitsch as heck. Didn't matter to her. She loved them.

"Either Patsy would come and pick me up or my mom would take me over there. Patsy was big on costume jewelry and I used to love to play in her jewelry box and walk around n those high heels of hers.

"Patsy liked being domestic. She was like I am now. She liked cooking but she wasn't the type who'd throw something together in an hour. If she had all day to do it right, she'd do it. She was just as much a perfectionist on that as she was on everything else.

"We had a good relationship and became close. Sometimes Dottie West would be over and we'd help Patsy with Julie or help her in the kitchen. And when I'd go over, Patsy and I would sing. I'd listen to her and she'd listen to me and then we'd both sing together. I'd ask her things about how she did certain things and vice-versa. Both of us sort of had the little hiccup thing—you know, our voice would crack on a certain note—and that growl effect that was often called yodeling.

"Patsy could yodel up a storm and I envied her that because I couldn't yodel at all. It was my dream. She tried to teach me, but I was a lost cause. Patsy wouldn't give up, but it was no use. She wanted to do it on her records except ole Owen wouldn't hear of it. Patsy'd yodel on her live dates, but except for that time in Texas, I never got to see her perform.

"Those were my formative years and Patsy had a big influence on me. It was wonderful, as I look back now, to be involved with someone like Patsy who was unique. Most people would not have bothered with a youngster. Patsy was so unselfish and not the least bit envious of anyone else. She didn't mind their successes. That was a good impression on me. I think, unconsciously, a lot of Patsy rubbed off on me. We had similarities in that we had both been working since we were quite young.

"People have said that Patsy was hard to get along with and difficult to work with, but I never saw that side of her. I've heard she was bitchy, but she wasn't. In the studio, she might not have always been easy to handle, but Patsy knew her music and what effect she wanted. She would try and communicate what she felt to the musicians and Owen.

"I was the same way. We were both perfectionists there, too. Owen and I never had problems. He tells me that when I was about fourteen he had to stop everything to tell me how to sing a line and that I got upset and told him, 'I don't tell you how to turn your knobs [on the mixing console], so don't tell me how to sing.' Owen said that from that minute on, he never did. He was far ahead of his time. I learned much from him, too. I had two good teachers.

"I learned some other things from Patsy, also—a few unusual words. I wouldn't say Patsy was rated X, but she would come in under an R! I don't mean that in a detrimental way, because Patsy was Patsy. She'd say just what she thought. She was honest and blunt.

"When I was on the road as a kid with Faron, Mel Tillis, and George Jones, they'd tell me jokes—none of which I understood. Then they'd say, 'Hey, Brenda, go tell so-and-so that.' I'd go up to whomever it was and tell the joke and they'd say, 'Lord, all that coming out of that kid's mouth.' Well, Faron, Mel, and George just thought it was downright funny.

"When Patsy cursed, I don't think anyone got offended because it was just her mode of talking. She didn't mean to be vulgar or common. I remember we used to wonder who on earth in her family she took after! But she didn't. She was just Patsy.

"Patsy was the most generous person you'd ever want to meet. I liked her so much more because of what she did for people. She did such a lot for Dottie, Loretta, Hank, Roger [Miller], and Barbara [Mandrell]. Patsy started out young. Her mother would take her everywhere so she could perform. She begged to be on shows when no one would halfway give her a break. So, I think, because of that she had a heart as big as the world. Patsy'd give you the shirt off her back. She really would.

"I loved her so dearly, and when she had Julie I said, 'Patsy, if I ever have a little girl, I'm gonna name her Julie after your little girl 'cause I love you so much.' She'd answer me, 'Oh, you will not!' and I'd retort, 'Yes, I am. You wait and see.' She didn't wait to see, but I did. Every once in a while I find myself crying when I stop to think about Patsy and the wonderful times we had. It was really so unfair. She was a real good girl. . . . "

Patsy's generosity and down-home nature gave way to the forming of a Country music clique that included Dottie and Bill West, Hank Cochran, sometimes Willie Nelson, Donnie Young (later named Johnny Paycheck), Roger Miller, Justin Tubb (Ernest's son), eventually Loretta and Mooney Lynn, and Ann Whiten (now Ann Tant, the director of promotion for Warner Bros. Records in Atlanta).

"I met Pat while I was talent coordinator of the 'Saturday Dixie Jubilee,' " said Ann. "This was an Atlanta based Grand Ole Opry-type show with Nashville guests and local talent—Jack Greene, Joe South, Ray Stevens, and Jerry Reed. Pat and Charlie would drive to Atlanta often starting in nineteen fifty-nine in their big, white Cadillac. Pat loved to laugh and all of us enjoyed a good time so there was never a dull moment backstage.

"Paul Strickland, a Jubilee producer with George Stromatt, adored Pat. He ran a company called S and M Sales—the name used to make Pat laugh and she'd kid Paul all the time—that carried novelty items. He gave Pat this cigarette lighter emblazoned with the Confederate flag. It was also a music box that played 'Dixie.' It became one of her treasured possessions. How she loved to go up to some unsuspecting soul and light their cigarette.

"Pat and I became good buddies so when I moved to Nashville in nineteen sixty-one to work for Mercury Records she was one of the first persons I contacted. It wasn't long before I was a member in good standing in the clique.

"Every Friday night after the WSM Friday Night Frolics and every Saturday after the Opry at the Ryman and half the nights during the week we'd stole into Tootsie's Orchid Lounge for a fun time. Tootsie was a wonderful lady with great gusto and a heart as big as all outdoors. It was no wonder she and Pat got on so famously. Tootsie kept us all together. She didn't know how to say no. She kept IOUs on half of us. I remember when Roger made it big, he gave Tootsie this huge freezer for all the IOUs she had on him. She busted out crying. We'd go in there for drinks and to eat. Tootsie had this great cook named Maggie who made the most wonderful red beans and cornbread.

"During the week we'd sit downstairs right up in the front, but weekends, when the upstairs artists' lounge or back room [with an alley level entrance that gave convenient entry from the rear of the Opry] was open, we'd be there. We'd often carry the party over to Sunday. It was nothing big—we couldn't afford that. Just hanging out."

Roger Miller commented on his friendship with Patsy, dating back from the days he was the drummer in the Country Deputies, Faron Young's band, and the clique.

"I was Patsy's friend because I amused her. She was a loner

of sorts. She didn't have a lot of close, close friends. I was a musician and I was a writer—one unlike any other in Nashville. Patsy thought my music was unique and wonderful and all that, and, of course, I agreed with her. That made two of us.

"Patsy was one of the first who appreciated what I could do. She wasn't making predictions for the future for me. I was just a musician she thought was pretty amazing for some reason. She thought the same of Doug Kershaw.

"I had been doing okay as a writer and had a couple of records that had done fair, but Patsy was a star. At that time there was a distance between writers and musicians and the so-called stars, but Patsy was not like that. She loved good talent and was a friend to all of us. She didn't have any head problems. Patsy always seemed to know where she was going!

"Patsy and I were not intimates. I was just a clown and made her laugh. I made everyone laugh, but Patsy's laugh was the greatest. It was a wild, raucous thing. Anytime anyone would ask Patsy Cline what she thought of Roger Miller or just mention my name to her, she'd throw her head back and laugh.

"She was the type who'd do anything for you. She didn't know the meaning of 'in harm's way.' A bunch of guys went into Juarez [Mexico] after a date in El Paso. Over there they bought a little grass and started to worry about how to get it back across the border.

"Patsy was too much. I don't think anything scared her. She said, 'What the hell y'all worried about when you got Patsy here? Give me that stuff. I'll take care of it.' And she did. She grabbed it and stuck it down her bra as a favor. She was one of us. Patsy didn't hold herself apart.

"The clique, as everybody started to call us, would gather at Dottie and Bill's house out on Highway Sixty-five across the Cumberland River. There was no bridge so we had to take a ferry to get over there. They didn't have any money. They just had a house. It was a place to get together. I remember Dottie clipped things out of *House Beautiful* and would say, 'Someday when I have money, I'd like to have a house like this one, or this one, or this one.'

"I looked over at this big scrapbook she had already compiled and I said, 'Well, honey, make up your mind soon or you're gonna be an architect's nightmare.' And Patsy chimed in, 'Or mother lode!'

"We loved to have picnics. They had this big porch with a swing and we'd all sit around sipping drinks and talking shop. Dottie was taking care of her kids. They were just toddlers. The girls would go crazy over those children. There was a comraderie then that you don't see much today. It was just a few writers and singers and one or two others we let in because they were in the business and we liked them.

"Sometimes Harlan and Jan [Howard] would come and be with us, but they kinda kept to themselves or ran with the Carter clan, Mother Maybelle's daughters, Helen, Anita, and June [now Mrs. Johnny Cash].

"Patsy, Charlie, and me were always the life of the party. Oh, Patsy and Charlie had some ups and downs, but nothing that much for the public to know. They were getting along pretty well at the time. Now that Charlie could get a bit rowdy when he was drinking. But I don't know what that entailed."

Dottie West cannot forget Tootsie's. "We loved to go there, if for no other reason than to have Maggie's luscious hamburgers and chili. With Tootsie keeping IOUs, we could have a good time no matter who was working and who was not. Even though we were appearing on the Opry, no one of us was making big money. You only got fourteen dollars a night in those days.

"We couldn't get out the back door of the Ryman fast enough—Patsy, Charlie, Bill and I, and all the gang—to get over to Tootsie's. As soon as she saw us, she'd send the drinks over, especially to Charlie. I bet that Tootsie had more IOUs on Charlie Dick than anybody. Now, Tootsie was another lady you didn't mess with. Charlie and a lot of others found that out.

"When Tootsie was ready to close, if the guys who'd had a little too much to drink wouldn't leave when she'd holler, she'd go around and jab 'em right in the rear with a hatpin. They'd jump, saying, 'Goodnight, Miss Tootsie!' just as she was saying 'Closing time!' I bet Tootsie used that hatpin of hers on Charlie more than anyone. When Charlie'd say he enjoyed a beer now and then, I'd razz him, 'And you've got the wounds to prove it.' "

It is easy to see the fierce loyalty Patsy generated among her peers. Loyalty was not uncharacteristic among her fans. Here is an engrossing replay of Patsy's visit with a not untypical fan, Mrs. Louise Everett Seger, formerly of Jackson, Mississippi, then and now of Houston, Texas.

"The first time I heard Patsy Cline sing she was in my living room and I was in the kitchen. That was January nineteen fifty-seven. I was not a big Arthur Godfrey fan, but my two kids, Donna and David, who were five and three, were. They watched 'Arthur Godfrey Time' every morning, while I was usually doing the breakfast dishes. We had a big Muntz black and white. The kids would lie with their feet underneath it, staring straight up.

"This particular morning, subconsciously, I was listening to the program. All of a sudden I heard a voice that absolutely stopped me in my tracks. I said, 'My god, that sounds like I've always wanted to sing. And I threw the forks and spoons into the sink and I went tearing off into the living room. I said, 'Get out of the way, kids!'

"And there stood this chunky little girl, leaning back and just leading into 'Walkin' After Midnight.' And I have never heard a voice that impressed me so. She was probably on Godfrey's morning show at least a week, and every morning found me and the kids right in front of that TV. One morning Godfrey said, 'Here's a little girl from Virginia that I think you people are going to be hearing a lot from.' Then she dropped out of sight, but I never forgot the voice and I never forgot the feeling it gave me.

"By nineteen sixty-one I was divorced and had taken a job as an electronics technician, and the man I worked for loved Country music. He kept a radio in the lab and it always stayed tuned to KIKK, one of our better-known Country stations. Again, I was doing my work and subconsciously listening to the radio. I heard *that* voice again and I absolutely stopped in my tracks. The announcer didn't say who it was, so I called the station and asked. They told me, 'That was Patsy Cline singing "I Fall to Pieces.' I said, 'My god, that's the same kid I saw on Arthur Godfrey.' I talked to Hal Harris, the disk jockey, while he was on the air, and told him, 'You play that song again.' And he played it for me.

"Patsy's music made me feel alive everytime I heard it. I worried that poor man to death. I would call him on an average of four or five times an afternoon. He'd play 'I Fall to Pieces' and say, 'Louise, I just played your song.' I'd call him and say, 'Well, turn her over and play the other side ["Lovin' in Vain"], and then, in an hour, play *my* song again.' I did this to that poor man for about two months. He thought I was a bit screwy to be so wrapped up in Patsy 'cause I never asked for anybody else. One day when I called in my request, Hal said, 'Incidentally, she's coming to town.'

"I said, 'What?' Hal replied, 'That's right. She's supposed to be at the Esquire Ballroom next Friday.' The Esquire, out on the Hempstead Highway, was a gigantic barn, similar to Gilley's now. It was to be on May twelfth and I told the guy I was dating, 'Patsy Cline is coming to town. We're going.' He asked, 'Who's Patsy Cline?' I told him, 'Never mind. You'll find out.' My boss said, 'I kinda like her. I wouldn't mind going.' I said, 'Great. I'll phone and make reservations.'

"I found out you just go stomping in and find a table, so I informed the group, 'We're just gonna be there early. We're wearing our western clothes and we're going to be there at six-thirty.' My friend said, 'But, Louise, the band doesn't get there until eight.' I said, 'But we're going to be there at six-thirty.' I wore my yellow cowgirl boots and my black and yellow cowgirl skirt and we went in what I called my 'sexy dude,' my pink and black Pontiac.

"There wasn't another car in the parking lot. Four acres of blankness! I told 'em, 'Well, I got a good place to park!' We walked in and they were still cleaning the place. Except for the folks at the bar, the ballroom was empty. We went tromping in and you could hear our boots holler. It was that empty! I dragged them right up to the edge of the bandstand. My boss said, 'Goddamn, Louise, you won't be able to hear yourself talk.' I told him, 'Now, look, we didn't come here to hear ourselves talk. We came to hear Patsy Cline.'

"Around a quarter to seven, when we were engrossed in beer talk, I looked up and saw this girl walk in quite a distance away. She stood around looking at the place—up at the ceiling, at the walls, down at the bandstand. Something in my mind went ding-ding-ding. She had on a tan-colored raincoat and white high-heeled pumps. I thought maybe this was an agent—I didn't know who the hell it was giving the place the once over.

"She walked across the dance floor and took a table about three over from us. Nobody else even noticed her. I kept watching her. She removed her raincoat and put it across the back of the chair. She had on a pink, two-piece, cotton suit. As I watched her it seemed our minds were talking to each other.

"It seemed like she was saying, 'I'm Patsy Cline. Who are you?' I punched the bunch and said, 'Do you know what that is at that table?' and they looked over and said, 'No, Louise, who is it?' I told them, 'That is Patsy Cline.' They replied, 'Oh, hell, don't be foolish. That can't be. The band doesn't get here until eight.' I watched her for a few minutes more and my heart told me I was right. I said, 'Well, just a minute.' My date and my boss and his date said, 'Louise, for God's sake, don't go over there and make a fool of yourself.' I told them, 'A fool I'll always be!'

"I walked up to her and said, 'Excuse me. Miss Cline?' She had a big smile and said, 'Yes?' I told her, 'My name is Louise Seger and I just wanted you to know how much I admire your music. I have "I Fall to Pieces" played for me everyday. I have some friends here who are also fans of yours. If you have time, I'd like you to come meet them.' She replied, 'Well, why can't I just come over and sit with y'all?' I answered, 'God, we'd love to have you!' And Patsy was just as us as we were.

"My friends nearly fell out of their chairs. Patsy ordered a Schlitz and we were talking like old friends. She was not a stranger to us. Patsy remarked, 'This is a damn big place, isn't it?' I answered, 'Yes, m'am, but boy it's gonna be packed.' She was a m'am to me. Patsy was a star. In my mind, the biggest star in the world! That was the beginning of the evening. Before it was over, it was 'Hey, gal.' We shared every secret either one of us ever had.

"Patsy wanted to know what the band was like, and I told her I didn't know a lot about them. She said, 'I'm worried. I don't know them. Do they know my music?' I answered, 'They must!'

"She said, 'I don't know. Do you know my music?' I told her, 'Yes, m'am, every word and beat of it.' Patsy asked, 'I wonder if you'd do me a favor then.' I said, 'Of course, what's that?' She wanted me to stand by the drummer during the show so he wouldn't rush her. 'He's the one who can really mess me up. If you know the tempo, you can tell him when he's rushing me.' I told her, 'I sure could.' She seemed greatly relieved."

Louise Seger recalled the remainder of the evening as follows.

"How long are you gonna be on?" Louise asked Patsy.

"I guess, I'll start when the band does and go to closing."

"You mean you're gonna be up there the whole time?"

"Well, I guess so."

"Are you traveling by yourself?"

"Yes, This is the first time I've been out on the road since my baby boy was born in January."

"If you don't mind my asking, how much are they paying you for tonight?"

"Three hundred and fifty dollars."

"Wait a minute. You got a hit record and you're gonna stand up on that stage and sing straight through for four hours with only a fifteen-minute intermission?"

"Nobody's told me anything."

"You just come with me."

"Louise," said her boss, "please don't make a fool of yourself!"

"Hell, my dad was a musician and I know a bit about these things."

Louise took Patsy by the elbow and marched up to see the night manager.

"Hello. I'm Louise Seger and this is Miss Patsy Cline. I'm representing her. I'd like to know the times you have Miss Cline scheduled for."

"Well, the band starts at eight," he said.

"Yes, but what times do you have Miss Cline scheduled? We figured two shows would be about right."

"Well, O.K., I guess probably a show at nine-thirty and eleven-thirty will be fine."

Lousie explained, "Look, I loved this gal and I wanted to talk to her. I couldn't let these people have her all night!"

Patsy and Louise returned to the table laughing. When the band arrived, Patsy went to meet them and distribute her music. When the show began, Louise did as planned.

"I just sort of tapped my foot and if the drummer started to rush Patsy, I'd reached over and with my fingers snap the rhythm she was accustomed to."

Patsy brought down the house, and the ballroom filled with screaming and yelling. After the show Patsy signed autographs and posed for pictures.

"Well, Louise, it's been nice but I better be getting back to the hotel. I have an eight o'clock flight to Dallas in the morning."

"How the heck did you get out here?"

"I came by taxi. I don't know anything about Houston and I had no other way."

"Where are you staying?"

"The Montague, where most of the acts stay when they play here."

"I can't believe Decca sent you on the road by yourself. You'll never get a taxi out here. We'll get you back, but first we're going to my house and have bacon and eggs."

"I'd love that!"

Patsy picked up her money and joined the others in Louise's Pontiac. At Mrs. Seger's, Patsy helped fry the bacon and eggs.

"She had on one of my aprons so she wouldn't get grease on her suit. We were there cooking and chattering away. It was like having the sister I never had. I had long since stopped the 'm'am' bit. Patsy was only eleven days older than me."

After breakfast, the babysitter left, David was put to bed, and the others left, Patsy and Louise sat at the kitchen table "and poured our hearts out sounding like two people writing Country songs. We talked about broken hearts, husband problems, children, loves lost, loves won—everything."

"Louise, where's your little girl?"

"Oh, she's spending the night with a friend."

"It must be tough raising two kids when you're divorced and working."

"Yes, it is. Tough and crazy!"

"I've been through it all. Charlie and I ain't getting along too well at all right now. His name is Charlie Dick and he is one! But I love my kids. They mean everything in the world to me. I'll stay with him just as long as I can for no other reasons than that. I'd love to leave him, but I don't have the guts. I always have to go to him."

Patsy told Louise of knock-down, drag-out fights she and Charlie had.

"Lots of times he bruised me up so bad I've had to work with my face or a black eye all covered up with makeup. I get so mad at him sometimes, I'd like to throw a skillet at him! But I'm afraid I'll break it! I'll go to pick up something and say, 'Oh, no. I just bought that.' "

They traded stories until almost four.

"Gee, Louise, it's late and I've got a plane to catch at eight."

"Patsy, I can never tell you what this night has meant. But, hey, since it's so late, why don't you just stay here? Mind getting up early? I've got a disk jockey friend who I know would want to interview you."

"Okay. Sure."

Louise called Hal Harris at his home. His wife answered, and then when Hal finally came on, Louise said, "Hey, I'm gonna bring Patsy Cline by for an interview in the morning."

"Oh, my God, Louise, what are you drinking?"

"Hal, I've got Patsy here at the house and she'll do an interview before she leaves for Dallas."

"Sure you do, Louise, and I've got Marilyn Monroe in bed with me. Now, honey, you go sleep it off and I'll play 'I Fall to Pieces' for you in the morning, which it appears to be already."

"Hal, Christ! I'm serious. She's sitting right here."

"I know you are, sweetie. Sure she is. Goodnight."

Louise went and told Patsy that everything was set.

"You can sleep in Donna's bed, if that's okay."

"I got nothing to sleep in."

"You ain't gonna be asleep that long, but I've got a pair of pajamas you can have."

Patsy changed and went to Donna's room.

"Hey, they look better on you than they do on me! They're usually too short for me. How tall are you?"

"Five-four and a half."

"Well, no wonder, I'm five-eight."

The alarm went off at five. Louise got up and called Hal at the station. He had just arrived.

"Damn, Louise, what are you doing still up? Did you go to bed?"

"Hal, fast, what's the oldest Patsy Cline record that you've got there?"

"Hell, I don't know. I'll look and see."

"Well, get an old one and play it next!"

"Louise, are you sober?"

"Yes, honey. Will you do that for me?"

"I guess I will if I want any peace for the rest of my life!"

"All right then."

Louise went into her children's room. David and Patsy were sound asleep. She turned the radio on between the beds with the volume low. When Hal began to spin the record, Louise turned the sound up loud. David remained asleep, but Patsy sat straight up in the bed.

"My god, what the hell is going on? Who is that?"

"Don't you know?"

"No, but she sure is loud."

"That's you, you fool!"

"My god, when did I ever record that?"

"I don't know, but Hal found it. Well, get dressed. We've got to hurry 'cause we've got to get downtown, get you packed, go out to the station, and then to the airport."

Louise and Patsy zipped through her room at the Montague. Patsy got dressed while Louise took things from all over—hair rollers, underwear, shoes—and literally threw them into Patsy's suitcase.

"Pack everything carefully."

"Carefully? Honey, it looks like a hurricane ran through here last night when you were getting dressed!"

Louise had on yellow western slacks, a yellow print western shirt, and cream-colored squaw boots. When Patsy came out, they could have passed for identical twins—only the colors were different. Patsy checked out, and the two headed toward the station in Pasadena on the Gulf Freeway.

They drove into the parking lot and there was one sports car sitting there. "Ah ha, you fool, are you in for a surprise!" Louise thought to herself. They went in the back door, which was left unlocked. Hal was in the control room in an old pair of Bermuda shorts, blue wool sweater that looked as if it had been washed and dried but never ironed, no socks, and tennis shoes with holes cut out for the toes.

"He wasn't shaved. He hadn't combed his hair. Everything looked thrown on. But there he was sounding very sexy on the radio at that hour and looking like death warmed over!"

Louise tapped on the window. Hal turned around, then did a double-take. He jumped up, came to the door, and was speechless.

"Hal Harris, I'd like you to meet Miss Patsy Cline. Patsy, this is the man who plays your music for me."

Louise put it very well when she said, "That man could have fallen through his asshole and hung himself!"

Harris was running around in circles. Then he went to the file, grabbed a record, and on the microphone said, "Ladies and gentlemen, I'm going to play a record for you by a young lady who was in town last night. And I have a big surprise for you. We have her here in the studio this morning. Here's Patsy Cline singing 'I Fall to Pieces.'"

After he started the record, Harris talked to Patsy, getting some statistics. Then they did a fifteen-minute interview. Hal said goodbye to Patsy and by 7:00 Louise had her on the way to the airport.

"Louise, I want your address. We're gonna keep in touch."

They exchanged addresses "but, like always, you figure that will be the end of that." Just as Patsy reached the top of the stairs of the ramp, she turned and waved goodbye to Louise.

"In less than two weeks I got the first in a long series of letters and phone calls from Patsy. That Country gal was a winner!"

Patsy's letter to Louise, dated May 29, 1961, from Nashville stated:

> Dear Louise and all:
>
> Wanted to take time to write a line or two to thank you folks for the nice way you treated this ole country gal while I was there. I sure do appreciate all you done, because if you hadn't been so nice I wouldn't have been able to go to the radio station. My sincere thanks and hope I can be as nice to you all sometime. Tell Hal "hello" for me.
>
> Hope this finds you well and things going great. As for me, the kids and myself are fine and hell is still a poppin' of course. Ha. Don't know how much longer I can stand this way of living, but the little ones always come first with me. Till then I'll grin and bear (sic) it. Ha.
>
> Now for the really big news. Well, I'm nearly up on the moon and didn't need a rocket. My record sold 10,000 in Detroit last week alone and is hitting all pop charts. It's #1 on both pop stations here in Nashville and is the #1 best seller at Decca and is already being put in 3 [premium] albums right away of different artists. I go to the 5 Star Jubilee [Friday nights, NBC-TV, Springfield, Missouri (Ozark Jubillee)] on July 7th, and it's in color. Swingin' huh? I think I told you I'm getting things in shape for the Dick Clark [show] but don't know the day yet. But I'll let you know.
>
> I'm going home next Tuesday and while there, they are proclaiming a Patsy Cline day in my home town. Ain't that a kick in the head? I wish they would just left it like it was, but I do appreciate the noise they are kicking up. So I guess I'll have to do what *they* want

that day. The mayor is gonna be there and recognize me and so on. Anyway, it sure is a good feeling. I can't really believe it.

Guess I'd better close and get busy with this ironing I've got here.

Be sure to kiss the boy for me. He sure is a doll and tell the couple that was there that night "hello" and I hope I didn't bore them with my troubles, and I think they are wonderful folks. I still want all of you to come down to see us and the Opry. So write soon and thanks again. (Dallas was a swingin' date.)

Hope to see you again soon.
Love and Luck,
Patsy Cline and Family

Then, in less than two weeks after receiving Patsy's letter, Louise was driving to work. As usual she had on KIKK, listening for Hal Harris to play her favorite Patsy Cline records. Instead she heard on the news broadcast that Patsy had been critically injured in an automobile accident in Nashville and was near death.

11
"Write Me in Care of the Blues"

Billy Walker: **"Patsy, let's bow our heads and thank God for sparing your life. . ."**

Patsy Cline: **"And Lord, please let these Seventh Day Adventists get some meat in this damn hospital. Amen."**

Patsy had only just returned from Winchester, where she attended her sister Sylvia's high school graduation. She flew up, but Hilda brought Patsy and the babies back to Nashville by car. She was accompanied by Sylvia and her 21-year-old brother Sam, whom Patsy often called John.

The next day, Wednesday, June 14, 1961, Patsy had Sam drive her to a shopping center near the Dicks' house on Hillhurst Drive in Madison, Tennessee, so she could buy dressmaking accessories.

"I was on the way home from the store," Patsy wrote in a series of letters, describing the circumstances leading up to the accident. "I had just finished buying buttons, ribbons, and thread to finish one of my show costumes. Suddenly there came a bad rainstorm, so brother John and I started home. It was just after 4:30. John was driving. We were going along Halls Lane when we came on top a bridge and then the road dropped in a valley for about a block. Then the road went up another little hill. Coming toward us in the other lane were two cars and, from out of nowhere, the second car, driven by this woman, pulled out of her lane to try and pass the car in front of her.

"There wasn't enough passing room in this little valley, and there was a double yellow line all the way. John blasted on the horn. I was just a-yelling. But she gunned her car and tried to get around, then ran smack dab into us, hitting our car head on. No way at all getting out of it for us. I went through the windshield and flipped back over the car."

Dottie West was at home listening to the radio. "I just couldn't believe what I was hearing when the news bulletin came on. The accident occurred in front of Madison High School, which was not far from where I was living at the time. I dropped everything I was doing and went to the site.

"That car accident showed me—in case I needed any proof!—a lot about the real Patsy Cline. When I got there she was still on the side of the road. She was so concerned about the others that were hurt, she insisted they be taken to the hospital first. I pushed through and got to Patsy and as soon as she saw me she made a joke. I said to myself, 'This lady is absolutely amazing!'

"I went in the ambulance to Madison Hospital with her and on the way I was picking a lot of the glass from the windshield out of her hair. She was a bloody mess. I was trying not to look at her because I didn't want her to see me crying."

Mrs. Ruby Nell Angell, 32, was dead on arrival at the hospital. Her death was attributed to head injuries. She was riding in the car driven by Mrs. Harold Clark, 22, who was admitted with numerous cuts and bruises and listed in fair condition. Mrs. Angell's son, Jimmy, 6, was listed in critical condition with injuries to his chest and not expected to live.

Sam Hensley suffered "a hole punched in the chest as big as a dime and about 3 in. deep," Patsy wrote. "Right through his breastbone and he cracked his front ribs and has a few cuts and bruises. The woman driving the other car broke all her teeth and had cuts on the lips and chin. It killed her cousin [Mrs. Angell] and her cousin's little boy.

"Of course, they don't have insurance, but John does. Three different kinds that will pay everything. So I hope to get $35= to $40,000 out of it. I'll get enough to buy a Cadillac, another home, and pay every penny I owe to anyone and have money in the bank, but this sure is a rough way of getting it.

"I never lost consciousness from the time it happened,

through the sewing up of my head, (saw the other lady die) and until they gave me gas to set my hip. I cut an artery and I lost lots of blood. They thought I was gone twice during the sewing up and had to give me 3 pts. of blood.

"I don't think I'll ever be able to ride in a car again. I just thank God above that I can see *perfect* and my *babies* weren't with me."

Patsy also wrote that the accident "was the other guy's fault and Patsy and Sam, were the 'fall guys,' " but in all police and newspaper reports the story of the incident follows the situation as Patsy outlined it.

Her scrapbook contained the following cutting from the WSM newsletter written by public relations director Trudy Stamper. "One of the reasons Patsy had such a long pull was that she insisted on the police and ambulance people taking care of the other people first—and she lost a lot of blood in the process—so it is taking her longer to build back up her strength. She's had a pretty bad time and will be in the hospital a while longer."

June 16, two days following the accident, Patsy's condition was still listed as "fair." Charlie told reporters at Madison Hospital that Patsy had been taken off the critical list.

"She's improving. Patsy's got an awful bad cut on her forehead, and one hip was dislocated," he said. "But she's conscious and talks okay. The doctor said it's going to take a lot of rest and time but we think she'll be all right."

Charlie noted that Sam was still hospitalized, but was now able to be up and in a wheelchair. Patsy received roses, telegrams, and cards from fans and well-wishers. "I Fall to Pieces" was rated second on the Country charts and was climbing on the popular music charts.

"We appreciate everybody thinking of us," Charlie said, "but the Madison Hospital switchboard has been kept pretty busy with calls." Patsy's doctor requested that she have no visitors except immediate family.

There was great concern about Patsy. Not only was she still very much known by the public because of "Walkin' After Midnight," which had sold over 750,000 copies, and her Godfrey and "Ozark Jubilee" appearances, but she was riding high with another smash. Patsy was even amused in the hospital when someone told her that a disk jockey introduced her record thusly, "Here's a gal who did just what her song says to make it a hit! Patsy Cline singing 'I Fall to Pieces.' Patsy, you didn't have to go that far! We love you. Keep those cards and letters coming to Patsy in Madison Hospital in Nashville."

The situation was touch and go. Patsy was not expected to live. "Through it all," said Patsy's Winchester friend, Jim McCoy, "Patsy's philosophy was 'They can't keep this ole Virginia gal down.' She was sustained by a great faith and hope."

Patsy told friends that she was stunned by the outpouring of concern of fans from every state—nearly a thousand cards, letters, and telegrams all total. Flowers came from Brenda Lee, Faron Young, Jan Howard, Bill Anderson, June Carter and the Carter family, Roy Acuff, Webb Pierce, Tex Ritter, Skeeter Davis and Ralph Emery, and WSM.

"To know her peers cared so much," said Charlie, "meant a great deal to Patsy." She seemed to be especially surprised to learn that "the whole Opry had been here and half of them from seven P.M. till two A.M. the night it happened to see if we were gonna be all right or not."

Patsy told Charlie and other close friends and family, "You don't appreciate home until you leave it and, let me tell you, you can't appreciate life until you've almost left it. Some people hope and still die with their song still in them. Oh, how I want to sing it. The pain is so unbearable sometimes that I thank God when I fall asleep. And when I can't, I still thank Him that I'm alive to be awake. This ole gal used to think happiness resulted when my earnings matched my yearnings. Not anymore!"

Hilda remained in Nashville to be by Patsy's side and to help Charlie with the children. Within a week Patsy was answering her fan mail.

On June 23, Patsy wrote Louise Seger in Houston to thank her for her cards, letters, and calls to the hospital. "I'm in bed and in traction so I hope you'll be able to read this . . . I didn't know there was so many people in this world that knew of me, but it sure gives me faith and a wonderful feeling to know how many fans and friends are wanting me well again . . . Plastic surgery will have to be done on me in 3 mos. . . . Dr. says I'll be home in 12 days and singing by the end of 2 mos. . . . I am out of pain now. Already got the stitches out 3 days ago. I've got black eyes and black and blue places all over."

Patsy kept saying to the nurses, whenever they commented on the volume of mail and flower arrangements, "I've got to send thank you notes and I'm gonna answer every single one of them letters." In spite of a cracked wrist and having her right arm in a splint, one nurse stated, "Patsy set about making good her promise. We were always handing her more stamps and putting her letters in the mail."

As a result of her accident and near death, extraordinary changes came about in Patsy's persona. Many strong friendships were forged, such as that of her and Loretta Lynn.

"The Opry was over about eleven-fifteen in those days," reminisced Ernest Tubb. "The stars would start coming over to my record store from Tootsie's just a little before midnight, when the broadcast ['MidNite Jamboree'] started.

"I remember Loretta and Mooney coming in. They hadn't been living in town too long. Loretta and I talked about Patsy's accident before the show. Loretta, God bless her, was real upset when she heard about what happened to Patsy. She was a big fan of hers. Loretta told me what she wanted to do, and I said I thought it would be real nice."

Loretta sang her newest single, "Honky Tonk Girl," and then said, "Friends, this is the Number One hit song by Miss Patsy Cline. I guess ya'll know that she's over there in the hospital 'cause she's been in a real bad car wreck. So I want to dedicate this song to her. Patsy, if you're a-listening, this song is for you, 'I Fall to Pieces.' I hope you get well real soon!"

Before going to the microphone, Loretta explained that she took an issue of *Country Song Roundup*, a magazine that, as its name implies, reprints the lyrics to hits on the country charts, and looked at the words to "I Fall to Pieces." "I loved that song, but I didn't know it by heart so when it came my turn to go on I did my song and then I held up the page from *Country Song Roundup* and stood there reading the words as the band played."

Indeed, Patsy Cline was listening. She had tuned in for the Opry and stayed tuned for the "MidNite Jamboree."

Charlie said, "Patsy was impresed, moved. She told me, 'Well, I'll be damned! That was pretty nice of that gal. Charlie, go down to the record store and thank her for me and tell her I want to meet her.'

"When I arrived at Ernest Tubb's I looked all around, then I saw this skinny girl in western clothes and I went up to her. I asked, 'Are you Loretta Lynn?' She answered, 'Yes, sir, I sure am. Who are you?' I told her, 'Well, I'm Charlie Dick.' Loretta smiled and said, 'Well, it's sure nice to meet ya!' There was a pause, and I quickly added, 'I'm Charlie Dick, Patsy Cline's husband. She sent me to thank you.'

"Loretta threw her arms around me and nearly hugged me to death. She hollered out, 'Doo, this is Patsy's husband, Charlie, and Patsy sent him down here to thank me for singing her song on the broadcast.'

"Mooney, which was a throw back to his moonshining days in the Kentucky hills, was standing near Loretta, who called him Doo, which was short for Doolittle, and I never had the nerve to ask him what that stood for. He came over and introduced himself. I told them, 'Patsy really enjoyed what you did and she wants to meet you.'

"Loretta nearly had a fit. She told Mooney, 'Oh, my goodness, honey, I just can't believe it. Patsy heard me and now she wants to meet me.'

"I spoke to them for a while. It was nearly one o'clock in the morning and since Madison Hospital was run by the Seventh Day Adventist Church they were very strict about keeping the rules. It was also quite a distance outside of the downtown area.

"So I asked Loretta and Mooney what they were doing later that afternoon and they said they had no plans. I told them I'd come and fetch them and take them by the hospital."

Loretta Lynn, of course, discussed meeting Patsy Cline and the influence Patsy's friendship played in both her life and career in her best-selling autobiography *Coal Miner's Daughter*. Here are additional details from a conversation with Loretta.

"Charlie took us up to the fourth floor and showed us in. The room was all bright and cheery. There were flowers all over the place. I remember thinking, 'My goodness, all the florists in this here town must be sold out.' Patsy was all in bandages. Her face was bandaged up from up around her eyes to her hair line. Her leg was in a cast hanging from a pulley. It was just pitiful. I was looking at her and trying to talk with her, but I could hardly keep from crying.

"I thanked Patsy for her thoughtfulness in inviting Doo and I to see her. She thanked me for my thoughtfulness. We sounded like a love duet! As bad off as she was, there she was asking me questions and being interested in my career. We talked a good while and became close friends right away.

That's the way it was with Patsy. But we were cut from the same cloth."

Charlie remembers, "Patsy and Loretta got on famously. They were talking a mile a minute. Patsy was bandaged up pretty good, but that didn't stop her from chattering away and laughing up a storm with Loretta. They talked about how hard it was for a girl singer in Country music, and Patsy and Loretta were trading stories back and forth about the politics of the 'Grand Ole Opry.'

"Finally Mooney and I went out in the corridor and talked. He told me what a hard time they had been having, but that things were starting to look good now that Loretta had a hit with 'Honky Tonk Girl,' met the Wilburn Brothers, Owen Bradley at Decca, and been on the Opry.

"I told Mooney that things had only just started looking up for Patsy, that 'I Fall to Pieces,' which was Number One then, was her first solid hit since 'Walkin' After Midnight.' We talked about how it was having a wife who was in the business and working on the road.

"They had resettled from Washington state to Indiana and had been coming and going to Nashville since Loretta first sang on the Opry a few months back [October 1960]. They were settling in town and Mooney was going to get a job doing automobile body repair work in order to make extra money.

"I told him, 'We ought to get together sometime and have a few beers and talk some more.' He was all for that, and we did that often. It was the beginning of a long and loyal friendship. And although Loretta was not the roaring type, Mooney enjoyed partying and they became regular members of the clique."

Loretta recalled that Patsy was really excited about having a Number One record. "She told me, 'I finally did it, hoss. I got me a Number One!' In spite of those stitches, she just smiled from ear to ear. She said, 'Oh, I never want to record again! I just want to enjoy this one song forever.' "

Patsy Cline became virtually a new woman. A change had come over her. When she would complain about her aches and bruises, Patsy would add, "But, as the Lord knows, there are no gains without pains." She told one friend from the music business who visited her, "Well, I learned that without faith a person can do nothing and with it all things are possible."

"My friendship with Patsy and Charlie dated from the time they first moved to Nashville and especially after Patsy was being managed by Randy Hughes, who was also my manager," reflected Billy Walker. "Patsy and I were not too friendly right off the bat. She kinda had a way of showing an overzealous spirit. Some wives didn't take to that, especially mine, so I kept my distance. But Patsy had a unique personality and eventually we got to be close. Most of the wives took it that she was after their husband when, in fact, Patsy just wanted to be one of the guys—most of the time. I got embarrassed by her language a few times, but that just egged her on more. She got the biggest kick out of that. She was pretty outspoken, to say the least.

"Our real closeness came when she was accepted as a member of the Opry. In our talks, I got to know more of the serious side of Patsy. They say the easiest way to spot a lonely person is in a crowd, and that sure was true of Patsy. We were all living in Madison at the time, and after the car accident I made a regular habit of stopping by the hospital to talk with Patsy and also to pray with her about her recovery. There was a time when the doctors had given up hope that she would live.

"The Reverend Jay Alford of the Madison First Assembly Church of God [Assembly Churches make up the largest organized Pentecostal group in the United States] visited the hospital on his rounds, and he and Patsy met and hit it off. He would come over to the hospital often to pray with Patsy.

"Patsy was really concerned about life because her life had almost ended. She had not been a particularly religious person prior to that to my knowledge, but that accident brought her into a real depth of the Lord. She told Reverend Alford and myself, 'I really feel uptight at times because the pressures of this business won't let me be religious when deep down in my heart I know I want to please God.'

"She told us that when she was a child she used to love to sing in the church choir with her mother back in Virginia. Boots [Sylvia Jean], who was my wife then, and I kept going back to see Patsy. We did a lot of praying and just plain visiting back and forth. We would stand around the bed and hold hands with Patsy and pray silently or together out loud. Sometimes Charlie would be there and sometimes he wasn't.

"Patsy, Reverend Alford, and I talked about healing through faith, our potential spiritual power to influence others through our life and deeds, the daily presence of the divinely conferred gifts in each of our lives, and the second coming of Christ. She said she wanted to accept Christ.

"The thing I admired about Patsy was her amazing faith and courage. Regardless of how desperate her situation got or how low she got in her feelings about what was going to happen, she seemed to always have a funny joke to tell and a cheery outlook."

AnnWhiten,of Patsy's clique, said that the star's sense of humor never failed her. "I waited until Charlie said it was okay to come by the hospital. I wanted to see Patsy but, because of her condition, it was not something I was looking forward to. I was more than a bit on the squeamish side. I get there and Patsy's head was all bandaged and she had black eyes. I hated hospitals to begin with so when I went in I didn't get too close. I could see more than enough.

"I kinda of spoke to Patsy from across the room. She told me, 'Come over here so I can talk to you without yelling.' Well, I went over and as soon as I got a good look at all the scars and bruises I got sick and fainted dead away, just passed out right there on the floor. When they brought me to, I put my head down and got nauseated.

"After I was better Patsy and I had a big laugh. She told me, 'Hoss, you got some nerve coming to the hospital to do this!' I said, 'Yeah, I know. Isn't this awful? I come here to cheer you up and go and pass out on your floor! I was so worried and concerned about you and now I got you worrying about me.' Patsy cracked, 'Well, there's one thing I'm glad of.' I asked, 'What's that?' She said, 'That I had enough sense to have my pictures taken before this. Now I can look at them and look into the mirror and it'll be just like the story of the beauty and the beast!' "

On July 3, Patsy wrote Trudy Stamper of the public relations department to thank her for her visit. "My operation last Tuesday week was a great step forward and the Dr. says after three mos. more, after this heals up and I recover good, I'll go back for another operation to have these scars cut out and pulled together again.

"I'll be as good as new then. But I'll be back to singing in between time now and that operation. A little makeup should make me presentable enough for people to stand me . . . I'll be cutting an album of some of my songs and some standards as soon as I can stand up. I've got to cut a single, too, because there's not *a* song in the can at all.

"Well, I'll close and turn up again for another needle. If someone poured water in me, I'd look like a flower sprinkler from the needles I've gotten . . . P.S., My thanks to Ira Louvin who had all the artists [from the Opry] sign two pages of autographs to me last Sat. nite. I'll always keep it. Sure made me feel great."

Patsy wrote a long letter on July 7 to Jim McCoy in Winchester. "I would have wrote to you all before this but I am now getting back to my self again . . . John stayed here two weeks and went home . . . I'm improving real good. The 4th they let me up in a wheelchair by someone lifting my body up. I'll be on crutches a month after I leave the hospital. I'm still a very lucky girl. Lucky to be alive, be able to see, and that my babies were not in the car . . . I'm writing this and details [of the accident] 'cause everyone has been so misinformed, and I wanted to straighten everyone out. It was entirely the other woman's fault and we have witnesses to prove it and pictures . . . "

In the newsletter of Patsy's fan club that July she advised, "I'm having surgery again today to have my face cleaned up. But it will take some fancy stitching to makeme all beautiful again."

There was concern and loyalty even among Patsy's rivals. Skeeter Davis, who was to follow the trend Patsy began crossing Country over into the pop field after her death, came to the hospital to visit Patsy a couple of times. Skeeter was probably the only other artist in town who could talk as fast as, if not faster than, Patsy. As soon as Skeeter came in, the jokes started flying. Patsy told her once, "Well, hoss, I hate to see you have to go. You really keep me in good spirits. We kid around so much and I laugh so hard I think these stitches are gonna bust!"

Hilda says, "You just couldn't hold Patsy still. All the time she was in the hospital, she spoke of nothing else but the day she could get up and start back to work. She was going to have to manage on crutches. It didn't bother her. That's when I realized how important her career was to her."

Dottie West said, "Oh, you couldn't keep that gal down! She was ready and raring to go. If they had brought a microphone to her room—and Patsy wanted them to at one time—she would done a song right there from that bed. I don't know how it would have sounded, though.

"You know, that hospital was operated by the Seventh Day Adventists and, through the years, a lot of stories have been circulated about Patsy having Charlie and other friends sneak bottles of beer in for her. Well, I can tell you that could not have happened. About the only thing Patsy wanted sneaked in was some down-home cooking. She didn't care for the food at all. Patsy was having soybeans for breakfast, lunch, and supper. She hated it!"

"Patsy had a zest for living," reflected Ernest Tubb. "She didn't slow down a bit even after that car wreck. As a matter of fact she couldn't wait to get back to work. She was just a-itching. She asked me if the Opry was ready to have her back and I told her how much we missed her over there. She said to me, 'Well, they're gonna have to put a ramp outside so Charlie can wheel me in to the stage!' I came up there once and Patsy wanted to know if I brought any red beans and rice with me. I told her, 'Patsy, if I had known you were hungry I woulda had one of the girls over at Tootsie's fix you up something.' She moaned, 'E.T., I don't even want to hear about it. That's how hungry I am!' "

Billy Walker and the Reverend Alford were in constant touch with Patsy. "She had made remarkable improvement," explained Billy, "and Patsy was very thankful to the Lord. She told me that she had told Him that many times while she had been in the hospital. 'Billy, I want to leave here and live a little bit better life than I have been living. I just wish the demands of the business didn't put so much pressure on me.'

"Patsy had pressures at home. Charlie was not an easy guy to live with. Charlie was just Charlie.

"More than anything, Patsy said she was really fighting to keep their marriage together and make it work for the sake of their kids. She would cry and say how much it would mean to her if she could have a decent home life. And we would hold hands and pray to God, asking for this.

" 'Patsy, let's bow our heads. Lord, help me to remember that nothing is going to happen to me today that you and I together cannot handle. And, Lord, we want to thank you for sparing this woman's life. And we thank you for breathing strength back into her body. We ask that you watch over and nourish her through the healing process. We also ask that you give a special blessing to her wonderful family so that, together, they might find the peace and happiness they deserve . . . "

"Then, as we were finishing, Patsy interrupted and added, 'And, Lord, please let these Seventh Day Adventists get some meat in this damn hospital. Amen!' "

Patsy came home to Hillhurst Drive on Monday, July 17. She was far from recovered, as she told Louise Seger in a letter on July 20. "Beings I have nothing to do but sit and lay around, thought I'd let you know the latest news which the Dr. told me just three days before I came home . . . I'll be on crutches for the next 5 to 6 *mos.* Can't put this leg on the floor for 3 mos., but I'll be singing *anyway.* Randy [manager] says he will tell the people who want me and not work me over 6 days at a time. And the Dr. said also that for the next 2 mos. I'll have to have someone with me on all trips. That's just great!

"I know Charlie won't be able to go with me on all of them, but I don't know who else will and can go. Anyway what the Dr. don't know won't hurt him . . . How about that 'Fall to Pieces'? No. 1 in 3 trade magazines and one more to go in.

"If it stays in the pop charts 2 weeks in the Top 20, I'll get to go to N.Y. to receive a *pop award* on it. Ain't that a kick in the head? Wee-ee-ee! I still can't hardly believe it's No. 1. Louise, I look at it and I cry I'm so tickled. I know I'll get 3 or 4 country awards in Nov. here at the convention. Sure will be great. Well, I guess I'd best close and get to sleep. I get tired real easy and I can't write halfanyway 'cause of this write [right] arm in the splint . . .

"I go back in 3 wks. for the plastic surgern [surgeon] to see what's got to be done and then in 3 months I go back to the hospital for the surgery. Sure hate that. Write soon. I go to Tulsa and Enid, Ok., the 29th and 30th of this month. Ha. Wish me luck. They say I won't make it but I'm gonna show them. Will be with Leon McAuliff . . ."

"In late nineteen sixty, when I decided to relocate in Nashville on a full-time basis, Willie Nelson moved to town with me," remembered Billy Walker. "I knew Willie from Texas, of course, and had recorded one of his songs. When we got to Nashville, Willie brought me a song he had written especially for me, 'Funny How Time Slips Away.' Well, Patsy, my ole and good friend, heard the demo and she told me she wanted to record it."

"Now, you just wait a minute," Billy scolded her. "It's mine. I'm gonna cut this one myself."

"Oh, come on, hoss," pleaded Patsy. "Let me have it!"

"Naw."

"Well, now, don't ya'll fight over it," laughed Willie. "I

got more. How about that song you cut the demo on?"

"Great," said Billy. "Patsy, it's over at Starday Records [another independent] and I'll get it for you."

"All right, but I'd rather have this one!"

"You ain't gonna do it! And that's final!"

Nelson lived with Walker for three months. During that time the singer tried to get Starday "and just about everybody else in town" to give the writer a house contract, which would have meant a weekly retainer of $50 a week. Willie said that he didn't care how much he received, he just wanted to get into the business any way he could. He had given Walker a song called "Crazy," which he had "just sitting around." They went to Starday and, with Nelson in the studio, Walker cut a demonstration record of the tune with only his guitar instrumental as background. When Billy and Willie found the record, Walker took it to Patsy.

"Hon, you can't cut 'Funny How Time Slips Away,' but I'm not gonna do this one. I've decided it's not right for me. I think you'll like it. It'll be great for you."

"You don't like it and won't record it, but you think this damn record is okay for the Cline! Billy Walker!"

"Patsy, really, I know you'll love it."

She hated it.

"I must admit that I was partly responsible for Patsy's attitude on 'Crazy,' " confessed Charlie. "In Willie's early period he talked a lot of his songs. He had given me a demo one night at Tootsie's for Patsy. I took it home and, after I had a little bit more to drink, played it on the hi-fi over and over again.

"Patsy came home and she said, 'Could you please turn that damn thing down?' So I did. When she got really sick of hearing it, she said, 'Honey, are you gonna play that damn thing all night? What's the name of it, anyway?' I told her it was 'Crazy' by Willie Nelson and that he had given it to me for her.

"The way it was originally conceived by Willie, it was meant to be a talker. Patsy hollered out, 'Well, I don't want anything to do with it.' So you can imagine her reaction when she came home with the demo Billy gave her and what she said when she put it on the record player.

"She said, 'I still hate it!' I told her, 'Patsy, it's a great song.' She replied, 'Then *you* record it!' "

But Patsy did. And it wasn't easy on Owen Bradley.

"Patsy had her songs and Owen had his," explained

Charlie. "Patsy'd say 'I'm gonna do this!' And Owen'd counter with 'Oh, no, you're not, young lady!' There were times when the sessions were cold. His ideas and Patsy's didn't always mesh. They could be like two immovable objects. Always in the end, however, they would give a little to get the job done. And, you know what? They never were that far apart to begin with."

Owen Bradley laughed. "Maybe, but that certainly wasn't the case with 'Crazy.' Patsy didn't like it and she was absolutely determined not to record it. 'Crazy' was early Willie Nelson, but I thought him to be a good writer from the time his material first started making the rounds. And I was terribly impressed with 'Crazy.'

"Patsy just thought it was terrible, period. I told her how much I liked it over and over again. I thought maybe the more she heard it, the more she might like it. Wrong. I'd put it on and say, 'See what I mean?' She'd reply, 'I don't care what you say. I don't like it and I'm not going to record it. And that's that.' She was quite emphatic, but I had a little talk with her and smoothed her feathers. I told her we were going to do it. She said no way."

Patsy did her first recording session in nine months at Bradley's on August 17, 1961. She hobbled in on crutches and propped herself against a stool at the microphone. The songs were the Bob Will's classic "San Antonio Rose," a remake of Bob Hillard and Milton DeLugg's "A Poor Man's Roses (Or a Rich Man's Gold)," and "True Love," the beautiful Elizabeth Zax and Vivian Berger number [which many assume was written by Cole Porter], sung by Bing Crosby with an assist from Grace Kelly in the film hit "High Society."

And there was "Crazy."

"Patsy still hated it," asserted Charlie. "She told me, 'I'm just not satisfied talking it.' She had made an effort to do it, and I admired that and so did Owen. She and Owen spent hours working on it to get it right for her, but Patsy's heart just wasn't in it. In Patsy's case that had to be an important element to consider.

"The night before the session she was at home complaining about the song again. I interrupted her, 'Well, honey, if you don't like talking it why the hell don't you just sing it all the way through?' She liked that idea and so did Owen. But there were troubles in the studio."

Owen said these problems were physical. "Even after Patsy decided to sing it, we spent a lot of time that day in the studio trying to make 'Crazy.' Nearly four hours on just that one tune, which was a lot for that time and a whole lot for Patsy. Usually we recorded Patsy live on three tracks and didn't even have to overdub. She would do her homework so well, one take was all we'd ever need. Of course, afterward, she wouldn't be satisfied and would tell me, 'Owen, let's try it one more time.' I'd gotten used to that and would tell her, 'No, Patsy, really it's fine, honey.' She'd counter with, 'But I'd like to—' and I'd tell her again, 'No, Patsy.'

"Everything about the way Patsy was doing 'Crazy' was great. I could see it was going to be one of her best recordings. She really picked up on the emotion of the lyrics. Patsy could really put herself into the story of a tune—and she'd do it with so much feeling. When you'd listen, you could pick right up on that.

"But Patsy was having a difficult time hitting the high notes because her ribs had been broken in the accident and were still raw with pain. She'd just been out of the hospital one month exactly. We finally did the track without her. You know, just laid down the music on the tape. I told her, 'Hon, you can come back in two weeks and do the vocal. Things should be better then.' "

Meanwhile Patsy wanted to do another song on the session and figured Owen would let her have her way.

"Owen called me at our offices just across the street from Bradley's Studio and next door to Decca," said Teddy Wilburn. "He said there had been a last-minute snag and that he and Patsy needed an extra song. 'Teddy, can you find the lyrics to that Gogi Grant hit you and Doyle did?' he asked me, referring to 'The Wayward Wind.' I told him they had to be around somewhere, and Owen asked me to locate them and bring them right over. So I did. And that's what I did. While I was there, and Patsy went over the lead sheets and talked about it to the musicians. Then they went right ahead and did it, just like that."

Owen noted that Patsy "came back less than a week later [the twenty-first] and did the vocal. She made it in one take! And that's the record you hear. She was just hitting her stride with 'Crazy.' It was really the height of her career."

In the hospital, Patsy had written Trudy Stamper that she was anxious to get back into the studio and get some material "in the can." She got her wish. Considering her still fragile condition, her output was amazing.

On August 24, Patsy recorded "Who Can I Count On,"

"Seven Lonely Days," Floyd Tillman's "I Love You So Much (It Hurts Me)," "Foolin' 'Round" by Harlan Howard and Buck Owens, and "Have You Ever Been Lonely (Have You Ever Been Blue)." On the twenty-fifth, she did "South of the Border (Down Mexico Way)," a remake of Donn Hecht and Alan Block's "Walkin' After Midnight," "Strange" by Mel Tillis and Fred Burch, and Hank Cochran and Jimmy Key's "You're Stronger Than Me."

Gordon Stoker, leader of the famed Jordanaires—which began as a gospel music quartet (including Ray Walker, Neal Mathews, and Hoyt Hawkins) in 1949, won the "Arthur Godfrey Talent Scouts" show in 1957, and later went on to appear on Elvis Presley's records, live dates, and in his motion pictures—has insightful memories of Patsy Cline.

"We began working with Patsy as early as the 1959 sessions. A lot of people remember and took Patsy to be a very unfriendly person, but she could be cold to those she didn't know. But that was rare. She had a lot of respect for those who worked with her, and we had a lot of respect for her. In fact, we loved her kinda like a sister. I liked Patsy because she was brutally frank. If you crossed her, she'd strike back like a snake. She was firm. She had a reason to be, because she had a very hard time coming up. Patsy really struggled.

"Wally Fowler, the gospel singer, was the one who really opened the door for Patsy [in 1948 with a WSM "Grand Ole Opry" audition]. He loved her singing, and he tried to promote her. Now, ole Wally had a reputation of doing all sorts of promotion and Patsy, knowing her, probably got his number fast. Patsy said that Wally had his eye on her. A lot of people had ideas on Patsy, but she knew how to handle herself.

"Patsy knew the ropes. She'd been up and down them enough. Patsy could be rough and then she could turn the charm on. She'd love you to death if you did something for her, but if you turned on her, forget it. She'd look at you and say, 'Don't you ever cross my path again, you son-of-a-bitch!'

"She never turned on us, but during the sessions she was all business. She could do everything but read music, but that never bothered her. She could sing any song, even standards and semiclassical numbers. Patsy could do anything she set her head to doing. She'd turn to us in the studio and say, 'Hey, I want you guys singing here and I want you to hum with me here. I want you to go ooh, ah, ooh, ooh here and ah, ooh,

ooh, ah here.' She'd stop very quickly and tell you if you were doing something she didn't like. But she was also quite complimentary. She knew her music so well, you only had to sing a song to her one time and she'd have it down.

"Let me say that Patsy was not conceited. She was humble about her talent. I don't think she really knew the impact she had when she sang. To her it was just a God-given gift. She had something and didn't know what it was. When she'd finish a song, she would come over and talk with us. I'd say, 'Oh, Patsy, what a great job!' She'd answer you with 'You really think I did it good?' And we'd all say, 'Are you kidding?'

"Patsy was a perfectionist, but again, I don't think she realized it. She just wanted to do it good, the best she could. She was sensitive. If you were talking and happened to be looking her way, she'd haul over and say, 'You guys talking about me?' We'd say, 'No, we were talking about the news.' She'd say, 'Oh, no you weren't! What did I do wrong?'

"Owen was very good to her and very good with her. He took care of her. He knew what she needed to do. Unlike many A&R men, he had musical ability. He could keep Patsy under control, or when he thought the moment right, he'd get her mad. He knew her capabilities and he also knew what would and what would not sell. And, oh, Patsy and Owen would get into it over material and the way things were being done time after time. Owen would station himself between the quartet and Patsy and just go to town laying it off on Patsy. And Patsy was laying it right back off to Owen. It was so much and so fast, I can't remember exact details.

"Owen would say, 'Young lady, you're gonna do this my way!' and Patsy would tell him, 'Oh, no, I'm not!' Then Owen would tell her 'Don't you forget I'm the one driving the wagon' and Patsy would fire right back at him with 'And don't you forget who's your best passenger!' Owen'd tell her he was running the show, and Patsy'd say, 'Well, damn it, I don't guess there'll be a show if there ain't a star on stage.'

"Then Owen might crack, 'I should have known you were the star with that light following you around the room,' and Patsy'd answer him back, 'Well, at least, it ain't no damn halo!' And all such things as that. Cutting remarks. They were both quick, but I don't think Patsy every got the best of Owen. He knew how to keep her in line. If you were playing your cards right, Patsy could be the sweetest person in the world.

And, thankfully, we had a close relationship with her.

"There were lots of times when Patsy was down because of Charlie. They'd have fights and she'd come in the studio bruised or with a black eye, which she tried to cover with makeup. After the car wreck and all, things seem to get better. But whenever she'd come in after being knocked about, she'd always have a good excuse. She'd tell us she and Charlie had a row and we'd ask, 'He didn't hit you, did he?' and she'd say, 'Well, somebody did.'

"But I've been around music people all my life. One minute they're kissing and the next they're fighting like cats and dogs. Patsy would confide in Ray Walker, our bass singer. Ray was a pretty handsome guy and Patsy was genuinely fond of him. Ray was married and had a family and was a very strict, religious person. He didn't fool around, but, at the same time, he was fascinated by Patsy and she was crazy about him. Because we helped and encouraged her, we had a beautiful and very special relationship. It was like we were family. We talked, we shared, and we cared."

Recalled Trudy Stamper, "Patsy had lots of special friends and she loved to go around town talking about her good days and her bad ones. She'd tell her joys and troubles to just about anyone who'd listen. She'd tell you how tortured she was one day and how happy she was the next. She had a hard time trusting people, and maybe because of that she trusted everyone. But when things went against her, Patsy wouldn't take it lying down. No, sir! She'd fight back. She didn't mind being pushed, but she wouldn't let you step on her."

"Patsy did cry on my shoulders," disclosed Teddy Wilburn, "but not about anything connected with Charlie. She used to call me and we'd get together so I could listen to her session playbacks. Patsy knew I'd give her an honest opinion and wouldn't put the shuck on her.

"She had come to Nashville very early in January nineteen fifty-nine [the eighth and ninth] to do session work—'I'm Moving Along' and 'Gotta Lot of Rhythm in My Soul' were among the songs. The Friday night she finished the session, she came by the Friday Night Frolics at the WSM Studios in the old National Life Building. She told me she had an acetate and she wanted me to hear it. There was a time problem that night.

"After the Opry Saturday at the Ryman, Doyle and I were either hosting the Mid-Nite Jamboree at Ernest Tubb's Record

Shop or E.T. had asked us to come down there and do a song on the show. Patsy was there and she asked, 'Well, hoss, when you gonna listen?' 'Tonight,' I told her. 'We'll do it tonight. I promise.' After everyone left, Patsy and I listened to four or five songs on one of the audition turntables. We discussed them honestly. She'd ask questions and I'd give my opinions.

"It became a habit after that. At times she'd call and be crying. It got to where I expected Patsy to be crying when she'd call. She'd be in trouble, as she put it—in a situation that she didn't know how to handle. In her mind, calling Teddy helped a little. She knew I wouldn't beat around the bush.

"Around the middle of November nineteen sixty, again on a Friday night, Patsy and I went to our old offices near the National Life between Frolic performances to listen to the session she had done that Wednesday. 'I Fall to Pieces' was on that one. I told her how much I liked the song, but that I didn't care for the guitar work. And that goes to show you how much I knew. That was part of what made the song a hit.

"Owen would call, too, to tell me there was new material on Patsy. Near the end of August nineteen sixty-one, he phoned or I was talking to him and he sounded concerned, which was not like him. Owen was adding strings to the sessions and he said, 'I want you to hear what I've just done on Patsy.' We went to the studio and he got the tape of Patsy doing 'Crazy' and we listened.

"He shut off the tape recorder very solemnly and asked, 'I want to know, do you think I've gone too far away from Country?' I replied, 'Naw, I don't think so.' I felt, by that time when Patsy had had a couple of really fine records—not just one hit—behind her, she had made her mark strongly enough in Country not to worry."

For her first appearances on the "Grand Ole Opry" after the automobile accident, Patsy performed from a wheelchair and then, as the weeks progressed, on crutches.

"She had a good attitude," recalled Gordon Stoker. "She'd sit on the sidelines and hold court and then go out on stage and sing. She was always all smiles. The only thing that seemed to concern her were the scars on her forehead. She used a lot of makeup to cover them and was planning more surgery.

"She told me it was a lot to pull through and I could just only begin to understand what she was talking about. She didn't look forward to more plastic surgery, but felt it was a career necessity. She only talked about this to friends. She didn't bring it up to make you have sympathy for her. If you stopped to think about what had happened, she had a marvelous attitude."

Pearl Butler and Jan Howard remember that on an Opry show after Patsy's hospitalization, she sang a number and got a standing ovation. Patsy kept getting encores. She still had her leg in a cast and she'd hobble offstage to the wings and then hobble back to the microphone.

Faron Young, standing in the wings, razzed Patsy out loud, "Some people will do anything to get applause!"

"No, Sheriff, it's talent and guts they're applauding!"

"Well, who wouldn't? They can't help it when you go out there with those sympathy sticks!"

"Why, you jealous little son-of-a-bitch! Here, you take 'em and you go out there with 'em!"

"Oh, no, honey, I wouldn't want to deprive you. Hark, your public is demanding you."

Says Pearl, "I thought if was funny and I have always felt that Faron was kidding around. He loved Patsy too much to be jealous. Patsy got a bit upset, but she might have been on edge, and later they hugged and it was forgotten. Only after that Jan and I and some of the others would ask Patsy if we could use her 'sympathy sticks' just for one number."

Loretta Lynn cannot forget Patsy Cline. "Patsy relished her success so because she came up rough, just sort of jerked by the hair of the head, I guess. But she never done anything any worse than anybody else, or as bad as most. So it's not right to say things about her. Patsy took a lot of my problems to the grave with her, and I'm gonna go to mine with a lot of hers.

"The first time I heard her was when I was living in the state of Washington, where Mooney and I went after leaving Kentucky. She had 'Walkin' After Midnight' out and, I heard, had just gotten married to Charlie Dick. I was always a fan, so meeting her the day after singing to her on Ernest's 'MidNite Jamboree' was quite a thrill."

Loretta's reminiscences, with Loudilla Johnson, the copresident of the Loretta Lynn Fan Club, about Patsy are poignant. "Patsy was my best buddy. She gave me clothes to wear 'cause I didn't have anything. She promoted me with the radio stations all she could. When I wasn't making any money, she offered to pay me just to go out on the road with her to keep her company.

"I remember Patsy was never a phony. A lot of people thought Patsy was harsh 'cause she'd tell you exactly what she thought. Patsy would do anything in the world to help you if she liked you. She'd known plenty of hard times trying to make it, and I saw her go from nothing to the top. I remember when she was having it rough and I knew her when she had everything.

"The things I remember most are just little everyday things. We'd talk, sharing all our happy times and our sad times. We shopped together. She taught me how to buy things, about bargains and how to get the best for my money. Patsy taught me a lot of pointers on how to start and end my shows. She always said, 'Give it a lot at the end.' She liked to open her shows with 'Come on In (Sit Right Down and Make Yourself at Home).' She wanted her audience to feel close to her.

"Patsy liked to embroider. She said it kept her from being nervous, especially after her car accident. Patsy was a real pretty girl, much prettier than any of her pictures. She loved pretty things in her home and beautiful clothes. And she was a good cook. She enjoyed cooking shrimp and would invite me and Mooney over for supper. She loved rabbit and Mooney would go hunting and bring back rabbits. Then Patsy would come over to our place and we'd all eat together. And, like me, she loved bologna.

"More than anything, Patsy loved her babies. The thing she hated most about going on the road was leaving the babies at home. We talked about that a lot, and we certainly had that in common."

In her book Loretta noted that Patsy "was really like Hank Williams, the way she got this throb in her voice and really touched people's emotions." Loretta explained that several events, career and marital problems, brought her and Patsy closer and closer. What impressed Loretta was Patsy's thoughtfulness and warmheartedness.

"Many times," wrote Loretta, "when she bought something for herself, she would buy me the same thing. She gave me rhinestones—I thought they were real diamonds—and I still have the dresses she bought me hanging in my closet. She gave me one pair of panties I wore for three years. They were holier than I am!"

More than a few people in Nashville have said that Patsy and Loretta were not as close as portrayed in Loretta's book. However, Lee Burrows said, "No matter what anyone says, Patsy and Loretta were more than just passing acquaintances. I remember when Loretta first came to town, Vivian Keith, who used to work with Hubert Long [the agent] and the Wilburns, brought Loretta by a dress shop on Fifth Avenue South. It was managed by Peg Schulman.

"Vivian told Peg, 'Loretta doesn't have anything. She looks pitiful. Can you do anything?' Peg gave Loretta a couple of dresses. When Patsy got wind of this, she called Loretta over and gave her a whole bunch of clothes. Patsy was like that. Patsy and Loretta were good friends, but with Patsy you didn't have to be. Anybody that was in need, she would help. God, Patsy was a very good person.

"On a trip to New York, when Patsy was staying at a budget hotel—she was doing Godfrey—I was working the road promoting records, she'd never let you pay for anything. When I'd go to pay for things like lunch or the taxi, she pushed my hand down and insisted on paying. And she wasn't loaded. She said, 'Let me spend it while I got it. I can't take it with me. Next time we may need your money!'"

One artist indicated that friends in the business were easy to come by. "I don't know how often Loretta and Patsy exchanged visits at each other's homes. Backstage at the Opry, it was another story. All of us girls would be together in the dressing room gossiping away. Once at convention time Loretta was on the Opry and Patsy was there. We were all ganged up on the side watching this Country bumpkin sing. She had been voted Most Promising Singer, and Patsy and us said, 'Promising what?' Oh, we were just being nice 'n' nasty, but Patsy was right in there with us.

"It galls me when people talk about Patsy and Loretta being so close. That's a crock of bull. They were friendly. Patsy had lots of friends, but few intimates. I don't think Patsy had any real close friends, except for Randy Hughes, her manager. She always impressed people as being a loner.

"But this thing of getting to know someone backstage at the Opry—and you do feel you know them to a certain extent—and calling them your closest friend, well—You don't know them until you work a tour with them, seeing them night after night and sharing confidences. And even then I wasn't given carte blanche at Patsy's."

Dottie West says that, along with herself, though at different times, which was Patsy's custom, Brenda Lee and Loretta Lynn spent time with Patsy at home. "And sometimes after the Friday Night Frolics and the Opry on Saturdays, when all the clique would gather at Tootsie's, Loretta and Mooney would be there with Patsy, Charlie, and us—though, please let me point out that Loretta did not drink anything stronger than a Coke.

"Not everyone was welcome. We'd fly over to Tootsie's through the back alley, grab one of the tables with the checkered tablecloths, have a few beers, and kid around. Charlie, Roger, Ann, Loretta, Mooney, Jan, Harlan, Hank, Justin, Bill, and I knew how to have a good time. And Patsy had a great sense of humor. She loved to laugh and, to be frank, she enjoyed the stardom and adulation and attention. Everyone enjoyed Patsy, but it would have been hard any way you look at it to try and take the spotlight away from her when she was in a roomful of people.

"Of all the people I've known, I don't think anyone had a heart as good as Patsy's. There was no barrier so tall that she would not leap for you, no problem—financial or otherwise—that she wouldn't help you solve.

"She enjoyed playing the role of mother hen. Patsy loved people and having them around her. Charlie and Mooney were friends and so were Patsy and Loretta. Whether or not, Loretta was Patsy's closest buddy, I don't know. I don't even know if I was and I was closer to Patsy than Loretta. But does it matter? One thing for certain, Patsy had deep affinity and affection for us."

Perhaps Loretta can clear up history when she says, "There were so many wonderful things about Patsy, so many. I'll say it this way, and let it rest, Patsy Cline was my closest friend. I know that she and Dottie, Jan, and Brenda were real close. I'm saying that Patsy was *my* closest friend. She was the one person, other than my husband, that I knew I could turn to in a crisis. There was a bond between us that time has not been able to separate. From the first moment we met, I knew ours would be a friendship that would never die. And it hasn't.

"The thing that stands out in my mind most about Patsy is that she was my pal even in jams. There was a lot of resentment about me when I first came to town, and I imagine that she had the same thing. There weren't no certain one, just a lot of the girls.

"It was just little things, like maybe one singer would be a little jealous, and I'd speak one time when I would have been better off keeping my mouth shut. But Patsy was strong-willed. She was always taking up for me. She knew how things were.

"In an interview Dottie did, she referred to Patsy as a boozer and a cusser. Patsy's not here to defend herself. And she wasn't like that. And it's nobody's business anyway. I got mad about that article. I ain't lying about that. What Patsy done, Patsy done. I never said she was no angel. She was my best friend and I didn't say she didn't do this or that she didn't do that. Or that she did. It was all immaterial. I did not say either way. Everybody does things in their lifetime. Nobody can throw stones. I ain't seen nobody throw any stones. The only thing I'm saying is that I won't say anything about Patsy. Except that I loved her."

Bringing to mind that time, Teddy Wilburn, who with his brother Doyle, was instrumental in establishing Loretta's career, said, "I would have imagined Patsy's closest friends were her business associates, like Randy. When you're in the rat race of climbing the last few rungs of the ladder to the top, which is where Patsy found herself during the time she was here in Nashville, you don't have a lot of time to associate with an awful lot of people, except backstage at the Opry and on the road. Patsy was not the type of person to spread herself too thinly in reaching her career goals.

"Being connected with Loretta from the beginning, I basically think I know most of her association with Patsy. What made the illuminous bond as far as the friendship between Patsy and Loretta was the fact that, after Doyle had gotten Loretta many guest appearances on the Grand Ole Opry [Loretta appeared on the Wilburn Brothers show and not, as pictured in the film "Coal Miner's Daughter," the Patsy Cline Show], probably more guest appearances—I think, eighteen in all—in a row than any other artists in the history of the Opry, the girl singers got quite up in arms about Loretta having so many spots so many weekends in a row.

"Right after this Doyle had a meeting with the Opry officials and got Loretta made a regular member. But the girls planned a meeting of their own for the purpose of, more or less, putting a stop to so many appearances by Loretta while the other girl singers were standing idly by waiting for their opportunity.

"There were only a few regular female Opry members—Kitty Wells, Jean Shepard, Doyle's [then] wife Margie Bowes, comedienne Minnie Pearl, Skeeter Davis and Patsy. Others, such as June Webb, who sang with Roy Acuff's band, worked with groups but were not presented as a star at the microphone for a solo spot. There were girls in town who had recording contracts and they vied for the guest spots. Weekends, especially when many of the acts and the girls would be working personal appearances out of town, the Opry wanted female talent so they'd pull from the waiting list, so to speak, of singers like Dottie, Jan Howard and Loretta. Because of the Wilburns, maybe there was too much of Loretta. And the girls decided if the situation was to continue, they would simply not be available for the Opry when the Opry needed them. They planned to put it to the management just that way. I have heard the meeting was at Dottie's though that has never been confirmed to me.

"It was probably less than a dozen of the girls. I assume Patsy was there and since it supposedly took place at Dottie's she was there. I don't recall if Loretta went and I can't say if Jeanie went. I know Kitty Wells was not there even though she was invited."

Charlie Dick says, "I understand the meeting was at night and since I was working nights those days, I didn't know about this so-called meeting until I heard about it from Loretta. Patsy never told me about it, but she probably would not have mentioned it to me, anyway, since I wasn't big on gossip. Loretta told me, and that was good enough for me. If Loretta said it happened, then it happened. There would be no doubt in my mind that it took place. I have asked Loretta where it took place, and she won't tell me."

Loretta noted that because of so many guest appearances one girl singer, whom she would not identify, "asked me who I was sleeping with to get on the Opry so fast." She added that when the meeting was called, Patsy was invited.

"There were about six of them," wrote Loretta in *Coal Miner's Daughter*. "Inviting Patsy was their mistake. She called me up and . . . told me to get my hair done and she came over to my house with a new outfit she had bought for me and she made me go. . . . We went in there, and they didn't say a word. That ended their plan. Patsy put the stamp of approval on me, and I never had any problems with them again."

"I'm a very straightforward person," announced Jean Shepard in her husky voice. "That's what I've been told. Well, a lot of things I'm going to say are probably going to contradict what Loretta has said.

"I've seen Loretta only once since that book came out. She's not on the Opry often now that she's a star. I waited for a few minutes to see her, but I never got the chance. If I ever do, I'm gonna back Loretta into a corner and I'm gonna ask her about that supposed meeting. I don't know where she was or who might have told her that, but I didn't know a thing about it. If Patsy told her, then Patsy was a liar.

"It's been embarrassing. A fan came up to me on the road not long ago and asked me, 'Jeanie, is it true all you women singers tried to keep Loretta off the Opry?' I asked, 'What are you talking about?' And she told me and I replied, 'You've got to be kidding me!'

"It's a bunch of bull. If I am guilty, I'll tell you, 'Yep, I was in on it.' But I know nothing at all about this and I'm glad we can clear the air once and for all.

"I think I knew Patsy Cline about as well as anyone, and Loretta made a lot of statements in her book that just don't hold water. I'm gonna say straight aboveboard, Patsy Cline was a loner. A lot of people thought Patsy was conceited, but she wasn't. A little on the brassy side. I got along well with her because I'm the same. But that was Patsy. Take her or leave her.

"But Patsy had no really super-close friends. I was close to Patsy—she and I were having babies about the same time and talking about motherhood and all, probably as close to Patsy as Dottie or Loretta but I would never go around saying I was her bosom buddy. She had none. And I think Charlie would say it, too. And Charlie is a truthful person. If something took place, even if it made him look bad, and it's truthful, he'll tell you. It amazes me that he did not know anything about this meeting. I think this is just one of Loretta's tales out of school, but it has stuck in my craw ever since that book came out.

"And I understand that Loretta got angry when Dottie said that Patsy was known to cuss and have a drink. Well, if Loretta wants to live in a rose-colored world, then that's her business. But if Loretta knew Patsy—and don't get me wrong,

I'm sure she did and fairly well—she ought to know Patsy did cuss and did drink and wouldn't give a damn who knew it."

Jan Howard said that "I wasn't around Patsy and Loretta a lot when they were together, but they were close friends. I love them both so much. I was glad they were friends, too. Patsy took Loretta under her wing. That's how Patsy was. She gave us a lot of encouragement—talked to us about how the men dominated the business and the perils a woman faced.

"I cannot recall any meeting of the Opry girls. I don't know if it took place or not. I've heard about it indirectly, but didn't pay much mind. Since I don't like gossip parties, I may not have been invited. I went to a girls luncheon at the old Hermitage Hotel and it was only a bunch of women talking away about everyone. I turned to them and said, 'This is nothing but a gossip club, so I'm gonna leave. And when I leave you feel absolutely free to tear me to bits.' And I walked out and I'm sure they did."

Del Wood said, "Who of the women on the Opry had time for that kind of garbage—holding meetings to protest another singer? We were gone most of the time, an average of three weeks out of five. Kitty was the big Country singer and Patsy was the hot, hot competition. There was Jeanie, of course, right there at the top. And Skeeter and Dottie.

"All the singers were individual with unique styles. Nobody sang like Kitty and nobody sang like Jeanie, and nobody wanted to sing like Skeeter. There I go trying to be funny! And nobody could possibly sing like Patsy."

Dottie West has her turn. "I want to clear the air about two things. In an interview [with Don Rhodes of the Augusta, Georgia, *Herald*] I was quoted as saying Patsy could drink beer and cuss, and Loretta made a snide remark about that in her book. I was really hurt. Loretta got upset and told me she didn't think I ought to be talking about the dead like that. I want it known that I don't think I said anything that harsh. And I don't know why Loretta fells she needs to be taking up for Patsy. At home and when we went out, Patsy would have a beer and she would cuss. It was her business. And if she was here today, she probably would, too. And I don't think she'd mind anybody knowing it.

"She's probably listening right now and saying, 'Hoss, tell 'em!' I'm just sorry Loretta felt she had to do that. I certainly meant no harm and did no damage to the image of Patsy Cline. No one loved Patsy more than I did. I was just talking about Patsy the way we all knew her. Even Loretta! Ask Hank Cochran, Roger Miller, Jan Howard, some of our old gang.

"Now rumor has it that the 'famous' meeting Loretta talks about in her book was not only instigated by me but that it also was held at my house. I have to say that I don't believe any meeting happened. I certainly was not invited. I don't know anyone who was. And, if any such meeting did take place, it *did not* take place at my house. I didn't even know any of the girl singers to be upset at Loretta period. We all adored her. And still do, damn it! Jeanie told me it was in Loretta's book that the girls had a meeting to try and have Loretta thrown off the Opry.

"I told her, 'Oh, my goodness, that's terrible.' Jeanie said, 'Well, don't you know about it?' I answered, 'No. I sure don't.' She said, 'Neither does anybody else, but it was supposed to have taken place at your house.' I yelled out 'What?' I was stunned.

"Sorry to say, it is legend now. But I know of no meeting and don't know how it got started. It's not in my heart to do that kind of thing. I have never had a group of girl singers at my house at one time. When I lived on Upland Drive, Loretta did come to my house—once—and that was for a baby shower I gave her when she was expecting her twin girls, one of whom she named after Patsy. Patsy was there for that, as were some of the other girl singers, but there was also Loretta's mother and her own sisters. And, I believe, that's the only time Loretta has ever been to a home of mine.

"That's one party I can never forget. I was home with a new baby myself. My mother-in-law and I had been doing some fixing up, and out on the patio the glass in this big table had broken. I said, 'Well, we'll be inside, so let's just put a tablecloth over it.' A while later Patsy arrived. We went out to meet her. I had my son Dale in my arms. Patsy came bearing all sorts of gifts for Loretta and me.

"I said, 'Let me put the baby down and I'l help you.' Just then Mom came out and said, 'I'll take Dale.' I took the packages from Patsy and sat them right on the tablecloth and they went all over the place. I told Mom and Patsy, 'I'm glad I wasn't putting the baby down!' "

Loretta Lynn, regarding the controversial meeting, said, "I can hardly remember anything about that. It's all very faint. I remember there was a lot of people a little upset 'cause I was on the Opry so much. What that meeting was—maybe what I was talking about—that a bunch of the girls was gonna go to Ott Devine, the Opry manager, and complain because I had been on the Opry so much. They didn't want me on. But I don't remember no meeting at a house.

"I got a telephone call from a man—and I won't say who the man was—and he told me there was going to be a bunch of the girls going to Ott Devine to make sure that I was not going to be on the Grand Ole Opry anymore since I was not a member. There was no formal meeting at anyone's home that Patsy took me to. About the only place Patsy and I went to was to town shopping. And we did a lot of that!

"I do remember some of the girls, but I didn't give names in my book. And if I had been gonna tell it, I would have said it then. That's been almost twenty years ago. I know there was a lot of resentment about my being on the Opry so often by some of the girls. It was just one of those jealousy things. It weren't no big deal. Who made it a big deal? It's all blown out of proportion. But that's just about the way it was. But do you know any singer who comes to town and don't have the same thing happen?"

Side Four

" 'Cause if you weren't there to share
my love,
Who cares if the sky should fall?
For anyone can see
How much you mean to me,
You're my life, my love, my very all..."

—"Today, Tomorrow and Forever,"
recorded by Patsy Cline, written by
M.G. Burkes and W. Burkes. ©
1955 by Four-Star Music Co., Inc.

12
"Stop the World and Let Me Off"

Dottie West: **"Oh, Patsy, I couldn't. This is your scrapbook of memories."**

Patsy Cline: **"I want you to keep it for me."**

Dottie West: **"I couldn't."**

Patsy Cline: **"Yes, you can. It ain't gonna do me no good. I'll never live to see thirty!"**

Patsy Cline turned 20 on September 8, 1961. On October 16, "Crazy," backed with "Who Can I Count On?", was released. When Patsy introduced it on the Opry, the response was tumultuous.

" 'Crazy' is my favorite Patsy Cline song," said Loretta. "When she did it that night she got three standing ovations. And when she left the stage after her third encore, Patsy was so moved she was crying. She said, 'I guess that's gonna be my song!"

At her shows, Patsy thanked fans for "the greatest gift I think a person can have"—the outpouring of affection after her accident and the encouragement to get better. "You came through with the flyingest colors. You'll never know how happy you made this ole country gal. And I just hope I don't try to live up to this 'Crazy' bit like I did the last one!"

Patsy's record was well received. She had a smash! It zoomed up the country charts, and by November 19 it peaked in the Number Two position. In the meantime, during the WSM "Country Music Festival" [the new name for the birthday celebration and disk jockey convention] that began November 2, Patsy was named "Favorite Female Vocalist" by *Billboard* magazine's D.J. Poll, "Female Vocalist of the Year" by *Music Vendor* magazine, and honored with six other awards.

On November 21, when Patsy's second album, the "Patsy Cline Showcase," was realeased, "Crazy" was still skyrocketing on the pop music charts.

Because of her unprecedented acceptance by popular music fans, Patsy was honored with an invitation to appear with "Grand Ole Opry" stars Minnie Pearl, Faron Young, Jim Reeves [who was the Country male crossover champion], Marty Robbins, Bill Monroe, and, among the 40 performers, Grandpa Jones at an extravaganza in New York's Carnegie Hall, the first full-fledged Country music production ever staged at that cultural bastion of classical music.

If the event on November 29 was not enough in itself to become a *cause célébre* among transplanted Tennesseans and other Southerners—not to mention the pop fans of Reeves' and Patsy's, lovers of bluegrass, and just plain musical curiosity seekers—Dorothy Kilgallen, the popular New York *Journal-American* and syndicated columnist ["Voice of Broadway"] and star of TV's "What's My Line?" made it one with her a remark about the coming of the "Carnegie Hallbillies."

On stage in Winston-Salem, North Carolina, Saturday, November 25, Patsy had a few words for Miss Kilgallen, whom she called "Miss Dorothy, the wicked witch of the east." "We're gonna be in high cotton next week—Carnegie Hall in New York City. That old Dorothy Kilgallen in the New York *Times* [Patsy did have her newpapers confused] wrote 'everybody should get out of town because the hillbillies are coming!' Well, at least, we ain't standing on New York street corners with itty-bitty cans in our hands collecting coins to keep up the opera and symphonies."

(This may have been a swipe at the fact that the show was a benefit for the Musician's Aid Society of New York, a pension fund for infirm musicians, or Patsy may have been referring to a fund-raising campaign she had seen in the city.)

"Miss Dorothy called us Nashville performers 'the gang from the Grand Ole Opry—hicks in the sticks.' And if I have the pleasure of seeing that wicked witch, I'll tell how proud I am to be a hick from the sticks!"

Kilgallen was considered one of the most powerful woman reporters at that time. A sentence in her column could make or break reputations, though with her personal life she had no business being a gossip columnist. She was addicted to music, loved all kinds — except Country. And she despised it.

In a newsletter found in Patsy's scrapbook, WSM director of public relations Trudy Stamper wrote, "At first it looked as if just everybody and everything was against us. New York folks who were supposed to know said, 'Nobody will come! We'd just make fools of ourselves.' One of the wheels called the Thursday before our Wednesday date and said he'd heard we'd called it all off. You can imagine what Mother told him!

"Anyway, we were scared. Ott Devine, the manager of the 'Grand Ole Opry,' and Bob Cooper, the WSM general manager, and me — we couldn't sleep, eat — are completely minus of fingernails — thought seriously about slitting our throats. We had practically no advance ticket sale. Thought maybe nobody would come."

Phil Sullivan reported this dispatch form New York to the Nashville *Tennessean* for the morning edition of November 29: "Several extra clerks were put on at the hall yesterday to take reservations and answer questions from callers. The 2,700-seat hall was half-reserved last night, but for every reservation made there were 10 calls asking for information, according to Nat Posnich, treasurer of the hall.

" 'We'll come within an ace of selling out,' he said. 'This is an entirely different type of crowd from what we have been accustomed to. These people don't ordinarily make reservations. They just call up for information then hang up and show up for the program.' "

Country music in New York was still a novelty, although Ernest Tubb had played Carnegie, and there were occasional Country shows at Madison Square Garden. Trudy Stamper's "small-town public relations sense" helped provide the last-minute rush. Somehow she got Jack Benny to come down to Carnegie Hall and stand in line as if to buy a ticket. While all the photographers clicked away, Benny said, "I should be buying a plane ticket to Nashville. I'm paying seven-fifty here for what would cost me one-fifty there!" The photo appeared in all the papers the following day.

The Opry stars, including the Jordanaires, fiddlers Tommy

Jackson and Buddy Spicher, Ben Smathers and the Stony Mountain Cloggers, and, as master of ceremonies, T. Tommy Cutrer [now Tennessee State senator], with two exceptions, arrived via a chartered TWA craft dubbed on the hatch side with the words "Grand Ole Opry Liner."

The exceptions were Mrs. Henry Cannon, better known as Minnie Pearl, whose pilot-husband flew her to New York on Sunday in order for her to appear on the "Tonight" show with Jack Paar and the "Today" show with John Chancellor; and Marty Robbins, who took the train because of his fear of flying.

Minnie came out to LaGuardia Airport on Tuesday to pose on the stairway ramp of the plane with Grandpa Jones, Bill Monroe, Joe Reeves, Faron Young, and Patsy for WSM "Grand Ole Opry" photographer Les Leverett.

That day the Opry stars also each received a golden key to the City of New York from Robert W. Watt, director of commerce, who was standing in for mayor Robert Wagner.

"We don't want to spread this business around about giving away individual keys to these people," Watt told a newsman. "If we do, then everybody will want them. Someday we'll look up and there'll be five hundred Elks wanting golden keys."

After a brief ceremony inside City Hall, the stars moved outside to the steps of the building in lower Manhattan for more picture-taking.

Sullivan noted in the *Tennessean* that "The Opry performers were enthusiastic over their appearance in Carnegie Hall. Some were hopeful they would be well received but others were pessimistic.

" 'They can't all afford to like us,' said Jim Reeves, 'especially the critics. They'll enjoy it, though.'

" 'I think we'll be well received,' said Bill Monroe. 'There is a great following of bluegrass music up here.' "

That afternoon the Opry members got a taste of what was to come at a lavish press party thrown at Carnegie Hall. There were lots of stars there, yes; but only one star with a bulleted record that, from all indications — in spite of the fact that "Crazy" stopped on the Country charts at Number Two, was heading for Number One.

The lovely, gilded bar of the hall was a mob scene of pushing, shoving photographers and reporters from the local press, wire services, and music trades, and with all the artists represented by various labels, music company executives.

Patsy was protected by Randy Hughes, who acted as a one-man flying wedge, but to no avail. Trudy Stamper was attempting to introduce Patsy to important writers and executives, but could hardly reach her.

"This goddamn place is like a zoo!" Patsy told Randy. "Why the hell is everyone bugging me? Tell 'em to go bug Marty and the Sheriff. Hey, Sheriff, loan me one of your guns. The blasting kind!"

"Well, honey," blurted Faron, "I got three like that!"

"No, you don't! You got two. The one between your legs don't count!"

Suddenly the crowd heaved backward.

"God, ain't this something!" said Randy.

"He can't hear you," quipped Patsy. "He's at the bar trying to get a drink. I don't know if the press turned out because the Opry's here or because there's an open bar. I feel like I'm in the middle of the Red Sea, the one that Moses just parted. I think Cousin Minnie and Gentleman Jim just went by in a blur."

Patsy was able to make an undetected early getaway back to the hotel, where she spent some time with her mother, whom she had flown to New York for the occasion.

The Carnegie Hall program notes stated, "Over 7,000,000 people have traveled to Nashville to see WSM's live Saturday night radio show, Tennessee's largest tourist attraction. Some one has said, 'More people go to more trouble to see the "Grand Ole Opry" than any other show in the world.' "

Patsy and Randy were awed by the great four-decked hall. "This is the prettiest hall I've ever been in!" exclaimed Patsy at rehearsal.

Patsy and Randy Hughes toured the backstage area extensively. Playing Carnegie Hall was a moving experience for Patsy. She told Dottie West, "As I walked from the dressing room to the stage up this flight of stairs, all I could think of when I touched the railing was of all the famous, fantastic people—singers and musicians of all kinds—who had walked up those stairs to the stage. I got a rush as I walked on stage and heard this mob cheering. I could feel the good vibes as I moved up to the microphone. You really don't need a mike in that place! The acoustics are so good, you can just stand there and be heard even by the people sitting way up on the gods—the last row of the uppermost balcony."

Bobby Sikes, a guitarist and backup singer with Marty Robbins, observed that Patsy "had a powerful voice. The mikes were hanging thirty feet away and Patsy's range was so fantastic that she didn't need those mikes. At Carnegie Hall, you walk out on stage and whisper and everyone can hear it. Patsy just blew the end of the building out when she started to sing.

"I am sure, for those who attended, it was an evening they will never forget—Patsy, Marty, Minnie, Grandpa, Jim, Bill, Faron. You know, for Patsy, especially, life was to be enjoyed. She was vibrant, bouncy. She took life with a grain on salt and it came over in her performance.

"The musicains have to get most singers cooking and driving, but with Patsy it was the opposite. She cooked and she drove the band. You just felt like playing up a storm when she was in the studio or on the stage with you. That's the way it was that night at Carnegie Hall. Nothing scared Patsy and she was willing to try anything once. And, on stage, she was innovative for her time. She was one of the very few Country singers—male or female—who moved. Most everyone stayed still and sang into the mike.

"Well, let me tell you, that night was a success. People were hanging from the rafters. They turned away hundreds. The ones inside were standing in their seats and the aisles yelling and screaming for more. And there's no way you could ever tell me that all those folks were hillbillies! Had to be at least one New Yorker in the bunch!"

Phil Sullivan critiqued the evening, "For one who knew Carnegie Hall only through reading of the great princely affairs that have gone on there, it was novel to see tattooed snakes moving down the halls on bare arms. It was that kind of crowd.

"Leather jackets mingled with mink stoles and clerical vestments. The Opry show, generally, was received courteously by the critics when it was noted at all. After indirectly twitting the show in advance, Dorothy Kilgallen in the *Journal-American* subquently ignored the performance. On Wednesday she had taken a poke at the show by writing and commenting on a letter from a Country music fan protesting her previously expressed attitude toward hillbillies."

The New York *Times* was favorable. Robert Shelton, later the co-author of *The Country Music Story,* wrote, "It was an unusual sort of opera . . . Its musical score was very much in the American idiom; its libretto was casual and folksy. Most of the recitatives were delivered by a radio announcer and there wasn't a coloratura or a basso in the house."

During the finale, the aisles were jammed with standees while the ushers, evidently not used to this type of carrying on, giggled in the nearby corridors. The New Yorkers seemed to love it, although it was at a time when most of them wouldn't have wanted their friends to know they loved Country music. Sitting in the boxes, as opposed to the Park Avenue set, were folks in cowboy hats and levis, just like at the Ryman, and downstairs, just like at home, the audience roamed up to the stage to take flash pictures of their favorites.

Gary Hollis, a 21-year-old usher from Wisconsin, revealed, "This is great. This is really great. I'm going to come South someday! Boy, oh boy!"

Another Carnegie Hall employee said snobbishly, "I didn't know New York had people who liked this kind of music."

The Reverend John E. Downs, an aide to Cardinal Spellman, was there and remarked, "I've been waiting to see it twenty-six years. I never could understand why it didn't come sooner or why it hasn't been on television here. I've always been a backwoodsman at heart. It was a smart move to bring the Opry to New York. The people here eat it up!"

"They did come. . . .they heard. . . .they loved it. . . . Nashville conquered New York," Miss Stamper wrote in her news letter. "The audience started clapping at the beginning of songs, in the middle and, of course, at the end. They clapped so much the show ran three hours [it was suppose to go two hours and ten minutes]. It was so late the last number of the entire cast singing 'Stay a Li'l Longer' couldn't be done.

"They never would have left. Jim Reeves was irritated because he couldn't sing all the songs requested—so he left 'em cryin' for more . . . . The 'hipsters' in New York knew that the Grand Ole Opry is the Big Time, and with the Good Lord willing, we'll go on forever. . . ."

It was noted that a front-row seat was reserved for Miss Kilgallen, who did not show. Patsy's comeback to that: "She was chicken to show her face!"

After the show everyone quickly returned to the Barbizon-Plaza Hotel at Central Park South to get their bags. They boarded a bus for LaGuardia and left at approximately 3:30 A.M. for Nashville.

"It was quite a night," said Sikes, "so coming back we broke out the booze. There really was enough excitement and energy on that plane to provide the fuel to fly us back to town. It was a real high. Everybody was having a big, big time. Roger Miller, a sideman in Faron's band, the Country Deputies, was running up and down the aisle mugging it up just like J. Fred Muggs, the 'Today' show chimpanzee. Faron was even flying the plane! And that was enough right there to tear anybody up or frighten them to death."

Explained Faron, "On the way home it was a very festive mood. I had a pilot's license for my Piper Cub, but this was a big TWA four-motor job. Captian Sam Lucky and I had gotten to know each other pretty well by then and he ran me up to the cockpit and let me have a look-see.

"He let me sit in the co-pilot's seat and I was discussing the controls on the flight deck with him. Captain Lucky said, 'Sheriff, you want to take over?' Well, I guess I could have gone through the roof of the plane. I was quiet excited. I was like a child with a new toy. It was only for a few minutes, and under Captain Lucky's watchful eye. But, from what I heard later, you would have thought once I took over the crew had to prepare everyone for a crash landing!"

Patsy was exhausted and had curled up in her seat to sleep. Randy had covered her with a blanket. When word drifted through the plane that Faron was at the controls, Randy woke Patsy.

"Honey, the Sheriff is gonna fly us back to Nashville." Patsy jumped out of her seat and exclaimed, "What?" Randy repeated what he had said. "Oh, my God!" said Patsy, rubbing her eyes, "I better stay awake for this trip. I can sleep when I get home. I sure as hell hope there's somebody up there with him—*and* somebody *up there* with us!"

"I don't know why everyone was so worried," Faron laughed. "I didn't fart with the controls. Just kinda turned it a couple of times. I was sorta Captain Lucky's co-pilot for a while. I heard I scared the drawers off Miss Patsy, though."

On Saturday, December 2, when Patsy played the "Dixie Jubilee" in Atlanta, Carnegie Hall was still very much on her mind. She opened the show with "Come on In," her theme song.

"Crazy" was approaching the Number One position on the pop charts and getting tremendous airplay across the nation, so there was cheering and an enthusiastic welcome for her at the end of the number.

Come On In

Words and Music by
Eddie Miller

Come on in
And sit right down,
And make yourself at home.
If I had one wish,
I wish I could
Go back to my ole neighborhood,
Where the good folks they
All love you as their own.
Then I'd go over to my neighbor's house,
Knock on the door and they'd all sing out
Come on in
And sit right down,
And make yourself at home.

I'd sing their praises long and loud,
'Cause they're all my folks and I'm mighty proud
Of the little ole town back home where I was born.
I wish I could hear them say
In the good old-fashioned, friendly way,
Come on in
And sit right down,
And make yourself at home.

Well, they don't lock their doors at night,
'Cause they all know they're doin' right,
And the good Lord's proud to have them for His own,
If I go back to hear them pray in the pine church,
They all would say,
Come on in
And sit right down,
And make yourself at home.

When I was a child of only three,
I said my prayers at my mother's knee,
And I knew right then from God I'd never roam.
When I get my summons on the judgment day,
I hope I can hear my Savior say
Come on in
And sit right down,
And make yourself at home.

"Oh, I tell you, you're sitting up tonight! Oh, dogies, you sound like Pappy [Bob] Wills on them good fiddles. Never heard such a swinging beat in all my life. Howdy, everybody! You having a good time? Well let your hair down and let's see what you look like. We're having a ball. Here's one that's a kinda true life story. [The guitar player auditions a key for Patsy.] Leave it right in the same gear as that, hoss, and we'll see what damage we can do to it. [Laughter.] There's a couple of horses out there. Hear 'em laughing?"

Patsy sang "A Poor Man's Roses (Or a Rich Man's Gold)," and again received a thunderous ovation. "Oh, I love you! I'm a telling ya. This ain't like New York, but it's uptown. Oh, dogies, you talk about a hen out of a coop. I really felt like one up there. I'm a telling you. But you know what? We made 'em show their true colors. We brought that Country out of 'em if anybody did. They were sitting up there stomping their feet and yelling just like a bunch of hillbillies. Just like we do! I was real surprised.

"Carnegie Hall was real fabulous, but, you know, it ain't as big as the Grand Ole Opry. You couldn't get 'em [the turn away crowd] in there. We were awfully proud of having the opportunity to go that fur up in high cotton. Well, I guess, I'd have to say that's the cream of the crop. And, believe you me, it really did my ole heart good, because little did I know who was sitting in the audience a-watching me, 'cause if I had I wouldn'ta been able to went on, I guarantee you.

"They had Jimmy Dean sitting in the audience and Jack Benny. I guess he come to see Tommy Jackson play the fiddle. He was there, anyway. [Actually, he was not.] Above all, and the most inspiring thing of the whole thing that excited me the most, was Princess Menassia [unclear to whom Patsy refers], who is the sister of the King of Persia [Patsy may mean Muhammad Reza Shah Pahlevi], the Princess of Persia, was there in the first box on my right.

"And after the show was over, she came to the fella who was in charge of all the doings, Doctor Brooks of the musicians union there in New York, and she told him—and I haven't gotten over it yet—she said, 'The girl that knocked me out—the whole acts were tremendous, but the most tremendous thing on the show—as far as I'm concerned, was the Cline girl.'

"Talk about it! Well, I was all shook up. They couldn't hold me. I said, 'Well, why didn't you tell me? We had WSM's photographer there and I'd a took a picture of me and her and hung it on the wall. . . ."

Patsy talked about her Carnegie Hall experience for weeks. "One of the reasons I wanted to play there," Dottie explained, "was because when Patsy came back she showed me the pictures and the write up. She went on and on about what a thrill it was to play that great hall. She built that Carnegie Hall up so much to me, I couldn't wait to play it. But it took a few years." (Dottie's wish was realized in 1979.)

In addition to an earlier bow on NBC's "You Bet Your Life" starring Groucho Marx, over the next few weeks Patsy was to appear on the Dick Clark Show "American Bandstand" on ABC-TV and "The Tennessee Ernie Ford Show," also on ABC, and regional shows, such as Buddy Dean's in Baltimore, singing "I Fall to Pieces" and "Crazy."

They were back-to-back smashes, for that December "Crazy" made it to the Number Nine position on the pop charts—a dynamic first for a female country vocalist.

"Patsy evoked quite a lot of jealously in town," noted Ralph Emery. "When a new artist, and she was relatively new, has a hit, it is not unusual. Then that artist has another, which Patsy did, and there's more jealousy. The third time around, when she has another hit, then everybody wants in on it. Suddenly Patsy was found to be very acceptable. Some of the jealously faded because she was steamrolling the business like no one we'd ever seen. There was nothing anyone could do about it. And Patsy was making great inroads in pop with a new type of country, one with a contemporary sound. So, you know, if you can't beat 'em, the attitude went, join 'em. It was that way with Patsy as a result of 'I Fall to Pieces' and 'Crazy.' She found a lot of respect in Music City."

Where there had been three, soon there was to be a fourth.

Patsy maintained an amazing, excruciating schedule—working far too much, too soon, too hard—as if to make up for the time lost while hospitalized. Soon she would be asking herself, "Is it worth the price?"

Patsy once explained that a show business career is a vicious circle, now she was living proof. There is an adage: "You're only as good as your last hit." With her dry spell following "Walkin' After Midnight," Patsy knew the truth of that entertainment proverb. It was not going to happen again. And to make sure of that, she surrounded herself with the best talent Music City could offer, and kept demanding, "God-damn it! I want to see some results!"

She did.

"After the Opry we'd meet in Tootsie's second floor back room and party," reflected Hank Cochran. "Then we'd go to Patsy or Dottie's for a while. On Sunday we'd get together for picnics or chip in and buy the fixings for dinner, and then sit around and talk shop. Whether it was just a casual party or the real thing, there was always somebody sitting on somebody's couch saying, 'Hey, I just wrote this.'

"None of us were really making it. You don't make money right off the bat. If I had a number one right now, I wouldn't make any money for at least a year. People tend to forget that. Patsy and Charlie were having a hard, hard time, even with him working. They were making house, car, and, most of all, hospital payments.

"I had left Mom Upchurch's and moved Shirley and the kids into a three-room house trailer. I was writing at record-breaking speed for me. And when I finished a song that I thought was right for Patsy, I'd call and either she'd come over or I'd go there. At her house, I'd waltz in and very coyly say, 'Boy, do I have a hit for you!' I did, but she didn't always like 'em.

"Patsy was getting ready to record again around the middle of December and she called me and asked me if I had anything. I told her I didn't and that I didn't know of anything really good floating the rounds. She said, 'I need a smash, especially now, so, hoss, look around for me. And, God, if you find one holler!'

"Pamper Music, for whom I worked, was located in a small house in Goodletsville, about twenty miles outside of Nashville. We had converted the garage into a studio. I couldn't get the fact out of my mind that Patsy needed a song, so I went out to the studio and worked. I was still sitting there around five or six when everybody had left for home. Then something hit me.

"I got to knocking around with the guitar and I came up with a thing I called 'She's Got You.' I rang Patsy and told her, 'I found the son-of-a-bitch!' She asked, 'Who?' I told her, 'No, honey, I got a hit for you! I found the son-of-a-bitch you been looking for.' Patsy hollered, 'Well, get your ass over here with it pronto!' I called Shirley and told her I wasn't coming home, that I'd be at Patsy and Charlie's. Then I hopped right into the sixty-two Falcon that Pamper owned and headed for Patsy's on Hillhurst Drive.

"I zipped in there and Patsy was in the kitchen preparing supper, and I looked over and saw a rear end sticking out of the refrigerator. It was Dottie. She was helping Patsy with dinner. Patsy went to the cupboard and got down a pint of whiskey. She slammed it down on the counter, grabbed some glasses, and she poured. 'Okay, hoss, let's hear this goddamn masterpiece! It better be good!' I told her, 'It is. It's great! You're gonna love it.'

"She poured us another drink and said, 'Sing it again!' I did. Then she poured us another and said, 'Hoss, sing if for me again.' And I sat there and sang it over and over until we drank that pint of whiskey. Then I did it some more. She wanted me to, so she could learn it. And she did.

"She just walked away and went to the phone and called Randy Hughes, her manager, and right then and there sang it to him over the phone. She knocked him out. He told her, 'Go with it, gal.' The next day we went in and did it for Owen and he liked it right away. They set a session to cut it."

That date was December 17, and "She's Got You" was the only song recorded.

Whereas the Dicks had more to celebrate the Christmas of 1961 than at any other time, it was not a joyful occasion. Patsy was suffering and finally on December 18 had to be restricted to bed for two weeks of rest. She had a nervous breakdown.

In her Christmas card to Louise Seger, which read "From the Four of Us," Patsy wrote, "I'm still kicking but slow. I haven't forgotten you for a minute, but I just don't ever do anything but go, go, go."

"You know, when I think back, I can't ever remember seeing Patsy sad," Pearl Butler indicated. "But she was a great person for hiding things—her feelings, her problems with

Charlie. Patsy could laugh, kid around, and carry on as if nothing was the matter even if something was bothering her bad. maybe she'd be crying on the inside. You wouldn't know it, though. She never let that part of her show."

To certain friends, that is. To others she revealed everything.

"Patsy used to love going around saying, 'Oh, Lord, I sing just like I hurt inside,' " related Trudy Stamper. "She was literally telling the truth. But on the outside you never could tell. Patsy could cry on both sides of the microphone."

In spite of everything, did Patsy and Charlie have a happy, a good marriage? It depends on who you ask. Quite obviously, for them to put up with each other's insecurities and troublemaking, they had to be quite madly in love.

"Ah!" bellowed Jimmy Dean. "What is love? That is the million-dollar question. Patsy and Charlie used to fight. I mean, fight! With an exclamation point. She'd call up and have the cops grab him. Hell, I remember that down there at the Capitol Arena.

"She'd keep saying, 'I'm leaving that damn son-of-a-bitch, that no-good-bastard!' But she didn't. She never left. I thought there might have been a small amount of masochistic tendency. I don't know. It was a very interesting situation.

"I think Patsy's name was most misleading of all—Patsy. She wasn't anyone's patsy. Well, maybe there was the one exception in Charlie. If ever she was a patsy, it was for him. They had a unique relationship—stormy as hell and all in love. It was amazing. She'd go crying to friends about what a brute he was, and then she'd go right back to him—*and* they'd be lovie-dovie until the next time he hit on her."

Dale Turner kept in touch with Patsy through the time of "I Fall to Pieces." "We would call or write once in a while, still caring about each other. At one point she wrote me a nine-page letter, and I didn't know to keep it. It's probably just as well, because she didn't have a lot of good to say. She had been hurt in several ways, but I'm not going into that. She told me about Ferlin and Faron, how little they paid her and how she had to keep them in line. Patsy talked about having problems with Charlie and, not dwelling on this aspect, she was real down and said she was giving so much and getting so little in return. And that was one of the last times I heard from her."

"As far as Patsy and Charlie are concerned," asserts Pearl Butler, "it was touch and go a lot, but I'll tell you one thing—every couple that gets married has their ups and downs. but with Patsy and Charlie you dared not say nothing about either one because you'd get it. Charlie could say what he wanted about her, and vice versa, but nobody else better utter a peep. If anyone did say anything in front of them, that was it!

"Rumors floated like crazy about Patsy and Randy having an affair. I don't believe Patsy was ever involved in anything like that. She never said a word about it to me. Patsy looked at Randy like she would her own brother. He was her manager and helped her. He took care of all those money problems and handled everything. She hated that aspect of the business. Randy took a big load off her back. I'm saying they were close, but they sure weren't in love.

"After Patsy's bad car wreck, Charlie left his job and started going out on the road with Patsy to help her and Randy. Sometimes they would take along Julie and Randy. Is a hanky-panky romance the type of thing you bring children around? I don't think so. Randy would come to Patsy and Charlie's like family, and the same with them over at Randy and Kathy's. People are always gonna talk about anyone that's close. They think because you're together, you're together. There weren't nothing.

"Charlie never abused Patsy when he was with us. He never called and bugged her, to my knowledge, when she was with us. I never saw Patsy bruised or beaten or upset. Now, Charlie Dick may have been the strongest man in the world, but I imagine if he ever took a notion to hit Patsy, he lived to regret it. She could hold her own with anyone, I'll tell you!

"Let me say something else about Charlie. Patsy was very career-minded. Driven. She'd say she wasn't gonna let another baby stand in the way of her doing personal appearances, television, and so on. She was gonna have the operation so she wouldn't have anymore children. Charlie loved her enough that he wouldn't let her do it.

"He goes and has it done himself [perhaps Charlie only spoke of doing this, as he did father a child in his marriage to Jamey Ryan]. Don't that prove something to you there? He told me he went and did it himself! I'm sure, like all of us, Patsy and Charlie had their problems. But a lot has been blown out of proportion."

Dottie says, " Charlie realized what he was like when he was drinking and he really put up an honest effort to stop. Oh, but when he was. Patsy'd be out on the road and he'd call her and accuse her of fooling around. I don't think he believed it for a minute. He just wanted to say something that would hurt her. He'd yell at her, 'You ought to be home with me and the kids!' And Patsy'd yell right back, 'Well, if I was, there wouldn't be anything in the house to eat. Somebody's got to make a living for us!'

"Part of their problem was that Patsy was a strong-willed woman. It could very well be that it would have been difficult for any man to have been married to her. It's hard for any man to be married to a girl singer or someone in show business, especially if that person is successful. I can honestly say that from my own experience. We work so hard to try and accomplish what we're after, and even though we are willing to share everything—any money, any fame—with the man, it is still difficult. And it's not the way most men would want it.

"As far as I know, and this is the truth in my eyes, Patsy was never unfaithful to Charlie. [When told Faron Young spoke of having a brief fling with Patsy, Dottie just reared her head back and laughed.] I didn't know of any fooling around. From what I observed, most of Patsy and Charlie's fights would start when he had a few drinks. they'd argue over nothing. And it could get dangerous being around them then.

"Charlie would go to hit Patsy and she'd pick something up and throw it at him. I think she was always careful not to throw something she really liked or could not replace. Patsy could kick back. Charlie knew that if he hit or kicked her, he'd get one, too!"

Ralph Emery speaks of marriage versus stardom. "It ain't easy. Whenever Charlie'd call Patsy and badger her, usually he was missing her and crying in his beer. She'd get upset and she'd start crying. According to Hubert Long, who worked with Randy and who booked Patsy, he kept her crying a lot.

"Patsy had a roughcut image and anybody who might see her at parties or partying around might say, 'Oh, she fools around,' but I don't think that was the case. You never know what goes on inside a person. Having been married to a quote unquote star [Skeeter Davis], I can say stardom is a hell of a thing to bring into the framework of a marriage.

"Suddenly this girl you were so intimately sharing every thought with is so damn busy with the phone always ringing incessantly with people wanting something—her to be here, to be there, writers wanting her to look at their songs, producers wanting her to record, other record labels trying to get her away from where she is now, photo sessions, personal appearances, photo sessions, agents, promotion tours, this deal and that deal. Bang! You have no more private life. A hit record can be devastating to a marriage and can cause a hell of a lot of adjustments.

"Patsy was more than just a star. She did something rather remarkable for that time. Kitty Wells was the unquestioned Queen of Country, and Patsy was the first girl singer to knock her out of that spot. Kitty won every year she had been singing. She always got the Female Vocalist of the Year Award. Jean Shepard was a threat, then Patsy came along with a fine voice and great songs and became the giant. And Patsy had the distinction of crossing over to pop before any other female singer. Later Skeeter was to do it. But Patsy opened the door. I got the impression that Patsy was all for Skeeter and Jean or anybody else.

"Now Patsy was no longer climbing. She had arrived, and thusly was on the road a lot. Charlie figured maybe she didn't love him anymore. He wasn't Number One. That can be possible in a society like ours where the man plays a dominant role. It is damaging to your ego. I'm sure that happened to him, and created problems for him and for them."

"Maybe so," offered Billy Walker, "but Patsy would have been a stronger wife had Charlie been a stronger husband. I believe that Patsy would have been much more of a settled person and not wanted to party if Charlie hadn't lent himself to the excitement of stardom as much as he did. Definitely, Patsy wanted the stardom. She wanted for the outward expression a performer has to have. And, yes, she wanted the money. But the money wasn't all of it. She wanted the success. It was an ambition. I always thought of Patsy as a little girl in search of a big dream. When the dreams became a reality she found trouble handling it all, especially when big performers tried to put the make on her.

"It wasn't that Patsy didn't want to be a true wife and mother and a sincere one at that. I just don't think she had the help from her husband that she needed. But that happened a lot in those days. And it could not have been that easy on Charlie. It was not a high-finance business then. From being absolutely nowhere, suddenly you could become somebody—and the money rolled in. It went to a lot of heads. And if you go into those strictly defined areas of male/female role playing, you can see where it would become doubly difficult."

Louise Seger, whom Patsy called often late at night "just to talk," explained, "Patsy must have been afraid of close friends. Afraid that they could hurt her. And yet she needed somebody. None of us can make it alone. She needed that closeness and very much needed somebody she could talk to and confide in, especially when she was down. Patsy needed someone to say, 'Get up, girl! I know you can do it. Come on, keep your chin up, kid! That's it.'

"I've never met Charlie. He may be the nicest guy in the entire world, but perhaps he could not offer Patsy that extra something she needed. And I'm speaking from the standpoint of the person on the other end of the phone—all the way in Houston—so I have to realize I was getting only one side. I'm sure he has his.

"But inevitably when we'd have our 'dining-room-table conversations' via long distance late at night, between eleven-thirty and midnight when the kids were long tucked in and asleep, it was just after Patsy and Charlie had some type of argument. She needed somebody to talk to. Maybe Dottie or Loretta were away. But Patsy knew I'd listen. That's all Patsy really needed and wanted, somebody to listen."

Teddy Wilburn, who became quite close to Patsy during long visits when they would both do a lot of soul-searching, stated that "even when I'd be there with them, they would be openly breaking each other up and down the wall. It was, I think, more or less, a way of life. They would put each other down and then turn around and pick each other up. They'd call each other names and start acting crazy. You'd think, 'What are these two doing living together if they feel this way about each other?'

"But there was something there. I'm sure they loved each other very much. Maybe neither one of them knew how to express their love. That wouldn't be unusual. Very few do. Sometimes we hurt the people we love the most. Someone does something the other doesn't like and then there is retaliation. The next thing you know, there it is in their lives on a constant basis.

"That's the way it probably was with Patsy and Charlie. But they had two beautiful kids and they *both* loved them dearly. And I know that Charlie has a deep love in his heart for Patsy that nothing and no one will ever fill."

Hank Cochran supposes that Patsy and Charlie are the type of people songwriters write songs about. "If Charlie made Patsy mad, she wouldn't let him walk over her. She didn't care. I saw her knock hell out of Charlie one day with a damn iron and anything in that house she could get her hands on. He'd drink, she'd have him arrested, then call everyone in town and tell them about it, and the next day she'd have him out back in her arms.

"God! In one breath she'd be tearing him down and crying how she was 'gonna put that damn son-of-a-bitch back in the jail,' and in the very next breath she'd be crying about how she couldn't live without him."

Lightnin' Chance recalls "Patsy and Charlie were constantly at each other's throat. It was like each was still searching for their own identity or establishing their I'm-King-of-the Mountain ground. God, this man loved Patsy. She was his world. And, consequently, Charlie, who's kind of like Mooney Lynn, played the background role. *But* this man, this little boy, deserved a crown, man!

"I knew from visiting in their home with Randy and being around them myself the cross that Charlie had to bear. The moods Patsy experienced—the goddamn-it-don't-forget-who's-the-star-of-this-family syndrome.

"Patsy was on the receiving end, that I know. She had bruises and black eyes and I'd look at her real strange with questions all over my face, but she always had a good one ready, like she had run into a door or somebody threw on the brakes in the car too fast. I'd tell her, 'That's a good story, Patsy. Stick with it.'

"Ole Charlie did hit it pretty hard and I loved Charlie good. He was a fine guy and deserves a lot of credit.

"And all of Patsy's big boisterousness and you-think-I-give-a-damn come-on was just a coverup for a heart as big as one side of the world and as soft as a bowl of jelly."

To put it simply and succinctly, Patsy once summed it all up, saying, "I've become a captive of my own ambitions."

Patsy did not allow her nervous breakdown to put a damper on the new year. The success of "I Fall to Pieces" and "Crazy" allowed Randy to ask for top dollar for his star.

Charlie was lending a hand on the road and with the business affairs. Patsy was finally making her way on her own two feet again without the aid of crutches.

If she was supposed to have slowed down on doctor's orders, you would never have known it from Patsy's letter to Louise Seger on January 22, 1962, while on a two-week tour with the reigning male star of country, Johnny Cash, and George Jones, Carl Perkins, Gordon Terry—formerly of the Bill Monroe band—and Johnny Western. "No, I'm not dead and I'm still thinking of you, but just don't get time enough to write...Got a 12-year-old girl who plays steel guitar out of this world. My ole ears have never heard anything like it. She also plays a sax and sings. Looks like a blonde doll. And, boy, what a showwoman. She's great. Her name is Barbara Mandrell. Wish you could hear her.

"Hope this finds you and yours well and not snowed in like I've been so much lately. I was in Canada and then South Dakota and then Chicago, then Indiana and now out here in Kansas City and Iowa and all these places. There's been so much snow, you can hardly move. I'm sick of it.

"Guess you've heard my new record 'She's Got You.' It's going into Billboard next week at Number 60 in the Top 100 pop. So hope it will get into all the charts. In some places the other side is taking off, 'Strange'...

"This tour ends in about seven more days and then I go home for 3 days, then to Toronto, Canada, for 2 days and then home for about four days, then start another tour. So see why I don't have time to write much?" The letter was written after a performance in Omaha, Nebraska, and mailed the morning following a show in Joplin, Missouri.

The Decca Records ad in *CashBox* read: "Don't Fall to Pieces but you'll be Crazy about Patsy Cline's newest two-sided smash 'Strange' c/w 'She's Got You.' "

"I was living in Madison the first time I heard the song, 'She's Got You,' " said Loretta Lynn, "and was on my knees waxing the floor. I had the radio down on the floor. Peggy Sue, my sister, was there with me and I told her, 'Well, this is gonna be a smash record.' And it wasn't long before it was a Number One. It was one of my favorites."

Owen Bradley was not letting Patsy burn too many bridges behind her before he'd have her back in the recording studio. On four dates in February, the 12th, 13th, 15th, and 28th, Patsy recorded an unbelievable 14 tracks. Bradley was attempting to package Patsy's third album for release later in the year.

If ever you wondered at the reason for Patsy's popularity, examine some of the songs she chose to tackle: "You Made Me Love You (I Didn't Want to Do It)," 1913; "Heartaches" and "That's My Desire" from 1931; "Anytime" and "You Were Only Foolin' " from 1948; the Hank Williams smashes "I Can't Help It (If I'm Still in Love With You)" and "Your Cheatin' Heart"; "Half as Much" and "You Belong to Me," 1952; and the new tunes, "Lonely Street," "When I Get Thru With You (You'll Love Me Too)," and "Strange."

"I visited with Patsy on a couple of the sessions," Dottie remembered, "and afterwards Owen would have us over to his office across the street at Decca for a little ritual. We'd listen to the playbacks and drink champagne. Patsy'd make a toast and then Owen would make a toast. Teddy, Hank, and Jan were there, too, I believe. And Charlie'd be with us.

"Owen would play a track and Patsy'd say, 'Owen, we'll have to do that one again!' He'd tell her, 'Nothing of the kind, young lady! It sounds great.' Then Patsy'd ask around to all of us there, 'Do you really think it's all right?' And, of course, we'd say it was fantastic, which it *really* was. And which she knew all along. Maybe she just needed reassuring, as we all do from time to time."

Said Owen, "The success of 'Crazy' might have scared Patsy. She was always in a dilemma when she wanted to use strings in her sessions over whether she was breaking out of the Country mold too much. She didn't want to do that. Patsy's voice had a magnificent, wide range. She could master anything, but she wanted to be a Country singer.

"She kept telling me, 'I want to yodel more.' She really liked that, and she thought if she yodeled or growled, she'd have one big Country hit. Patsy had a real loud growl which many of the girl singers used back then. It was like the blues singers used to sing. But hers was a different kind of growl. She had a quality about it and it was almost as if her voice was about to break on a high note. Very effective.

"We had quite a lot of discussions about the fast songs and Patsy wanting to yodel. I'd look at her and cry, 'Oh, no, Patsy! No more yodeling.' The next thing you know there she was wanting strings, like on a pop music section. She had such a romantic voice.

The interesting thing about Patsy as an artist, I think, was that as she progressed more and more as a singer and stylist, she attempted to get deeper and deeper into her musical roots instead of just going along with what everyone thought would sell. You'd have to put her at the forefront of the innovators, and there weren't many, for that period."

Patsy's outlook and style were a great influence on Dottie West and completely changed Loretta Lynn's whole attitude toward the staging of her show. "Patsy talked to me abut how to apply makeup," explained Loretta, "and about what to wear, when to do uptempo numbers, and when to do the ballads. Pacing the show was all important, she said.

"Patsy never recorded too many fast songs. She seemed to prefer the slow ones and maybe that was because she could really put her heart and soul into them. And nobody did that like Patsy."

Patsy was working such a rigorous schedule for a reason. Because of her huge hospital bill she had borrowed considerably on her royalties. So she had to go out and work the road for her "pen money"—the money for the house and car payments. And Patsy and Charlie's Hillhurst Drive home was getting smaller and smaller. Patsy and Charlie began the search for Patsy's dream house. And Patsy was banking so much of her weekly road take for the down payment. "Patsy had to have her status symbol," said Charlie.

That February Patsy was on tour in Canada and appearing with her was a very young Bill Anderson, who vividly remembers how unselfish Patsy was in championing the cause of all the singers on the bill. "Patsy was a real spunky lady. She could be as feminine as you wanted, and she could get a bit rough. She was smart enough to know the difference between the two. We had not been paid by this particular promoter we'd been working for. And we were booked into Toronto. When no money for any of us appeared before the show began, Patsy called over the promoter and mentioned that none of us had been paid yet. He said he couldn't come up with the money right away.

"Well, Patsy walked out on stage and when the applause died down, she asked for the house lights to be turned up. She told the audience, 'Folks, we've been working the past few days for this promoter and we've not been paid. Country folks have to eat, too. and since we aren't being paid, I'm sorry to tell you, as much as we love you, we just can't perform for you tonight. I hope you understand.' As soon as Patsy got back to the wings, he was there with our money! She was something!"

March 1962, Patsy was booked with old friends Jimmy Dean and George Hamilton IV on a series of dates in the Northwest and Canada. "Jimmy had a hit with 'Big Bad John' and was riding high with 'P.T. 109,' " spoke Hamilton wistfully, "and Patsy was on her third doubleheader hit in a row." "She's Got You" went into the Number One spot on the country charts March 3 and, that same month, to a high of Number Fourteen on the pop charts.

"Marlin Payne, a Montana promoter booked us into several Canadian cities. We were the package and I was thrilled to be working with the old gang. A friend of Marlin's drove us around in this limousine. We were in the back, Jimmy on the left, Patsy on the right, with me in the middle. Though I had been in Nashville, I was still a bit green compared to Patsy and Jimmy. One of them produced a bottle of liquid refreshment. We had a couple of hundred miles to go in blizzard conditions. They were sending this bottle back and forth across me, and before I knew it, there I was sitting between two people who were becoming increasingly intoxicated. And there I was cold sober. I had an occasional beer or wine but never had a tolerance for whiskey so I was not partaking. Patsy'd take a drink and start reminiscingl Jimmy's take a drink and start telling another story.

"There was no mix, mind you. They were just drinking it straight out of the bottle. They were sitting there alternately crying and laughing about the years in Washington, the comings and the goings, the good times and the bad. It was sentimental, funny at times, and poignant.

"Jimmy had gone his way with the CBS network show and had split from Connie B. Gay, who was bought out by the network, Patsy had gone hers and was making headlines as the female Country innovator of the time, and I had left rock 'n' roll and gone my way as a Country artist. But still there was that comraderie of having shared similar roots. Well, that bottle was going from hand to hand, and then, suddenly, it got very quiet.

" 'What's the matter, hoss?' inquired Patsy. 'You ain't having anything to drink with us?'

" 'I beg your pardon, Patsy. Are you speaking to me?'

" 'You see anyone else I'm looking at?'

" 'No. I'm sorry. It's just that I was deep in thought.'

" 'What else is new? Listen, you little son-of-a-bitch, are

you gonna sit here cold sober while Jimmy and I drink and talk about the good ole days?'

" 'No, I'm not,' I let out, overtaken by Patsy's statement. 'Pass me that bottle!'

" 'Now you're a talking! Jimmy, pass ole hoss here that damn bottle!'

"I took a big swig and Patsy's face lit up.

" 'Hoss, take it easy. Go slow. Don't overdo it.'

"I took another swig.

"Patsy cautioned, 'Well, dogie, I hope to hell you know what you're drinking. It ain't milk!' "

By the time the trio arrived that early evening at their next performance date, says George, "we were all three thoroughly out of it! We weren't stoned or unable to walk, but we were feeling no pain. I would love to have a tape recording of the conversation that took place that day. It must have been unique. To say nothing of the show that night. It would have to be one of the funniest shows of all time. Patsy and Jimmy held their liquor well, but not me. I was roaring. I was the drunkest of the three!"

Patsy was to see a lot of Jimmy Dean that March and April. Just after the Canadian tour, they played the annual firemen's benefit in Houston. Backstage to greet Patsy as she arrived was friend Louise Seger.

"It was like I had seen her just the other day," bubbled Louise. "It was like we had never been apart. She came running up to me and threw her arms around me. 'My God, Louise, it's great to see you. It's been much too long. How the hell are you?' Well, I must have driven her batty with hundreds of questions about how she was doing, how she was making out now that she was riding high and hard, and how she was mending.

"She reached into her travel bad and waved this absolutely gorgeous silver fox at me, saying, 'Look what I bought me in Canada!' She was just as proud of it as she could be. She told me, 'Now I want you to hold it for me while I'm on stage. I don't want anybody to get off with it.'

"So I went out into the hall trying to look real suave and calm, holding this great long thing—it must have been all of six feet!—and trying to fold it up into my lap so nobody would see me with it. Patsy was phenomenal that night. She did all the songs from way back when and all the current hits. There was a hush over the audience as she sang 'Crazy.'

"Afterwards in the dressing room when Patsy was changing, she took off her wig and a lot of the makeup she used to cover the scars from the wreck. I was trying not to look. I hated to even think of what she had gone through. But, God, she was amazing! She hadn't changed and it seemed as if she had just come in from crossing the street. I helped her with some of her things and she invited me back over to the Montague Hotel with her and Jimmy Dean. It was my first time to meet him and, him being a good ole Texas boy to begin with, I was thrilled.

"We all had drinks up in the room together. But Patsy didn't hang around very long. And the part that surprised me was that neither did Jimmy. There I was sitting and sipping and looking forward to having a nice long conversation with Patsy again after all those months and she had something else in mind. They looked like they were pretty wrapped up in each other. Patsy got up and Jimmy got up and they both headed for the door. As she walked out, Patsy looked back over her shoulder at me and winked—I'll never forget it!—and said, 'Keep in touch, Louise.' And I said, 'You bet.' How could I forget? That's the last time I saw Patsy."

Later, in Peoria, Illinois, as co-stars of WIRL's "Shower of Stars," Jimmy and Patsy did separate interviews. Patsy told the reporter she had been singing for fourteen years and that it was while appearing on a local radio program originating in Winchester [perhaps Patsy meant Arlington or was misunderstood by the reporter], Virginia, that she was discovered by Jimmy, who liked what he heard and hired Patsy.

Patsy said that soon one of her very favorite songs would be released, "Imagine That." She noted that she liked peppy songs herself, but that her fans tended to like her slower or melancholy songs better.

How had her life been affected by her success? "I never have any time to spend with my family," Patsy told the writer from *The Limelight*, a school paper. "I am very nervous due to my automobile accident last year. Many times I have to leave a crowd and take a fifteen-minute rest." Patsy talked of Julie and Randy and claimed that her "two greatest buddies are Jimmy Dean and Ferlin Husky."

"I have gotten more than I asked for," acknowledged Patsy, discussing her goal in life to become a star. "All that I ever wanted was to hear my voice on record and have a song among the Top Twenty."

Patsy advised teens interested in a show business career, "If you can define in life what you want to do, set your goal and don't change it. Work toward it and listen, above all, to your parents, because you never have but one set. Make them proud and you will achieve your greatest wish in life."

"When times got good in nineteen sixty-two," said Charlie, "all Patsy would ever talk about was the day she'd find or build her dream house—a real Nashville showplace. One time or another, we must have looked everywhere. We finally found it fifteen miles outside of town. Randy told us about one particular house that he thought was just what Patsy was looking for—lots of room and lots of grounds.

"So we went driving around Goodlettsville off Dickerson Pike, a four-lane section of Highway Forty-one. The house was on Nella Drive off Cunniff Parkway in an area overgrown with beautiful trees. We were driving along and Patsy was attempting to search out the one Randy had told us about.

"She yelled, 'Charlie, stop the car! Turn around. That's it, baby!' I parked and we got out. There was this huge house under construction. We looked it over and Patsy just loved it. She traipsed through it, and I just couldn't get her to leave. 'Just goes to show you,' she kinda said aloud to herself, 'if you wait long enough, it'll all come your way. Oh, baby! This is gonna be fantastic.'

"About the only thing more fantastic than the house was the price tag. It was thirty thousand dollars unfurnished, but Patsy didn't care. She said, 'We can afford it and if we can't, I'll get Randy to book me some big dates so we can have this. Nobody's gonna deny me my dream house. Let's take it!' The lady spoke and the lady got her house."

Patsy and Charlie had reason to be optimistic. "When I Get Thru With You (You'll Love Me Too)," backed with "Imagine That," had been released as a single and was approaching the *Billboard* Country Top-10 [reaching the Number Ten position, its high, on June 2] and looked as if it might be another winner in the pop field [it only got to Number 53, however]. And by the end of the month, the B-side was beginning to take off up the Country charts and make a bit of noise in pop.

The house was of a beautiful red brick construction. It was nicely set back off the street and in the backyard there was a farm within shouting distance. As a matter of fact, until the housing development began, the entire area was farm and grazing land. There was a small portico entrance with white laced wrought-iron supports. On the inside there were three levels, the first and second story and a full lower floor that combined a huge den and adjacent garage. This floor opened onto a stone patio. There were fireplaces on the basement and upper levels.

"Patsy threw herself into fixing up that house day and night," Charlie laughed. "And it was something to see! She wanted an American Heritage touch, she said, so she was doing everything in Colonial furnishings. She had a mural painted on the living-room wall. Everything was the best, and super elegant. Patsy ordered custom-made furniture, drapes, and carpeting. There was a fancy dining-room table and another table, in Colonial design, in the dining nook next to the kitchen.

"The master bath was spectacular. Patsy had seen something in some movie where someone had wallpaper speckled with gold, and she always said, 'Boy if ever I get me a house, I'm gonna do that.' Well, she had her house, and she did it. Only she didn't stop with the walls. She even had the marble tops sprinkled with real gold dust."

Donn Hecht remembers Patsy talking about what she would one day do with her dream house. "We were in California in the Four-Star offices. She was telling me how she hoped to make enough money to buy her mother a real beautiful home. Once and only once did I ever hear her talk about wanting luxury for herself. 'When I was little,' she told me, 'I went to a movie and there was this rich dame taking a bath in a fancy marble tub. And you shoulda seen the wallpaper!' Her eyes shone brilliantly as she talked about it. 'Somebody said it was speckled with real gold and, somehow, I've always wanted a bathroom with wallpaper like that.' "

Charlie explained that everything in the house had to be "just so so, and Patsy could drive a hard bargain. When the special three-piece couch came, she looked at it and told me, 'Honey, the arm's in the wrong place on this section. It's on the left. I wanted it on the right. Call the store and tell 'em to come pick it up and make it right!' When I reminded her how many weeks it took just to get it like that, and how many more we'd probably have to wait now, Patsy just declared, 'I don't care. I paid for it, damn it, and I want it the way I ordered it!' "

George Hamilton IV and his wife Adelaide were often at the Goodlettsville furniture store where Patsy shopped. "Adelaide was a good friend of the owner, but when we saw what a hard time Patsy was giving the poor man, we didn't say too much about knowing her. We didn't want him to hate us! She ran that man ragged. Patsy was very precise in what she was ordering and she wanted things to be a particular way, and God help him if they weren't. From the way Patsy was always carrying on about 'I don't care how much it costs!' I got the distinct impression nothing was too good for that house. Well, she did deserve the best. And she waited long enough to get it."

There was an intercom system, a full kitchen on the main level, and a mini-kitchen in the den, which Patsy dubbed the music room, below. Upstairs in the beige master bedroom Patsy had a rug in the shape of a Gold Record. There was a short half-Louis XIV, half-Regency style chest of drawers festooned with acanthus leaves. In not so traditional style, Patsy just slapped a frame of a mirror atop it. Her closets were filled with pullover sweaters, pedal pushers, western costumes, gowns and spiked slippers and boots. Around the house, Patsy's favorite footwear was a pair of gold lamé "chug-a-boots" slippers. In a place of honor was her silver fox stole.

Since the accident, and because Patsy had not made time to follow through on the plastic surgery to remove her forehead scars, she had begun collecting wigs in blond and brown colors. They were horrendous, but it was the lesser of two evils. Patsy was self-conscious about the scars and would use hair from the front portion to pull down over her brow.

There were bedrooms upstairs and off the hall leading from the living room. The kitchen was separated from the dining room by a serving counter. Adjacent was a cozy den, furnished almost exclusively in Colonial style.

Brenda Lee talked about Patsy at home and about the couple's "music room." "Whenever Patsy was in town she was just a-fussing and a-fixing up that house. When I'd come to help or visit, what impressed me was the way Patsy doted on Julie and Randy. I'd look at Patsy when she was playing with those kids. They were the light of her eyes. Somehow I always felt that Patsy had a trait that is common among show business folk, that she was lonely. She was a terrific mother. If nothing was too good for that house, that went doubler for those kids. She said once, 'They're all I'm working my butt off for, anyway.'

"Of course, I never can forget that house. It was a second home. Downstairs, in Patsy's 'music room,' she had a parquet floor with all different shades of wood. There was a padded bar with the words 'Patsy and Charlie' studded into the leather covering. On the bar was a cowboy-boot cigarette lighter, a covered-wagon planter with a snake plant, and ceramics of a toy poodle and a Brahma bull. She also had this black ceramic cougar. Behind the bar was a refrigerator and on top was a tape recorder.

"Patsy had her two album covers—and later a third one—hanging on the wall along with those of Webb Pierce, Red Foley, Burl Ives, the Wilburns, and one of mine. There was this huge recliner chair we all loved and a hi-fi on one of those roll-about tables. Patsy had record albums everywhere. And there was a daybed that was made up into a couch.

"There was a fireplace downstairs, too. Glass doors opened on to what was a huge backyard. Back in the room, a door opened right into the garage and a large storage room. That 'Music Room' impressed me as being one of the nicest and most comfortable rooms I'd been in. You'd feel right at home at Patsy and Charlie's, just the way she sang in 'Come on In.'

"Some of the things Patsy bought, as I've said, were kitsch. But Patsy wasn't out to impress anyone—even with that house, I don't think. This was her prize for all her hard work and struggle. She figured she owed herself something.

"And then there was what I called 'the conversation piece,' the big bathroom on the main floor. Patsy had a marble tub with gold dust sprinkled through it. It was the talk of the town. Folks weren't in the house two seconds before they had to go to the bathroom. And Patsy always directed them into 'the conversation piece.' I'd get such a kick out of their reaction and Patsy and me'd just laugh.

"I used to tease her, 'Hey, Patsy, what did you buy for the house today?' And she'd tell me! Oh, well, this was her dream house, the one Patsy had waited for. She enjoyed it and, oh, how she loved it. I felt good for her.'

"Patsy and I had one thing in common. We gained weight so easily and were always trying to lose. She was an excellent cook. Loretta and Dottie were over and they'd exchange recipes and talk about the road while they prepared things to eat. That never helped our diets."

Dottie West would look forward to Patsy's return from tour dates so she could go over to the new house. "I loved Patsy like a sister. And though she was only about a month older than me, I looked up to her. I had her on a pedestal. I'd do anything for her. I'd be there waiting when she'd come home from tour to help her clean and cook—to do anything, really, just to be with her.

"I loved to watch her with the kids. She pampered them to no end. You couldn't get Patsy away from her babies. That's what she called them. The only thing she hated about the business was that she had to leave them behind when she worked. She told me, 'I feel guilty every time, but I know they understand.'

"Patsy kept that house spic 'n' span. She liked nice things and, when she was able to afford them, nothing gave her greater pleasure buying them. And she loved to go out and get some new piece of furniture to surprise Charlie with. Back in those days, when I'd visit with Patsy, I felt that house was a mansion. It was her proof that she had arrived.

"When you walked into Patsy and Charlie's there was this little foyer and Patsy'd wax it and wax it until you could almost see your face. If someone walked over it, she'd grab the dust mop and touch it up. Charlie used to kid, 'Yeah, we have someone come in and help Patsy.'

"One day, just after they moved in, when I was over Patsy said, 'Come outside with me.' We walked out into the front yard and she kept going toward the street. She turned around and just stood there looking at the house all the while crying these big tears. I asked, 'Patsy, honey, what's the matter?' She said, 'I just love this house, hoss. I waited so damn long. Now I have something that's made the waiting worth it. This is my blood, sweat, and tears.' "

Patsy's last statement to Dottie was literally the truth. The big money had not started rolling in from royalties since Patsy had borrowed on her monies. She was working herself ragged to keep up all her payments. Patsy, Charlie, and Randy had a meeting and it was decided to up her asking price to $1,000 a night on dates not already booked. Certainly with a fourth hit record to her credit it was not asking too much. But there was balking. Randy's attitude was, "If you want Patsy Cline, you have to pay for her."

After Carnegie Hall and her Dick Clark and Tennessee Ernie TV appearances, Patsy's next biggest engagement was a special concert in Los Angeles at the Hollywood Bowl on Friday night, June 15, 1962. The Bowl was jammed for this first and largest combined "spectacular" of folk, Country and

Western, and bluegrass performers to be held on the West Coast. The show headlined Johnny Cash, then the top-draw Country star and a much-exposed, best-selling artist on Columbia Records.

Cash had just completed an eight-day sell-out engagement in Las Vegas at the Mint Casino. Starring at the Bowl besides Patsy was George Jones, Don Gibson, Mother Maybelle & the Carter Family [including June, Cash's future wife], Leroy Van Dyke, Cash's group, the Tennessee Three, and, from Patsy's recent tour of the Midwest with Cash and Jones, Johnny Western and Gordon Terry.

The Bowl engagement began another series of one-nighters for the Cash cavalcade. Stops included Phoenix on the 16th, Tucson on the 17th, then Douglas and Safford (Arizona), El Paso, and Albuquerque.

In the Hollywood audience was Patsy's mother, Hilda, whom she had flown out for the occasion. "You know, Patsy never accepted the fact that she had made it. She always liked to have me with her for the big shows, and, of course, it was a thrill. At concerts she'd be so insecure, she'd make me sit in the audience so I could tell her what people were saying. I'd hear a man say she was great,then a woman would say she didn't think Patsy was so hot. At the end of the shows, before she'd close with 'Lovesick Blues' [which she recorded in 1960], Patsy'd say from the stage, 'One of the best friends I have in the world is here tonight. I want you to meet her—Mrs. Hilda Hensley from Winchester, Virginia, my mother.'

After the Bowl concert Patsy and Johnny Cash had a surprise. Jan and Harlan Howard, also close friends of the Carters, got the family together and came out for the show.

"When I think back," said Jan, "I realize how lucky I was. What a lineup of talent on that show! It was a show I'll never forget. And for another reason, too. It must have been one of the coldest nights in Los Angeles' history. From the professional point, we were seeing less and less of each other, so afterward we had an extensive 'yak' session backstage."

That July, following the Cash tour, Randy got Patsy a job that could have led to new career directions. Patsy and Charlie joined Dottie, Webb Pierce, and Sonny James for two weeks in Deland, Florida, where Patsy and the artists were to star in a Country musical film. According to Dottie, "The plot was simple and built around the artists making appearances to do their big hits. It was a copy of the rock 'n' roll movie formulas.

It was fun. We had expenses picked up and had several days to relax on the beach. In the end, it was one of those stories you used to hear about a lot in Country. The producer ran off with the money, we were never paid, and the movie, or what was made of it, never saw the light of day."

One night later that month back in Nashville Dottie's phone rang. It was Patsy. She was crying and quite upset. She and Charlie had had another argument.

"Patsy sounded terribly scared and asked me if I could come over and spend the night with her," Dottie recollected. "I told her I'd be right over. When I got there I figured, as usual, everything would be all right. It wasn't. Patsy and I hugged and she was shivering. I asked, 'Honey, what in the world is wrong? Where's Charlie? Patsy, what happened? Are the children okay?'

"She told me, 'Oh, yeah, they're fine. He wouldn't dare do anything to those kids!' I replied, 'Well, I know that, Patsy.' She said they were sound asleep. But Charlie, well, let's just say that Charlie wasn't there. [In fact, Patsy had called the police and had him arrested.] He had gone out for the evening."

Dottie calmed Patsy down. They went to the music room and had a drink. Before you knew it, they were talking shop.

"Hoss, it's really hard out there for the girl singers," proclaimed Patsy. "The amount of damn work you do and still you have nothing to show for it. You work, work, work and still you're not really making it or being accepted like the men."

"The men have it easier," Dottie observed.

"They sure as hell do and they lord it all over you! Can't think of too many of them who are married to girl singers who are active. It's bad enough for a girl trying to make it in this business, but it's really difficult when the girl singer is married."

"To someone in or out of the business."

"That's the honest-to-God truth, hoss. Don't matter. They don't understand and they don't want to understand!"

"Well, we could all pray that things get better!"

"You said it. And do something about it, too! God, I really wonder sometimes if it's really worth what we go through, what we have to put up with?"

"I don't know, girl. Sometimes you do wonder!"

"The kids are compensation enough. I know we need to go out and work one-nighters, but I just hate to leave Julie and Randy. My girl takes good care of them, but I cry when I have to say goodbye to them and they pull on my dress. They want to know why I'm leaving them. Julie starts crying and says she wants to come with me. She just cries, 'Please, Mommie, don't leave me. Let me go with you. Please, Mommie!' That just tears my heart out!"

Patsy got up and mixed she and Dottie another drink. Then she pulled down the scrapbook they put together and constantly updated of articles about Patsy, her chart listings, sheet music of her songs, Decca ads from the trades, the WSM newsletter that Trudy Stamper put out, and pictures of herself, Ferlin, Faron, and Elvis Presley. She loved Elvis and kept "my special portrait" of him inside the back cover. It was a huge color picture from a magazine.

She would tell Dottie again and again, "Of all 'em, this is my favorite picture. The time I got to meet Elvis [at the opening of the St. Jude Hospital in Memphis with Danny Thomas and Ann-Margret] was one of the greatest moments in my life."

Patsy came to a picture of Jimmy Dean on the Town and Country Jamboree and told Dottie about Billy Grammer, George Hamilton IV, Mary Klick, and Dale Turner.

"This show was responsible for really putting the Cline on the map! We had some problems there, but we had a helluva lot of good times." She pulled out several clippings of chart listings. " 'I Fall to Pieces' made it to Number One on the *Billboard* Country charts. Remember that song 'Michael' by the Highwaymen? That kept me out of the Top 10. But, hey, this is the week it got to Number Twelve."

Patsy read Dottie a *Cash Box* review of her single "She's Got You" and "Strange."

"God, what's this doing here?" Patsy picked up the sheet music from "Walkin' After Midnight" and "A Poor Man's Roses." The latter had a photo of her in her western outfit with a kerchief around her neck. "They don't belong back here. I've been looking for these for a couple of weeks."

Patsy turned the page and unfolded a newspaper clipping. "Well, looka here. Remember when I went back to Winchester after 'I Fall to Pieces' to sing at the drive-in? Here's nearly a full-page ad for that. And here all the Decca gang is in the hospitality suite at last year's D.J. Convention. Look at the way I got my legs crossed! Who was I trying to turn on? This is a big article one of the papers did after I got out of the hospital. 'Patsy Cline Is Back in a Big, Big Way.' Heck, I wasn't pregnant then!"

"Oh, Patsy!"

"It says here, 'You can't keep a star away from those hit records.' And you know something, hoss, that's the truth. We just got to keep on pushing and shoving. Can't get down."

"Yeah, but your problem is you don't practice what you preach!"

"Yes, I do, or I wouldn'ta got this far!" Patsy snapped the scrapbook shut. "Would you look at me! Here I am doing all the talking *and* about me. How things going with you, hoss? You and Bill staying busy?"

"Things are okay. There's not a whole lot going on, as you know. We're trying to keep our heads above water."

"I know you are. It's gonna happen for you, hoss. And soon. Just you wait!" Patsy got up from the couch. "Excuse me a second. I've got to go to the john."

"You just went."

"Must be that whiskey."

Patsy went upstairs and into the darkened living room. She walked to the large picture window that looked out onto the expanse of yard. She pulled back the drapes and peered into the early-morning darkness. A strange mood overcame Patsy. She stood in the darkness as if she was alone and helpless. If there is only one effect nighttime can have on you, it is to make you feel more helpless and cut off from everyone—those you like and those you love—than you really are. She stared into the void wondering what all she had done and sacrificed to get to the point in her life of having a scrapbook filled to overflowing with all sorts of clippings. She was a star. Tonight she was nothing. How cruel life can be when the spotlight is switched off!

She quickly turned and let the curtains fall back into place. Patsy went down the hall to her bedroom and sat at the dressing table. She pulled out some papers and began writing something. When she finished, Patsy folded the paper into her hand. She got up and walked back to the flight of stairs that led to the music room. Dottie had put one of Patsy's records on the hi-fi.

Patsy paused for a moment. A slight feeling of uneasiness overcame her. "Oh, hell, it's nothing," she told herself. It was something, but Patsy could not pinpoint it. It was a fleeting glimpse, a vague, distant, very far-off perception that something was not right. It wasn't wrong, but it wasn't right. Whatever it was, it only bothered her a few seconds. She paid it no mind. Then she had it. It's a premonition of what was coming. Maybe not tomorrow, or the next day, or the next week. But soon. Soon enough.

She walked briskly down the steps and into the music room.

"Patsy, are you okay?"

"Sure. I'm fine."

"You were gone a long time."

"Had to take care of some business, and look in on the kids."

"They okay?"

"Oh, sure. Hey, where's the scrapbook?"

"I put it on the top of the bar."

Patsy picked the book up and tucked the paper from her hand inside. She took the book and turned to give it to Dottie.

"Hoss, I want you to take this—"

"What?"

"I want you to have this."

"Oh, Patsy, I couldn't. This is your scrapbook of memories."

"I want you to have it and keep it for me."

"I just couldn't!"

"Yes, you can."

"I can't do that. You should save this and give it to your grandchildren someday."

"You gonna argue with the Cline?"

"Yes!"

"That don't make sense and you know it!"

"Oh, Patsy!"

"I want you to have it. Anyway, it ain't gonna do me no good 'cause I'll never live to see thirty!"

"Oh, my God, Patsy! Don't talk like that."

"Well, it's the truth. I'll never live to see thirty."

"My goodness, let's change the subject!"

"We can if you'll take this."

"Okay, Patsy. I'll keep it for you. You know where it will always be."

"You know it's nearly daylight?"

"You're kidding! I gotta go. You gonna be okay?"

"I'll be fine. Thanks a bunch for coming over. I needed to talk."

"Charlie coming back in the morning?"

"Oh, yeah. He'll be back."

Dottie drove home and sat down at her kitchen table with the scrapbook. She looked out the window. The sun was starting to come up.

"I thumbed through the pages and I started to cry—for both of us. I wondered what on earth possessed Patsy to give me her cherished scrapbook. She was real down because of the argument and fight with Charlie. She was trying to be a good wife and mother in addition to being a singer—and the best one there was. 'It ain't easy,' she'd say, 'and no one seems to appreciate it.'

"There was the picture of Patsy and Jimmy. I turned the page and there was this paper folded up. I opened it. I didn't know what to think. It was a check for seventy-five dollars with a little note Patsy had written, 'I know you're having it hard and that you're not working. You can use this to pay the rent. Love, Patsy.'

"I don't know how Patsy knew. She had so many of her own problems, I didn't want to bother her with ours. Bill and I had been trying to get enough money together to pay the rent and hadn't been able to. That Patsy! What a lady!"

13
". . . And Then Goodbye," Reprise

Sam Hensley: **"Hey, I told you Patsy is not on any plane!"**

Hilda Hensley: **"Wait a minute! Patsy was on a plane!"**

Patsy Cline's third album, "Sentimentally, Yours" was released August 6, 1962, and on September 8 and 10, Patsy recorded seven new tunes: Harlan Howard's "That's How a Heartache Begins," "Why Can't He Be You?" and "When You Need a Laugh" by Hank Cochran, "Leavin' on Your Mind" by Wayne Walker and Webb Pierce, Bob Montgomery's "Back in Baby's Arms," "Tra Le La Le La Triangle," and "Your Kinda Love."

Untrue to her statement to Dottie, Patsy did live to see her thirtieth birthday. It was also the occasion of Patsy and Charlie's first big party in the new house.

"Parties, began Billy Walker, "have always been a prevalent thing in Nashville music society. They were more prevalent then. You always invited your constituents—you know, your peers—and the parties were eagerly looked forward to as it was a way to see everyone together just like backstage at the Opry. We were a very close-knit community in those days. Of course, there were a lot less of us.

"There was a feeling of concern for one another. We were still budding, building an audience. This was especially true about Patsy. She was everyone's biggest booster. As far as she was concerned it was 'All for one, and one for all.' And with Patsy, the people she worked with, she loved."

"Patsy and Charlie loved to give fun parties," recalled Bobby Sikes. "And it was always a pleasure to go to their house. They were gracious hosts from the time you walked in. The house was literally yours. You never had to want for anything to drink or to eat. Patsy was a fabulous cook and, if I'm not mistaken, she usually prepared almost everything."

Patsy had enjoyed entertaining before, but this was a very special occasion—and she was celebrating more the debut of the house than her birthday. The guest list included Randy and Kathy Hughes, Dottie and Bill West, Loretta and Mooney Lynn, Jan and Harlan Howard, Hank and Shirley Cochran, Wayne Walker, Del Wood, Teddy Wilburn, Wilma Burgess, Billy Sikes, and, among the 75 guests, Faron Young.

"Like at all parties," Faron said, "we sat around and had some drinks and then someone would grab a guitar and we'd take turns singing."

A few nights later Patsy called Dottie and asked her to come sit with her.

"Well, hoss, we've shared a lot of secrets, haven't we?"

"I guess," replied Dottie, understating the case.

"I got another one for you tonight."

"Okay. What is it now? Let's hear it."

"You sure you can keep a secret?"

"Cross my heart!"

"Well, I've been putting aside something for a rainy day. Something that's just mine. I don't want even Charlie to know about it."

"Not even Charlie?"

"Nope. I don't want Charlie to know about it. This is between you and me."

"Patsy, what the heck are you talking about?"

"My stash."

"What do you mean?"

"I've got me a stash."

"A what?"

"A stash."

"Oh, my God, Patsy! I don't believe this."

"Well, it's the honest truth. I found me a hiding place behind one of the bricks in the fireplace in the den. I've been putting some money in there every week. Don't you dare tell anybody. You're the only other person that knows. I just want you to know about it in case anything happens to me."

"There you go again! Patsy, why do you feel you have to hide money?"

"It's my business, hoss. It's for a rainy day. Remember, mum's the word."

And it was, until Patsy was killed and Charlie sold the house.

The Eleventh Annual WSM Country Music Festival got underway on Wednesday, November 7. Friday afternoon, following a presentation to WSM founder E.W. Craig by Governor elect Frank Clements, the visiting disk jockeys were set loose on the Country stars for interviews to air on their respective stations back home. At the taping session in WSM's Studio C were Minnie Pearl, Flatt & Scruggs, Roy Drusky, Jimmy C. Newman, George Hamilton IV, Charlie and Ira Louvin, Cowboy Copas, Pearl and Carl Butler, Skeeter Davis and Ralph Emery, Jim Reeves, Del Wood, Faron Young, Jimmy Dean, and Patsy Cline.

Patsy did at least a hundred mini-interviews. She was asked what it was like being hospitalized for 35 days after her car accident. Her in-depth answer to the visiting d.j. was "Awful!" When asked why she went back to work in a wheelchair and on crutches, she replied, "I just couldn't stay home."

At the awards ceremonies held Saturday afternoon in the Maxwell House Hotel [destroyed by fire in 1964] Patsy came away the big female winner. She took honors from *Music Vendor* Magazine [which later became *Record World]* for Female Vocalist of the Year for "Crazy" and "She's Got You"; from *Billboard* for Favorite Female Artist; from *CashBox* for Most Programmed Album of the Year, "Patsy Cline Showcase," and Most Programmed C&W Female Vocalist; and from Music Reporter for Female Vocalist of the Year and Star of the Year. There were other citations from other sources for a total of ten.

"It's so unbelievable," cried Patsy, who was attired in a gold brocaded evening suit and spiked heels. "My new house is gonna have wall-to-wall awards! It's wonderful, *but* what am I going to do next year?"

Jimmy Dean was named *Billboard's* Country and Western Man of the Year in a brief ceremony on that night's thirty-seventh anniversary broadcast of the Grand Ole Opry.

In the Sunday, November 11, 1962, edition of the Nashville *Tennessean*, Julie Hollabaugh wrote: "Singer Patsy Cline, the spunky girl with a golden voice, is 1962 queen of the country music field with sweepstakes awards from leading musical publications and official title of 'Star Performer of the Year'...The story behind Patsy Cline's success is one of a determined young woman who wouldn't give up, even in the face of overwhelming odds."

For the second year in a row, Patsy had unseated Kitty Wells. She had finally received her recognition.

The following Saturday night, Lee Burrows was at the Opry with her 11-month-old baby. "I hadn't been to the Opry in a while and I was speaking with a bunch of old friends. Suddenly I heard someone say, 'Hi, snob!' I looked up and there was Patsy. 'What's the matter? Don't you speak anymore?' I said, 'Well, hello, Patsy. I didn't see you. Congratulations, by the way! It finally happened. You are really up there now! I'm so happy for you.'

"We talked for quite a while, pure and simple backstage girl talk. I told her I'd been away from Nashville, living in Arkansas. She wanted to see my baby. She told me about hers and carried on about Monette. I'll never forget, I kept looking at her facial scars from the auto accident and wondering what kind of doctor had done the work. It was just horrible!

"Before Patsy left to go on, she said, 'We got to get together and talk soon.' She waved goodbye. I guess I'll never forget that. It was the last time I saw Patsy."

Faron Young noted that, after "I Fall to Pieces" and "Crazy," when Patsy was attracting so much attention and in as much demand on the pop music circuit as she was in Country, Patsy changed her image. "She realized she could be a lot more commercial and be hotter copy without a hayseed image. She left that Country girl look in those western outfits behind and opted for a slicker appearance in dresses and high-fashion gowns. From the way I saw it, and I told her and Randy, she had the potential to become a Kay Starr or Patti Page.

"She was also getting the big head! Patsy and I worked a lot of concerts together on package shows. Hell, she was out on her own a long time by now. I could no longer afford to pay what she and Randy were asking. But when you're hot, you're hot. In nineteen sixty-one I had a hit with 'Hello, Walls' and it did well with the pop crossover play.

"We were driving along to some date and we'd be tuning up and down on the car radio trying to see if we could find our songs. Now Patsy had 'Crazy' and 'She's Got You.' Every one of the stations would be playing her tunes and I yelled, 'God-damn it! Where's "Hello, Walls?" They haven't forgotten me in less than a year, have they?' Patsy said, 'You're old hat, Sheriff. They don't want to play you no more.' I told her she better watch it or she could get out and walk."

As a member of the Opry house band and a freelance musician, Lightnin' Chance worked with Patsy on many appearances. He describes Patsy as far from a big head or a conceited entertainer. "Faron and Patsy were close and he was just kidding around. The Patsy I knew was constantly nervous before she went out on stage. But I've been in this business far too long and I've never gone out to open a show yet without butterflies in my stomach. Patsy'd have knots in her stomach. Patsy would keep a handkerchief in her hand because her palms would be as moist as anything from sweating just before she'd perform. Sometimes, if she was nervous, she'd smoke. I remember after the accident, Patsy got frequent headaches. And around the time she was having those scars worked on, she'd keep some type of band around her hairline to apply pressure or to keep the stitches in place.

"On stage, no one could come close to Patsy. She was amazing. A star. Really. That's such an overused word, but Patsy was the epitome of a star. She had that special something. She did. I worked with her when she wore those cowgirl outfits and when she wore fancy dresses. And, you know what? It didn't matter what Patsy wore or didn't wear. It didn't make a damn bit of difference because when Patsy opened her mouth at that mike not only did she get attention, she demanded it. Patsy had charisma. It was like Red Foley when he did the gospel hymns and Hank Williams with his heart broken and bleeding. Patsy was at her finest, I think, when she sang the heart songs, the you-done-me-wrong-dang-you type. From the moment she hit that stage, and it didn't matter where it was, Patsy had so much power and expression in her voice. She was telling her story, and to tell the truth, she was telling the story of the ladies out there in that audience. She was damning those men for doing those ladies dirty.

"When Patsy finished she was wrung out like a wash rag. But it was a joy and a privilege to have known and worked with her. She could be testy, but she was a great gal. Patsy was pretty good with the audience rap, but mostly the funny things that happened at shows involved her snide remarks to us guys in the band, her 'dogies,' as she called us.

"In those days you would stand on your head, gobble peanut butter from a ceiling fan, and pee in your vest pocket and all kinds of stuff, anything to be a little different. Showmanship. Patsy didn't have to worry. She was unique, the way she moved when the others would stand like statues and the way she sang.

"But, as far as the band was concerned, Patsy being Patsy would demand, if I can be modest, the best, and we had to come up with little things to please her all the time. I had developed my squeaking bass—some people say I made the darn thing cry—as an applause-milking gimmick. We weren't using drums back then, so I had a rim cut out of a piece of seasoned ash, took a tiffany head and wet it, and stretched it over the wood. When it dried, it was real tight and I attached it with springs to the side of my bass. So for making musical comment or to pick at the artist to have some fun, I took this drum brush, reached in back, and dragged my hand up—while I was still playing with my thumb and finger of the other hand. It delighted audiences. And Patsy especially got a kick out of it. When I'd do it, she'd act real scared and say, 'Hey, little dogie, you trying to scare the bosslady?' "

Patsy often called the home she and Charlie purchased on Nella Drive "the house that Vegas built." Since Patsy's Decca earnings were coming in slim payments because of hefty advances the company had made to the singer, Patsy desperately needed money to keep the house. Randy booked her into the Merri-Mint Theatre in the Mint Casino, which was owned by the Sahara Hotel, for an extended engagement of thirty days.

Teddy Wilburn remembers, "Patsy called me in early November and told me about Vegas. She was totally beside herself. This was at the time when Elvis had gone there and totally conquered it. She told me she had spent five thousand dollars on arrangements and on a choreographer who had taught her some steps to do in her act. She was set to work with Claude King and the Glaser Brothers—Chuck, Jim, and Tompall. The Glasers had been on Godfrey, too, and now were recording for Decca. They were to back Patsy vocally and as a band.

"She told me she wanted to get together with them while

they were in town and rehearse. She couldn't get them to do it. It wasn't in their contract. She was real upset. I told her, 'Hey, Patsy, cool down. Ferguson's, where you'll be staying, has a couple of big rooms available where you can rehearse. So relax. There's nothing to worry about.'

"Doyle, Loretta, and I had worked at the Mint lounge, and she was asking some advice, information, and pointers. I said, 'Well, first of all, throw away those arrangements and forget about the choreography. Just get everybody together and meet out at the motel a few days early and plan what you're going to do. That way, it will be fresh on everybody's mind. If you do it here, they'll forget everything before they get out of there.' She paused and said, 'Well, I never thought of it that way.'

"I said, 'And you've got nothing to worry about yourself, either. You just get up there on the stage and sing like I know Patsy Cline can sing and you'll knock 'em dead—even the high rollers.' No matter what I said, Patsy was still worried.

"I told her, 'You've got nothing to worry about!' There are some artists who need to do a lot of movement or exciting things to get an audience with them. But not Patsy. She was that good. I knew that, but I really don't think Patsy knew. She had a lot of insecurities. They manifested themselves in her person in the way she talked. The way she'd try to gun you down. Outwardly, she was as hard as nails; inwardly, she was just like mush."

Patsy opened at the Mint on the downtown Strip Friday, November 23, with Hilda and Charlie in the audience. Throughout her five-week run Charlie remained with Patsy and, for the most part, so did Randy. For sure, Patsy missed home but she was a hit, though, because of the self-serving nature of the Las Vegas newspaper columns, there was little in-depth reporting on the show, Patsy's phenomenon, or her amazing up-and-down life and career. The Las Vegas *Review Journal* ran a WSM press release that was a virtual rewrite of the Country Music Festival awards story in the Nashville *Tennessean.*

The following appeared in the Las Vegas *Sun* "SUNdial" column on November 27: "ALL ROADS LEAD TO VEGAS—Patsy Cline made her local debut before an SRO throng and delivered the goodies. She's described as a 'switch-hitter' since topping both popular and country ballad balloting by *Music Vendor, Music Reporter, Billboard,* and *CashBox* magazines. The crowd enthusiastically applauded for more at the conclusion of a solid session which included songbird Patsy's interpretations, including: 'I Fall to Pieces,' 'Heartaches,' 'Crazy,' 'I Don't Want a Ricochet Romance,' 'Am I a Fool!'

"Miss Cline's accompanists did a whale of a job too, as the singer moved efficiently from one ditty into another. 'This is the song Connie Francis made famous,' she said, introducing 'Stupid Cupid' and credited 'the late Hank Williams' as she dipped into 'Your Cheatin' Heart.' Humor was injected into the performance through the words of a rendition, viz: 'You've Beeen Foolin' Around on Water Skis, You're Gonna Get Water On Your Knees,' (etc.)."

Patsy Cline, to the Vegas press and audiences, was a big record star. Her single of "So Wrong" and "You're Stronger Than Me" in August had gotten to Number 14 on the Country charts and to 85 in the pop Top 100. Her current single of "Heartaches" and "Why Can't He Be You?" wasn't making any Country waves but was Number 73 on the pop charts.

Publisher Al Gallico visited with Patsy in Las Vegas. "She put on one hell of a show for a country performer at that time. The powers in Vegas could see her potential.

"One night while I was there, Patsy was asked to appear at the Sahara to get a feel of the room and she didn't seem to be too keen on the idea. She told me, 'They want me to work the Strip, but, hoss, that's too uptown for me. I ain't gonna do it.'

"I told her she was bananas! But Patsy explained why. 'I won't do it because I'm afraid to work up there. They're not my kind of people. I don't want to wear fancy gowns. I want to wear my cowgirl outfits.' I said, 'Patsy, your kind of people are all over!' "

Dale Turner recalls Patsy telling her how upset she became in Las Vegas. She took the engagement because she needed the money badly. One of the reasons she was so down was that she had to be there over the Christmas holidays, and that just tore her up having to be away from the kids. You know, with Patsy, the audience knew right where she was coming from. Onstage she was very direct. On Christmas night, or Christmas Eve, she just broke out crying right in the middle of the show. She said, 'No matter what, I will never do this again. This is the time to be with your family, not away from them.' "

Donn Hecht surprised Patsy at the end of the run when he came from Los Angeles to see the show. "She startled me by interrupting her performance to formally introduce me. Patsy called me 'a fine Country writer who's played an important role in my career.' I had never written Country, but having the distinction of being termed that by Patsy because of 'Walkin' After Midnight' was one of the greatest compliments I've ever received.

"Backstage we visited for quite a while. She was exhausted, pale, unsure. Only the heart was there. At first, I thought it was overwork, but the lines on her young face spelled much more. She, Randy, and I were going to eat that night but Patsy abruptly canceled because, as she puts it, 'I need some rest more than I need any food.'

"Patsy persuaded me to just stay and talk to her. She went to get up, stood, and reeled with a slight wobble. She complained of not feeling well, which she attributed to the flu bug. While she was fixing her hair, looking at me through the mirror, she brought up Bill McCall. She was still bitter, but she dropped it as fast as she brought it up. Patsy looked at me and said, 'I meant what I said out front, Donn. You are a fine Country writer—you and Alan [Block]. And you're a good person to come all this way just to see me. Hey, you gotta come to Nashville soon and visit us. I got my gold-speckled bathroom!'

"We talked about doing some special session work together and before you know it I was making plans to come to Nashville and we got Randy and even set a tentative date. When Patsy went to turn around, she complained of some tight aching muscles over her shoulders and neck. She wanted to know if I couldn't do anything. I approached her from behind, folded her arms over her chest, and gently lifted her from where she was standing in bear-hug fashion to stretch her back and help relax her. With a pop or two, she said, 'Okay, you can unsqueeze me. I feel better already.'

"The thing which had always amazed me about Patsy was her unnerving ability to switch topics and trains of thought. Right then, in a tone and manner that appeared somewhat strange and ominous, Patsy began talking very softly about her life and things she needed to take care of when she got home the following week. It was like a person who intended moving to another city and was going through the motion of settling accounts."

"And I owe you a lot," Patsy told Donn, "in more ways than a song."

"How's that, Patsy?"

"Oh, just a lot of ways. Your way of thinking things out and all. About music being music and crossing fences to see that people and things are like they really are, and not like you think they are."

"That's nice of you to say, Patsy, but it's not true that you owe me. We learn and mature from relationships we have with the people we meet along the way. I can say the same about you—that you taught me about pure guts and taking on the world and about winning. You're a champion of a winner. Look at what you've accomplished. I just feel proud knowing you, and that I've had the opportunity to share in some small way."

"There was nothing for me musically before 'Walkin' After Midnight.' My one regret was that one had to be shoved down my throat!" Patsy and Donn laughed, thinking back at what everyone went through to get her to record that song. "It must have been like giving medicine to a baby! The baby says she doesn't want it and you're saying, 'Oh, baby, but it's good for you.' I owe you!"

"Oh, no you don't."

"I want to record some more of your material."

"We can work that out."

"We have to because I owe you, hoss!"

"You owe me nothing. A piece of flint comes in contact with a piece of steel at exactly the right time and a spark appears. And both are better for it. If I have another song that I think is right for you, I'll submit it to you or Randy. If it's in the cards, as they say in Vegas, it's in the cards. Maybe we can make sparks again!"

"Do send me some stuff. Send it to Randy! He's the decision maker in the family. Think we could get rolling soon?"

"In about a month?"

"Fine."

"I could use the money from a Patsy Cline hit!"

"So could we!"

Hecht told Patsy and Randy he would put some material in the mail immediately. When Randy left them, Donn noticed

Patsy's mood and personality changing yet again.

"You know, I don't understand it at all, Donn."

"What, Patsy?"

"I know people all around me who don't have half my talent—oh, they might have regular schooling and all. And they seem to have everything good happen to them without even half trying."

"Yeah, I've seen that, too."

"Hell, all my life it's been uphill! It's uphill even now. I tried to do everything the right way without stepping on or hurting anyone—*even* if it meant hurting me. *But*, let me tell you something, Donn, all that's going to stop. Experience is a hard teacher. She gives the tests first and the lessons come after."

"When it's much too late!"

"Right. I've got a lot of living to do, with people I want to do it with and for *once* in my damn life I'm going to do it!"

"Hell, Patsy, go to it, girl!"

"Hey, you remember back in nineteen fifty-seven, about this time of the year, we recorded your song 'Cry Not for Me'?"

"I sure do."

"And McCall wouldn't release it until Fifty-nine! He didn't want to spend any money promoting it."

"Actually, that song was Bill's Patsy Cline insurance. He was thinking you might be planning to fly the coop and go to another label."

"From his thoughts to God's will! There's a big interrelation between that song and my life."

"How can that be? That's absolutely ridiculous. At long last, you're a star. One that will shine for a lot of years. Hell, Patsy, if Donn Hecht is remembered at all thirty years from now, it'll be because I knew you! This is not a time for crying. You've reached a place in the sun that hundreds of would-be singers would envy."

"I'm not so sure. Don't kid yourself, Donn. I don't. Every time I've had what I've wanted here [she held out her palm], something somewhere has always pulled the rug out from under me and I've fallen flat on my Country rearend. Sickness, car accidents, hospital bills, and Bill McCall. It's happened before and it'll happen again. Watch and see. But I don't give a damn about it now, because, hell, I'm used to it."

"Patsy, you're talking crazy!"

"No, I'm not. Listen. 'Cry not for me, when I am far away, there's nothing more to say, cry not for me...' And that's really the way I feel, you know, because when I go, I don't want anybody to cry for me."

"And why not, honey?"

"I just don't."

"What do you expect the people who love you to do?"

"Just listen, that's all. Listen to the songs and how I did my damndest to learn the words and sing them right."

"That they will, Patsy! You're a songwriter's dream. But, my goodness, you've got a hell of a lot of songs to sing yet! And a hell of a lot of time to sing before you'll be joining in any choruses in 'Hillbilly Heaven.' "

Patsy reared her head back and just laughed. Hecht said it was the first time all evening she had laughed. "Well, if there really are a bunch of hillbillies there, you can be damn sure I'll get in!"

"It's getting late, Patsy, and I'm going to have to head out."

"Come on, let's find Randy and we can all go."

Outside on East Fremont Street, Patsy and Donn hugged. She said, "I'll see you in Nashville, hoss!" Patsy and Randy walked down the street. Then Patsy turned and said, "Donn!" He answered her. "Goodbye. Have a safe trip."

Hecht explained that he was bothered by some of the things Patsy told him in the dressing room. "They were strange to the point of being weird.

"I cannot arrive at any other conclusion than to say that logic followed that perhaps Patsy and Randy were more than client/manager, and that things had not been going well in her marriage. They walked down the street in a way that suggested much more than a business relationship. Perhaps, at last, she had found *the* man in her life."

Patsy and Randy. Some people said, "Oh, yes, very definitely." Others, "My God, never in a million years." Kathy Hughes said that her marriage was a good, solid one and that there was no romance between Patsy and Randy. She told of the strong dependence Patsy had on Randy "and, yes, there was more than a client/manager relationship. They were the best of friends. Why does that appear ugly to some people?"

Randy was always there for both Patsy and Charlie, according to Kathy. He just wasn't Patsy's friend. She told of an occasion, when at 2:30 on a Sunday morning, Patsy called Randy at home and told him she and Charlie had a fight after they got home from the Opry. "Patsy told him, 'It's a knock-down, drag-out fight! You better get over here!' And he did. Just like that, got out of bed and went. He said, 'Those two are at it again!' He would have done anything for either one of them. This was a way of life with Patsy and Charlie. She was always threatening to leave him. But anything Patsy said about that or getting a divorce, I doubt if that was true. And she certainly wasn't leaving Charlie for Randy!"

Billy Walker, Randy's client also and a friend to them both, says, "Patsy and Charlie separated for a while, and Patsy and Randy had made overtures about the situation but I think they had resolved it. I don't know for sure. I don't think anybody knows for sure, except those two. Even Charlie. And, if he does, he ain't tellin'."

"I believe it was common knowledge that Charlie had a girlfriend," said a source close to all the parties. "Patsy and I talked about this. She said on numerous occasions she was going to divorce Charlie. But I don't know. I always figured that was just Patsy talking, because every time you turned around she and Charlie were together. Who's to say what was in their minds?

"As far as a romance between Patsy and Randy, I think they had a crush on each other but it didn't go any further than that. Their friendship went further than that. Maybe it was misconstrued. We were together a lot and they were genuinely fond of each other, but I never took it for 'love.' People in this town, like everywhere, love to grab on to something and they sure did on that.

"I'm sure the thought may have entered Patsy and Randy's minds. But both of them knew it wouldn't work. He was Patsy's manager, number one, and Randy was very much in love with his wife, Kathy. More than anyone, I think Randy would know that Patsy would have been hell on wheels to live with. In spite of everything, she and Charlie were a 'thing,' and, you know what, everything she said aside, nothing could have broken them apart."

Lightnin' Chance says, "No, it never went as far as that. Definitely! You heard rumors and all kinds of stuff. But, you know, I could tour with Kitty Wells, probably one of the most happily married women in the entire world, and the first thing you know is that we're sweet on each other. There's always going to be a rumor started."

Gordon Stoker brought up the situation with Randy. "To Patsy, Randy was the greatest. And he was also kinda stuck on her and she was kinda stuck on him. I kidded him, 'Hey, man, don't get too interested in your merchandise.' I picked at him about it, because I really loved Patsy and Randy and I wanted to get at the truth from the source. And, heck, Randy was like a member of the family. I knew they were together quite a lot. Well, Randy got tired of me bugging him and he finally said, 'Gordon, there's one thing I was told many, many years ago by a man who knew and it's something I've never forgotten—and don't you ever forget that I told you this. He told me, 'Son, don't ever put your cock in the payroll!' He made that remark so firm and so sincere to me that I really believed him. Randy was not carrying on with Patsy on the side."

Dottie West disbelieved the rumors and the subject never came up between her and Patsy. "Patsy and Randy were such close friends, so close that it would make you wonder if anything was going on between them. There was a very close attachment, but nothing more. Charlie was a little afraid and jealous of Patsy's relationship with Randy. He stuck pretty close. It caused problems for sure.

"There is a certain love and dedication between a client and a manager. You love him for working so hard for you. But I can't say I ever saw Randy and Patsy even embrace. There were times when I would talk about everything that was on her mind and she never once brought up anything like this. If there was something, I believe she would have told me. She did love Randy, but it was love for the man who helped make it happen for her—helped her achieve what she had wanted for so much of her life."

Not long after Patsy's single of "Leaving' on Your Mind" and "Tra Le La Le La Triangle" was released, January 7, 1963, she and Loretta spent the day together. "She and Charlie had a fuss that day. She came over to pick me up and we were going into town to pick up a bunch of new long gowns that Patsy had ordered. That was back in the days when the girl singers wouldn't wear long dresses.

"We were driving along and her song '(If You Got) Leavin' on Your Mind' came on the radio and she had been talking about what was going on between her and Charlie, so I said, 'Well, it looks like you're leavin', girl!' And we broke up laughing. She weren't going nowhere. Sure they had their squabbles. The marriage had its rocky moments, but there were pressures from several directions."

Patsy's mother said that in those final weeks, Patsy had an attorney draw up trust papers for the children and was considering beginning divorce proceedings. Charlie refutes this, saying, "This simply was not true. Patsy talked about trust funds for the children and I agreed we should do it, but we never got around to it. I told her, 'Heck, we've got plenty of time for that. We can do it the next time you have a breather.' And if Patsy was considering a divorce, she had a funny way of showing it. She wanted me with her constantly, and I was there."

Sums up Jean Shepard, "I've heard the rumors, but as far as a separation between Charlie and Patsy, that was never the case to my knowledge. I wasn't privy to Patsy's confidences. We were just friends. To say it was the happiest marriage in the world, well, that would be telling a lie. But when you see people day in and day out, you get a gut feeling about things. And Patsy was trying to have another baby. I know, because we had the same doctor, Homer M. Pace. One day he was telling me 'That Cline woman has some temper! You know, Virginia Dick.' I thought for a minute, and said, 'Oh, Patsy!' He went on, 'Yeah. She came in here to be examined and couldn't be bothered waiting when she arrived for her appointment. She demanded to be waited on immediately. I told her I'd be with her as soon as I could. And she waited.'

"Doctor Pace finished examining me and as I was about to leave he said, 'And if you see Patsy tell her to come in as soon as she can. That dame has the most screwed-up female problems of anyone I know.'

"Patsy and Charlie had some battles. She'd have him thrown in the drunk tank one night and the next she'd have forgiven him. It was a crazy marriage, but sometimes love is crazy!"

Sometime in mid-to late January 1963, Patsy and Charlie were returning to Nashville late at night from an engagement. "Jackie DeShannon came on the radio singing 'Faded Love,' the Bob Wills song," Charlie said. "I thought Patsy was in the back seat asleep, but she popped up, scaring the devil out of me, saying, 'Everybody's modulating down these days. I wonder why Jackie did it?'

"I told her, 'Probably the song is not in her key. If it's too high for her, it would have been hard to do without bringing it down.' Patsy replied, 'No, it wouldn't. I can do it.' I answered, 'Oh, you can, huh!' She said, 'Yep, I sure as hell can!' At her last session, Patsy took 'Faded Love' and made the high notes a half step higher, and sang it all the way through without the least bit of modulation. 'I told you I could do it,' she boasted. I was fairly amazed and a little impressed, though, by then, I knew she could do anything she set her mind to. And if you dared her, oh, my god! She was really something."

The last sessions were held February 4 through the 7th. Patsy recorded "Faded Love" on the first day, followed by "Someday (You'll Want Me to Want You)," and the Pat Boone hit "Love Letters in the Sand."

Over the next three days, she did the Bill Monroe, Irving Berlin, and traditional standards, "Blue Moon of Kentucky," "Always," and "Bill Bailey, Won't You Please Come Home."

New Tunes were Don Gibson's haunting "Sweet Dreams," "Crazy Arms," "He Called Me Baby" by Harlan Howard, "You Took Him off My Hands," co-written by Howard, and, the last tune of the Thursday, February 7th session, "I'll Sail My Ship Alone."

On Wednesday, Teddy Wilburn found Patsy in Owen Bradley's office listening to playbacks and asked him to join her."I was wondering how Las Vegas worked out, so I asked Patsy. She had given me a big hug, but hadn't said a word about anything concerning the engagement. I said, 'You haven't told me how things went in Vegas.' She replied, 'Fine. We knocked them out, hoss. Knocked them out!'

"I retorted, 'I told you so!' She was showing me pictures of the Las Vegas performances. I asked, 'Did you do what I told you?' She was real suave and answered, 'There weren't no problems, hoss, Things came off real well.' Patsy knew what she could do but sometimes she was not secure with the knowledge. I think the Vegas folks were interested in having her come back. They were in the process of negotiating a return engagement with Randy."

Patsy called Jan Howard on Thursday morning and asked, "Hey, where have you been? You gonna come to the studio tonight, arent't you?"

"I don't honestly know," replied Jan. "But I don't think so."

"Why not, damn it?"

"Well, I've got some things I need to take care of and really, Patsy, I don't want to bug you when you're working."

"Ah, shit, bug me!"

"Are you sure?"

"Oh, my God, yes. I'd kinda like to have you there."

"Okay, then I'll be there."

Jan and Harlan attended the session along with Dottie West. Randy and Charlie were there.

"After the session Patsy was kidding around with the Jordanaires and telling them what a great job they had done. They always did. Patsy was elated, she was so thrilled at how things had gone. And, for once, happy with what she had done. She couldn't have done it better or greater, as far as I was concerned.

"We went over to Owen's office to listen to the playbacks. Patsy went into Harry Silverstein's office—he was Owen's assistant and a Decca producer who died very young—and came out with a forty-five r.p.m. record."

Patsy said, "Well, here it is." She held up the record.

"What are you talking about?" asked Owen.

"The record."

"What record?" asked Jan.

"Here's 'A Church, a Courtroom and Then Goodbye.' It's the first and the last."

"Don't say that," scolded Jan.

"Oh, hoss, I just meant here's the first record that came out and here we are listening to the last one."

Jordanaires leader Gordon Stoker noted, "I didn't think, from some of the strange things she said, that Patsy was planning on being around long. It all goes back to a remark she made during the 'Crazy' session when she was trying so hard to hit those highs in spite of her injuries. She was amazing in that she always seemed to make the best of any situation, no matter how bad it was.

"She walked into the session on her crutches and looked at us and said, 'Well, fellas, the third time is charmed.' I asked Patsy, 'What in the world are you talking about? You've got a cat's nine lives!' We all laughed and Patsy got to talking about some accident or illness years ago, and about the car wreck she and her brother had survived and said again, 'The third time is charmed. The third time I go. If I have another accident, it's going to be all she wrote!' "

Remarked Brenda Lee, "I've always felt that Patsy had a premonition that she didn't have a whole lot of time here to do what she had set out to do, and that accounted for her amazing drive. Patsy and I would discuss our style of singing and how not to compromise how we sang for our beliefs and not for those of others. She was the first woman singer in Country to make the industry and the men singers realize we weren't chattel.

"We talked about our status in the business and labeling that was rampant then—if you weren't this, you had to be that. We were in that unique category of not being rock 'n' roll and not being Country either. Patsy transcended the labels and appealed to the public's taste. She wondered over the fact that she was neither fish nor fowl, and if her lot was a yoke around her neck.

"Patsy finally came to the realization that it was not her choice and that she was just Patsy Cline. Which was all she needed to be. Patsy loved singing and she enjoyed her work immensely. I remember, especially after the accident, that she was itching to get back to work. I said, 'Take it easy. Rest. You've got plenty of time. You need to heal first before you do anything.' She didn't listen. She was just a-itching to get out again and sing as if it was going to be her last chance.

"She had to do another road tour, another session, another this, and another that. She was trying to cram a lot of living into a short space of time. I used to let that really worry me. But it didn't bother her!"

Monday, February 11

"Carl and I were booked to do a two-week tour in California," remembered Pearl Butler. "He had costumes, but I didn't. Goldie Hill, the Decca star from the 'Louisiana Hayride,' who retired after she married Carl Smith in nineteen fifty-seven, told me, 'Patsy don't want her costumes no more. Why don't you call her and see what she's gonna do with hers. I think she's planning to give 'em away.'

"We were at Les and Dot Leverett's—Les is the WSM Grand Ole Opry photographer—and I called Patsy right from there. She asked me, 'Pearl, what do you want my old costumes for? I've worn them for years and pretty well out!' I said, 'Well, honey, I ain't got nothin' to wear for this trip to California and I just thought you'd let me borrow a couple.'

"Patsy got real angry, 'Well, Pearl Butler, I am ashamed of

you for even thinking you have to ask! Just get your tail over here and we'll go through the closets."

When Pearl and Dot arrived, Patsy was castigating Charlie, yelling, "What kind of man are you anyway?" When they looked up and saw the visitors, all was quiet and Patsy brushed past Charlie and took Pearl upstairs.

" 'Is that all you want?' she asked me. I said, 'Oh, honey, it's more than enough, I don't know how to thank you.' Patsy slapped me across the back and exclaimed, 'Now, hoss, don't go and get sentimental on me. You, of all folks, don't have to thank me. I'm glad I can do something for you. You can have 'em all—boots and everything.

"I told her, 'Oh, no, Patsy, I couldn't.' She said, 'Well, I don't know why not.' I persisted, 'Thank you so much, but I really just couldn't.' We hugged. She gave me a real tight squeeze and said goodbye. And that was the last time I ever saw Patsy. I was really so proud to be wearing those outfits. I felt like a million dollars on all those shows."

Wednesday, February 13

"When I was the all-night disk jockey at WSM," informed Ralph Emery, "I used to say people would come see me because everything else had closed and I had the only open place in town. I thought about putting a sign outside the station that read, 'Ralph's Place—Open All Nite.' Patsy and Charlie and some of their buddies would come up in a party mood around midnight. I tried to interview Patsy over the air, but it never worked. Too many inside jokes among friends and no content for the air. It was frustrating. I was at the end of the party.

"Now this one particular Wednesday night Patsy came up by herself. Charlie and the gang didn't show. She and I began rapping and it was really good, one on one. We covered the spectrum of her career and she was real down and in a talkative mood. Patsy said she had played hard, but that she had worked hard. I kick myself everytime I think about that interview. I thought it would be like all the other times. My interviews with Patsy had been disasters. I didn't roll the tape machine!"

Saturday, February 16

"I was in town and Patsy and Charlie invited me to come over to their new home for a party after the Opry," said Al

Gallico, the music publisher. "Randy and I got to talking about road dates and he was bragging about the plane he had purchased that summer. I told him, 'Hey, do me a favor, please. Why don't you give up that shit box you fly in before something happens?' Randy answered, 'Hey, Al, don't worry. I don't take chances.' "

Friday and Saturday, February 22 and 23

"Patsy and I were working on a Country package show in Lima, Ohio, on the Friday before we did Birmingham and the Kansas City benefit," noted Billy Walker. "Charlie and Randy were with us, but that Charlie seemed to have gotten uncontrollable. He'd get drunk and be very abusive around Patsy. It was embarrassing and a shame. Randy and I tried to do something but you just had to hope he'd go off by himself.

"The next night in Toledo the whole show was simply Patsy and the orchestra. I don't think Randy knew this. I came to see the show since we were working together the night before. I wasn't on the bill in Toledo. At least, I wasn't supposed to be. This was not an unusual situation with Patsy, to play a Country gig one night and then turn around and do a pop concert the next day or so—all in the same area.

"She could hold an audience in the palm of her hand in either arena. Everyone liked Patsy. Of all the female Country singers that have been, Patsy could adapt to any type of song. She was my favorite. Audiences felt a real closeness to Patsy.

"She was a down-home-type person—no phoniness or pretensions, just warmth and a lot of heart in her music. Loretta Lynn has a lot of the same attributes as Patsy had. And Patsy enjoyed the autographs and picture-taking. As a matter of fact, she was a hog about it! I used to kid her, 'Well, are you coming or are we gonna have to stay here until you sign autographs for every last person in the hall?' We would watch each other's shows when we worked together and make comments. Patsy took criticism well as long as it was presented in the right way.

"Anyway this Saturday night when she found out she was the whole show, she came to Randy and me and asked, 'What do I do?' I said, 'Well, hey, you want me to help you out?' I had some pop crossover, especially with 'Charlie's Shoes.' Patsy said, 'Oh, hoss, would you?' I replied, 'My goodness, Patsy, sure I'll help you. You don't even need to ask.' With just one artist it would have been rough to do a two-hour show. It takes weeks of preparation. Patsy could have done it—before the accident. But since that car wreck she was having a bad time with aches and pains and headaches. She got nervous real easy and had to rest. Patsy asked me to open for her. I did an hour and then she came on and did an hour and fifteen minutes. That was a long show in those days."

Thursday, February 28

"Patsy had a seamstress make some drapes for Loretta and Mooney's little Goodlettsville farmhouse," said Teddy Wilburn. "She'd also had two of those big ottomans made to resemble dice and she was going to take them over, too, the day before Patsy left on the last tour. She surprised Loretta and Mooney with the drapes and helped put them up. The dice did not come in, and she planned on taking them over when she got back to town."

Loretta recounted the story of that evening in her book and to Loudilla Johnson. "That same night, Patsy called me and Mooney and asked us to come over to listen to the sessions she had just completed just a bit over a week ago. We got up out of bed and went over. She was all excited and so proud. Patsy told us, 'Now, I want ya'll to listen to this and see if you think maybe I'm getting out a little too far from Country.' Patsy had been worried about that. Me and Doo sat in Patsy and Charlie's music room and listened. As we listened to the tapes, Patsy embroidered a tablecloth. Her little boy Randy was on a rocking horse. When the tape finished, I told her, 'No, Patsy, it's beautiful.' What else could you say. That's what it was. It was fantastic! But, of course, Patsy was fifteen to twenty years ahead of her time in her singing and her music.

"Patsy told me she'd give me fifty dollars if I'd go with her on that Kansas City benefit date Sunday, but I told her, 'I have a date Saturday that pays seventy dollars, so I better go on and take that one.' We made plans to go shopping when she returned from the weekend. Just before we left her house around midnight Patsy said she had something for me. Then she gave me some long gangly sparkling earrings and a whole big box filled with clothes.

"When we went out to the car through the music room door to the garage, I said to Doo, 'Oh, I forgot to say goodbye to Patsy.' He told me, 'Well, hurry up and go ahead and tell her. It's midnight and we need to be going.'

"I sat the box down on the hood of Patsy and Charlie's

Cadillac and went back in. I hugged her and kissed her, and as I went back out the door Patsy hauled off and hit me a little bit. She said, 'We're gonna stick together, aren't we gal?' That was the last time I ever saw Patsy."

Saturday, March 2
Birmingham

Mr. and Mrs. Bill Holcombe of Alabaster, Alabama, parents of beautiful blond singer/musician Wendy Holcombe, went to see the Country superstar-studded show that Saturday night in Birmingham that headlined Tex Ritter, Charlie Rich, Jerry Lee Lewis, Flatt & Scruggs, and Patsy.

"Plain and simple, the reason I wanted to go," Helen Holcombe reminisced, "was to see Patsy Cline. I first saw her on the Arthur Godfrey TV shows and liked her and, of course, had heard her records. I told Bill, 'Hey, we only go out once a year. Am I due for my big treat?' He said he guessed so, but that he didn't have much money. I told him I thought he'd be able to scrape enough together for the Country show starring Patsy.

"We lived way out in the country, so eating out was a big enough treat, but also getting to see Patsy, well that was fantastic. We even had to take Wendy with us. She was about one. We were able to leave our other baby, Bill Jr., with my mother-in-law. When we got to the City Auditorium, I asked Bill to buy me a Patsy Cline photo so I could try and get it autographed later. He said, 'Oh, honey, we can't afford it.' I didn't push. I knew I was lucky getting the tickets the way things had been.

"The show was great when it really began for me when Patsy came on. She wore this beautiful white dress with rhinestones. She sang her hits, 'I Fall to Pieces,' 'Crazy,' 'She's Got You,' and her song, 'Come on In.' But when she did 'Walkin' After Midnight,' the place went wild. When she finished Patsy got a standing ovation.

"Patsy said at one point, 'Any of you gals out there have weight problems?' Of course, there was a loud roar. She went on, 'I been busy trying to lose weight, too. And this is the first time in a long time I've been able to wear white.' She told us how much she now weighed and how much she had lost. We all applauded. 'I'm telling you!' she yelled out. 'Don't it just look good. Of course, got another problem now. I can't look at any food!'

"At the end Patsy quieted everyone. She was genuinely touched by the response that night. She said, 'I have really had a good time with you. God love you! I've done a lot of things that I'm not happy about. And in the short time God gives us on this earth, I'm doing something about changing all that. But I sure do appreciate you sticking with me and buying my records. Y'all been good to ole Patsy!' And, of course, everyone was on their feet giving her another ovation.

"It was, needless to say, in spite of Wendy squirming all over the place, an evening I'll never forget. And Bill's never forgotten he didn't get me that photo. I kid him all the time, 'It was only a dollar!' "

Nashville

One thing became quite clear, if everyone who says they were asked by Patsy to go on the Kansas City benefit for Jack Call were, indeed, asked, Randy would have had to fly a cargo plane to get them all there.

However, it is a fact that Loretta Lynn was asked and declined because of a prior engagment; that Billy Walker was set to fly with Patsy, Randy, and Cowboy Copas, and when he had to cancel at the last minute and take a commercial flight, that Hawkshaw Hawkins was asked to fill in his place.

It also appears that before Walker confirmed he would ride in Randy's Comanche, Lightnin' Chance was invited by his partner and Patsy. "Randy and I were going to fly everyone up and then go on to our friend Buddy Baer's game farm in Missouri to do some quail hunting with his bird dogs. Then Ferlin got hung up down in Coco Beach and Cape Kennedy (Canaveral) for a front man and emcee and I had to come to the rescue and Hawkshaw ended up taking my place."

Sunday, March 3
Kansas City, Kansas

"We sat in the dressing room between the second show of the afternoon and the evening performance," reflected Dottie West. "Patsy was ironing the blouse she wanted to wear to a two-piece lace dress her mother had made. I said, "Why don't you let me do that, and you get some rest. You already got a bad cold and you know how easily you get tired.' But she just kept on ironing, hardheaded as usual.

"On the night show Patsy wore this lovely white gown. She closed the show. I had been on long ago to do my songs. One of them was my record of 'Touch Me' by Willie Nelson. I idolized Patsy so much, I would never miss the opportunity to watch her perform. But I didn't just stand in the wings. I went out front, into the audience, and watched Patsy's whole set. She was magnificent, as usual. Patsy was a star. When she did get to that point in her career she was elated. But she never took that star status for granted. She ate it up and made the most of it, but Patsy never gave an audience short shift. No matter how late it was or if the show was running overtime, Patsy, when she was closing the show, did all her big songs.

"That night in Kansas City, Patsy had the audience on their feet giving her standing ovations and screaming for more. She was moved to tears and thanked the audience and told them how much they meant to her and that she'd be nowhere without them. Since I was standing in this ocean of humanity who were pouring their hearts out to Pasty the same way she'd done for them, it is a night that is indelibly etched in my memory. But, then, how could I ever forget that night?"

Monday, March 4

"When we hugged and kissed goodbye," observed Dottie, "Patsy said, 'Don't fret. Hoss, if that little bird goes down, I guess I'll go down with it.' I remember thinking about that all the way home in the car. The storm was bad. It was a rain that looked like it was never gonna stop. It was a thick, murky rain. As Bill and I were driving, there were many times when we couldn't see the tops of the telephone poles. I kept saying over and over, 'Now, I hope they don't go and get crazy and decide to go ahead and try to leave.'

"I cannot say I had a premonition that anything terrible or tragic was going to happen, but I recall being quite concerned. All the way home I drove Bill crazy, saying, 'Honey, you do think they'll wait, don't you?' and 'I wonder how the weather is back in Kansas City?'"

Tuesday, March 5

"Why don't you stay the night?" asked Bill Braese, manager of the Dyersburg, Tennessee, airport.

"Naw," said Randy, "Hell, I've already come this far. It's only another ninety miles [by road, actually, some 120 miles]. We'll be there before you know it."

"I don't know. I think you're taking a chance. Why don't

you take the airport car? It's a Plymouth station wagon. 'Sixty-one. But it'll get you there. I'll bring your plane to your tomorrow and pick up my car."

"That's nice of you but we're going on. I'm gonna take care of it and if I can't handle the situation, I'm gonna come back."

"The car'll be waiting."

Hughes signed the receipt for the gasoline and took his copy, folded it, and put it in his money bag. The plane had enough fuel to stay in the air three and a half hours.

They taxied off at 6:07 P.M.

Dottie and Bill West arrived in Nashville about that time. "We came directly home," said Dottie, "and it took some sixteen hours, even with both of us driving. We said goodnight not too long after six to Grandmother West [Bill's mother], who was staying at the house taking care of the children, and we went in to go to bed. I was exhausted. I wondered what time Patsy and Randy had gotten back and decided I'd call her later that night if I woke up or the next morning. I figured she was sleeping, too."

The weather in the area between Dyersburg and Nashville was described as "extremely turbulent." According to the Federal Aviation Authority, at least one commercial liner saw fit to change course.

Randy headed due east past Huntington with a heading toward Bruceton, across the Tennessee River, Waverly, and Nashville. The green-and-yellow single-engine Comanche was equipped with radar so there was nothing to worry about as far as Hughes was concerned. The winds were high, and bucking them slowed flying time considerably. It was getting darker and Randy was not an instrument-rated pilot. Time was of the essence.

Near Camden, some 85 miles west of Nashville, the plane encountered dense clouds from the storm front in the area of the river and south of Kentucky Lake. When rain became so heavy that it rocked the plane, Hughes turned the craft around. His plan probably was not to return to Dyersburg, but instead to cross back over the Tennessee River and scout quickly for a landing spot. He saw a narrow, twisting rural road but needed a long, level stretch amid these woods of the northeastern Tennessee hills.

As Hughes grappled with the control wheel, he looked at his watch. It was 6:22 P.M. All he could see was dense woodland. And gray clouds from the storm front. The rain stopped, but the clouds lingered. Randy spotted a clearing, and instinct told him to go for it. There was a fire-prevention lookout tower at the top of a hill and the area around it appeared to be as good a location to attempt an emergency landing. First, he had to try to place an SOS call.

Normally, Patsy would ride "shotgun," or in the co-pilot's seat, but since Hawkshaw was six-foot, five she gave up her place to him and sat directly behind, next to Copas.

Hughes advised everyone to make sure they were strapped in and to brace themselves. He needn't have. They were holding on for dear life. And praying.

The plane descended lower and lower and rushed over utility poles and farm houses. Sam Webb, whose farm was located in the dense woodland area, saw a plane circling his home a few minutes after seven and noted that "it was revving up its motor . . . going fast and then slow, like it was attempting to climb. Then I couldn't see it anymore."

Randy frantically worked the controls. He managed to climb but flew right into a cloud. Not being able to read the instruments, and unable to see out of the window beyond the cloud, Randy did not know if he was flying level, upward, or downward. As he attempted to determine direction from the instruments the situation became worse and worse. "Maybe I should fly low and follow a road, any road!" He descended lower. "No, that's bad to do. It's better that I gain altitude."

"My God, Randy, we're flying upside down! Randy!"

The propellor tore into the trees and sawed their tops off. The thick brush grabbed the plane and ripped at it, tearing gaping holes in it. They bounced and skidded across mangled trees and hit with considerable impact straight into the ground.

Randy Hughes' Piper Comanchre 250 crashed at approximately 7:00 PM. There were no survivors.

The major road Randy was looking for, Highway 70, lay not quite one mile away.

Kathy hung the phone up after speaking to Randy. She was about to call Charlie and Jean when the phone rang. It was Billy Walker again. He had called Monday night to see if everyone had arrived back in town. Kathy told him they would be leaving Kansas City about two o'clock on Tuesday. He had still not heard anything and was concerned.

"I'm really worried about Randy," Billy told Kathy. "Have you heard anything?"

"He just called, Billy. They've just refueled in Dyersburg and will be leaving any minute."

"Thank God, I didn't know what to think."

"I'm going to Cornelia Field right now to have 'em turn the lights on."

Kathy spoke with Charlie and Jean, then she and her mother Lucille went to the airport and, as Randy had instructed, asked that the runway lights be put on. "Then we sat and waited, and waited. Then we got worried. It shouldn't have taken Randy more than fourty-five minutes to fly from Dyersburg. We began to suspect something had gone wrong. We asked the attendant if he had heard anything and he said no.

"Then something snapped in me; I knew immediately that something had, indeed, gone wrong, but I didn't know what. One of the men suggested it might be better if we went home and waited for further news. All we could think of was that Randy might have turned back. Everything but the most obvious ran through our minds.

"We came home and turned the radio on. A little after eight there was a report that said the plane was missing. Another said the plane had gone down. The phone started ringing about eight-fifteen and it never stopped. We all spoke back and forth. When things began to look desperate, friends started to come over."

Charlie Dick said, "Kathy had called so I knew they were on their way home. I was there playing with the kids and waiting to go pick Patsy up. They were due around seven. Around seven-thirty I got worried. No one called from the airport to say Randy and the gang had landed. I made a couple of calls. Nothing. Then some friends came over around eight. They had heard on the radio that something had gone wrong."

"About an hour after the call from Kathy," said Jean, "I took my baby Don Robin and put him up in the kitchen sink to give him a bath before I put him to bed. I was eight months pregnant so the kitchen sink allowed me to stand up. A little after seven this weird, completely weak feeling came over me for about ten minutes. I was afraid to move away from the sink because I thought I was going to faint.

"Don was splashing water all over the place, but I just kept bathing him. My first thought was, 'Oh, my God, the baby.'

Then I just froze and held on the edge of that sink. There was no one with me. Then I said, 'No, the baby's not due for another month. What's the matter with me? What am I going to do?'

"A cold sweat broke over me, then it passed and I said, 'Oh, Hawk, get home pretty soon!' When he wasn't home by nine, I really began to get upset. I had low-blood problems and tired very easily. I was a borderline case with leukemia."

At 9:10 the phone rang again at Kathy Hughes' home. "The party asked to speak to Mrs. Randy Hughes. I told him he was. It was a gentleman from the Civil Aeronautics Board office. Randy's departure from Dyersburg had been confirmed from the gasoline purchase receipts. He asked me all sorts of questions—who was on board, the plane identification number, and so. They were planning to mount a search query over the radio. After that I was never contacted by any official spokesperson."

"When it got to be ten o'clock," remembered Jean, "I told myself, for the safety of the baby and my own health, I had better get to bed. I wasn't overly concerned because Kathy had told me if the weather got bad they might turn around and go back to Dyersburg. I was nervous but not upset. I laid in bed and thought, 'Well, maybe, they did go back.' I must have fallen off to sleep.

"The next thing I recall was the phone ringing. I got out of bed slowly to answer it. As I went to the phone I looked at the clock. It was eleven. It was some of Hawks fans—fans we had gotten to know well and who'd become friends—calling from Minneapolis. I slept very deeply, almost as if I was drugged, and was listening to them, but really still in bed.

" 'What are you doing, Jean?' my lady friend asked. I was a bit upset at being woke up. I replied, 'Well, my God, I'm doing what every sensible person would be doing at eleven at night. I'm sleeping.' She asked, 'Are you in bed?' I told her, 'I was. Is there a better place to sleep?' She wanted to know, 'Have you got the radio on?' I answered, 'Naw, I don't have the radio on.'

"Then there was silence. I heard her starting to cry. She said, 'Oh, my God, Jeanie!' That's when I knew. I knew what was wrong. I knew. The plane was down. She told me that Grant Turner on WSM had just announced that the plane believed to be carrying Hawk, Cowboy, and Patsy was lost. She was so upset I couldn't get her off the phone. I finally told her, 'Eileen, I'm by myself. I've got to call somebody. Let me get off the phone, hon.'

"I stayed pretty cool for about an hour. I called Smiley and Kitty Wilson, two of our closest friends in the business—they once played and sang for Ferlin, and their line was busy. When I got them they told me they had been talking to Kathy to find out if what they'd heard was really so and then tried to get me. They came right over.

"It was an all-night vigil. No authorities phoned me or came to the house to tell me, 'Your husband is missing —nothing. It was a nightmare. It was hell!"

The Wilsons called Jean's doctor and asked him to come over. Governor Frank Clement sent a highway patrol car to the houses of each of the families and stationed it there through the night.

"It was a good thing, too," noted Jean, "because some weird things went on. A woman I didn't even know walked into the house before the patrolman arrived, and started asking me questions about the crash. My doctor finally had to sedate me and put me to bed. He stationed the patrolman right outside my door and told him not to let anyone bother me.

"Minnie Pearl and her husband Henry Cannon came to the house when word got out that the plane was presumed missing or crashed. They asked to see me. The patrolman knocked on my door and came into the bedroom. He said, 'Ma'am, I don't know what to do. Minnie Pearl's here to see you. Should I let her in?'

"The doctor was monitoring the baby's heart beat every half hour. I asked him if it would be all right to see Minnie and Henry and he said yes. So they came on in. Minnie was pretty broken up. It was like that all night."

Charlie was at home awaiting word and jumped each time the phone rang. Julie and Randy kept asking him where their mother was. "Is Mommie coming home tonight?" asked Julie.

"It was one of those tough situations," explained Charlie. "I had not given up hope and I did not want to burden them. They would not have even understood. I did not want to lie to them. I didn't know what to say. I tried to get them to go to sleep."

Wednesday, March 6

It was midnight. Jan Howard was home sound asleep. The phone started to ring. Still half asleep, she answered it.

"Jan?"

"Yes—"

"Oh, thank God!"

"Who is this?"

"Jan, this is Hank. Are you all right?"

"Yeah, I'm all right. I was asleep, Hank."

"Then it's Patsy—"

"What are you talking about?"

"If you're all right, then there's something wrong with Patsy."

"Hank, what on earth are you talking about?"

"I'm in Fred Foster's office at Monument [Records] and a few minutes ago two albums fell off the shelf—one of yours and one of Patsy's. I just had a gut feeling that something was wrong—"

"Where's Patsy?"

"I don't know. Don't you worry. I'll call you back."

"Hank, please let me know if something is wrong with Patsy."

"I'll talk to you later."

Roger Miller heard the news. "I used to just cruise around town at night in my old 'Forty-nine Dodge and think and write music. I was everywhere at once. I tuned in to WSM and Grant Turner was saying that the plane carrying Patsy, Cowboy, Hawk, and Randy was late arriving at Cornelia Field and presumed missing. That was about one A.M.

"They had not announced that the plane had crashed, only that it was overdue. Grant promised to keep listeners posted, so I stayed tuned. Then, at one point, Grant announced the flying time from Dyersburg to Nashville and pinpointed an area around Camden where a farmer had seen a plane that looked like it was in trouble and also where an explosion had been reported. It was said that when a communications check by radio had failed to locate the plane or bring any response, Federal Aviation officials, the state and local police, and the Civil Air Patrol were forming a search party."

Shortly before midnight a party of 15 men centered their search efforts in a three- to four-mile radius of Sandy Point, a village about four miles west of Camden. The police dispatcher there said that around 7 P.M. he had received calls from several farmers around Sandy Point stating a plane was circling with its engine cutting out.

The callers reported hearing the engine die, and a few

minutes later, they said they heard what sounded like a crash of some kind. Most of those phoning the police and the state highway patrol office centered the "explosion" and "crash" around one particular object, the tall fire tower off Mule Barn Road in Sandy Point.

The discrepancy in the story is the time of the sightings of the crippled plane. Most of the reports say 7:00 and 7:30. A report listing results of the Civil Aeronautics Board investigation appearing in the Nashville Banner says, in the body of the story, without crediting the CAB, that the crash occurred "about 20 minutes after it took off."

"I heard a plane backfire around seven-thirty," said R.C. King of Route 2, Camden, to Gerald Henry, the staff correspondent for the Nashville *Tennessean,* the next day. "Then I heard something pop a little after seven. The dogs ran out. My wife heard a roar and a pop and then nothing."

Add to these reports the fact that Patsy's watch supposedly stopped at 6:20 and Randy's at 6:25. The exact time of the crash is conjecture, but undoubtedly, from the facts, it appears the 20-minutes-after-take-off theory was a miscalculation.

When Roger Miller heard of the forming of a search party, "I suddenly realized that I had to go there. The blood came rushing to my head and I speeded around town, going from door to door to all the guys I knew well, trying to get someone to go help me. I wanted to get over there and join in the search.

"It was a rainy night and I had visions of them crashed, but maybe hanging from the seats and not being able to help themselves. I had all kinds of visions of them out there in the rain and hurt, still alive, with nobody to help them. Me and another boy, Don—oh, I don't believe I can't remember his last name, who I got to go, headed straight there."

Carl Perkins, the famed guitarist and one of the originators of rockabilly (he wrote "Blue Suede Shoes") who toured regularly with Johnny Cash and had worked with Patsy, also left Nashville about the same time to join the search party.

Miller indicated that he drove north of Camden, out along Highway 70. "Then I stopped. I looked out and there was this farmhouse standing right there. I can see it clearly even now. It was about two-thirty or three, but the lights were on. I got out of the car and knocked on their door. A lady opened it and I asked her about anything she or her husband might have seen or heard that sounded and looked like a plane crashing or in trouble.

"She told me, 'No, we ain't heard no plane crashing. We been up here watching this storm and seemed to me I heard a noise that sounded like a clap of thunder a few hours ago right here behind the house. I thought it went with the rain.' Don and I went running into the woods just a-yelling and a-screaming."

At three Jan Howard's phone rang. She was still awake, tossing, turning, hoping, praying. It was Hank. "'Oh, Jan, this is horrible,' he told her. 'Randy's plane is missing and he was carrying Patsy, Hawk, and Cowboy Copas! It's been confirmed on the radio.' I was stunned. I couldn't say anything. 'Jan! Jan! Are you there? Are you okay?' I couldn't think. Finally, I said, 'Yes, Hank, I'm okay. This is a blow. I can't believe it. There are no other reports? Where did it happen?' Hank was very excited. He said, 'Hon, I've got to see what I can do. Turn the radio on.'

"Harlan and I had been over to Hawk and Jeanie's a day or so before they all left for Kansas City. We were sitting around playing a game of Crazy Eights, and Jeanie was so big with the baby she was very uncomfortable. Hawk took us out and put his show horses through some tricks. They were the first people to befriend me when I got to town. I turned the radio on to find out any details. I still couldn't believe it. 'No, it couldn't be true,' I thought. Somehow there had been an error. The news didn't say anyone had been killed. All I could do was pace and pray. Then I thought of Jeanie and realized I had to go and be with her."

At 4 A.M. the phone at the Hensley home in Winchester, Virginia, rang. Patsy's brother Sam ran out of his bedroom to answer it.

"Hello. Who is it?" Sam heard someone talking, but was not really very attentive. "What did you say?" A friend of the family was trying to explain what he had heard on the radio. "Hey, is this some kind of joke?" Sam asked angrily. "Patsy's not on any plane. Why don't you go back to sleep?"

He slammed the phone down. Mrs. Hensley had jumped out of bed and come into the living room. "Who was that?" The phone rang back at once and Sam grabbed it. "Hey, I told you that Patsy is not on any plane!"

"Wait a minute," exclaimed Mrs. Hensley as she snatched the phone from her son's hand. "Patsy *was* on a plane!"

Sam had to hold his mother. How could this be when they waited out the storm? As quickly as she could, Mrs. Hensley turned the radio on for news of what had happened. Moments later Jim McCoy, near hysterical himself; called from the station WHPL to confirm to Mrs. Hensley and Patsy's family that the Hughes plane was, indeed, missing. He advised that he would call Hilda with reports before putting them on the air.

It was 5:30 and for nearly two hours Roger Miller and his friend Don ran through the woods yelling, "Patsy, Hawkshaw, Cowboy, Randy" at the top of their lungs. "The briar was so bad it had torn our clothes and we'd been cut here and there. We kept at. Then at daybreak we came to this clearing and I spotted this fire tower station and climbed up. When I got to the top I looked out over the area. And there it was. About twenty yards from where we were, I could see that the trees had been all chewed up and I could see debris and metal hanging from the branches.

"There were people gathered back in the area on the main road, sitting on their cars waiting to be directed into a search party. I went back to them and told the highway patrol, 'I found something over here.' And I led the way. I went running as fast as I could. I ran through the brush and the trees and I came up over this little rise and, oh, my God, there it was."

Pearl and Carl Butler were returning from their string of California dates, where Pearl had worn some of Patsy's western costumes. They pulled a small utility trailer behind their Cadillac. It was packed with instruments, amplifiers, assorted stage gear, and Carl and Patsy's outfits.

"We were almost back home, driving through the sticks of the Tennessee hill country, when we heard Grant Turner play one of our songs on the radio. It was always our policy, no matter where we were, whenever we could, to call the disk jockey at the particular station and thank them for playing one of records. They always got kick out of that. They also remembered to play more of your records, too. We kept looking and looking for a telephone booth on our side of the highway. It was nearly daybreak, but it was raining so hard and the wind was blowing so fierce, you just could hardly see a thing in front of you.

"'There's one, Carl!' I yelled, scaring him half to death. 'Pull over so we can call Grant.' He got as close to the booth as he could, and I got out. I could hardly get the door open, the wind was blowing so hard. I started to make a run for the phone, and the wind was blowing the rain all over me. I got inside and dialed the operator. She came on and told me, 'Ma'am, if the phone booth starts to blow over, don't worry about hanging up. Just you get out.' The rain and wind was just a-howling all around us. It was bad!

"When I got through to Grant, he asked, 'Pearl, where are y'all?' I told him, 'Well, what ya want to know for? You wanna come and meet us for coffee?' He sounded excited. 'Pearl, just where abouts are you?' 'Heck, I don't know. Not far from Nashville. Just a minute.' I yelled for Carl, but he didn't hear me. I told Grant, 'Hon, I think we're someplace right outside of Camden. Know where that is?'

"He said, to me, 'Pearl, that's just about where the plane crashed!' My first instinct was to look up and then out of the booth, but I couldn't see no place. I asked him, 'What plane? Who crashed?' 'You mean, you don't know? Thought you had the radio on.' 'We just turned it on when we heard you playing one of our songs. Who crashed? Somebody you know?' 'Yes,' he said, 'you know them.' I asked, 'Them?' And he told me what happened and I just couldn't believe it. I prayed to God it wasn't so. I didn't know how to tell Carl. Oh, my, he loved Hawk, and Cowboy, and Patsy.

"Grant said, 'You can't be far from where they think the plane may have crashed. If you see anything let me know.' The rain had stopped. I got back in the car. Carl asked, 'What did ole Grant have to say?' I told him and all he did was keep shaking his head in disbelief."

It was about 5:30 and Dottie was in such a deep sleep she didn't hear the phone ringing. "I finally woke to this knocking on the door. It was Grandmother West. I was half asleep but I could see she was quite upset. 'What's wrong?' She said, 'Oh, my God, Dottie, wake up! Their plane is down.' I asked, 'What plane?' She told me, 'A small plane has crashed and they think for sure it's the one Patsy's in!' I threw the covers back and jumped up, 'What?' 'Honey, that plane Patsy, Hawkshaw, Cowboy Copas, and Randy were coming home in has crashed somewhere up in the hills.' I woke Bill up and we turned the radio on and started to make calls to see what we could find out. We lived in the country and were quite isolated. I had to know."

Roger Miller says he was the first to arrive at the crash site. "I walked up to it and wanted to turn back. It was ghastly. That's the only way to describe it. The plane had crashed nose down. It just plowed into the earth on this steep hillside. The engine lay at the bottom of a five- or six-foot wide crater that was filled with water. The explosion people had heard was not from a gasoline explosion. There had been no fire. It was just the natural explosion of the impact of the plane hitting. It was awful. It was all twisted metal and pieces of bodies. It was especially horrible when you knew them all. Evidently Randy contacted vertigo. He thought he was climbing at full power and, instead, he was going down."

This is another discrepancy. Published reports in the local press credit members of the search party in the fire tower using field glasses and, almost simultaneously, ground searchers W.J. Hollingsworth and his 20-year-old son Jeners, corn and cotton farmers in the Sandy Point area, and brothers Lewis and Claud Bradford, who also had a farm near the scene of the crash.

It seems that, from the newspaper accounts, the Hollingsworths might have been the first on the crash site, but an interesting sidelight lends credence that the Hollingsworths and Miller and his friend might have passed within a few feet of each other at about the same time. The elder Hollingsworth was walking south along a ridge to the upper end of an area called Fatty Bottom, best described as a succession of woods, hills, hollows, and swamps. The terrain was, and is still quite rugged. He happened upon the crash at about 6 A.M.

"I almost had a nervous breakdown when I ran down and saw the bodies," Hollingsworth told the *Tennessean*. "I had to sit down on a log and then walk out to the road 'til help came." Mr. Hollingsworth called his son and sent him for the searchers.

State Trooper Troy Odle, who was up all night helping with the search, was the first official at the scene. "I've never seen a wreck as bad," he said.

Many of the searchers had walked within three to four hundred feet of the accident in the early hours when the search began, but could not see it or, since there was no fire, smell smoke. The wreckage was deep in the hollow and shrouded in nightfall.

There was, however, plenty to see in the light of day and the gawkers came in droves—some with infants in arms, one man on crutches. Cars piled up along the twisting, graveled Mule Barn Road as word spread of the discovery. The line went back over a hill and around the curves and bends in the road as far back as the eye could see.

When the rescue team reached Hughes' plane, Odle found the tail and radioed the identification number, N700P. It was confirmed that this was the craft owned by Hughes. Debris and pieces of the bodies were strewn over a 250-yard area through tangled vines and briar and the scattered debris of the fuselage.

Stations in Nashville and across the country interrupted programming to report the tragedy as soon as the wire services passed the story. Just after six, Grant Turner burst into the music he was playing to announce, "Ladies and gentlemen, this is the hardest thing I've ever had to do." He reported the plane had been found and that "there were no survivors."

In Winchester Mrs. Hensley received a call saying that the wreckage had been spotted, but there was still no news of survivors. Because of the weather and terrain, the search party was having a difficult time getting to the site. Then the Hensley phone and the phone at the Dicks' home in Nashville started to ring constantly and unmercifully.

"Everybody was expressing their concern about Patsy," Mrs. Hensley said. "They kept telling me not to give up hope. There was still hope. But nothing they said helped. The waiting was a nightmare."

Then the Hensley and Dick phones rang again. It was the news Hilda and Charlie and anyone else who loved Patsy, Hawkshaw, Cowboy, and Randy did not want to hear.

"All night long we got these horrible reports," stated Kathy Hughes. "One farmer heard this, another heard that, one saw this, and another saw that. We just kept hoping and praying for some good news. It never came. Just after the six o'clock news, Grant Turner broke in and confirmed our worst fears. It was a terrible way to find out, but I don't know if there is any good way. And if I could go back, I don't guess it would have mattered how we learned. I had lost my father and my husband. For my mother and me, it was the end of a terrible nightmare."

Pearl Butler and her husband Carl continued on down the highway after speaking to Grant Turner. "Then no more than ten miles later Grant came on and announced the plane had been sighted and that there were no survivors. We were both terribly upset, shook up. These were our friends. Carl turned off the highway and onto this gravel and dirt road that twisted and turned every which way. He stopped and we pulled ourselves together.

"All I could think of was that in the trailer behind the car were the costumes Patsy had given me and of something Patsy had told Carl and me one night when we were driving back from a date. She had been up in Winchester for a visit with her family and she said, 'Everyone wants me to sing for nothing. That's especially true back in my home town. I want you both to remember this, because one day you'll be able to tell it. The next time I go to Winchester, Virginia, everyone in that town will know that Patsy Cline has been there.' Whenever I recall that it makes cold chills run all over me. There may have been other times since, but when they took her body back for burial I said to myself, 'Well, girl, everybody did know it!'

"When we started up to leave, we were lost. Didn't know where we were. Carl turned around and headed back until we hit the highway. I've tried and tried to find that road and, to this day, I've never been able to. I used to think, 'My goodness, did we go on a road that didn't exist?'"

In a way the Butlers did. They had turned onto the roughhewn Mule Barn Road, which is not much of a real road. Had they proceeded another mile onward, they would have encountered the cars from the search party and the pitiful remains of the three stars they loved so.

Raymer Stockdale of Stockdale-Milan Funeral Home, Camden, was quoted in news reports, "Identification of the men could be made only by their billfolds—which miraculously weren't torn away." Patsy's was the most intact of the bodies, the back of her head, upper shoulders, and her right arm. Because of the flight path of the plane through the heavy brush and trees and the impact of the crash, the bodies were terribly dismembered. Civil Defense official Dean Brewer, when asked by the Nashville *Banner* reporters "if all four of the bodies had been located," replied, "There's not enough to count . . . They're all in small pieces."

Camden Chief of Police Aubrey Pafford said, "For reasons of investigation into the cause of the accident or its contributing factors, the Memphis Air officials [the CAB] have requested an autopsy be performed on the remains of the pilot."

"There were pieces of instruments, guitar stings, sheet music, Patsy's cosmetics, and clothing littered all about," pointed out Miller. "It was a maddening experience. I was yelling at people. It got to be where souvenir hunters were combing through the wreckage. I would see people picking up things and I screamed at them."

Randy's money bag with the receipts of the weekend shows was never recovered.

A soft slipper, gold and muddy, from the pair Patsy was reported wearing in Dyersburg, pointed to the impact spot. A silver expansion watchband, broken, rested near the Flyers' Bible. On a piece of notepaper in red ink was written the lyrics "Boo Hoo Hoo Hoo." There was Patsy's mascara wand, hair brush, and her beloved "Dixie" cigarette lighter. A black sock and a red slip fluttered with other remnants of clothing from tree branches.

Metal from the plane hung from the trees. Part of the fuselage was twisted around a tree. Among the broken musical instruments, pieces of plane, and the broken bodies was Hawkshaw's cowhide belt with his name written out across the width in hand-tooled lettering, his famed Hawk jacket, his Stetson hat, and one of his boots. A few feet away lay the broken black and silver neck of his Gibson guitar. Underneath the torn guitar strings was pearl inlay, saying "Hawkshaw."

Nearby was Patsy's fringed cowgirl jacket and western hat and, several yards away, her white belt inscribed with the black-tooled lettering "Patsy Cline." Scattered pieces of a multi-colored jigsaw puzzle littered the sloping landscape. Compared to the massive puzzle of jagged metal, and torn flesh, it would have been simple to solve.

Randy was 35, Cowboy, 49, Hawkshaw 41, and Patsy 30. She had lived to see her thirtieth birthday after all.

14
"Today, Tomorrow and Forever"

Sammy Moss: **"The last resting place for the late, great Patsy Cline is Shenandoah Memorial Park. Anytime you're in the area, stop by!"**

Paul Harvey News,
broadcast of March 6, 1963

"Three familiar voices are suddenly silent today. And over an ugly hole on a Tennessee hillside, the heavens softly weep. No more mournful ballad was ever sung on the Grand Ole Opry than the one which was hammered out on the nation's newsprinters this morning.

The Nashville Country music stars Hawkshaw Hawkins and Cowboy Copas and Patsy Cline and her manager. They'd flown in a one-lung Comanche to Kansas City for a benefit performance. For the benefit of the widow of a friend who'd been killed in a car wreck.

And they were returning to home base—Nashville, Tennessee. They'd refuelled at Dyersburg. Some severe thunderstorms had been raking that area along the Tennessee River. At least one commercial airliner had detoured. Precisely what happened thereafter will be subject to conjecture forever. And what terror there was toward the end we'll never know. But there was no pain. When they found the plane this morning its engine had entered the earth straight down.

> Somebody will write a cow-country classic about this night ride to nowhere. Because hill folks are a sentimental lot. But the highest compliment their eulogies are likely to include is that the somber citizens who converged this day on that ugly scar in the woodland where pieces of four bodies lay, that there are real tears in their whispered words. And that they refer to each of the suddenly deceased by his or her first name. For none of them ever thought of Randy and the Cowboy, Hawkshaw and Patsy any other way than as homefolks, kinsfolks, friends."

Loretta remembers her reaction to the news of Patsy's death. "I had gone to bed early Tuesday night instead of listening to the radio as I usually did. I got up real early Wednesday to clean my house so I've have plenty of time to get ready and be able to go shopping with Patsy. We had a date for Tuesday, but I heard they would be late coming back. I wanted to be ready for her now.

"I thought, 'I'll call that lazy thing and get her out of bed.' Just as I lay my hand on the phone, it rang. I said, 'I wonder who the heck that is? It's Patsy. She must have come in last night.' But it wasn't Patsy. It was [agent] Bob Neal's wife calling to tell me the bad news. I froze. I couldn't believe what I was hearing. I said, 'What? What are you saying?'

"I'll tell you how I felt when I lost her. I felt that probably I would not make it 'cause she was my buddy. I went to her for advice and she'd give it to me. When she was killed, the thought ran through my mind, 'What am I gonna do now?' When Patsy died, I lost the most wonderful friend I'll *ever* have."

Hank Cochran was driving back into Nashville later Tuesday when he heard the news report about the plane being missing. "I had to pull over. I was pretty well shook. I really loved that gal. I was supposed to be on that plane with them. Patsy had asked me if I wanted to go and I said yes, but at the last minute a meeting came up with Timi Yuro, who was in town looking for material. So I stayed in town and worked all weekend."

Cochran followed the WSM broadcasts into early Wednesday when it was announced that the plane and bodies had been found. When he heard that it was true, he ran out of his trailer and went berserk, screaming through the trees surrounding his place, "It's not true. It's not true! Please, God, don't let it be true!"

Brenda Lee was touring in Germany and heard the news on an Armed Forces Network broadcast. "It really stunned and hurt me. I couldn't believe it. She was gone just like that. It seemed so unfair after all she had gone through. I called Owen in Nashville and asked him what I should do. He told me even if I could cancel the dates, I would miss the funeral. He said, 'Hon, Patsy, would understand.' The thing I kept saying to myself was, 'She hadn't even seen her peak in the business!' Probably, had she lived, Patsy'd be bigger than even she ever dreamed!"

Donn Hecht and his wife were driving back from Los Angeles International Airport, where he had just bought his ticket for the trip to Nashville. "I was tuned to a Country station and when they interrupted with the news, I was too overcome to continue driving. I pulled off to the shoulder of the freeway. My wife was trying to comfort me. I recall looking up through my tears and seeing the cars whoosh by and thinking, 'How can they go along as though nothing has happened when part of my world has ended?'

"Then the disk jockey very inappropriately put on 'I Fall to Pieces,' and I was rendered completely incapable of operating the automobile. My wife drove on home and I consumed a third of a bottle of cognac. My wife said, 'It's none of my business since it was a long time before you knew me, but I'd like to know. Was there anything between you and Patsy?' 'Why do you ask?' 'Well, I've never seen you like this. You're about ready for the hospital!' My answer was a truthful one, 'Honey, there was *everything* between me and Patsy!"

Up in Frederick, Maryland, Patsy's friend from the old days Fay Crutchley called bandleader Bill Peer, Patsy's former mentor and lover, to say how shocked and saddened she was upon hearing the news. Bill said, "My God, Fay, I can't believe this. I had no way of knowing. I was only kidding Saturday night." "I had forgotten all about what he was talking about," said Mrs. Crutchley, "then I remembered when we were talking about Patsy Bill said, 'As far as I'm concerned, Patsy can just fall to pieces!'"

Granville "Shorty" Graves, fondly known around the Phillips-Robinson Funeral Home in Madison as "the last man to let you down" because of his job as an assistant funeral director, went to the Stockdale-Milan Funeral Home in Camden Wednesday morning at ten to bring the bodies back to Nashville.

"I paid the four hundred dollars in charges for the work they did, swapped bags, and headed back between noon and twelve-thirty. I had a Tennessee Highway Patrol escort coming back. Each time I would cross a county-line—from Dickson, to Cheatham, to Williamson, and on into Davidson—there would be another car waiting to take me on."

While Hubert Long helped the families with the funeral arrangements, friends from inside and outside the music community gathered, as Ann Whiten said, "as one big family, all together, all caring—one of the traits I love so much about our business," at the homes of the deceased bearing, in the Southern tradition, cakes, pies, fried chicken, baked hams, potato salad, home-made biscuits and rolls, bottles of beer and whiskey, and assorted soft drinks.

It was Charlie's decision "to bring Patsy home for one more night since she loved that house so much and had gotten to spend so little time in it."

A prayer service was set for Thursday afternoon at 5:00 at Phillips-Robinson for Patsy. Her friend, the Reverend Jay Alford, would officiate. Afterward, Patsy's body would be flown to Winchester via a Tennessee National Guard airplane for services on Saturday afternoon. Interment, at the request of Mrs. Hensley, was to be in the new Shenandoah Memorial Park outside of Winchester.

Joint services for Copas and Randy were scheduled for 10:00 Friday morning, with Hawkins' rites to take place at 3:30. It was decided to place a framed photograph of each of the deceased on top of the casket.

Dottie West was in bad shape. She even found herself angry with Patsy. "I was sitting at the kitchen table crying and staring off into nowhere. My face was a mess, but I didn't know, didn't care. I was sipping black coffee and I'd put the cup down and I'd say, 'Well, damn it, Patsy, why didn't you come with us? You always had to be so damn hardheaded. Gotta do everything the way you want to do it!'

"Bill tried to get me out of my stupor. He told me I had to get up and pull myself together and get dressed. 'Hon, we've got to go over to Kathy and Jeanie, and then we've got to go and help Charlie.' I said, 'What?' Bill said that we had things to do. Charlie. Oh, my God, Charlie! There I was sitting, feeling sorry for Dottie and I had forgotten about what Charlie must be going through.

"I got cleaned up and dressed and we headed over there. I

wondered how Charlie was doing with the kids. Both of them were babies. Each time I tried to call him the line was busy. We pulled up in front of the house and I could not help but be reminded of that day Patsy asked me to go outside in the front yard with her. She stood there looking at that house and crying. She was so proud of that house.

"And the day after she moved in, she took me on a guided tour, just to show off her 'castle,' as she put it. All I could think of then was her words to me that day. She said, 'Hoss, when I die tell 'em to bring me right on here to my castle and lay me out!'

"That's what Charlie had decided to do. Oh, my, Patsy would have liked that!"

If things had not been traumatic enough for Charlie, they quickly became worse. As a matter of fact, he was so distraught there was a fear among his close friends that he might try to kill himself.

"Let there be no mistake about the fact that Charlie Dick loved that Patsy," said an associate from the industry. "I only wish all those Doubting Thomases had been there to see how broken he was and the exemplary way in which he conducted himself. My heart really went out to him. He looked drained, pale. Like a lost soul. He had lost his Patsy."

Charlie had the black lady who worked for him and Patsy at home to help him with the kids, but it was an ordeal.

"Randy had only just turned two that January," said Charlie, "but explaining the loss of her mother to Julie, who was four and a half—oh, God, that was the hardest thing I've ever had to do. Some of our friends were terrific with the kids, trying to keep their minds occupied, but they knew something was not right.

"Julie especially knew. She didn't know quite what had happened, but she knew it was not the normal, everyday thing. She'd ask me, 'Is my mama ever coming home again, Daddy?' Randy was sick with bronchitis. There was no way I could make him understand. As sick as he was, he kept running through the house crying for his mother. That made it doubly bad. Oh, boy!"

"Charlie had the gold-finished casket placed in front of the draped picture window in the living room," said Ann Whiten. "There was a photograph of Patsy on top. WSM and the Grand Ole Opry sent a huge casket spray. At first, I thought it was a bit morbid having the casket at home with the kids and all, but Patsy did love that house and everything was handled in the very best of taste.

"If Charlie and the lady who worked for him had their hands full with the children, saying that things became a total disaster when Patsy's family arrived, well, that would be an understatement. Hilda and three carloads of family and friends arrived Wednesday evening. Mrs. Hensley, of course, knew Patsy was dead, but when you come face to face with that coffin it does not get any easier.

"By this time some of the clique had been at the house long enough to work on Charlie, but now we really had a problem with Hilda and Patsy's sister Sylvia. One would pass out and as one came to another would pass out. They were a beautiful, close family. It was a horrifying experience. Seeing the closed casket, knowing the condition of the body, seeing the photo, seeing the kids who had no more mother. You add it all up!"

Patsy and Charlie's friends showed en masse: Dottie and Bill West, Loretta and Mooney Lynn, Jan and Harlan Howard, Owen Bradley, Del Wood, Roger Miller, Hank and Shirley Cochran, Doyle and Teddy Wilburn, Faron Young, Ferlin Husky, June, Anita, and Helen Carter and, of course, Ann—and from outside the close circle came Charlie's buddies and poker mates from the newspaper, and such concerned stars as Minnie Pearl, Roy Acuff, Billy Walker, Carl and Pearl Butler, Skeeter Davis and Ralph Emery, to name but a handful.

Everyone took on certain chores. Del and Mooney scrambled eggs and made toast. Jan and Dottie carved ham, opened Cokes, and served up potato salad and stuffed eggs. Anita Carter and Jan went into Madison from the Goodlettsville house and bought a Barbie doll for Julie and toys for Randy.

"People told me they were talking to me and I seemed to be in space," recalled Dottie. "I probably was. I was like a zombie. I just could not bring myself to believe that Patsy was gone until I saw the casket in the living room. Then I completely broke down. Bill didn't know what he was going to do with me. He was afraid at one point he was going to have to put me to bed. Patsy Cline had been my friend. Heck, she was more than that. It was not easy accepting and it would not be easy going on without her. But Patsy was gone.

"Charlie was getting upset with me. He and Bill forced me

to sit down. I was sitting on the couch next to Loretta. Oh, she was so upset she was shaking. I rubbed my hand across the fabric of the couch and I said, 'Charlie, this is the sofa Patsy just had made.' He was down and answered, 'Yeah, Dottie.' I said, 'She was so proud of it.' Charlie laughed, 'She drove 'em crazy until they got it the way she wanted it!' I looked up on the wall and saw the portraits of Julie and Randy that Patsy had just had done. I started to cry and so did Loretta.

"We thought taking turns playing with the kids would help us. But Julie and Randy were running to Charlie, hugging his leg, and asking, 'Daddy, where's Mommie? Is she coming home tonight?' That did something to me. It made me never take my family for granted. Each time before I leave for a date I always spend a few special moments with them. You just never know. Julie and Randy didn't understand and that made it worse on all of us that did.

"Everytime Julie'd start to cry, Hilda, Loretta, and me—we'd start crying. And, oh my, Hank was taking it real bad. All the music people were going from Charlie's to Jeanie's to Kathy and Lucille's. Everyone who was in town was at one house or the other all that night and into the morning."

As the night wore on, Charlie had spent very little time just being with Patsy. He wanted that very much. He finally asked everyone to leave so he could "be alone with my girl." The highway patrolman stayed on duty at the front door. It was just Charlie, Hilda, and the immediate family.

The attendance at Patsy's prayer service, the service for Cowboy and Randy, and that for Hawkshaw has gone down on records as the largest funeral in Nashville history. "For each of the services," claimed "Shorty" Graves, "we had to close off part of Gallatin Street in front to traffic. There were over a thousand people at each of the funeral rites. The inside of the home was jammed, and we had to put loudspeakers outside to supplement our permanent porch speakers. Even though the services were at different times, all four of the caskets were displayed together in the same room.

"All total there were six hundred and fifteen flower sprays, and by the morning of the Hughes-Copas funeral, we had to tell the florists to take the flower arrangements directly to Forest Lawn Cemetery on Dickerson Road. At the request of her family, all the Patsy Cline flower arrangements went to the funerals of the other three after her service was complete. Many people and companies sent one spray of flowers for all three, also. Telegrams poured in from all over the nation and all over the world—Europe, Africa, and Australia—expressing regret to the families. Each of the Nashville funerals had over six hundred cars in the procession. We'd never seen anything like that."

Teddy Wilburn is one who will never forget the Patsy Cline Thursday prayer service. "You literally had to fight your way through the surging crowds in the street and the crowd inside. We were standing there, milling around, talking in low, hushed tones waiting for the Reverend Alford to begin. Suddenly there was this commotion and word filtered in that Jack Anglin [of the famed Johnny (Wright) & Jack duo] had been killed. He had been to the barber shop for a trim before coming to the service and on the way he was involved in an accident.

"I totally broke down. I absolutely lost control. A lot of people were upset and horrified at the news. It was too much. Now we lost a fifth star. I had known Sleepy McDaniel from Hank Snow's band, Patsy, Cowboy, and Hawk, but Doyle and I went all the way back to the 'Louisiana Hayride' with Jack. I was wiped out from Patsy's death and had two funerals to go, and now Jack. I fell apart. Two people finally had to help me outside. Someone sat me down in the front seat of a car so I could pull myself together. I don't think I did for several days."

Dottie said that Jack Anglin's death totally nonplused everyone. "Bill was holding me up and I heard people gasping. I looked up and someone said, 'Jack Anglin's just been killed.' It buzzed through the crowd like that. Oh, what a shock that was. What another shock! That was all we needed. I remember that Johnny was there with [his wife] Kitty Wells and when he heard the news about his partner he became hysterical. The three of them were like family. No, they *were* family. It was just like a black cloud had fallen over Music City."

Each of the stars killed in that March 5th crash and in the March 7th accident was beloved by fans and industry folk as well. WSM and many of the Opry members debated whether or not to have a Grand Ole Opry Saturday night.

"It was finally decided to go on with the show as they would have certainly wanted," explained Ralph Emery, then an Opry announcer in addition to his work at the station. "And then we pondered how to handle the incidents of the deaths on the broadcast. It was a sad, sad night for us all. Backstage at the Ryman things were quite subdued. People were talking, but I honestly don't think they knew what they were saying.

"Someone said there must be a jinx on the Opry. Another said there was a hex on Patsy—you know, to have recovered from the car wreck in which she nearly died and to be involved in another horrible accident."

Teddy Wilburn reflects on the impact of the deaths. "The Country music industry had gone for almost ten years without any tragedy. Everyone was living on and on, and no one tremendously important in the business had died since Hank Williams passed on. And his was a natural death, so to speak. It was amazing, especially in view of the way we traveled—no buses to speak of, everyone mostly driving Cadillac limos and pulling trailers with costumes and equipment. The law of averages caught up with us. But it didn't make it any easier to accept."

Emery compares that bleak week to something akin to the later assassination of President John Kennedy and the aftermath of depression that followed. "Suddenly the impact was hitting everyone, and some got ideas to commercialize on it. At the funeral for Hawk, one of the record executives told me he was asking me and asking all the disk jockeys at the Country stations not to play any records that might attempt to morbidly commemorate what had happened. Within a week, word leaked that at least three were planned. When they did come out, the d.j.s laid off them and they disappeared from the scene."

Opry executives and members chose to have a brief memorial to the departed stars on the 8:30 portion of the program. The stage was filled with music, laughs, and pure Opry entertainment for the first hour "for Patsy, Hawk, Cope, Jack, and Randy...would want us to keep smiling—and to recall the happier occasions."

Then at 8:34 Opry manager Ott Devine began a simple spoken tribute after all the evening's performers gathered on stage. Standing at an announcer's podium at the far-right-hand side, Devine intoned: "We won't be having no big to-do. They sure wouldn't have liked that. What do you say when we lose such friends? We can reflect on their contributions to all of us through entertainment, their acts of charity and love. We can think of the pleasure they brought to the lives of millions and take some comfort in knowing that they found fulfillment in the time allotted to them. They will never be forgotten."

Devine bowed his head, and throughout the great hall the 3,500 people assembled began to stand and bow their heads. There was a moment of silent prayer.

"Patsy, Copas, Hawkshaw, Jack and Randy never walked on this stage without a smile and they would want us to keep smiling now. Let's continue in the tradition of the Grand Ole Opry!"

The Jordanaires at stage left began the final tribute, a moving rendition, accompanied by a lone piano, of "How Great Thou Art." Audible sobs broke the stillness. More than a few women dabbed away with handkerchiefs—and men ever so slyly wiped—at tear-filled eyes. Then at exactly 8:39 Roy Acuff and his Smoky Mountain Boys stepped to center stage and struck up a rousing fiddle tune of farewell, attempting to turn a sad occasion into one of joyous remembrance. The stars filed offstage with long faces and some tears of their own.

Tears welled up in the eyes of Minnie Pearl, who was due to go on next. Acuff went to wave her on, and she motioned to him to let her have another minute to compose herself. She swallowed hard, wiped her eyes, signaled Acuff she was ready, and he brought her on to wild applause. Cousin Minnie rushed out on stage with her famed greeting, 'Hooowwwdddeeeeee! I'm so proud to be here."

Declared Emery, "That Cousin Minnie was something. When she went out the Ryman was an ocean of handkerchiefs. Minnie is a sentimental and gentle lady, but she performed to the highest traditions of the Opry and brought the house down with howls of laughter.

"I can only imagine how she felt in her heart. At the Opry almost everybody looks upon everybody as family. All five who died were close to Minnie—to us all, really. As she left the stage with the audience still in stitches, I could see that Minnie had tears rolling down her face. She looked up at me and said, 'Oh, Lordy, we lost some good friends!' It is a mental image that I have never been able to erase. One that I would never want to forget."

And across the width and breath of the nation that night Minnie Pearl's sentiments were shared by hundreds of thousands of Country and pop music fans.

It would be polite merely to say that Patsy's funeral on Sunday was a three-ring circus. Charlie had to attend the services for the other deceased in Nashville, so Patsy's funeral was moved to Sunday afternoon to not only give Hilda and members of the family but also Charlie time to get safely to Winchester. Though it was certainly not what the family wanted, the service attracted thousands of fans and, worse, an unruly mob of curiosity-seekers and media personnel covering the "event."

The situation was so unmanageable that old friends of Patsy's, such as the Crutchleys, the Deytons, Bill Peer, and Jumbo Rinker, could not even get into the Jones Funeral Home.

Sammy Moss, a Winchester disk jockey and bandleader who had also known and befriended Patsy, noted on his annual Patsy Cline memorial broadcast in 1972: "This country d.j. had never expected anything like this. I had been asked to be a pallbearer along with other friends of Patsy's...As I arrived...about two forty-five it looked as though something big was about to happen. Streets were jammed with people. Traffic was almost at a standstill and when I arrived at the Jones Funeral Home I could see what all the commotion was about. It was the general public wanting to participate in the final rites of Patsy Cline. The Jones Funeral Home was a large establishment with two large rooms, and both rooms were filled to capacity with persons seated and standing. The doors were locked quite a while before services began because this place was filled beyond expectation."

The memorial leaflet distributed by the family quoted Tennyson:

> "Sunset and evening star,
> And one clear call for me!
> And may there be no moaning of the bar,
> When I put out to sea,
> But such a tide as moving seems to sleep,
> Too full for sound and foam,
> When that which drew from out the
> boundless deep
> Turns again home."

The Reverend Nathan Williamson conducted the service and delivered the message when the service began at 3:30. At 4:30 pallbearers—Jim McCoy of WHPL; Moss, WRFL; Billy Graves, a Nashville producer; Bill Allison, WINC; Dick Dovel,

WFTR, Front Royal, VA; and Eddie Matherly, WKCW, Warrenton—began moving with the casket toward the hearse. As the doors to the funeral home opened, a burst of excitement thundered through the throng. People yelled, "There she is! There's Patsy!" There were hundreds packed and jammed in front of Jones. The pallbearers could not maneuver the casket through at first. Police finally cleared a way. Cameras continuously clicked; flashbulbs popped.

An estimated 25,000 persons lined the funeral route, which wound some four miles from downtown to the Shenandoah Memorial Park south of Winchester. Hundreds of Virginia State Police had to clear the way for the cars in the procession, and several times cars not belonging in the lineup attempted to break in.

Fay Crutchley arrived at the funeral home and found the doors locked so she and her family started for the cemetery, but found traffic so congested, they pulled off to the side of the road and parked.

Jack Cummins described the funeral and atmosphere in the Winchester *Star:* "And people who knew her, knew of her or just wanted to see the affair out of some morbid curiosity, packed the area...Cars were lined up from the edge of the city all the way to the cemetery...A small fortune in flowers of every description was delivered at graveside.

"And before Patsy—the small-town girl who made good as the number one country music singer—was in the earth, the people who trampled and jammed the soggy cemetery field were beginning to steal sprigs of lilies and roses or other flowers.

"The effect of the first stolen flower hit the crowd like an electrical shock. The people—jammed in close to the small tent over the grave—began snatching, literally from the side of the grave, everything and anything they could lay their hands on, short of the gold-finished coffin.

"Several women surveyed the racks of flowers and wreaths with a critical eye, and began a methodical selection of the items they wanted—as if it were dollar day at the department store.

"One blondish woman, perhaps in her early forties, managed to pick several wreaths clean of decorations and plastic emblems, and even made herself a little collection of cards from the various wreaths and garlands of flowers, banked high beside the grave.

"But it's unlikely that Patsy... would have minded. These were 'her people,' her fans, the people who made her famous. One of the honorary pallbearers, speaking of the thousands of people, probably summed it up best when he said, 'It's like a religion with them. They're very emotional and that's one of the reasons so many people are here.'

"Those who came to see only the celebrities who were supposed to be on hand were disappointed. According to another of the honorary pallbearers, none of the people named to serve in that capacity was notified of his obligations. Consequently, he said, they apparently didn't know they were supposed to have been there.

"After the services, as the people flooded back to their parked cars like a tide rolling out, a colossal traffic jam developed, tying up autos and trucks for miles on either side of the cemetery. Many of the onlookers appeared to have just slipped into any old clothes they could fine for the trip to the cemetery. They ranged from infants to bent, wrinkled elderly men and women....

"And it seemed nearly everyone at the cemetery had a camera of one kind or another—movie cameras, expensive 35 millimeter models, and $5 box types. Occasionally, while a solemn-faced pastor intoned the words of ritual over the casket, the crisp buzz of a movie camera could be heard in the hushed mob.

"Several hundred yards away, on the side of a big white barn, a photographer had perched himself halfway up, apparently by scaling the wall. At a restaurant a few hundred yards north of the cemetery the proprietor, in white apron, was surveying his driveway, packed with cars of onlookers. In exasperation he called to a state policeman to 'Try and do something about getting my driveway cleaned out.'

"When it was over—about an hour later—the highways were still jammed for hours. A squad of state policemen was sent to important intersections and remained there, directing the crush of cars through the early evening.

"But apparently the drivers and their passengers didn't mind too much—they had seen what they wanted.

"Patsy got a funeral worthy of royalty."

On his 1972 broadcast, after noting several times that Patsy Cline "was my very good friend," Sammy Moss made the following statement: "The last resting place for the late, great Patsy Cline is Shenandoah Memorial Park just a few miles from

Winchester, Virginia. Anytime you're in the area stop by. Tributes have been paid by many of Patsy Cline's followers, but the place and the name will remain forever. Remember it's Patsy Cline, Shenandoah Memorial Park, Winchester, Virginia!"

What is not commonly known is that Gerald Cline attended the funeral and went to Charlie afterward to extend his condolences. And through the years, Gerald has remained a friend to Hilda and often visits with her.

And so it was.

Time heals what reason cannot.

> "Someone said that time heals sorrow
> But I can't help but dread tomorrow,
> When I miss you more today than yesterday . . . "
>
> —"I Miss You More Today,"
> recorded by Loretta Lynn,
> written by Lorene Allen and Loretta Lynn.
> Sure-Fire Music Company, ©1972.

The letter received by Mrs. Jo Walker, director of the Country Music Association, on March 13, from Shaun Gooderham of Middlesex, England, was a typical fan reaction to the cataclysmic events of the preceding week.

6th March, 1963

Dear Mrs. Walker,

I have just learned of the death of Miss Patsy Cline, Cowboy Copas and Hawkshaw Hawkins, a great and tragic shock to all.

Each of these truly great artists have made their mark on the music scene, and they will be sorely missed by every 'country fan.'

Miss Cline seemed fated from the start. It is such a pity that after her motor accident this should happen, just when deserved success was coming her way. She had so much to live for.

Cowboy Copas, perhaps the best known, was a veteran in the country style. He will be missed most of all, I think.

Hawkshaw Hawkins in my opinion was the best singer of country ballads next to Hank Williams. He had a voice of amazing depth, quality and realism which could sing a country song better than anyone else.

That this terrible tragedy should happen just now, when country music had a real hold on the music world is a blow from which, if it wasn't country music, it would perhaps never recover . . . Let everyone know that they will be missed just as much in Britain as in America.

Finally may I say how sorry I am for the relatives. The hearts of many people go out to them I am sure. One thing, they have the satisfaction of knowing they died for a cause, 'Country Music.' They lived and died country music. To them country music came first, and it was there at the last.

May God always keep their memory alive.

The week after the funeral, Paul Cohen rushed into the studio with Rusty Adams to do a song about Patsy, Hawkshaw, Cowboy and the crash.

"I cussed him out about that!," spewed Ernest Tubb. "I didn't blame Rusty. He was just a kid. I blamed Paul for capitalizing on the deaths of three of our folk.

"I told Paul, 'That record will not be played on the Ernest Tubb Mid-Nite Jamboree or sold in my store.' If they had waited, that would have been different. Justin, my son, wrote a song about Hank Williams and I said, 'Son, it's good and I'll do it. But in about a year. Not now.'

"But this song by Rusty was released ten days after the funerals. That's the only falling-out I ever had with Paul. We were good friends, but I said to him, 'How in the hell could you, of all people, do something like that?' He replied, 'This is a business, E.T.!' I said, 'Naw. Naw! We don't have to be that desperate for a buck. Don't be that money-hungry! We go around saying ours is a business with a heart. Sometimes I wonder.' "

The Rusty Adams record died a quick death. Files show the Adams release "Angels from the Opry" and "Dateline Disaster" to be a Briar record release on March 30, 1963. Cohen didn't realize there was a conspiracy afoot to keep the record from being played.

Jan Howard informed that she, too, was approached to make an album of Patsy's songs. " They asked me and I said, 'My God, no! I couldn't do it.' I refused. 'There is no way I'd go in and do Patsy's songs for money. That's a disgrace.' He said, 'Well, if you don't, someone else is going to and they're gonna make a mint.'

"I told him, 'Well, if their conscience will let them, tell them to go right ahead.' No one ever did, though, until Loretta put out her tribute album in 1977, which was not at all what they wanted me to do, wanted me to commercialize on Patsy's memory. Some people will do anything for money.

"In the first place, I never could have done Patsy's material justice. Frankly, no one ever will be able to. Secondly, my heart just wouldn't let me do something like that. When Patsy sang, she got you right in the gut. Me, too. Take 'Sweet Dreams.' Who can listen to that without getting cold chills? 'Faded Love' is another. I was in the studio when she recorded that, and I was in awe of Patsy. You know, afterward you're supposed to say something nice. I couldn't talk. I was dumbfounded."

Tommy Dee, a singer/songwriter and West Coast television personality, had a million-seller in 1959 with "Three Stars," a tune about the deaths of Richie Valens, Buddy Holly, and the Big Bopper. In March 1963 Dee wrote and recorded, with Bonnie Owens, "Missing on a Mountain" for Pike Records.*

"Missing on a mountain
Coming home from a show
Three of our greatest singers
Gosh, we'll miss you so
Missing on a mountain
After a good deed
You'll always be remembered in our fondest memory!

Narration—
On the left stands Hawkshaw Hawkins or 'The Night Hawk' as he was called—
When it was his turn to sing a song, they had to lift the mike for he was mighty tall—
Then he would sing his greatest songs and the crowd would yell 'More!'—
Then he would smile and humbly tip his hat and say 'Here's the song you asked for—
Now God has called him to a land beyond the blue,
Hawkshaw, you made our life richer by knowing you.

Narration—
On the right stands Cowboy Copas—a giant among men—
In every walk of life Cope had a million friends from his latest to his greatest—
Each song a hit—And the way he sang 'Alabam' we'll never forget—
Cowboy Copas often sang hymns that told of God's great love—
Now he has a fulltime job singing in God's chorus up above.

Narration—
In the middle stands a wonderful girl—the whole world knows her fame—
For speak the words 'I Fall to Pieces' and Patsy Cline they're both the same—
She became a star overnight or so it seems—but she worked so hard
And God smiled down and answered her dreams—Maybe that's the reason why God called her
Because her star did so brightly shine—and He needed a new star in heaven—
And called it Patsy Cline.

You'll be remembered in our fondest memory!"

The doctor who began Patsy's plastic surgery after her automobile accident remembers the singing star. "I was so proud of the job and the way things were turning out," he said, "and then she went and got herself killed. That's something!"

Billy Walker attended the prayer service in Nashville for Patsy, Hawkshaw, Cowboy, and Randy, but, because of road commitments, did not take part in the Opry memorial. Immediately after the accident, Billy told the Nashville *Banner,* "God was on my side. Else how can you explain my being here and Patsy, Copas and Hawk and Randy gone? No, I was not scheduled to ride the plane. Actually there wasn't enough room for me in the four-seater. So I went out and back on a commercial flight."

There was nothing said about his dad having a heart attack, and Billy calling Hawkins and asking him to let him have his plane ticket, thus putting Hawkshaw on the plane in his place. Billy was happy, at last, to set the record straight. "For a long time I was in a deep depression because I thought I was partially responsible for what happened since I had encouraged everyone to come to Kansas City to help the Call family. The benefit cost them their lives.

"But looking back now I realize there was no way I could have foreseen any of what happened. That didn't help me then, however. I was thankful I was alive, but, of course, I certainly had guilt feelings. They were gone; I was still here. Cowboy was a dear friend, and I had gone a long way back with Hawk. And Randy and Patsy were like family. Randy was like a brother to me. It just wasn't in God's plan for me."

Through some source with access to the *Banner* and *Tennessean* photograph file, several radio stations secured prints of the crash and funeral pictures and offered them for sale over the air.

In a more appropriate remembrance, Hap Peebles and Tex Ritter led a moving tribute on March 17, 1963, at the Memorial Auditorium, in Kansas City, Kansas. Peebles spoke of the good deed Patsy, Hawkins, Copas, and Hughes performed and of the deaths the week of March 3 of SleepyMcDaniel of Hank Snow's band and Jack Anglin. Tex Ritter then came out and sang a special rendition of "Hillbilly Heaven" with the names of the recently departed.

Needless to say, rumors of all kinds about Randy Hughes circulated around Music City after the crash—that he was not a licensed pilot, that he did not heed warnings, that he lived and flew his plane dangerously. "I heard many things from many people," deplored Kathy Hughes. "But in my mind I am certain Randy felt he was doing the right thing. The CAB report noted that even pilots who have had hours of flying get in the same predicament. It was one of those things [a storm] you couldn't predict. [In fact, Hughes was warned and the storm was in the forecast.]

"The autopsy cleared the mind of any wrongdoing. It was said by many that Randy and the others had been drinking. There was no trace of alcohol or drugs of any kind."

In a ruling on May 21, 1964, the Civil Aeronautics Board claimed that Randy Hughes flew in adverse weather though untrained in the use of instruments, and this was the probably cause of the crash. Their investigation showed that the plane was intact and that the engine was developing substantial power and there was no failure or malfunction before the impact. The report made no mention of "vertigo," though this is the term used often when a pilot loses control of a craft in dense clouds or bad weather, or that the plane, again as has been commonly stated, was flying upside down at the end. The CAB did say Hughes received a thorough weather briefing and "was informed that the en route weather was unfavorable and the destination weather was below VFR (visual flight rules) minima with further deterioration indicated before any improving trends could be expected."

Sturvesant Insurance Company of Allentown, Pennsylvania, filed for a declaratory judgment, claiming it was not liable for full damage or personal liability of the insured aircraft while piloted by Hughes. Mrs. Hughes filed a $2.5 million suit with the executors of the other three estates filing counterclaims of $750,000 each.

"The crux of the insurance matter," said Kathy, "was that Randy had bought some insurance [for the plane] through a broker here in Nashville, and there was some question to them—Sturvesant—as to whether he should have been flying without a flight instructor.

"Also, it was reported that I had told Randy, when he called me from Dyersburg to ask about the weather, 'Why, it's so clear you can see the moon and the stars.' This came up at the insurance trial, but I never said anything like that and that has really been exaggerated. Certainly if it was a cloudy day, you couldn't see the moon and the stars! I told Randy that it had cleared to the point where it wasn't raining."

In the end, in May 1966, an out of court settlement was reached, whereby Sturvesant paid each beneficiary $33,333 and another $15,000 to Mrs. Hughes for the plane.

By the fall of 1964, Charlie had begun the construction of a memorial entrance way to Shenandoah Memorial Park in Winchester in memory of Patsy. The cemetery did not permit monuments on the graves. On the side of the huge granite wall facing into the park, on a scroll with musical notes, Charlie had inscribed: "This entrance way is dedicated in remembrance of Patsy Cline, one of America's best beloved singers by her husband Charles Dick, their children Julie and Randy, and her family."

Hawkshaw Hawkins' rhinestone-studded "Hawk" jacket was donated to the Country Music Hall of Fame along with the hat he wore on the day of his death. Though very little was recovered from the souvenir hunters at the crash site, eventually Carl Perkins, at the urging of Roger Miller, donated Patsy's hairbrush, still grasping remnants of hair, and mascara case to curator and director of the museum, Dorothy Gable.

Miss Gable then received a call from Mrs. Todd Francis of Hendersonville, Tennessee, the beautician who dressed Patsy's hair and wigs. Patsy had left her favorite wig for repairs just before departing on that fateful Kansas City benefit. After several notices to the family went unheeded, Mrs. Francis donated the wig to the Hall of Fame.

A resident of Paris, Tennessee, who was combing the crash site found Patsy's "Dixie" cigarette lighter and, while hearing Miss Gable discuss the Hall of Fame displays on a tour, came forward to contribute the lighter. Pearl Butler donated one of the Patsy Cline western outfits she had been given to the museum in 1980. Gordon Stoker of the Jordanaires was given a piece of the plane's floorboard by a friend and he has donated it to the Hall of Fame collection.

Patsy Cline's catalog of albums was selling approximately 75,000 copies a year but with the release of "Coal Miner's Daughter" there was an amazing rekindling of interest in her product. Owen Bradley removed Patsy's vocals from the original three-track master tapes and, with new musicians and background singers, created ultra contemporary tracks using today's sophisticated computer technology.

The results were not totally satisfying to diehard fans but these "new" recordings brought Patsy a cult following, especially among teens and pre-teens too young to have known her great successes except through "Coal Miner's Daughter."

Many singers—Patti Page, Connie Smith, Charlie Rich, Troy Seals, Emmylou Harris, Diana Trask, Linda Ronstadt, Loretta Lynn—have recorded songs that Patsy introduced and made famous. And immediately after her death, there was a campaign to develop another Patsy Cline. Says Charlie, "MCA had loads of gals who tried to imitate her. I won't mention names, but they were standing in the wings. But none of them could come close to touching Patsy."

In spite of her sales record, Patsy has yet to be awarded a Gold Record. "They were unheard of then in Country," explained Charlie. "Only Patsy Montana had been awarded one. And, if anybody had ever bothered to count her sales, Kitty would certainly have received one for 'It Wasn't God Who Made Honky Tonk Angels.' To be sure, Patsy would have been awarded one on the strength of 'Walkin' After Midnight,' not to mention her later records of 'Crazy' and 'I Fall to Pieces.'"

The lifelong devotion of Loretta Lynn to Patsy resulted in a warm, amusing chapter in *Coal Miner's Daughter* and a portrayal in the sanitized, often fictionalized film version. Sissy Spacek won the 1980 Academy Award as Best Actress for her outstanding characterization of Loretta.

In spite of heavy industry promotion, Universal Pictures failed to get Beverly D'Angelo nominated as Best Supporting Actress for her superb performance as Patsy. The film, of course, became one of the smashes of 1980 and 1981.

So much interest occurred in Patsy that producer Bernard Schwartz immediately began talks with Universal for a film biography. Several scripts later, company brass vetoed the project. Undeterred, Schwartz made a deal months later with Silver Screen Partners, a division of E.F. Hutton and HBO, the pay-tv arm of Time-Life, Inc.

The new script, titled "Sweet Dreams," after Patsy's 1963 recording (released after her death), was penned by Robert Getchell, nominated for a 1974 Academy Award for his screenplay "Alice Doesn't Live Here Anymore." Developed in cooperation with family and industry associates, "Sweet Dreams" is quite selective in depicting many aspects of Patsy's life, loves and career. It rather concentrates on her romance and subsequent rocky marriage to Charlie.

Jessica Lange, Academy Award winner as Best Supporting Actress in "Tootsie" and Best Actress nominee for "Frances" and "Country," was the unusual choice to play Patsy. Since she does not sing, she lip syncs to Patsy's voice.

Loretta, for one, was not happy with the choice. "I've wondered why they didn't get the little girl (Beverly D'Angelo) that did Patsy in my movie. She's something. I mean, this girl acts. Even her movements bothered me when I was around her. I would forget that it wasn't Patsy, and I would start to say something that only Patsy and I would be knowing. And I'd catch myself. It was a weird feeling."

The singer made it clear she was not connected with "Sweet Dreams." "They didn't even ask me what I thought about Patsy Cline, let alone anything else." Though she wasn't asked to be a consultant, Loretta said she was able to read the script.

"I know Jessica Lange is a good actress—and to me, that's about all the filmmakers have got. I hate to say that, but I ain't gonna lie about it."

Czechoslovakian-born, British-reared Karel Reisz, a former film critic and the acclaimed director of "Saturday Night and

Sunday Morning," "Night Must Fall," "Morgan," "Isadora" and "The French Lieutenant's Woman" was the more unusual choice to helm the $13-million picture, set in Virginia and Tennessee, about a country singer. He cast Ed Harris, so good in "The Right Stuff," "Swing Shift" and "Alamo Bay," for the role of Charlie; and that eclectic comedienne of state, screen and television, Ann Wedgeworth for the only other key dramatic part, Patsy's mother Hilda.

Without a doubt Patsy Cline would have been the female country giant of the 60s—and had considerable pop music impact—had she continued in the same recording trend. Certainly, if the hits kept coming, she'd have become a superstar along the lines of Loretta, Dolly Parton and Barbara Mandrell.

Dottie West is also very definite. "I still think Patsy was the best girl singer that ever came out of Nashville! It's that simple. She was so kind to me. I will never forget that she forgot all other considerations and introduced me around town to get me known and was always working with me and teaching me. There will never be another Patsy. And in a way I'm thankful for that."

Loretta Lynn still feels the spirit of Patsy Cline guiding her career and protecting her from harm. "When the time came to record my tribute album, memories of Patsy grew stronger within, and I found it difficult singing her songs. At one point I began crying and just got up to leave. Owen told me, 'Loretta, hon, try it one more time.' I walked back to the mike and the strangest feeling came over me. It was like Patsy herself was telling me how ashamed she was of me—telling me to 'go to it, girl!—and I sailed through the session without a hitch."

In January 1978, Loretta told the *Star:* "I know some people will think I sound crazy, but I have had ESP all my life and I can feel Patsy around me." She went on that while in Las Vegas she was having throat problems, "I felt Patsy's hand on my arm patting me and holding me. I knew right away that it was her up on stage with me, even though it surprised me. I could feel her saying, 'Don't you worry, Loretta, it's gonna be fine.' And it was."

Sums up Jan Howard, "Heavens, she'd still be a big star today. My God, what she could have achieved had she lived! Since it meant so much to Patsy, I was glad she achieved what she did in her short life. Thank God, we still have her records. It would be a shame to deprive the public of so great a voice."

Louise Segar had left Houston and was living temporarily in Manaus, the capital and a port of the Amazonas in northeastern Brazil, when she heard the news of Patsy's death. It was something she would not let herself believe at first.

"There were a lot of people around the hotel from Oklahoma who worked the oil wells and they liked Country music. We'd get a few under our belts and we'd start singing. I'd always do some of Patsy's songs. A man had come in on a plane from New York that day and when I finished singing 'I Fall to Pieces,' he said, 'Louise, who'd you say sang that song?' I told him, 'Patsy Cline,' He said, 'My God, that's the girl that was killed in a plane crash not long back, isn't it?' I just absolutely went cold. 'No, un-huh, you're talking about somebody else. It couldn't be Patsy.'

"He replied, 'Well, I'm almost sure of it.' I told him, 'No, you must mean somebody else. You don't mean Patsy.' 'Louise, I'd almost swear to it. I was reading it in *Life* on the plane down this morning.' I said, 'I don't care what you were reading, you've got to be making a mistake.' He told me, 'Look, the magazine is in my room. Here's the key. Go see if you don't believe me. Honey, I'm not lying to you.'

"I opened the room, found the magazine, and started turning the pages until I came to the article. It's impossible to tell you what I felt, how I broke. It really was true, but I just couldn't believe it. But, for me, Patsy is still with us. We have her music. And every day I thank God for that. Yes, I do."

Trudy Stamper, formerly of WSM, explained, "I like to think of Patsy as I saw her last. She came by the office only a few days before the accident (February 19) to tell me about her latest recording session. At that time we had a group of senior citizens on tour of the studio and I asked Patsy if she wouldn't like to go in and sing for them.

"She said, 'Sure. You think they'd like "Bill Bailey"?' I nodded, 'Yes, of course, they would. That would be great.' She turned and went into the studio and without rehearsal or anything she just sang. She sang her heart out and with lots of soul. I'll never forget how those people gathered around, showering her with love and affection. It was beautiful and for a brief moment I realized why she wanted so desperately to be a star. She had so much to give."

One of the most poignant tributes to Patsy Cline was paid by Jimmy Buffet in his song "I Miss You So Badly"*:

> "I've got a head full of feelin' higher
> And an ear full of Patsy Cline
> There is no one who can touch her
> Hell, I hang on every line . . ."

In a moving tribute, presided over by Dottie West, Patsy was elected to the Virginia Country Music Hall of Fame in 1981 with Hilda in attendance.

Charlie Dick has never been able to forget Patsy Cline. It became more obvious after her death that Patsy was his love and his life. For several years, until she sold the house on Nella Drive, Charlie left their bedroom as it was. He remarried in September 1965 to singer Jamey Ryan.

"Hilda felt mixed emotions about me," remarked the former Mrs. Dick (they were divorced in 1972). "I was nineteen and marrying the father of her two grandchildren. Her attitude was 'What kind of kid is coming in here and taking care of my grandbabies?'

"She kept the children for the year and a half before we were married. After a couple of years of marriage to Charlie, Hilda knew I loved the kids and cared for them very much. I don't talk to her on a regular basis now, but we do stay in touch and are friends. Lots of things happened between Charlie and me over the years, and it was a sad thing our marriage did not work out, but . . .

"Charlie and I have a son, so good, bad, or indifferent, I have to accept Charlie. I know he did try. It was not easy. But he was a good father, and still is. I loved Julie and Randy as if they were my own and I still see them. This is one of those things we all have to learn to live with."

Charlie's preoccupation with the memory of Patsy was apparently a contributing factor to the marriage breaking up. Charlie played Patsy's records to the point where it caused friction between him and Jamey. On one occasion, when Charlie was listening to Patsy sing "Faded Love" and she

* ©1977, Outer Banks Music Company.

came to the final monument in the song where she pauses after completing the high note for a breath, he yelled out to Jamey, "Listen, she's not dead! Here she is living, breathing!"

Patsy's childhood home still stands in Gore, Virginia, though it is overgrown with weeds. The house she grew up in on South Kent Street in Winchester is there, too. Through the years, from various individuals and politicians, an effort was made to erect markers and a gateway sign denoting Winchester as the hometown of Patsy Cline. There was much talk about a museum in town and/or Nashville.

Mrs. Hensley, a remarkable and active woman even in old age, often spoke of how Patsy's friends forgot her. "One of the singers she helped always used to say she wanted to come and visit Patsy's grave. Well, finally, she called and told me she'd like me to accompany her to the cemetery so she could lay some flowers. She told me something about looking real nice. I asked her if she was going to have pictures taken, and she said yes. I told her the only way I would agree to go was if ther were no pictures. She said she'd call me back. I never heard a word from her for several years!

"I'd like to see a museum. I've got Patsy's costumes. One contains three thousand rhinestones, each and every one placed by hand. The Country Music Hall of Fame has never asked for any of her things. Their painting of her is awful. If you had never seen Patsy, you'd never know what she was like.

"Singing was her life and I know more than anything, Patsy would consider her election to the Hall of Fame the greatest honor of her career. It's an honor I treasure in my heart. I was disheartened that I let her down in her biggest moment, the night she was elected. She was the only woman nominee, and when Tex Ritter went to read the announcement, I fainted. I came to in Jo Walker's (CMA executive director) arms. (Charlie does not recall Mrs. Hensley fainting, only Patsy's sister Sylvia letting out a scream of shocked surprise.)

"I was angry that nobody told me and they had to know since the plaque had to be cast. No one said anything in her behalf. That was the least I could have done for her after all she did for me."

"Sweet Dreams," of course, is Hilda's dream come true and she was thankful she lived to see that type of recognition for Patsy.

Hilda met Jessica Lange in Martinsburg, West Virginia, at

the Rainbow Road tavern set for a sequence in which the star, outfitted in a gaudy, skin-hugging outfit of the type Patsy favored and with her blond hair tucked beneath a brunette wig, lip synced Patsy's "Foolin' 'Round."

Locals filled the dance floor in 50s swirl skirts and pleated gabardine pants. Lange emoted and, behind the cameras, Hilda observed this momentous occasion. When shooting wrapped, Hilda seemed pleased, stating, "Jessica was superb. She belts out the songs just like Patsy did."

In Martinsburg or on stage of the Ryman Auditorium in Nashville, home of the Grand Ole Opry when Patsy was alive, Lange had no problem stepping into the part. Thirty-five-year-old Jessica especially brought 29-year-old Patsy to life when walking in spiked heels and creating a slight, sexy swagger—two of the trademarks of the tough-but-tenderhearted Patsy.

For the Opry scene where Patsy does her "I Fall To Pieces" hit, Stonewall Jackson, veteran Opry and country star who had a million-selling hit with "Waterloo," was cast as an announcer. He brought Lange, costumed in a tight-fitting green beaded sheath, on in true Opry tradition, prodding the audience of extras, hands waving, to give a rousing welcome.

"I knew Patsy well," Jackson said, "from our many appearances on the Opry, when I had the pleasure of often introducing her, and the backroom hangout at Tootsie's. Jessica Lange was great in how she captured her spirit. She looked out of sight and moved the way Patsy did on stage."

Jackson remembers Patsy as "a talented woman who'd speak her mind as easily as she'd say good morning. Six months before her death, she was telling my wife and I about someone giving her a hard time. Patsy was on the hefty side. 'If I can get one more hit,' she said, 'they can all kiss my fat a-double crooked letter!"

Charlie Walker, whose hit "Pick Me Up On Your Way Down" was a Patsy favorite, got the part of Cowboy Copas after Reisz and Lange saw him on the Opry. "I'm tall—6'1"—and wear a western hat like Cowboy, so I guess I fit the bill. I'm only in the sequence that ends with the crash. It's one of the key spots and we recreated it as close as possible to a life and death situation.

"Reisz and Jessica were super people to work with. She's so fantastic that it almost intimidates you working with her. I have a feeling she can do about anything. The part I played was natural, having been in the business all my life and knowing all four people. But Jessica really pulled it off. She's something else as Patsy."

David Clennon is Randy Hughes, James Staly portrays Gerald Cline, Frank Knapp appears as Hawkshaw Hawkins and the Riders in the Sky as the Jordanaires. Country singer Boxcar Willie plays a vagrant Charlie lands in jail with.

Walker noted someone told him that Charlie went out and tried to get the job playing himself. "They said 'No!' It's just a rumor, but I think it's true!"

Patsy and Charlie's children live in Nashville. Julie married Michael Connors, a representative for an automobile-related resale business. In 1980 they were able to purchase a handsome home in a stellar neighborhood with the income from the trust set up by the estate. Thanksgiving Day, 1980, Julie gave birth to her first child, named Virginia (after Patsy's given name) Lee. Randy, who is especially close to his father, graduated high school. There may be more show business blood in the family: Virginia Lee made her on-camera bow in a 1984 Nashville-produced music video.

Charlie and Jamey had a son, Charles, Jr., in 1966.

After Patsy's untimely death, emotions flared and there was some bitterness between Hilda and Charlie. Mrs. Hensley said that when she came to Nashville with her grandchildren she was not welcome at Charlie's home. Charlie says, "Oh, that's Hilda talking. She knows she was welcome as far as I was concerned. If she chose to stay in a motel, it was of her own doing. There was a misunderstanding between her and my wife, Jamey, but that was cleared up. Today, we are all very, very good friends."

Many of Charlie's mementos of Patsy and a collection of candid photographs were destroyed by water flooding from a broken pipe.

Reminisced Mrs. Hensley, "We've had a lot of heartaches, but we have some beautiful memories, too. It's not at all sad reliving the past. Patsy was a wonderful daughter. I saw her start from nothing and watched her accomplish one of her dreams—becoming a country singer. I was awfully proud of her! God in heaven knows, she did it the hard way—and had very little to show for it, except her children."

Jim McCoy received the following poem from Hilda for one of his annual March 5th memorial broadcasts:

"I wonder if you've ever stood beside a casket
flanked with flowers,
And asked the Lord to help you thank Him for
the hours
When she was a child at your knee.

For your tender loving care,
For a voice that was filled with laughter and
a will to do,
For all the little things that meant so much.

And when she came home late
I'd be waiting at the window
Or leaning on the gate.

Yes, I remember that day forever,
When God said, 'It's moving day.'
He knew my darling daughter was already
on her way
To a new home with Him in Heaven.

And now when we come home late,
She'll be waiting at God's window,
Or leaning on Heaven's Gate."

You'd have to be a parent to understand, but there is nothing like a mother's love.

"Strange
You're still in all my dreams.
Oh, what a funny thing,
I still care for you.
How strange . . ."

—"Strange,"
recorded by Patsy Cline;
written by Mel Tillis and Fred Burch.
©1961, Cedarwood Publishing Company.

People still talk about Patsy Cline's greatness and her contributions to the music scene. Some say she was one of a kind—unique in the annals of the entertainment business, that she has yet to be equaled.

"Patsy was a great, great lady," said Barbara Mandrell. "She touched me deeply. I could stand and watch her perform for hours." Kay Starr, who was one of Patsy's favorites, remembers her as "a lady who lived a lyric. Those of us touched by her were the lucky ones. Patsy was busy being a woman while the other ERA dolls were trying to figure out what it was. In a race for space, she could have outdone Dolly if she had set her mind to it—had they been on the same track at the same time."

It is ironic that Patsy is more famous in death than she was at the peak of her triumphs.

> "Listening to the music of Patsy Cline
> Is an art form that's very fine . . .
> It's all in the song,
> And that isn't wrong . . .
> Patsy was such a talent, it was a shame
> She had to be caught in that ole plane . . ."
>
> —Carrie McNeill, Vancouver, B.C., Canada;
> "A Fan Remembers Patsy Cline."

This classified ad, misspelling intact, appeared in the Wednesday, October 15, 1980 edition of The Winchester *Star,* Winchester, Virginia:

> CEMETARY lots (4)
> Shenandoah Memorial Park,
> adjoins Patsy Cline. 1-304-
> 725-3884.

Within days, the lots were sold.

Patsy's grave site is marked with a simple bronze plaque that reads: "Death cannot kill what never dies." Patsy Cline was a star when she left us, and a star she remains.

Appendix A

PATSY CLINE'S RECORDING HISTORY

Session Date	Selection Recorded	Original Record Number	Release Date
January 5, 1955	"I Love You Honey"	C-61583	2/5/56
	"Come On In"	61583	2/5/56
	"I Cried All the Way to the Altar"	NR	
	"I Don't Wanta"	NR	
June 1, 1955	"Hidin' Out"	61523	11/5/55
	"Turn the Cards Slowly"	61523	11/5/55
	"A Church, a Courtroom and Then Goodbye"	61464	7/20/55
	"Honky Tonk Merry-Go-Round"	61464	7/20/55
April 22, 1956	"Stop, Look and Listen"	D-29963	7/8/56
	"I've Loved and Lost Again"	29963	7/8/56
	"Dear God"	NR	
	"He Will Do For You (What He's Done For Me)"	NR	

Numbers preceded by lettered prefixes indicate albums
Symbols: C = Coral Records
D = Decca Records
NR = Not released during Patsy Cline's lifetime

Session Date	Selection Recorded	Original Record Number	Release Date
November 8, 1956	"Walkin' After Midnight"	30221	2/11/57
	"A Poor Man's Roses (Or A Rich Man's Gold)"	30221	2/11/57
	"The Heart You Break May Be Your Own"	NR	
	"Pick Me Up on Your Way Down"	NR	
April 24, 1957	"Today, Tomorrow and Forever"	30339	5/27/57
	"Fingerprints"	DL-8611	8/5/57
	"A Stranger in My Arms"	30406	8/12/57
	"Don't Ever Leave Me Again"	DL-8611	8/5/57
April 25, 1957	"Try Again"	30339	5/27/57
	"Too Many Secrets"	DL-8611	8/5/57
	"Then You'll Know"	30504	11/18/57
	"Three Cigarettes (In An Ashtray)"	30406	8/12/57
May 23, 1957	"Write Me in Care of the Blues"	NR	
	"I Can't Forget You"	DL-8611	8/5/57
	"Hungry for Love"	DL-8611	8/5/57
	"That Wonderful Someone"	DL-8611	8/5/57
	"Ain't No Wheels on This Ship"	DL-8611	8/5/57
	"I Don't Wanta" (remake)	30504	11/18/57
December 13, 1957	"Stop the World and Let Me Off"	30542	1/13/58
	"Walkin' Dream"	30542	1/13/58
	"Cry Not For Me"	30846	2/3/59
	"What a Wonderful World"	NR	

Session Date	Selection Recorded	Original Record Number	Release Date
February 13, 1958	"Just Out of Reach"	NR	
	"I Can See An Angel"	NR	
	"Let the Teardrops Fall"	30659	4/28/58
	"Never No More"	NR	
	"If I Could Stay Asleep"	NR	
	"Come on In" (remake)	30659	4/28/58
January 8, 1959	"I'm Moving Along"	NR	
	"I'm Blue Again"	30929	7/20/59
	"Love Me, Love Me, Honey, Do"	NR	
January 9, 1959	"Yes, I Understand"	30846	2/3/59
	"Gotta Lot of Rhythm in My Soul"	30929	7/20/59
July 3, 1959	"Life's Railway to Heaven"	NR	
	"Just A Closer Walk With Thee"	NR	
January 27, 1960	"Lovesick Blues"	31061	3/7/60
	"How Can I Face Tomorrow"	31061	3/7/60
	"There He Goes"	31128	8/1/60
	"Crazy Dreams"	31128	8/1/60
November 16, 1960	"I Fall to Pieces"	31205	1/30/61
	"Shoes"	NR	
	"Lovin' in Vain"	31205	1/30/61
August 17, 1961	"True Love"	DL-4202	11/27/61
	"San Antonio Rose"	DL-4202	11/27/61
	"The Wayward Wind"	DL-4202	11/27/61

Session Date	Selection Recorded	Original Record Number	Release Date
	"A Poor Man's Roses (Or A Rich Man's Gold)" (remake)	DL-4202	11/27/61
August 21, 1961	"Crazy"	31317	10/16/61
August 24, 1961	"Who Can I Count On?"	31317	10/16/61
	"Seven Lonely Days"	DL-4202	11/27/61
	"I Love You So Much It Hurts"	DL-4202	11/27/61
	"Foolin' 'Round"	DL-4202	11/27/61
	"Have You Ever Been Lonely"	DL-4202	11/27/61
August 25, 1961	"South of the Border"	DL-4202	11/27/61
	"Walkin' After Midnight" (remake)	DL-4202	11/27/61
	"Strange"	31354	4/20/62
	"You're Stronger Than Me"	NR	
December 17, 1961	"She's Got You"	31354	4/20/62
February 12, 1962	"You Made Me Love You (I Didn't Want To Do It)"	DL-4282	8/6/62
	"You Belong to Me"	DL-4282	8/6/62
	"Heartaches"	31429	10/8/62
	"Your Cheatin' Heart"	DL-4282	8/6/62
February 13, 1962	"That's My Desire"	DL-4282	8/6/62
	"Half As Much"	DL-4282	8/6/62
February 15, 1962	"Lonely Street"	DL-4282	8/6/62
	"Anytime"	DL-4282	8/6/62
	"You Were Only Fooling (When I Was Falling in Love)"	DL-4282	8/6/62

Session Date	Selection Recorded	Original Record Number	Release Date
	"I Can't Help It (If I'm Still in Love With You)"	DL-4282	8/6/62
February 28, 1962	"You're Stronger Than Me"(remake)	31406	7/12/62
	"When I Get Thru With You"	31377	5/7/62
	"Imagine That"	31377	5/7/62
	"So Wrong"	31406	7/12/62
September 9, 1962	"Why Can't He Be You?"	31429	10/8/62
	"Your Kinda Love"	NR	
	"When You Need A Laugh"	NR	
	"Leavin' on Your Mind"	31455	1/7/63
September 10, 1962	"Back in Baby's Arms"	NR	
	"Tra Le La Le La Triangle"	31455	1/7/63
	"That's How A Heartache Begins"	NR	
February 4, 1963	"Faded Love"	NR	
	"Someday (You'll Want Me to Want You)"	NR	
	"Love Letters in the Sand"	NR	
February 5, 1963	"Blue Moon of Kentucky"	NR	
	"Sweet Dreams"	NR	
	"Always"	NR	
February 6, 1963	"Does Your Heart Beat For Me?"	NR	
	"Bill Bailey, Won't You Please Come Home?"	NR	

Session Date	Selection Recorded	Original Record Number	Release Date
February 7, 1963	"He Called Me Baby"	NR	
	"Crazy Arms"	NR	
	"You Took Him Off My Hands"	NR	
	"I'll Sail My Ship Alone"	NR	

Appendix B

SONGS RECORDED BY PATSY CLINE

Only three of Patsy Cline's albums were released during her lifetime: "Patsy Cline," August 5, 1957; "Showcase," November 27, 1961; and "Sentimentally Yours," August 6, 1962. Since her death there have been many additional albums from Decca/MCA and various other companies containing mixed selections. Some songs appear on only one LP, others on several. The following is a list of all the songs Patsy Cline ever recorded as well as the albums on which each song can be found.

ALBUM KEY

A.	Patsy Cline	Decca 8611
B.	Showcase with the Jordanaires	Decca 74202/MCA 87
C.	Sentimentally Yours	Decca 74282/MCA 90
D.	The Patsy Cline Story	Decca DK88-7176/2-MCA 4038
E.	A Portrait of Patsy Cline	Decca 74508/MCA 224
F.	That's How a Heartache Begins	Decca 74586
G.	Patsy Cline's Greatest Hits	Decca 74854/MCA 12

H.	Patsy Cline's Golden Hits	Everest 5200
I.	Encores	Everest 5204
J.	In Memoriam	Everest 5217
K.	Today, Tomorrow, and Forever	Hilltop 6001
L.	I Can't Forget You	Hilltop 6016
M.	Stop the World & Let Me Off	Hilltop 6039
N.	Miss Country Music	Hilltop 6054
O.	In Care of the Blues	Hilltop 6072
P.	The Heart You Break	Longines Symphonette 93489
Q.	Gotta Lot of Rhythm in My Soul	Metro 540
R.	Country Music Hall of Fame	Pickwick 6148
S.	Patsy Cline Remembered	Tee Vee 1026
T.	Here's Patsy Cline	Vocalion 73753
U.	Great	Vocalion 73872
V.	Stop the World	Longines Symphonette 93488
W.	Always	MCA 3263
X.	Portrait of Patsy Cline	CBS Musical Treasures P255280
Y.	20 Golden Pieces of Patsy Cline	Bulldog Records 2003
Z.	Greatest Hits (of) Jim Reeves & Patsy Cline	RCA AHL1-4127
A1.	Remembering Patsy Cline & Jim Reeves	MCA 5319
A2.	The Legendary Patsy Cline (from England, but available in U.S.)	MFP Records 50460
A3.	"Sweet Dreams" soundtrack	MCA Records

Ain't No Wheels on This Ship (A-H-N-U-R-X)
Always (E-W)
Anytime (C-S)

Back in Baby's Arms (D-G-A1)
Bill Bailey, Won't You Please Come Home? (F)
Blue Moon of Kentucky (E)

A Church, a Courtroom and Then Goodbye (K-R-V)
Come on In

Come on In (remake) (J-L-P-R-X)
Crazy (B-D-G-S-W-Z-A3)
Crazy Arms (E)
Crazy Dreams (F-M)
Cry Not for Me (J-X)

Dear God (N-P-X)
Does Your Heart Beat for Me (E-W)
Don't Ever Leave Me Again (A-I-K-O-Q-U-X)

Faded Love (E-G-S-W)
Fingerprints (A-I-K-R-X-Y-A2)
Foolin' 'Round (B-D-W-A3)

Gotta Lot of Rhythm in My Soul (M-Q-X)

Half as Much (C-S-A3)
Have You Ever Been Lonely (B-Z)
He Called Me Baby (F-S)
He Will Do it for Me (N-P-X)
The Heart You Break May Be Your Own (H-N-O-P-R-X)
Heartaches (C-D-S)
Hidin' Out (J-N-R-X)
Honky Tonk Merry-Go-Round (J-M-Q-X-Y-A2)
How Can I Face Tomorrow (M-T)
Hungry for Love (A-H-L-P-U-R-Y-A2)

I Can See An Angel (H-L-P-Y)
I Can't Forget You (A-H-L-P-U-X-Y-Z2)
I Can't Help It (If I'm Still In Love With You) (C)
I Cried All the Way to the Altar (J-M-O-P-R-X-Y-A2)
I Don't Wanta
I Don't Wanta (remake) (A-H-K-U-V-Y)
I Fall to Pieces (B-D-G-S-W-Z-A1-A3)
I Love You Honey (I-N-V-X-Y-Z-A2-A3)
I Love You So Much It Hurts Me (B-D-W)
I'll Sail My Ship Alone (E-W)
I'm Blue Again (R-K-R-V-X)
I'm Moving Along (F-M)
I've Loved and Lost Again (I-L-O-P-T-Y-A2)
If I Could See the World (H-T)
If I Could Stay Asleep (J-L-O-X-Y-A2)
Imagine That (D-S)
In Care of the Blues (A-H-O-T-V-Y)

Just A Closer Walk With Thee (L-O-T-V-X)
Just Out of Reach (A-H-N-O-T-V-X-Y-A2)

Leavin' on Your Mind (D-G-S-A1)
Let the Tear Drops Fall (J-L-Q-X-Y)
Life's Railway to Heaven (L-P-T-R-X)
Lonely Street (C)
Love Letters in the Sand (C)
Love Me, Love Me, Honey, Do (F-K-O-X-A3)
Lovesick Blues (F-K)
Lovin' in Vain (F)

Never No More (J-N-P-Q-Y-A2)

Pick Me Up on Your Way Down (J-Y-A2)
A Poor Man's Roses (Or A Rich Man's Gold) (I-K-P-R-X)
A Poor Man's Roses (Or A Rich Man's Gold) (remake) (B-D)

San Antonio Rose (B-D)
Seven Lonely Days (B-D)
She's Got You (C-D-G-S-Z-A3)
Shoes (F)
So Wrong (D-G-S-A1)
Someday (You'll Want Me To Want You) (E-S)
South Of the Border (B-D-W)
Stop the World and Let Me Off (H-M-T-V-X-Y-Z)
Stop, Look and Listen (I-M-X)
Strange (C-D-G)
A Stranger in My Arms (I-K)
Sweet Dreams (D-G-S-Z-A3)

That Wonderful Someone (A-I-U)
That's How A Heartache Begins (F)
That's My Desire (C-W)
Then You'll Know (A-I-K-U)
There He Goes (F-M-O-Q-V-X)
Three Cigarettes (In An Ashtray) (A-H-N-U-R-V-Y-A2)
Today, Tomorrow and Forever (I-K-R-X-Y)
Too Many Secrets (A-H-L-U-Y)
Tra Le La Le La Triangle (D)
True Love (B-D-S-W)
Try Again (I-M-X)
Turn the Cards Slowly (J-N-Q-V)

Walkin' After Midnight (A-H-J-K-R-V-Y-A2)
Walkin' After Midnight (remake) B-D-G-S-A1-A3)
Walkin' Dream (J-T)
The Wayward Wind (B-D-S)
What A Wonderful World
When I Get Thru With You (E-C)

When You Need A Laugh (E-S)
Who Can I Count On (E)
Why Can't He Be You (D-G-A1-A3)
Write Me In Care Of The Blues

Yes, I Understand (K-Q-T-V-X)
You Belong to Me (C-D-S)
You Made Me Love You (C)
You Took Him Off My Hands (E)
You Were Only Foolin' (C)
You're Stronger Than Me
You're Stronger Than Me (remake) (D-G)
Your Cheatin' Heart (C-D-S-A3)
Your Kinda Love (E)

Some Patsy Cline selections were featured also in special packages marketed by the Ernest Tubb Record Shop in Nashville.

Acknowledgements

Deep gratitude to: Mrs. Hilda Hensley and Charles Dick.

No book of this nature would be complete without photographs. Amazingly, the bulk of Patsy Cline photographic memorabilia was taken for WSM/the Grand Ole Opry by one man, veteran cameraman Les Leverett. Since candid photos of Patsy are all but rare, without Mr. Leverett's work, his untiring cooperation, his drive for perfection in the processing stage, and his dedication—not to mention his prized friendship and support—this book would not have been realized.

To Irene Tuchapsky, for rendering the transcription of countless interviews—many in a dialect foreign to her ear; Karleen Sebastian, Bonnie Rasmussen, and Elaine Hughes for their inexhaustible services, assistance, and encouragement.

No words of thanks can express the appreciation and esteem I have for Joseph and Catherine Shewbridge for their selfless interest in wanting to see the record set straight on the beginnings of Patsy Cline's professional career. I thank Mrs. Benny Birchfield, the former Mrs. Hawkshaw Hawkins, and Mrs. Marvin Hughes, the former Mrs. Randy Hughes, two of the warmest individuals this writer has ever met, for sharing, with remarkable, frank, and detailed recall, events before the plane crash and those in its aftermath, some of which proved to be of a highly personal nature. To Louise Seger, for the sharing of her correspondence with Patsy Cline. To Dottie West, for interrupting her more than hectic schedule at a time of crisis in her own life and sharing hours of wonderful memories of Patsy Cline. And to Del Wood, for her straight-from-the-hip bluntness, Woodisms, and so much more.

For their valued cooperation: NLT, Inc. of Nashville, parent company of WSM and the Grand Ole Opry; the Country Music Foundation Library and Media Center (Robert Oerman, Don Roy, and Kyle Young);the Country Music Association; WSM, Inc.; the Grand Ole Opry (Jerry Strobel, public relations), MCA Records (Jerry Bailey, Nashville; Anne Boyd Lewis, photographic services, Universal City; Lynn Kellerman, Diane Smith, New York); Universal Pictures (Burt Solomon, Edward Z. Epstein, New York); the Nashville *Banner* and Nashville *Tennessean* newspapers (Joe Rudis, photographic services; Bill Hance; Laura Eipper); the Winchester *Evening Star,* Winchester, Virginia (Cookie and Larry Sullivan, Laura Cameron, Mitch Heironimus); Harry and Fay Crutchley, Frederick, Maryland, for stories of Patsy and Bill Peer and photographs of Patsy; Ronnie E. West, for establishing contacts with the family of Gerald Cline; Carol Darst, for her thoughtfulness; Dale Turner Westberry for photograph of Patsy Cline and Jimmy Dean; Roy Deyton, for photographs of Patsy and Bill Peer; Dorothy Gable, charter curator of the Country Music Hall of Fame and Museum; Ralph Grubbs, Winchester, Virginia, for early photographs of Patsy; H.R. and Barbara Nash, Nashville, for access to Patsy Cline artifacts; Alfredda Rhoades and Erma Schofield, Kansas City, for sharing personal mementoes of the stars' last concert; the Loretta Lynn Fan Club (Loudilla, Loretta, and Kay Johnson, co-presidents); Ralph Emery, for always leading me in the right direction; Larry Peer, Mrs. Mark Yontz, and Mrs. Charles Spiker, for photographs of Patsy, Bill Peer, and Gerald Cline; Paul Harvey for permission to reprint broadcast; and Jimmy Bowen of the Patsy Cline Fan Club.

For file and source material: the Nashville *Tennessean* (Gerald Henry, Julie Hollabaugh, Phil Sullivan, Eugene Dietz, and Steve Korpan); the Nashville *Banner* (Larry Brinton, Clay Hargis, Red O'Donnel; library research, Stacy Neher, Sandra Roberts); Melvin Shestack, the *Country Music Encyclopedia;* the *Kansas City Star;* the Winchester *Star* (Jack Cummins); Joint Universities Library System of Vanderbilt for access to Patsy Cline artifacts; Robert Shelton and Burt Goldblatt, "The Country Music Story"; the Clark County, Nevada, Library (Allan Goldberg); The Denis Archives, Riverdale, New York; Record Research, Inc.; the Augusta, Georgia, Herald (Don Rhodes); Bernard Geis Associates, publishers of *Coal Miner's Daughter* by Loretta Lynn with George Vecsey;

the New York Museum of Broadcasting; and the New York City Library for the Performing Arts, Lincoln Center.

For kind permission to quote from song lyrics: Irwin A. Deutscher, Nashville, trustee (Janice Blackwell), for Four-Star Music Company, Inc., for "A Church, a Courtroom and Then Goodbye" by Eddie Millier, © 1954, "Walkin' After Midnight" by Donn Hecht and Alan Block, © 1956, "Come On In" by Eddie Miller, © 1955, "Just Out Of Reach" by V.P. Stewart, © 1953, "Hungry For Love" by W.S. Stevenson and Eddie Miller, © 1957, and "Today, Tomorrow and Forever" by M.G. Burkes and W. Burkes, © 1955, all rights reserved; Cheerleader Music Company, Leon Beaver, Chattanooga, for "Sundown In Nashville" by Dwayne Warrick, © 1969, all rights reserved; to Teddy Wilburn of Sure-Fire Music, Nashville, for use of lyrics from his composition of "Dakota Lil"; Sure-Fire Music Company, Lorene Allen, Nashville, for "I Miss You More Today" by Lorene Allen and Loretta Lynn, © 1972, all rights reserved; Eightball Music Company, Leon Hart, Bakersfield, California, for "Missing On A Mountain" by Tommy Dee (Donaldson), © 1963, all rights reserved; Outer Banks Music Company, Nashville, for "I Miss You So Badly" by Jimmy Buffet, © 1977, all rights reserved; Cedarwood Publishing Company, William Denny, Nashville, for "Strange" by Mel Tillis and Fred Burch, © 1961, all rights reserved.

In addition to those artists, fans, and music industry executives, past and present, who so generously gave of their time and memories, I would like to extend sincere thanks to Art Maher, whose faith in a magazine series on Patsy provided the impetus for the project; Jim Albrecht, Country Style Magazine; Lee Rector, Music City News; and Jane Ayer; Rona Barrett; J.D. Bell; Henerietta Betheil; Becky Blevins; Archie Bleyer; Teresa Brewer; Michael Brokaw; Willie Bruffy; Lee Burrows; Elizabeth Casey; Mary Reeves and Terry Davis; Billy Deaton; David Fluke; Shirley Freland; Richard Gordon; Daniel Hsu and Belinda Smith (Country Music Wax Museum, Nashville); James Hughes; Charles Lowe; Joan McGriff; the Mandrell Sisters; Michelle Marino, BMI, Inc., New York; Margarite Renz; Mrs. A.L. Ritter; Amanda Ruben; Jim C. Scott; Andrea Smith; Bob Thiele; Blanche Trinajstick; Belatha Wright and Mrs. Johnny Virgin.

And I must extend special appreciation to Loretta Lynn for remembering Patsy in her autobiography, *Coal Miner's Daughter*.

Photographs, interview transcripts, and research materials from *Patsy Cline* are being donated to the Country Music Foundation Library and Media Center, Nashville.